DATE DUE

MR 29 '05			

DEMCO 38-296

Too Many Enemies

Rosemary Sayigh

Zed Books Ltd
London and New Jersey

lped

Too Many Enemies was first published by Zed Books Ltd,
7 Cynthia Street, London N1 9JF, UK, and
165 First Avenue, Atlantic Highlands, New Jersey 07716, USA, in 1994

Cover designed by Andrew Corbett.
Typeset by EMS Photosetters, Thorpe Bay, Essex.
Printed and bound in the United Kingdom
by Biddles Ltd, Guildford and King's Lynn.

A catalogue record for this book is
available from the British Library

US CIP data is available
from the Library of Congress

ISBN 1 85649 055 6 Hb
ISBN 1 85649 056 4 Pb

Contents

Acknowledgements

I should especially like to thank Umm Mustafa, who first sponsored me in Shateela; and Ahmad Haleemeh, without whose help this book could not have been written. Others who were particularly generous with their time were Dr Muhammad al-Khateeb, Abu and Umm Muhammad Farmawi, Jihad Bisher, Abu Mujahed, Abu Makarem, Abu Mustafa, Hajji Lateefeh Sarees, Ustadh Khaled Sarees, Abu 'Ali Abbas, Abu and Umm Isma'een, and Nuhad Hamed.

Thanks to Wafa' Yasseer and NPA staff for never-failing support with logistics, production and *zuhoorat*.

For patient explanation of Palestinian politics, I would like to thank (besides Yusif and Yezid) Shafiq and Bayan al-Hout, Salah and Samira Salah, and Suhayl Natour.

In the hope that what I have written will not embarrass him, I would also like to thank Abu 'Ala, director of SAMED and the PLO Directorate of Economic Affairs, for his kind and unconditional help with recording and translation expenses.

Finally, thanks to the friends who helped to translate the tapes, and whose enthusiasm and comments have been a valued input: Najla Fahd, Suhayr al-Uzm, Somaya Kuttab and Riham Hindi.

Note on transliteration
In general I have adopted a system of transliteration that tries to render as closely as possible for English readers how words are spoken in (Palestinian) Arabic. For example, for the long vowel classically transcribed as 'i' I have substituted 'ee' (as in Shateela). I have used the mark ' to indicate both *'ayn* and *hamza*. Inevitably there are inconsistencies: in the case of names already familiar to Western readers (for example, Khalil, Walid) I have left them in their conventional form; also the names of well-known figures such as Chamoun and Chehab.

Note on names
People whose real names appear have given their permission. In the case of people who could not be contacted, I have given fictitious names.

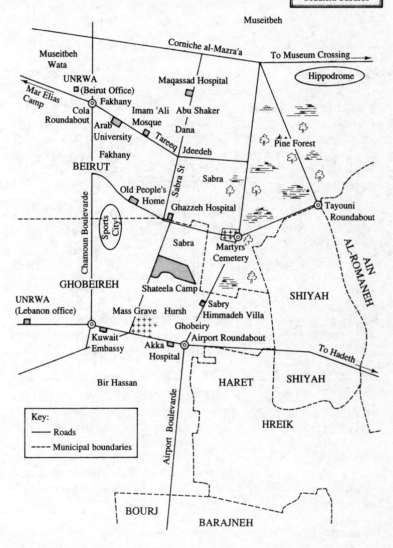

Map 1
Shateela in Beirut's
Southern Suburbs

Museitbeh

Corniche al-Mazra'a   To Museum Crossing

Museitbeh
Wata   Hippodrome

Mar Elias Camp   UNRWA
                      (Beirut Office)   Maqassad Hospital
                      Fakhany
          Cola
          Roundabout   Imam 'Ali   Abu Shaker
          Arab   Mosque
          University   Dana
                        Tareeq   Jdeedeh   Pine Forest
          Fakhany

BEIRUT   Sabra

                Old People's
                Home   Tayouni
                        Ghazzeh Hospital   Roundabout

          Sports
          City   Sabra   AIN
                              Martyrs'   AL-ROMANEH
                              Cemetery
GHOBEIREH
                Shateela Camp
UNRWA   SHIYAH
(Lebanon office)   Mass Grave   Hursh   Sabry
                      ++++   Himmadeh Villa
                      ++++   Ghobeiry
          Kuwait   ++++   Airport Roundabout
          Embassy   Akka   To Hadeth
                    Hospital
      Bir Hassan   HARET   SHIYAH

Key: HREIK
—— Roads
- - - Municipal boundaries

                                  BOURJ
                          BARAJNEH

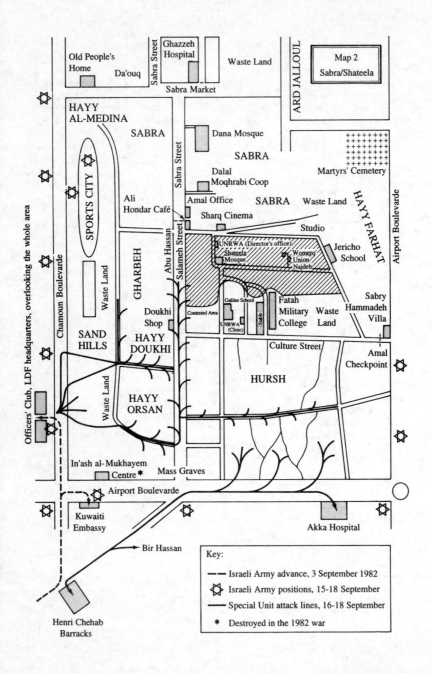

Map 2
Sabra/Shateela

Map 3

Low-income Palestinian
Settlements in Lebanon, 1992

SYRIA

TRIPOLI
8.0 Nahr al-Bared
Baddawi

MEDITERRANEAN

BEIRUT
28.1 Dbeyeh*
Mar Elias Tell al-Za'ter
Sabra Jisr al-Basha
Al-Jnah Shateela
Bourj Ta'labayyeh
Barajneh
Barr Elias
SIDON Iqleem al-Kharroub
50.4
'Ain Helweh
Miyyeh-Miyyeh

BEQA'
7.8

Ba'lbek
Wavell

SYRIA

Abul Aswad
Al-Bass Nabatiyyeh
TYRE Qasmiyyeh
Bourghaliyyeh
5.7 Shabriha
Ma'shouq
Bourj al-Shemali
Rashidiyyeh

Key:

◎ Lebanese cities

● Palestinian camps (UNRWA)

▲ Destroyed camps

▼ Old Palestinian settlements
(quasi-camps)

■ Recent settlements of
Muhajjareen (War displaced)
(= more than 100 families)

5.7 Percentage of total
Muhajjareen in each area

ISRAEL

(*Dbeyeh camp was overrun in 1976;
most inhabitants were killed or evicted.
Today 25% of it's population is Palestinian.
Some UNRWA services are offered.)

The one thing none of us can forget is that violence has been an extraordinarily important aspect of our lives. Whether it has been the violence of our uprooting and the destruction of our society in 1948, the violence visited on us by our enemies, the violence we have visited on others, or, most horribly, the violence we have wreaked upon each other – these dimensions of the Palestinian experience have brought us a good deal of attention, and have exacerbated our self-awareness as a community set apart from others.

Edward W. Said, *After the Last Sky* (1986)

Should we not have some other task
Than digging graves
And seeking new words for a eulogy
To make it seem unlike the one
That we'd just written?
How small these flowers are
How deep is all this blood.

Mahmoud Darweesh
(translated by R. Kabbani)

There are those who build palaces and those who dig graves.

Proverb current in the Palestinian camps

Prologue

Beginnings

The idea to research and write this book came after the first Amal attack against Shateela and the other Beirut camps in May/June 1985, when I climbed into Shateela through hills of rubble to find friends. I had visited Shateela occasionally before 1982, but only began frequent visits afterwards, with the intention of researching the experiences of Palestinian women. By 1985, after a difficult initiation period, I was beginning to feel at home. At this time, too, Shateela and Palestinians in Lebanon seemed to have come through the worst of the violence unleashed against them by the Israeli invasion and its aftermath. To see this small community attacked again, this time by 'brothers', was so shocking that I put aside other work to try to grasp it, both as an objective event with historical causes and as an inner experience that only survivors could recount.

My sense of shock was political as well as moral. The attackers and the attacked were fellow Arabs and fellow Muslims, and had fought together against the Israeli invasion in 1982, and in resistance to the occupation of South Lebanon. Further, this battle was fratricidal in class as well as national and religious terms: the Amal movement represented a subordinate group within the Lebanese class/sect system, and Amal fighters came from the same broad socioeconomic strata as camp Palestinians. Death and destruction on both sides were staggering, with Amal casualties even higher than those of the Palestinians; yet, in spite of this, the Amal attacks continued with Lebanese Army support for three years, a duration that differentiated this episode from the brief clashes between allied militias that occurred on both sides of the 'Green Line' in Lebanon's Civil War. The 'Battle of the Camps' seemed to illustrate only too well how low-income strata in 'pluralist' societies are manipulated to attack each other; the fighters die while the leaderships stay in place. The length and seriousness of the episode suggested the need to examine the connections between external powers, internal leaderships, economic interests and popular political culture that cause confrontations such as this.

Shateela in mid-1985 was not a fortress bristling with Resistance fighters but a small cluster of low-income housing filled with families, among whom a handful of ex-fighters had individual weapons. The camp's small size, less than 1 square kilometre, deprived it of strategic depth. Surrounded on two sides by higher ground, its innermost alleys were visible to Amal and Army snipers posted in high buildings all around. Only a few buildings inside the camp were more than one or two storeys high, their walls of breeze blocks and thin cement roofs offering the flimsiest of defence against heavy artillery. Four small semi-underground shelters could not hold more than part of the population, particularly in the later sieges when Palestinian inhabitants of the surrounding area fled into Shateela. The first attack was so sudden that there was no time to make fortifications. People say of the fighters, 'They defended Shateela with their flesh.' It is true. In rational military terms, Shateela was indefensible. Surrounded, outnumbered, outgunned, cut off from all supplies, pounded for six-hour stretches by missiles normally used against armies, Shateela should have fallen not once but many times. The fact that it did not challenges our frames of analysis.

It is important to remember, too, that Shateela's resistance was not the result of a leadership decision nor even of 'revolutionary discipline'. Certainly a long history of national struggle and Resistance movement ideology played a role. But the siege testimonies make very clear the spontaneity and fragility of the organization of defence. There was no conscription: people were free to flee or stay, to fight or sit in the shelter. Whereas official accounts would have edited out shortcomings, betrayals and internal conflicts, thereby reducing courage to the level of a taken-for-granted nationalism, people's accounts show that morale and morality were not invariably high. There were moments of despair, and internal political conflicts. There were accusations over the distribution of supplies. There were some people who exploited shortages, or stole from public stocks, or spied for Amal. Rather than detracting from the epic of the sieges, this frankness enhances the *sumood* (steadfastness) of ordinary people because it shows them resisting in spite of shortcomings within their own group. The siege testimonies are valuable in the way that they show a small Palestinian community acting under crisis and more or less cut off from national-level leadership. A part of the cultural substructure of Palestinian popular struggle is revealed here in a way that would not be possible in official histories.

The terms used by Shateela people themselves to explain their *sumood* draw on a religious and nationalist language: 'our faith in God'; 'our belief in our cause'; 'we were in the right'. This broad popular view is well expressed by one of many Umm Muhammads:

We were besieged five months and the world said, 'Let them be destroyed.' But *insh'allah* we shall remain strong and hold our heads high. We have a cause. Our goal isn't Lebanon. If they offered me the whole of Lebanon, I'd tell them it's not equal to one Palestinian olive.

Another very widespread, religious-based idea is that the aggressor is in the wrong and thus is bound to fail. That people do not readily offer what in the West would be considered 'rational' or 'realistic' explanations does not mean that they discount the material resources, technical means and human qualities needed to resist – on the contrary, these are carefully weighed and described in the siege narratives. It is important that secular readers should not take such remarks as signs of an unchanging essence, 'fatalism', that characterizes Muslims. Equally they should not be dismissed as 'self-deception' or 'pious formulas'. We can be sure that religious/nationalist faith does help people survive ordeals – the accounts suggest some of the ways in which this was true – but we can also be sure that faith did not protect people from moments of fear and despair. There is also evidence of breakdown, though this mainly occurred after the sieges ended.

Hardly aware of Shateela's history when I chose it as a research milieu, I discovered only gradually the reasons that, with Sabra,[1] it was singled out to bear the main force of Amal/army attack. One reason was its strategic position close to large, mainly Sunni quarters of West Beirut, and between Beirut and the mainly Shi'ite southern suburbs. Another was its history, with Sabra and Fakhany, as the *mantaqa ra'isiyyeh* (headquarters, centre) of the Resistance movement up to 1982. Third, its small size made it appear to the attackers as the 'weak link' in the chain of defence of Palestinian autonomy in Lebanon, the easy prize whose fall would demoralize and weaken all the other camps. Instead, the opposite happened: by pinning down a large proportion of the attacking forces, Shateela helped the other camps to resist or avoid similar attacks. Only Da'ouq, the tiny unofficial camp in the heart of Sabra, having just two alleys with about sixty families, was overrun.

The *sumood* of Shateela and the other besieged camps, Bourj Barajneh and Rashidiyyeh, altered the course of Lebanese and Palestinian history in several ways. In Lebanon, Amal's bid to monopolize the representation of the Shi'ite community was aborted both by its attack on the camps and its failure to crush them. Syria's project for a new order in Lebanon, based on the three main sectarian militias, was also frustrated, in spite of the Tripartite Accords.[2] The 'Battle of the Camps' had deeper consequences in the Palestinian political arena, further discrediting Syria (seen as the real originator of Amal attacks) and breaking up the Syrian-backed National Salvation Front which had threatened to split the Palestine Liberation Organization (PLO). It was during the third siege that the Popular Front for the Liberation of Palestine (PFLP) and Palestine Struggle Front (PSF) left the Palestine National Salvation Front (PNSF) to rejoin the PLO Executive Committee. The resistance of the camps thus contributed directly to the reunification of the PLO, realized at the 18th PNC meeting in Algiers in April 1987. It had been suggested that the 'Battle of the Camps' also fed into the anger and pride that fuelled the Intifada spirit in the Occupied Territories.[3]

However, my own concern was less with the political consequences of Shateela's resistance than to record the experiences of its people – fighters, cadres, volunteer defence workers, mothers, children – of each siege episode as it ended. Most of the siege recordings were carried out in the first week or two after cease-fires, so that the phases of the sieges – their ups and downs – as well as individual incidents and feelings were still fresh in people's recollections. After the ending of the third siege, the Syrian Army set up a checkpoint at the entry of the camp and it became increasingly difficult to enter. It was then that I began work for the other two main sections of this book: one is a historical analysis of developments in the Lebanese arena between the Israeli invasion of 1982 and the beginning of the 'Battle of the Camps' in May 1985; the other is a reconstruction of Shateela's history from its establishment in 1949 up to the invasion. Although conditions were not conducive to the making of an ethno-history, I used the same method of oral recording as I had used for the siege experiences, intending thereby to give a voice to different social sectors and political points of view.

Necessity and problems of Palestinian oral history

The many kinds of cultural manifestation that have accompanied the Intifada point to the political importance of such work in reflecting, sustaining and amplifying political action. The Palestinian press has provided written and photographic coverage of the daily events of revolt and repression in spite of censorship, closures and the arrest (sometimes assassination) of journalists. Films have been made, art exhibitions have been held, popular drama groups have given performances. Realization of the importance of popular resistance has produced new kinds of research, media and political/social writing, for example close-up reports of small milieus, the Women's Resource Centre in Nablus, and a popular women's magazine published by the Women's Studies Centre, Jerusalem.[4] News from the Intifada speaks directly to other struggles, whether national, class or racial/ethnic. The Palestinian struggle should have its place in world 'oppositional literature'.

Oral history is a valuable tool for recording popular struggles but it is one that has so far been little used by Palestinian historians.[5] There are many reasons for this, both circumstantial and cultural. Exile and dispersion separated the Palestinian intelligentsia from their historic environment, from each other and from the mass of refugees in the camps – at many times in Lebanon those wishing to visit camps have had to apply for official permits. In Lebanon also, national archive collections have been attacked and pillaged. In other areas national cultural work has been discouraged by state surveillance. Among the cultural reasons are a tradition of history writing that values written sources over popular speech, as well as the assumption that it is to leaderships that historians should look in explaining causality in history. However, one of the most striking characteristics of the Palestinian national struggle has been the spontaneity of its uprisings, and the problematic relationship between these and the national leadership. Early peasant uprisings against land sales to Jewish colonists occurred before the formation of a national leadership, in the Ottoman period.[6] The Great Revolt of 1937-39 was peasant-based and largely autonomous.[7] Even in periods without any national leadership, for example between 1948 and 1964, the Palestinian people sustained many kinds of political action in many parts of the *menfa* (exile, dispersion). The necessity of recording this widespread and multiform struggle is more urgent now than ever. On the one hand, the generation that can remember the Great Rebellion, the exodus and the first years of exile or Israeli rule, is vanishing. At the same time the diaspora is widening, with old settlements of refugee Palestinians being broken up by new waves of migration. Any settlement of the Middle East based on limited autonomy for the Occupied Territories is likely to be followed by repression of Palestinian communities and national cultural work throughout the Arab region.

One of the values of oral history that possibly accounts for the coolness towards it of state cultural institutions and national leaderships is its potential for revealing social struggles contained within the history of nation-states or national liberation movements. In the Palestinian case, these are not always revealed directly but may be read 'between the lines' of the narratives of ordinary people. Even in regard to gender, a sensitive issue which is kept out of the arena of controversy by an array of ideological means, kinds of protest emerge woven into the strong nationalist feelings that Palestinian women express. Protest against class hierarchy is also revealed, not only explicitly by members of progressive Resistance groups but also implicitly by others who may profess to abhor communism on religious grounds. Often such protest is articulated in the form of proverbs which offer a vehicle for ideological debate in popular milieus. It was from pious, middle-aged women that I heard several highly radical proverbs. One is quoted at the beginning of this book: 'There are those who build palaces and there are those who dig graves.' Two others are: 'The rich eat chickens, the poor fall in the thistles', and 'The rice is honoured, the *burghul* can go hang himself.'[8] Another form of class struggle is the drive for education:

reading the Shateela histories we can feel how much this drive, always couched in national terms as necessary for confronting the Israeli enemy, is also in part a struggle of the ex-peasant class to acquire a better life, and of women to gain the tools to speak and write and act politically like men.

Oral history takes its place in the frame of political action rather than academic work, yet its methods and interpretation need to be subjected to several kinds of scrutiny. People's memories of the past – recent or distant – cannot but be affected by certain factors, which researchers and readers need to take into account. There are obvious questions concerning the representativeness of particular speakers – the effects of class, political affiliation, age or gender on what they say; but there is the more important question of the effect on speech and memory of the situation at the time of the recording, with 'situation' including overall and local political conditions, mood, the particular moment and place of recording, and the researcher's identity and relationship with the history-givers. Particular phases of the past may seem good or bad depending on their relationship to the present. People may speak differently depending on whether they are in offices or homes, among family and neighbours or alone with the researcher. The researcher's nationality, class and gender is likely to affect responses. Beyond such basic situational factors, how people tell history is necessarily shaped by culture: oral histories should not be read primarily as a source of historical 'fact' but rather of historical experience and the cultural frameworks through which it is lived and recollected.[9]

The situation of Shateela people during the period of recording (1985–89) was one of great insecurity and economic hardship. Most of the homes in the camp had been destroyed or heavily damaged; many families were living outside in ruined or unfinished buildings. Amal militia attacks remained a danger until the end of 1987, and from early 1987 the Syrian Army in West Beirut began carrying out mass arrests of Palestinians accused of being 'Arafatists'. The future, whether of Shateela, the community in Lebanon or the PLO, was clouded in uncertainty; only the beginning of the Intifada in December 1987 brought a glimmer of hope. The problems of daily life – finding housing, employment, schooling, health care, news of prisoners – weighed on everyone. Inflation added its weight to other worries. If people were at all ready to record their history in such a period it can perhaps be attributed to pride in the resistance of Shateela and in the Intifada that followed. Conditions that made it dangerous to speak also made it necessary to bear witness.

The question has to be considered of the effects on speech and memory of Syrian control over West Beirut at the time of recording. In particular, how did this affect people's recollections of the period of Resistance movement autonomy: was this seen as a 'golden age' in contrast to the present? Or had critical views of the leadership been sharpened by PNSF campaigns against

Arafat's 'capitulationist' policies? There were few signs of fear: refusals to record were minimal, although some requested anonymity and others agreed to speak if politics was excluded. How people 'edited' their speech is another question. It is to be expected that among oppressed groups caution in speech becomes almost unconscious, eliminating or euphemizing any reference likely to be dangerous. But speaking frankly or circumspectly also depends to a great extent on individual character, and in small communities such as Palestinian camps this character difference seems to become deeper, with some people being known as *jaree'* (daring) and others as fearful. Nonetheless it was not easy to find Fateh loyalists in West Beirut – those who had survived the camp battles were mostly in Syrian prisons, or 'Ain Helweh. For the sake of balance, I was forced to take special measures to find people ready to record from a Fateh perspective.

If recollections of the 'Days of the Revolution' tend to be critical, sometimes bitter, this was not, I am sure, from fear of the Syrians but for other reasons rooted in the politics and special situation of 'Lebanese' Palestinians. The present coloured views of the Resistance movement period because that period had not merely preceded the present but also in some sense caused it. The 'Days of the Revolution' had begun with high hopes of return to Palestine; it had ended with the evacuation of the *feda'yeen* (guerilla fighters) and the massacre. There were also political fears that a 'diplomatic solution' in the shape of a state in the Occupied Territories would leave 'Lebanese' Palestinians with nowhere to go. Another factor possibly accentuating criticism is the rootedness in the Lebanese camps of the Arab Nationalist Movement (ANM)/PFLP, the main opposition within the Resistance movement to Fateh's predominance.

In a broader sense, too, recollections of the past must be affected by the emotions of the moment in which they are recorded. The bleakness of the period in which the histories of Shateela were recorded is reflected by the speakers in different ways. Many express nostalgia for the past, not only 'the days of Palestine' that few can now remember but also, in some cases, the first years of settlement when 'UNRWA [United Nations Relief and Works Agency] ruled, and no one had guns, and we were all one family'; or for the early years of the Resistance movement, between 1965 and 1973, before corruption by money and competitive recruitment. Such presentations were characterized by a sharp differentiation between 'before' and 'after', with these marked by a particular event such as 1948, the year of the exodus; or 1967, the year when the defeat of the Arab armies allowed the Palestinian Resistance movement (PRM) to take the initiative; or 1973, the year when Egypt and Syria won a partial victory in the 'October war'[10] with mainly negative consequences for the PRM. Another concept of Palestinian history encouraged by the moment of recording was as a series of defeats and tragedies, a special destiny of persecution. One man said about the

Palestinian experience in Lebanon, 'We never had a bronze age, let alone a silver one.' Where people begin their stories and how they sequence them is shaped by their vision of the destiny of the people to whom they belong. Thus one very old woman began her recollections with a description of British soldiers beating the men of her village with strips of prickly pear, and then jumped back to her marriage during World War I, when her husband had to flee to Hawran to escape conscription by the Turks. Such dominant modes of presentation arise from historical experience itself, not from situational factors such as the Syrian presence in West Beirut, or my own identity as researcher and the way my project was perceived.

In certain, mainly practical, ways my gender and ambivalent outsider/insider status helped me. That I was married to a Palestinian and the mother of Palestinian children probably helped reduce suspicion that I was a spy for any of a number of enemies; and my being a foreign made it easier to believe that I was not a supporter of any specific Resistance group, nor partisan in the Fateh split. Being a foreigner and a woman also made it less likely that I would be tracked down and stopped by any of the Lebanese or Syrian military bodies that ruled the area. The national boundary was useful also as an element in building rapport, especially in the way it overrides class boundaries. When I went visiting in Shateela with an UNRWA staff nurse, people invariably made us sit on chairs, a symbol of status and power; as a foreigner I was free to sit on the floor.

The question, however, is not so much whether my foreigner status was an obstacle or a help in carrying out the research project, but rather how it affected its guiding concept and methods, its proprietorship. The idea of the history had not originated in the research community, and in the circumstances in which we were living there was no way it could be transformed into an ethno-history. In a more normal situation, I could have taken steps to 'indigenize' the project, for example through consulting with representatives of different sectors of the community to discover their concepts of their history, along with its phasing and critical moments, and to resolve the sensitive issue of who should 'speak for' the community. If I had been an indigenous researcher, sharing the same national history and political culture as the research community, I would have been able to take some of these steps intuitively, and I would have had easier access both to their historical experiences and to the cultural frameworks through which these are remembered. Although I do not think that my foreignness reduced empathy or distorted what people told me, it did affect the questions I asked, my interpretation of what people told me, what I chose to emphasize and what I left out. Only through necessarily slow processes of comparing my interpretations with theirs could this defect have been overcome. In First World/Third World cultural politics, a narrow line separates pre-emption from facilitation. There is always the danger created by international power asymmetry of imposing Western frameworks on Third World people's conceptions of their own culture and history.[11] The only really authentic histories are those that groups involved in national or social struggle produce themselves as an intrinsic part of political action.

The question of proprietorship apart, the histories given by Shateela people point to kinds of cultural shaping that need to be made explicit for non-Arab readers. There is, for example, a dominant mode for telling the Palestine crisis, one produced by the national intelligentsia in the course of a long struggle, with its focal points in the exernal world, the history of Zionism and Great Power politics in the Middle East, the Basle Conference, the Balfour Declaration, etc. Only the highly educated can fully master this complex body of knowledge, which reaches popular levels through politicization more than through schooling (UNRWA and Arab school textbooks do not adequately cover Palestinian history) and is assimilated in a way that separates 'the Cause' from the lives of ordinary people. Religious/nationalist discourse sustains this separation by emphasizing the sacredness of 'the Cause' and the importance of sacrifice for the homeland. That it is ordinary people who mainly sustain the cause and suffer its setbacks is an idea foreign to this discourse. Even though exile has greatly modified the social structure that reproduces this language, we still find remnants of a separation between the political and the personal in the way people narrate history. It does not come easily to them to see their own lives as a part of history. This makes their accounts sometimes impersonal and anonymous, a tendency that is reinforced by the 'collectivization of experience', the process through which members of small communities exchange fragments of individual experience (or, put differently, the domination of collective experience) is achieved, and how it is reflected differently in different social sectors. The point I want to emphasize here is that transposing the personal (experiences, feelings, ideas) into the public, political record is itself a political process that *can* be undertaken in research, but that does not occur by itself, without the use of a specific methodology. Personal stories occur spontaneously all the time, as mothers talk to their children, or friends visit. But the artificiality of the recording session tends to suppress these personal anecdotes, through which outsiders could better grasp the way the Palestinian tragedy has affected particular lives.

As we attempt to reach the local and individual levels of popular struggles, we can never forget that these are encompassed and constrained by larger territorial and systemic frameworks that ultimately mesh with the 'world system'. Our interest in Palestinian communities arises from the way they form a vital ideological and social base for contestatory action. As an unachieved national liberation movement, the Palestinian struggle still contains a capacity for challenging power arrangements in the Middle East;

anti-imperialist and social reformist themes are still strongly voiced within it, by intelligentsias and ordinary people. But Palestinian communities, whether in Israel, the Occupied Territories or in the Arab diaspora, exist within a political/economic/cultural framework characterized by its contradictions, one in which Palestinian goals and organizations clash to a greater or lesser degree with the 'host' authority (Israeli or Arab), each with its own legal system, definition of the Palestinians, military/administrative bodies, and educational and other systems. Although the Palestinian Resistance movement jumps over Arab state boundaries, it is also constrained by its Arab environment and enmeshed in its conflicts. While Palestinian communities participate in this transnational movement, they simultaneously exist in a variety of authoritarian systems and respond to local economic and political pressures. It is to the specifics of Lebanon as host country and its susceptibility to Arab and other external forces that Chapter 1 is directed, since it is against this background that Shateela's history needs to be read.

Notes

1. Sabra is not as is often thought a camp, but an area in which a high proportion of residents are Palestinian. Camps are officially designated areas for which the state often pays ground rent and where UNRWA provides a camp director and other services.

2. See Chapter 6, p. 69.

3. Y. Sayigh, 'The Intifadah Continues', *Third World Quarterly*, vol. 11, no. 3, July 1989.

4. See for example S. Khalifeh, 'Our Fate, Our House' with introduction by Penny Johnson in *Middle East Report*, no. 164–5, May/August 1990; B. Doumani, 'Family and Politics in Salfit', in Z. Lockman and J. Beinen (eds) *Intifada: The Palestinian Uprising against Israeli Occupation* (Boston: South End Press for MERIP, 1989). See also reportage in *Race and Class*, e.g. 'Gaza: "This is no rebellion – it is a war"' by M. K. Makhul, vol. XXIX, no. 4, Spring 1988.

5. An exception is N. Nazzal, who interviewed refugees from villages in North Palestine for his book *The Palestinian Exodus from Galilee, 1948* (Beirut: Institute for Palestine Studies, 1978). B. al-Hout used interviews for her study of the Palestinian leadership, *Al-Qiyadat wa al-mu'essessat al-siyasiya fi Filasteen, 1917–1948* (Beirut: Institute for Palestine Studies, 1981). T. Swedenburg and S. Nimr collected oral histories in the West Bank for dissertations on the Great Revolt.

6. R. Khalidi, 'The Palestinian Peasantry and Zionism before World War I', in E. Said and C. Hitchens (eds), *Blaming the Victims: Spurious Scholarship and the Palestinian Question* (London and New York: Verso, 1988).

7. T. Swedenburg, 'The Role of the Palestinian Peasantry in the Great Revolt (1936–1939)' in I. Lapidus and E. Burke (eds), *Islam, Politics and Social Movements* (Berkeley: University of California Press, 1988).

8. In the third proverb, the classes are denoted by the food they eat, the wealthy by rice, the peasants by *burghul*.

9. See the Popular Memory Group, 'Popular Memory: Theory, Politics, Method', in R. Johnson *et al.* (eds), *Making Histories* (Minneapolis: University of Minnesota Press, 1982). L. Passerini's work is seminal: *Fascism in Popular Memory: The Cultural Experience of the Turin Working Class* (Cambridge: CUP, 1987).

10. Sometimes referred to as the War of Yom Kippur, the October war set in motion Kissinger's diplomacy and Sadat's 'peace initiative'.

11. T. Asad makes this point in his 'The Concept of Cultural Translation in British Anthropology' in J. Clifford and G. Marcus (eds), *Writing Culture: The Poetics and Politics of Anthropology* (Berkeley: University of California Press, 1986).

Part I:
An Oral-Based History of Shateela Camp, 1949–82

1. Palestinian Refugees in Lebanon: A Historical/Political Overview

To understand this oral-history-based account of a single Palestinian refugee camp in Lebanon, we need to set it in a larger political and historical framework that can explain its origins, its sustainment and the ruptures that divide its history up to 1982 into three distinct phases, the basis of the three chapters to follow. This introductory overview will attempt to lay out the main sets of factors that constitute this framework, allocating to each its distinctive role and demonstrating how their interaction causes the high level of fluctuation and crisis that has characterized the Lebanese arena: first, the creation of the 'refugee problem' testifies to the dynamic entry of a new factor into Middle East and world politics, the state of Israel, which has retained the military/political initiative over its Arab neighbours throughout the period covered by this book; second, the United States, without whose diplomatic, financial and military support Israel would not have been able to maintain its primacy – engaged in a world superpower struggle with the USSR, the United States has acted since the end of World War II to 'freeze' the Palestinian issue in such a way that solutions other than those acceptable to the Zionist movement/Israel would not be pressed outside the Arab League and its occasional allies.

Third, Lebanon's characteristics as 'host' for the Palestinian refugees have been shaped both by its own specificity as a sectarian state/society and by commonalities of history, geography and culture which, though harder to define than Lebanese specificity, are nonetheless real as factors that form and disrupt political equilibria. Lebanon's sect/class system was reflected in every aspect of the situation of the refugees: their legal status, the zoning of the camps, mechanisms of control, and modes of integration into the political and economic system. Commonalities have been expressed through political support for the Palestinian struggle by a substantial segment of the Lebanese population.

Its sectarian structure has also made Lebanon highly susceptible to regional power centres and transnational movements that constitute the fourth parameter in the framework within which camp histories have unfolded.

This characteristic Lebanese 'permeability'[1] existed before the Palestine crisis but was exacerbated by it, both as an Arab regional issue reflected with particular intensity in the Lebanese political arena and through the presence after 1948 of a substantial Palestinian refugee minority. Both individually and jointly as the Arab League, the 'Palestinian policies' of the Arab states have had varied, often intense repercussions in Lebanon, producing fluctuations both in Lebanese state policies towards the refugees as well as in attitudes towards them of different sectors of Lebanese society. Among the Arab states continuously influential in Lebanon are Egypt, Syria and Saudi Arabia. After 1967, the Palestinian Resistance movement must be counted into the framework as both an external and internal factor. Towards the end of the period under consideration a non-Arab regional force, Iran, enters the picture. Simply to enumerate states, however, does not exhaust the elements of the fourth parameter, which include transnational movements and ideologies, variants of Arab nationalism, Islamism and Marxism. The regional parameter has, in turn, been dominated throughout the period under consideration by the 'Cold War' rivalry between the United States and the USSR, in which the Middle East was of major importance to both superpowers.

Such a framework is inherently unstable. From 1948 onwards, a whole chain of regional events – changes of regime, uprisings, wars – were reacted to immediately and antithetically by different Lebanese groupings; Palestinian reactions were as strong, though muted until 1969 by state repression. It needs to be noted that in most cases regional events had their main impact on Palestinians in Lebanon not directly, but mediated through the state or ultra-Maronite groups hostile to the Palestinian presence. A clear example is the stiffening of state repression of the camps during the presidency of General Chehab, a result of the regime's fears of the mobilizing effects of the regional upheavals of the 1950s on Lebanese Muslims and 'Opposition' parties. The major regional event of the 1960s, the 1967 war in which Israel defeated three Arab armies and occupied the West Bank, Sinai and the Golan Heights, had more complex and far-reaching repercussions in Lebanon, rousing the ultra-Maronite groupings to reassert the hegemony that Nasserism had jeopardized, and at the same time leaving scope for the Palestinian Resistance movement to emerge, with its mobilizing effects on Palestinians and many sectors of the Lebanese.

Interaction between the different elements of the framework was speeded up after 1968, as PRM action was increasingly restricted to Lebanon, while Israel's Lebanon policy became increasingly retaliatory and destructive, supported by US suspension of condemnation. The Arab states, increasingly divided, continued to intervene in Lebanon, though without deterring Israeli attack; among them Syria gradually emerged, with tacit Arab consent, as hegemonic. Lebanon's own political forces were further polarized into anti- and pro-Palestinian segments. The stage was thus set for the explosions that have engulfed both peoples for two decades. The Israeli invasion of Lebanon, with which the first part of this book ends, is another historic watershed that points to the way that slight shifts in elements in the framework – a Likud government, Sharon as Minister of Defence, Reagan in the White House and Haig in the Pentagon – can produce devastation for Palestinians and Lebanese in Lebanon.

From the perspective of the people of the camps, the closest 'layer' of this interacting framework has been the Lebanese state (usually the army) and the refugee management apparatus (laws, ministries, UNRWA, the Directorate of Palestinian Refugee Affairs, etc.). The rest of the Palestinian community in Lebanon, with other camps and emerging national institutions,[2] formed a second layer. Furthermore, each camp is situated in a specific regional, economic and social setting, with neighbours who have been friendly or hostile depending on the historic moment and degree of sectarian mobilization. Beyond the immediate neighbourhood lies Lebanon's political arena, with its plurality of parties, movements and leaderships, each with its specific Palestinian 'stand', and the Lebanese economy and labour laws that have pressed Palestinian labour into the 'informal' sector and emigration. Beyond Lebanon lies the Palestinian diaspora with which camp people maintain close family and political links. The oral-based histories of Shateela camp are contained within and shaped by these external layers, which are not always made explicit by the speakers. The purpose of this overview is to make them so.

Israel and Lebanon

Israel's first major act of aggression against Lebanon was through population transfer. Before and during the war of 1948, between 700,000 and 1,000,000 inhabitants of Palestine fled or were expelled into neighbouring countries, among them Lebanon. Portrayed by Israel as an accident of war, this exodus has been shown by Israeli and Arab scholarship to have been the result of Zionist planning.[3] The substantial number of refugees – round 110,000[4] – who fled to Lebanon came mainly from the villages of Galilee and the coastal cities (Jaffa [Yaffa], Haifa and Acre [Akka], their access facilitated by a long common border, a major motor road and sea routes. Familiarity also played a role: many kinds of social and economic exchange linked the people of northern Palestine and southern Lebanon. The refugees formed a ratio of about 1:10 to the Lebanese population,[5] a heavy burden for a country poor in natural resources, with a high level of unemployment and outmigration.

However, long before the war of 1948 an interest in Lebanese water and land resources had been a part of Zionist movement thinking. At the Paris Peace Conference of 1919, Zionist leaders presented a map of the future state showing its northern border running from the coast just south of Sidon across the Litani River to Mount Hermon: South Lebanon's copious river systems were considered essential for the economic development of the Jewish state.[6] Israeli 'ultras' still view the Litani as Israel's 'natural' border.

Future Israeli military leaders acquired familiarity with South Lebanon during the 1937–39 Great Revolt, and again in 1940/1, when the British organized cross-border raids first against Palestinian *mujahideen* (guerilla fighters), and later against Vichy France.[7]

The Lebanese Army took almost no part in the war of 1948 but by the end of hostilities Israel had occupied eighteen Lebanese border villages, expelling the villagers by methods similar to those used in northern Galilee. These were eventually restored by the Rhodes Armistice Accords of 1949, a document that has ruled Lebanese–Israeli relations ever since, at least according to the Lebanese.[8]

For more than a decade after the 1948 war, the Israeli–Lebanese border remained tranquil as Israel focused on other areas, launching raids against the West Bank and Gaza, and joining Britain and France in 1956 in the tripartite attack against Egypt (the Suez War). The tranquillity of the Lebanese border was in large measure due to the Lebanese Army's effective control of the border zone, with Palestinians forbidden access. As late as 1967, during the 'Six Day' war, this border saw no military activity.

However, Lebanon continued to figure in Israeli strategic thinking. In 1954, Ben-Gurion strongly advocated a policy of destabilization of Lebanon, aimed at setting up a purely Christian state closely allied with Israel; in 1955, Dayan proposed 'winning or buying' a Lebanese Army officer willing to carry out such a scheme.[9] Although the Prime Minister at the time, Moshe Sharett, opposed 'adventurism' in Lebanon, this possibility persisted in Israeli strategic thinking, winning advocates among Israeli Defence Forces (IDF) commanders such as Eytan, Gur and Sharon, and possibly also in Mossad.[10] However, such moves did not find a favourable conjuncture until much later, after the emergence of the PRM and its transfer to Lebanon.

Israel's policies towards its Arab neighbours in the 1960s may be summarized as (i) consolidating its ties with the United States encouraging American–Arab alienation; and (ii) building up its military superiority. Military actions up to 1967 were directed mainly against West Bank villages, ostensibly in retaliation for 'infiltration' but with an underlying dual aim of either provoking the Jordan Army to intervene, or discrediting it through failure to do so (a similar approach would be used against Lebanon after 1967). Relations between Jordan and Egypt, already strained, were made worse when the Arab League failed to act to prevent

Israel's diversion of the River Jordan. In June 1967 Israel seized a favourable international conjuncture to launch a lightning attack against Egypt, Jordan and Syria, crushing their armies and occupying all that was left of historic Palestine as well as Sinai and the Golan Heights. Around 20,000 new refugees were created, some of whom reached Lebanon.

After the beginning of Resistance operations from South Lebanon, in 1964/5, Israel launched occasional retaliatory cross-border raids; but the full force of its retaliatory, destabilizing policies was not directed against Lebanon until after 1968. It was when the PRM in Jordan began to present a serious political challenge that Israel began to carry attacks deep into Lebanon, hitting Lebanese as well as Palestinian targets, notably Beirut International Airport on 30 December 1968, when eleven civilian aircraft were destroyed. Such attacks continued to escalate and were a major factor in bringing about the Civil War of 1975/6.[11]

In addition to military/strategic reasons for Israeli attacks against Lebanon, there was the fundamental political aim of destroying the Lebanese sectarian equilibrium and, by pushing the Maronites towards partition, proving that a pluralist polity and society could not exist in the Middle East, thus vindicating Israel's Jewish separatism. This objective gained in importance from the declared early aim of the Palestinian Resistance movement to establish a democratic secular state in Israel.[12]

Escalating after 1968, Israeli attacks against Lebanon included air raids such as the one that laid waste Nabatiyyeh camp in May 1974, part of a series carried out by Phantom planes against Palestinian camps and Lebanese villages in the South. There were also commando operations such as that in which three Palestinian leaders were assassinated in April 1973. Limited cross-border raids were numerous, while in 1978 the Israeli Army carried out the 'Litani Operation', an invasion in retaliation for a PRM sea attack, during which an estimated 1,000 civilians, mainly Lebanese, were killed. Artillery bombardments from land and sea were continuous, increasing after the establishment of the Israeli-controlled 'border zone' and South Lebanon Army during the Civil War.[13] Utilizing its massive military superiority, Israel encountered little obstacle in realizing Dayan's threat: 'We will make life impossible in South Lebanon.'[14]

Several factors combined to bring about the invasion of 1982. First, the formation of a Likud government under Begin in June 1977 increased the likelihood of massive intervention in Lebanon; so did the appointment of Ariel Sharon as Minister of Defence in August 1981. The upcoming presidential elections in Lebanon in September 1982, with Bashir Gemayel a candidate, renewed Israeli ambitions for a separate peace with Lebanon. The planners of the invasion certainly took into account the pro-Israeli leanings of the Reagan/Schultz/Haig team in Washington. The Arab political scene suggested the unlikelihood of militant reactions. Only a *causus belli* was needed. Since the Palestinian–Israeli cease-fire negotiated in July 1981 by special envoy Habib had been adhered to by the PRM, the Israeli government was forced to announce that it would consider any attack on any Israeli or Jewish target anywhere in the world as cause for an attack against the PRM in Lebanon.[15] Thus when on 3 June the Israeli ambassador in London was shot at by unidentified gunmen, the stage was set for the largest military operation ever mounted by Israel against any of its Arab neighbours, one resulting in massive loss of life, destruction and displacement.[16]

The United States: present/absent superpower

American policies towards Lebanon, more often implicit than explicit, have formed a basic determinant of developments from 1948 onwards. Scholars have noted the deep contradictions of US policy: on the one hand, support for a country whose liberal economy, pro-Western orientation and parliamentary system qualify it for recognition as 'friend'; on the other, practical disregard whenever Lebanon's interests have clashed with those of its southern neighbour. Both in brief periods of active intervention (1958, 1982–84) as in longer periods when Washington has relegated Lebanon to the 'back burner', the United States has exercised a quasar-like influence over events in Lebanon. Differences between one White House occupant and another have been ones of style rather than substance, hardly altering a basic view of Lebanon as an 'expendable ally'.[17]

Before 1948, Lebanon had formed a historic entry point for American influence in the Middle East. At first predominantly cultural, American interests took a more economic form after 1945 when Lebanon's independence from France left the country open to world finance and trade. Few other countries in the world practised such minimal protectionism, with almost no barriers placed to the entry of foreign capital and businessmen. The United States was among the first to benefit in terms of its share of Lebanese imports, as well as permits to establish bank branches and enterprises. Lebanon also offered the United States a stepping stone for contact of all kinds with the rest of the Arab region, facilitating a rapid expansion of its financial and trade transactions as well as its cultural and political influence. What had been in 1948 a small legation became the largest US embassy in the region. A steadily rising flow of students from the whole area left the American University of Beirut (AUB) to study in the United States, enhancing American cultural and economic influence in the Arab region and beyond.[18]

In spite of these growing interests in Lebanon, Washington did not intervene during the 1948 war or after to bring about a repatriation of the refugees. During protracted negotiations on this issue, American diplomats on the spot repeatedly called on the Administration to convince Israel to accept at least 250,000 returnees in a bid for an overall settlement. Israel refused and Washington backed off from applying the necessary pressure. Three aspects of this critical episode, which 'froze' the refugee issue for decades to come, are instructive in pointing to a long-term pattern in US–Israeli and US–Arab relations: (i) American officials on the spot urging compromising measures were overridden by Washington after Israel had expressed opposition; (ii) the problems faced by the host countries in integrating the refugees were not weighed in the same scale as Insraeli objections to repatriation (in the case of Lebanon in particular, the Administration ignored early warnings of the dangers presented by the refugees to the country's sectarian 'balance'); (iii) rather than put pressure on Israel to reach a settlement satisfying legitimate Palestinian claims, the United States used its power to stamp Israeli *faits accomplis* as 'irreversible' and Arab opposition as 'unrealistic'. All American effort was deployed in having the refugees absorbed by the host countries.[19]

Lebanon's *laissez faire* economic system has often been the subject of accolades from Washington, but US recognition of its parliamentary system and pluralist society has been less frequent. When America has intervened in Lebanon it has not been in defence of Lebanese democracy but with underlying regional aims in view. The first forceful US intervention, a Marine landing, was ordered by President Eisenhower on 15 July 1958. Ostensibly in response to appeals for help from President Chamoun, under attack since May by 'Muslim rebels', the landing took place twenty-four hours after a bloody insurrection in Iraq had overturned the pro-Western Hashemite monarchy. The intervention worked at the local level to ease Army Commander General Chehab into the presidency, while on the regional level it sent a signal to Iraq's new ruler, Colonel Qassem, that the United States was not indifferent to his policies on oil or regional and international issues.

After 1968, as the first clear indications appeared of the crisis that would drag Lebanon into civil war, American inaction was directly linked to Lebanon's marginality in US Middle East policy, focused on maintaining the status quo, Israel's security and the free supply of Arab oil to the Western world. Viewing the rise of the Resistance movement as a threat to its own hegemony as well as Israel's, Washington scaled down its concern for Lebanon in proportion as the Lebanese government proved incapable of 'disciplining' the PRM *feda' yeen* active in South Lebanon. Even if at times reluctantly, the United States went along with Israel's policy of retaliation against Palestinian and Lebanese targets in Lebanon, although these were always disproportionately destructive in relation to the provocation. For example, when the Israelis attacked Beirut's civilian airport (December

1968), Washington did not condemn this high-profile raid even though it caused a government crisis, bringing Lebanon closer to the civil war that would eventually overtake it.

Far from curbing Israeli attacks against Lebanon, the United States facilitated them through financial and military aid programmes and, more importantly, through protecting Israel from criticism in the United Nations (UN). Over seventeen years, successive US administrations used the veto or abstained on forty-three Security Council resolutions condemning Israel.[20] In 1978, when a unanimous Security Council resolution called for Israel's withdrawal from South Lebanon, it was US support that allowed Israel to avoid compliance. American reactions to Israeli settlements in the West Bank, the bombing of Iraq's nuclear reactor in June 1981 and the annexation of the Golan Heights in December 1981 were so mild as to be negligible.

As for the invasion of 1982, US prior knowledge and agreement has not been seriously questioned. The invasion began only a week after a visit by Sharon to Washington where he met Secretary of State Haig and Pentagon officials. The United States was the only country that did not condemn it, vetoing a Security Council resolution calling for immediate withdrawal, and claiming the invasion was 'defensive'. In the first quarter of 1982, the United States had supplied Israel with military equipment worth 40 per cent more than in 1981. Israel's use during the war of forbidden weapons (e.g. cluster bombs) caused only a temporary US suspension of arms shipments.[21]

Lebanon as 'host'

The formation of modern Lebanon under the French Mandate left a deeply sectarian imprint on its state and institutions; this shaped both Lebanon's integration of the refugees as well as the effects they would have on Lebanese politics. The weakness of the state, constructed to allow free play to sectarian institutions and mercantile interests, was a factor determining methods of refugee management. The small size and non-conscript nature of the army, supposedly aloof from politics, was another factor shaping Lebanese reactions to the refugees, eventually giving rise to anti-Palestinian militias, a phenomenon absent from other Arab host countries. Maronite hegemony over the state was guaranteed through monopoly of the presidency and the army command, and to a lesser extent through a fixed parliamentary majority. Next to the Maronites in size and influence, the Sunni Muslim community had challenged Maronite predominance throughout the Mandate; but in 1943, on the eve of independence, Maronite and Sunni leaders reached an unwritten power-sharing agreement (the 'National Pact') through which the highest positions in the state were allocated permanently to representatives of the major sects. As part of the pact, the Maronites were to give up their close relationship with France, while the Sunnis would abandon their calls for union with Syria. It was this precarious 'equilibrium' that the Palestinian refugees, in the majority Sunni Muslim, jeopardized.[22]

Lebanon's initial acceptance of such a large influx of refugees reflected this brief moment of Maronite–Sunni *entente*, personified in President al-Khoury and Prime Minister al-Solh, architects of the National Pact. Except for Archbishop Ignatius Mubarak, no Maronite figure made an open protest, although some are said to have expressed their misgivings to Western diplomats.[23] We can assume that this was because of the widespread assumption that the refugees would be repatriated. Only as such hopes faded did signs of resentment begin to appear. In 1951, Minister of Labour Lahoud attempted to illegalize all employment of Palestinians. That same year, campaigns began in the National Assembly to prohibit the employment of Palestinians in large companies or institutions.

Lebanon's primary impact on the refugees was to separate them out by sect and class. Middle-class urban Palestinians settled freely in Lebanese cities and encountered little difficulty in obtaining employment. Christians among them were at first easily granted Lebanese nationality, facilitating travel, engaging in the 'free' professions (medicine, law, engineering, pharmacy), and the establishment of businesses or companies. Middle-class Muslims could also obtain nationality by paying lawyers and proving Lebanese ancestry,[24] but this route was barred to the mass of poor rural and proletarian refugees. Few restrictions were placed on Palestinian capital, other than the legal obligation to employ three Lebanese workers to every one non-Lebanese. While middle-class Palestinians benefited, at least until 1975, from Lebanon's liberal regime and many institutions of education and training, the mass of rural and poor city refugees suffered material hardship, economic exploitation and loss of civic as well as national rights.

This refugee mass settled in seventeen official camp sites (recognized by the state and managed by UNRWA), as well as in a number of 'quasi-camps', low-income agglomerations mainly in the rural South but also near Beirut (Sabra and Qaranteena are examples). By providing rent-free space, shelter, basic rations, facilities (water, sewage disposal) and social services (clinics, schools), UNRWA-managed camps played a basic role in the economic survival of the refugees, especially in the first decade of low wages and limited employment. The provision of free schooling (for six- to sixteen-year olds) was particularly important in enabling occupational change and gradually improving levels of income and expenditure. However, no new camp sites were provided after the early 1950s in spite of natural population increase and the destruction of four of the original camps by war.[25] Such space restrictions put pressure on the refugees to build or rent accommodation outside the camps, or to migrate from Lebanon, and can be seen as political in origin.

The original siting of the camps was a product of several factors: an official zoning policy made itself felt through Lebanese Army moves to reduce the number of refugees in the South, especially near the border; this was done by transfer to other areas (mainly the Beqa') and by declaring the border a military zone, prohibiting civilian access. A second aim that became gradually apparent was to prevent a refugee build-up around Beirut. Prohibition of permanent housing and restrictions on the supply of water were early signs of this policy towards the Beirut camps.

Lebanon's sectarian map and the needs of its economy also played a role in the choice of camp sites. The bulk of the refugees remained in mainly Muslim, mainly agricultural areas (near Tyre, Nabatiyyeh, Tripoli and Ba'lbek), where they provided seasonal agricultural labour. Camps were also set up near predominantly Muslim urban areas ('Ain Helweh near Sidon, Baddawi near Tripoli, Bourj Barajneh in Beirut's southern suburbs) where they formed a cheap labour pool for public and private construction. Whenever they could manage to, Palestinians migrated to the urban camps because of the better chances these offered of employment and education, and the easier climate. Thus the urban camps – especially those near Beirut – became receiving areas for Palestinians from the rural hinterlands. The authorities used every means to stem this flow, from eviction to refusal to transfer registration, but failed for reasons that a man who moved to Shateela in the 1950s will later make clear.[26]

There was a sharp contradiction between state attempts to prevent concentrations of Palestinians around Beirut and the demand of Lebanese industry for cheap labour. Lebanon's foremost industrial zone was located in Mkalles, in what would become known as the 'Maronite enclave', and it was this that attracted so many Palestinian and Lebanese Muslim workers to settle in camps and shanty towns in East Beirut – Tell al-Za'ter, Qaranteena, Jisr al-Basha, Bourj Hammoud. During the Civil War of 1975/6, all these would be attacked, razed and their inhabitants expelled by the Maronite militias. After 1976, the only Palestinians to remain in predominantly Maronite areas were Christian.

Lebanese laws formed a basic source of constraints upon the refugee community. Defined as 'foreigners' with rights to indefinite residence, all those refugees who kept their Palestinian identity were obliged to apply for work permits, effectively confining them to work avoided by Lebanese labour, i.e. agriculture, construction and the 'informal sector'. In addition they were barred from working in government and foreign companies or institutions, and could only practise the 'free professions' by joining syndicates, conditional on Lebanese nationality. The absence of a clear code regulating Palestinian rights and duties allowed the state to operate a 'politics of convenience', using the Palestinians' need for vital documents (mainly work permits and travel documents) as a means of exercising political pressure, or individual extortion. The supply of work permits also responded to fluctuations in the Lebanese economy's labour needs. Departments of the state that dealt with the refugees – mainly the ministries of the interior, labour and foreign affairs – could issue their own decrees, enabling officials to exploit refugee needs for their own ends. Rules, procedures and fees were constantly changed, producing a situation of confusion and dependence on *waasta* (connections, bribes).

A basic element in management of the refugees was the division of labour between UNRWA, the UN agency established in 1950 to maintain them, and the Lebanese state which controlled them. State control was carried out through an array of bodies that changed over time, depending on presidential regime and the dictates of national security. Two major shifts in state policy caused sharp transitions in political conditions in the camps, dividing the period from 1949 to 1982 into three separate 'chapters'. The first of these came towards the end of the 1950s, with the change from President Chamoun, who relied mainly on general security and the Mufti's following for indirect control of the camps, and President Chehab who installed the Army's Intelligence Bureau directly in every camp (the foreign and domestic policy reasons for this move will be discussed later). The second major shift came in 1969, after a series of camp uprisings supported by the Lebanese National movement (LNM) forced the authorities to withdraw, leaving the camps as 'liberated zones' in the charge of a Palestinian force, the Kifah Musellah (Armed Struggle), in accordance with the Cairo Accords of November 1969.[27] The autonomy of the camps lasted until the Israeli invasion of 1982.

Though disenfranchised as refugees, the Palestinians were 'written in' to the Lebanese political system even before their arrival. As already noted, Christian Palestinians were encouraged to take Lebanese nationality (just as Armenian refugees had been before them). Several parliamentary leaders, Muslim as well as Christian, tried to recruit Palestinian followings by offering them naturalization. But in general Palestinians were attracted to the secular nationalist/progressive parties which, for convenience, I shall group together under the label 'Opposition'. Although attraction to the 'Opposition' parties affected all Palestinian strata, membership was mainly an urban, middle-class phenomenon; people in the camps were too absorbed by the daily life struggle, and distrusted parties as destructive of national unity. Shateela people's histories suggest that they were exposed to political recruitment earlier than other camps because of closeness to Beirut. Among the parties and movements appealing to Palestinians were the Parti Populaire Syrien (PPS), the Lebanese Communist Party (LCP), the Ba'th, and the Arab Nationalist movement (ANM). Apart from their activism, the source of the appeal of all except the LCP was the centrality they gave to the Palestine issue. It was, however, Arab nationalism in its Nasserist form that had most effect on the people of the camps, especially after the Egyptian President's nationalization of the Suez Canal (1956).

Nasserism appeared threatening to the authorities and most of the Maronite leadership not so much because of its effect on the Palestinian refugees, but because it offered a catalyst of fusion between the Palestinians and the Lebanese Sunni 'street',[28] as well as the other 'Opposition' groupings. Perceptions of this threat coincided with the rise to national prominence of the Kata'eb Party. Formed in 1936, it had remained marginal even in the Maronite community, its leaders not part of the oligarchic elite. Its chance came in 1958 when President Chehab (1958–64) brought Pierre Gemayel into the government; the Kata'eb benefited from its association with the Chehab regime, building ties with the Army's Intelligence Bureau, the new president's chosen instrument to break the power of the oligarchs, and control the increasingly politicized Muslim masses. Predisposed from the beginning to perceive the refugees as a threat to Maronite hegemony, the Kata'eb became the ideological and military spearhead of a civilian anti-Palestinianism unique to Lebanon,[29] which would reach its climax during the Civil War of 1975/6, and in the formation of the Lebanese Forces (LF) under the leadership of Bashir Gemayel. Contacts with the Zionist movement preceded the establishment of Israel, feeding into Kata'ebi anti-Palestinianism and laying the grounds for cooperation in 1975/6 and again in 1982.[30]

Lebanon as a polity had far more complex and fluctuating effects for Palestinians than did the more authoritarian regimes of Jordan and Syria. On the one hand they enjoyed the benefit of a pluralist political system, of which a substantial segment supported them; in addition, there was Lebanon's relatively free press and the scope allowed to Palestinian cultural institutions. On the other, there were episodes of violent suppression by the Lebanese Army and by sectarian militias, first Maronite, then Shi'ite. Given Lebanon's built-in sectarian tensions, such a pattern of support and attack could hardly have been avoided. But it was external forces that made this dialectic so much more uncontrollable and devastating.

The regional framework

Lebanon's 'permeability' is rooted in a long history of foreign intervention, stretching back to Ottoman times; in a population fragmented into sects traditionally linked to foreign or regional powers; and in a weak state constructed (as noted earlier) so as both to leave power to sectarian institutions and to preserve Maronite domination. The crises that have shaken Lebanon since its independence can only be understood by situating. the country within an international and regional framework that continually generates shifts which, because of its history and sectarian composition, have effects on different sectors of the Lebanese people. Palestinians have been only one element in this continual interaction between external and internal forces.

Every state in the region has had its 'Lebanon policy', and a complete discussion could not omit the interventions of Saudi Arabia, Jordan, Iraq, Algeria, Libya and Iran as well as those of Egypt and Syria: interventions that have taken multiple forms, such as financial or military aid to one or more of the conflicting parties, recruiting followings, subsidizing newspapers, sending armed forces and attempting mediation. Most regional states have equally carried on policies towards Palestinians in Lebanon: sending donations, making statements of support, allowing or refusing entry to migrant workers. Three forms of intervention have been particularly important: first, the opening of military training bases to Palestinians; second, President Nasser's campaign to establish the PLO and have it recognized by the Arab League; third, the formation or backing by certain Arab states of specific Resistance groups.[31]

But more important than specific state policies (with the exception of Syria and Egypt) have been the political upheavals and wars which have altered regional balances, established new regimes or created new mobilizing currents. Such events have been far too numerous to be listed in this brief introduction so I shall take only three examples, one in each decade, all of them producing changes in the Lebanese political arena, and in the situation of Palestinians.

In the 1950s, as a result of the defeat of 1948, a series of upheavals took place throughout most of the Arab region: the Egyptian revolution of 1952, Egyptian–Syrian union in 1957, the Iraqi revolution of July 1958, and the collapse of the US-sponsored Baghdad Pact. Chamoun's relatively casual control of the refugees had been partly based on his confidence in the predominance of the Western powers (in particular the US) in the region. The rise of Nasserist Arab nationalism shook this predominance and effectively ended Lebanon's brief immunity from Arab pressures. Chehab's response was dual: to placate Lebanese Sunnis through a pro-Egyptian Arab policy, and to install a regime of surveillance and repression in the camps. This was aimed at preventing two kinds of political action: recruitment of Palestinians into Lebanese 'Opposition' parties and movements, and the formation of Palestinian Resistance cells, through which camp youth was sent for military training in other Arab countries.[32] Stiff control of the camps also helped placate Maronites angered by Chehab's pro-Egyptian foreign policy. In addition, it deterred contact between the Palestinian intelligentsia outside the camps and the masses within.[33]

The most important regional event of the 1960s was Israel's defeat of the armies of Egypt, Jordan and Syria in the 'Six Day' war, with widespread repercussions throughout the whole area. Israel now occupied Sinai and Golan as well as the West Bank and Gaza, shifting the strategic aims of these three neighbouring Arab states to a recovery of national territory. The defeat of 1967 also marked the decline of Nasserism as a political force in the Mashreq, a decline already presaged by the failure of unity negotiations between Egypt, Syria and Iraq. A third result was that the formerly clandestine Palestinian Resistance movement was enabled to capture the initiative and become a force in regional politics. The multiple and profound effect of the PRM on Lebanon will be outlined in the last section of this chapter. But it should be noted here that it was moves made by Jordan and Syria in 1970/1 to exclude or constrain the *feda'yeen* that brought about their transfer to Lebanon.

Of regional events in the 1970s, undoubtedly the most far-reaching in its effects for Lebanon as well as for the PRM was President Sadat's 'peace initiative', beginning with his visit to Jerusalem in November 1977 and ending with the Camp David Accords (September 1978). Sadat's defection terminated Palestinian and Arab pressures on the Carter Administration to convene a Middle East peace conference which would recognize Palestinian national rights.[34] Parts of the Accords regarding the Occupied Territories – an end to Israeli settlements and self-rule – were not implemented. This development also deprived Lebanon of a balancing factor in the Mashreq, one that might have restrained Syrian intervention, which took a decisive turn during the 1975/6 Civil War, and perhaps also might have deterred the Israeli invasion of 1982. Syrian hegemony was to become, along with Israeli attacks, the dominant feature of Lebanon's post-1975 existence, accepted by the Arab League states and the superpowers. The formation of an anti-Sadat Steadfastness Front composed of Syria, the PLO, Yemen, Algeria and Libya did not pose a serious obstacle to Israeli aggression because of bitter conflict between Syria and Iraq.

A second 1970s regional event with repercussions in Lebanon was the Islamic Revolution in Iran in 1979. Although Palestinians saw the fall of the Shah as a defeat for US influence in the Middle East, the emergence of a theocratic Shi'ite power centre also had negative effects for the PRM, widening the rift within it between Islamic and progressive/secular currents, and reinforcing the sectarian consciousness of Lebanese Shi'ites.

The Palestinian Resistance movement: external/internal factors

In gestation between 1948 and 1967, the Resistance was enabled to emerge in 1967 in a moment of Arab defeat and disarray. Its call for immediate armed mass action appealed to exiled Palestinians, especially the young, the intelligentsia and the people of the camps. But the PRM also appealed over the heads of often unpopular governments to many sectors of Arab populations, generating media coverage, volunteers and support groups. Lebanon was deeply affected, not so much because of its large Palestinian community, although this was a factor,[35] but also because the rise of the PRM as a regional force coincided with deepening crisis in Lebanon, a crisis that had social and cultural aspects as well as politico-economic ones.[36]

The emergence of the Resistance movement after 1967 was preceded by the official Arab League establishment of a representative 'entity', the Palestine Liberation Organization (PLO). It was President Nasser who sponsored this vital step, calling the 1st Arab Summit Conference (Alexandria, January 1964) which gave Shukairy his mandate to consult the scattered Palestinian communities. Shukairy convened the first Palestine National Council (PNC) in Jerusalem in May 1964 from which issued the PLO, the Palestine Liberation Army (PLA) and the Executive Committee. Because of King Hussein's claims to represent the Palestinians, a second important step for the PLO came when the 7th Arab Summit (Rabat, 1974) recognized it as 'sole legitimate representative of the Palestinian people'. The PLO's representativeness was reinforced by its growing acceptance by the Palestinians of the Occupied Territories. International recognition was won when the PLO was admitted to the UN as an observer (November 1974, Resolution 3236).

The Resistance (or 'Armed Struggle') movement had different social roots from the PLO, originating with Palestinians who, after 1948, joined various Arab armies. Fateh gradually emerged as the dominant one among a number of small, scattered clandestine networks, a primacy based on the solidarity of its core group, organizational skill and commencement of attacks inside Israel in 1964/5. Fateh also initiated resistance in the West Bank in the wake of the 'Six Day' war. In addition, Fateh took more pains than other groups to build the social infrastructure needed for a long struggle. The main opposition to Fateh within the Resistance movement orientation and, after 1967, turned towards Marxism. The Democratic Front for the Liberation of Palestine (DFLP) split off from the PFLP in 1969, growing similarly out of the ANM but taking less irredentist stands. Other smaller groups were generally the creation of Palestinians close to one or other of the Arab states, and did not propose radically different ideologies or strategies.[37]

An important step for both the PLO and PRM was their fusion at the 5th PNC (Cairo, 1969), when Arafat was elected PLO chairman. Relations between these two distinct sectors of the post-1948 national movement had not been cordial. But each brought to the partnership something the other lacked, the PLO contributing its Arab and international legitimacy, the

PRM the power of arms and popularity with the Palestinian masses.

Fateh's decision to launch resistance inside the West Bank after 1967 made Amman the temporary capital of the PRM, from where the groups recruited and sent out mobilizing messages. Lebanese as well as Palestinians from Lebanon joined the movement; the first Lebanese to die in action, Khalil Jamal, was given an enormous funeral procession (April 1968).[38] Lebanese popular anger against the Army's attempts to prevent *feda'yeen* operations from the South reached its peak during this period, fuelling widespread demonstrations which deepened the crisis. It was Lebanese mass support that gave the people of the camps the courage to rise against the Deuxième Bureau during the autumn of 1969. Signed by the Lebanese Army Commander and Arafat, the Cairo Accords authorized PRM action in coordination with the Army, and guaranteed Palestinian civic rights.

In September 1970, tension between the PRM and King Hussein, sparked by a PFLP hijacking coup, brought about a bloody confrontation at the end of which the PRM was forced out of Jordan, transferring the bulk of its fighters and cadres to Beirut.

Although formally an external factor, the PLO/PRM had so many bases of support in Lebanon that its transfer in 1971 was minimally opposed, even though the years of Franjiyyeh's presidency (1970–76) were ones of mounting Lebanese–Palestinian confrontation. To understand this ease of transposition we need to see the PLO/PRM as an internal factor in Lebanese politics even before 1967. Lebanon had been one of the cradles of the post-1948 national movement permitting, as Jordan and Syria did not, early Palestinian social and cultural institutions.[39] There was also a high degree of integration between Palestinian and Lebanese intelligentsias. From the early 1950s close ties were formed between Palestinian nationalists and members of the Lebanese 'Opposition' groupings. These, led by Kamal Jumblat, formed the Lebanese National movement (LNM) in 1969 which supported, and was supported by, the PRM (or parts of it) in its struggle to reform the Lebanese state and political system. Another base for PLO/PRM rootedness in Lebanon arose from state neglect of the mainly Shi'ite South, and the failure of the Army to protect it from Israeli attacks and encroachment. This situation at first created a strong bond between PRM fighters and southern villagers.

After the Cairo Accords and autonomy for the camps, the Lebanese Army continued to try to control the PRM in the South and in Beirut. Israeli attacks were a pressure towards Army–PRM confrontation. An Israeli commando raid, killing three Palestinian leaders in West Beirut on 10 April 1973, brought a storm of protest against the failure of Lebanese security forces to intercept the raiders, and from there to the resignation of Prime Minister Salam, followed by a month of Lebanese Army attacks against the camps. Clashes between the PRM and the ultra-Maronite militias in the eastern sector became increasingly frequent. Mounting social protest, including the movement of Imam Musa Sadr to voice Shi'ite grievances, added to the pressures leading to the explosion of the Civil War in the spring of 1975.[40]

The PLO/PRM survived the Civil War in spite of Syrian military intervention to prop up the Maronite rightist forces, but it suffered two serious setbacks: the expulsion of thousands of Palestinians from the 'Maronite enclave' and the destruction of camps and low-income settlements there; and the creation of an Israeli-controlled border 'strip' in the South from which a renegade Lebanese Army officer (Major Sa'd Haddad) bombarded the whole of the South. Although PLO/PRM relations with Syria improved after 1976, the PRM/LNM alliance suffered a loss of *élan* and of mass popularity. In addition, the formerly pro-Palestinian Shi'ite movement became increasingly hostile (a development that will be discussed in Chapter 7).

To conclude: however brief, its period of relative autonomy in Lebanon allowed the PLO/PRM to consolidate and expand. Its most important gains were diplomatic, signalled by Arafat's appearance at the UN General Assembly in November 1974, and by the opening of PLO offices in dozens of capitals throughout the world. A second kind of self-development was the building of civil institutions – economic, social, cultural – of a future state. Less tangibly, the PLO/PRM gave structure to Palestinians' sense of 'peoplehood', embodying their capacity to surmount defeats and turn them into a new phase of struggle. The 'Lebanon period' was also one of internal conflict and debate out of which, as Alain Gresh tells, emerged the adoption of the goal of a 'national authority' on any part of Palestine that could be liberated (12th PNC, Cairo, 1974),[41] and the acceptance of negotiation as a form of struggle (13th PNC, Cairo, 1977), developments that prompted the PFLP to leave the PLO Executive Committee and form the Rejection Front.

The period between the end of the Civil War and the Israeli invasion was one of diminished intra-Resistance group conflict. It was also a period of expansion of the 'Palestinian economy' and of PRM social projects in camps. What was dangerous about the situation was that the Lebanese in the area controlled by the PRM/LNM joint forces bore the greater part of the costs of destruction and political stagnation, while the PLO/PRM benefited disproportionately. It was this that gave rise to the accusation that the Palestinians' objective was not to liberate Palestine but to take South Lebanon as a 'country of exchange'. In the face of crisis in its relations with its Lebanese support base, the PLO/PRM proved unable to impose on itself sufficient discipline to nurture rather than exploit its Lebanese environment. When Walid Jumblat dissolved the LNM at the height of the Israeli siege of West Beirut, in August 1982, it was a clear sign that the crucial alliance no longer existed.

Notes

1. See R. Khalidi, *External Intervention and Domestic Conflict in Lebanon, 1975–1985*, working paper no. 65, International Security Studies Program, the Wilson Center, Washington DC, June 1985.

2. Palestinian official institutions in Lebanon included the Mufti himself, who lived here after his expulsion from Egypt until his death in 1974, and also offices of the Arab Higher Council, from before 1948. After 1964, the PLO and some of its unions (workers', students', womens') had offices. The PLO Research Centre opened in 1965, and the PLO Planning Centre in 1968.

3. For a discussion of the idea of Arab transfer in Zionist thinking before 1948, see B. Morris, *The Birth of the Palestinian Refugee Problem, 1947–1949* (Cambridge: CUP, 1987), pp. 23–8.

4. Between 1948 and 1951 the number of refugees in Lebanon fluctuated between 105,100 and 130,000. However, this did not include about 3,000 Palestinians who did not register with UNRWA because they did not need relief: Y. A. Sayigh, 'Implications of UNRWA Operations', MA thesis, American University of Beirut, 1952.

5. No census was carried out in Lebanon after 1932, but A. Hourani gives a total of 1,126,601 for the Lebanese population in 1944: *Minorities in the Arab World* (London: Royal Institute of International Affairs, 1947), p. 63.

6. In a letter to Lord Curzon dated 3 February 1919, Chaim Weizmann wrote: 'The irrigation of Upper Galilee and the power necessary for even a limited industrial life must come from the Litany.' Quoted in F. Hof, *Galilee Divided: The Israel–Lebanese Frontier, 1916–1948* (Boulder: Westview Press, 1984), p. 13.

7. D. Peretz, 'Israeli Foreign Policy Objectives in Lebanon', paper presented at a CIIPS workshop, Ottawa, June 1991.

8. Hof, *Galilee Divided*, pp. 56–9.

9. See L. Rokach, *Israel's Sacred Terrorism* (Belmont MA: AAUG, 1980); also W. Khalidi, *Conflict and Violence in Lebanon* (Cambridge MA: Harvard Center for International Affairs, 1979), p. 171 n. 174.

10. For the suggestion that Mossad carried on contacts with ultra-Maronite groups independently of the government, see A. Yaniv, *Dilemmas of Security: Politics, Strategy and the Israeli Experience in Lebanon* (New York: OUP, 1987), p. 35.

11. See T. Petran, *The Struggle over Lebanon* (New York: Monthly Review Press, 1987), pp. 142–5; also K. Salibi, *Crossroads to Civil War* (New York: Caravan Books, 1976); and W. Khalidi, *Conflict and Violence*, pp. 90–92.

12. W. Khalidi analyses this aspect of Israel's Lebanon policy in *Conflict and Violence*, pp. 90–92.

13. Between May 1968 and April 1975, Israel committed more than 6,200 acts of aggression against Lebanon: Petran, *Struggle over Lebanon*, p. 142.

14. *Le Monde*, 14 April 1974.

15. Statements to this effect were made by Ministers Eytan (7 May) and Sharon (10 May): *Monitoring Israeli Broadcasts*, Cairo, 8 and 11 May.

16. See I. Abu-Lughod and E. Ahmad (eds), 'The Invasion of Lebanon', special issue of *Race and Class*, vol. XXIV, no. 4, Spring 1983; S. Nassib and C. Tisdall, *Beirut: Frontline Story* (London: Pluto Press, 1983); also Petran, *Struggle over Lebanon*, ch. 18.

17. This telling phrase comes from I. Gendzier, 'The Declassified Lebanon, 1948–1958: Elements of Continuity and Contrast in US Policy towards Lebanon' in H. Barakat (ed.), *Toward a Viable Lebanon* (London: Croom Helm with the Center for Contemporary Arab Studies, Georgetown, 1988).

18. For details of Lebanon's post-1948 'boom' see M. Hudson, *The Precarious Republic* (Boulder: Westview Press, 1985), pp. 61–3. Founded in 1866 by American missionaries, AUB has remained a major teaching and cultural institution for the whole Middle East.

19. See Morris, *Birth of Palestinian Refugee Problem*, pp. 254–66. Morris notes how the Israeli government used the refugees as bargaining counters.

20. See N. Aruri, 'The United States and Israel: That Very Special Relationship' in N. Aruri, F. Moughrabi and J. Stork, *Reagan and the Middle East* (Belmont MA: AAUG, 1983).

21. See J. Stork, 'Israel as a Strategic Asset', in Aruri, Moughrabi and Stork, *Reagan*.

22. On Lebanon's sectarian system see Hudson, *Precarious Republic*, pp. 21–34; also G. Corm, *Contribution à l'étude des sociétés multi-confessionelles* (Paris, 1971); and A. AbuKhalil, 'The Politics of Sectarian Ethnicity: Segmentation in Lebanese Society', PhD thesis, Georgetown University, 1988.

23. See B. Morris, 'The Initial Absorption of the Palestinian Refugees in the Arab Host Countries, 1948–49' in A. Bramwell (ed.), *Refugees in the Age of Total War* (London: Unwin Hyman, 1988).

24. Ease of naturalization for middle-class Palestinians ended in the mid-1960s. Every application had to be passed by every member of the Cabinet, giving Kata'eb ministers the power of veto.

25. Destroyed camps are Nabatiyyeh, Dbeyyeh, Jisr al-Basha and Tell al-Za'ter.

26. See Chapter 2, pp. 65–6.

27. For the text of the Cairo Accords see W. Khalidi, *Conflict and Violence*, Appendix 1, p. 187. The Accords were never published or ratified by the Lebanese National Assembly.

28. Lebanese Sunnis were not initially more welcoming to the Palestinians of the camps than other sects: H. Hashan, 'Attitudes of the Lebanese Sects towards the Palestinians', MA thesis, American University of Beirut, 1987.

29. Until anti-Palestinianism became evident in Kuwait. This began before the Iraqi invasion of August 1990, nurtured by militias employed by the ruling family (B. Sirhan, personal communication).

30. A comprehensive account of Israeli–Maronite contacts is given by Yaniv, *Dilemmas of Security*, pp. 57f.

31. See H. Cobban, *The Palestine Liberation Organization: People, Power and Politics* (Cambridge: CUP, 1984), ch. 7.

32. Arab countries that offered military training to Palestinians were (in order of time): Egypt in Gaza, Syria, Iraq, Egypt, Algeria.

33. PLO representative al-Hout recounts how, before 1969, he went to make a speech in a camp on some Palestinian occasion and found no one assembled to listen except a few children. He addressed them as the generation that would liberate Palestine. Gradually adults felt ashamed and joined the gathering. (Interview, 17 October 1989.)

34. Cobban, *Palestine Liberation Organisation*, pp. 92f.

35. A demographer's estimate for the number of Palestinians in Lebanon in 1970 is 247,000 (G. Kosseifi, 'Demographic Characteristics of the Arab Palestinian People' in K. Nakhleh and E. Zureik [eds], *The Sociology of the Palestinians* [London: Croom Helm, 1980]).

36. See Petran, *Struggle over Lebanon*, ch. 9, 'The Gathering Storm'; E. Picard, 'De la "communauté-classe" à la résistance "nationale": pour une analyse du rôle des chi'ites dans le système politique libanais', *Revue française du science politique*, vol. 6, no. 35, December 1985, has a perceptive description of economic, social and cultural changes which challenged the Lebanese system in the early 1970s.

37. See Cobban, *Palestine Liberation Organization*; also Y. Sayigh, 'The Politics of Palestinian Exile', *Third World Quarterly*, vol. 9, no. 1, January 1987.

38. See R. Brynen, *Sanctuary and Survival: The PLO in Lebanon* (Boulder: Westview Press, 1990), p. 47. Brynen and Cobban (*Palestine Liberation Organization*) are excellent sources for the PLO/PRM in Lebanon.

39. A branch of the Palestine Arab Women's Union reopened in Beirut soon after 1948. Another early independent Palestinian cultural institution was the Institute of Palestine Studies, established in 1963. The 1967 war stimulated several new social, cultural and informational associations: In'ash al-Mukhayem, Friends of Jerusalem, the Fifth of June Society, and others.

40. For the PLO/PRM in the Civil War, see Brynen, *Sanctuary and Survival*; Cobban, *Palestine Liberation Organization*; and Khalidi, *Conflict and Violence*.

41. A. Gresh, *The PLO: The Struggle Within* (London: Zed Books, 1985).

2. The First Decade: Remembering Palestine, Learning Lebanon

The founding of Shateela

A few refugee families scattered in the pine woods to the south of Beirut formed the nucleus of the future camp. Among them was a man whose energy and connections marked him out as the founder, Abed Bisher, a *mujahideen* leader who was in Lebanon on an arms-buying mission for the Mufti on 15 May 1948 when the Israelis closed the border. His son Jihad was nine or ten years old at the time:

> When we came we had almost nothing. My father never worked, he only fought. Payment was irregular, our only property [in Palestine] was a small house made of mud. Hajj Amin wasn't here, and most of my father's *mujahideen* comrades were in Damascus. We were in a desperate state; my older brothers worked but we couldn't pay the rent of the small room we were living in. So my father went to al-Nahar and bought a big tent and put it up in al-Hursh [the Forest]. There were around twenty people in that tent, all my father's family and the families of my two older married sisters. . . .
>
> My father got the idea of gathering the people of his village, Majd al-Kroom, together in one place. So he went to the Arab Higher Council. He also had contacts with the [International] Red Cross which was preparing at that time to hand over to UNRWA. He wanted to suggest finding an empty space and putting up tents in it. But before going to the AHC and the Red Cross, he went to see someone called *al-Basha* Shateela who lived in a large villa somewhere in the area. My father thought he was the owner of the land on which Shateela now stands. It seems that the real owner was someone from Shweifat who was out of the country at the time. Anyway *al-Basha* Shateela gave my father permission to use the land. It had nothing to do with UNRWA, he got it himself.
>
> So then he managed to procure twenty tents from UNRWA – it had started then – and he went to all the places where Majd al-Kroom people

were scattered and brought them to Beirut. The twenty tents were taken, more people came, my father got more tents. He had to keep in continuous contact with UNRWA for things that Palestinians needed – distributions of milk and rations, tents and so on. Then the offer came from UNRWA to my father to become camp leader[1] for a salary of LL75 a month. At the time this was great. My father had no objection, we needed the money badly. So he was officially appointed on condition that he agreed to take in around twenty-five families from Yaffa who were occupying Kraytem Mosque.

Although there were other candidates for the post of director, Abed Bisher had the backing of the Mufti, who had influence within UNRWA. A high agency official who had been instrumental in appointing Abu Kamal explained, 'I didn't want clerks, I wanted someone who could control the people.' Small in stature, Abu Kamal had leadership qualities; even those who disagreed with his politics, or criticized him for favouring his own following, acknowledged this.

Of all the Palestinian camps in Lebanon, Shateela is the closest to Beirut,[2] only just outside the municipal boundaries and not far from the predominantly Sunni Muslim quarters of the city (Museitbeh, Mazra', Basta). The plot of land donated by the Basha was not much bigger than a field, a narrow oblong about 200 by 400 metres. In 1949, no one could have guessed that the whole area would become a target for wave upon wave of rural migrants, Lebanese as well as Palestinian. Nor could anyone have foreseen the strategic nature of Shateela's location, for this would only gradually become apparent through the upheavals – economic, political and demographic – that were to come.

At the beginning of the flight of Palestinians into Lebanon, most remained in the South, waiting for repatriation which they believed to be imminent, resisting transfer to other areas as best they could. Urban Palestinians came to Beirut, but not the rural masses. Abed Bisher travelled about Lebanon, to the South, to Shaheem and Barja in the Shouf – even, it is said, to Aleppo – looking for people from his own village of Majd al-Kroom, and encouraging them to settle in Shateela. Besides his co-villagers, Abu Kamal brought in people from nearby villages: relatives, friends and associates from his past as a *qa'id* (leader). Although he actively recruited his own people, Abu Kamal did not turn anyone away.[3] He wanted Shateela to grow as rapidly possible, aware that the larger its population, the harder it would be to move people away. In early 1950 there were around twenty families; a few months later the number had grown to sixty. By the early 1960s there are said to have been 3,000 people in and around the camp.

Although more than half of Shateela's original population were from Majd al-Kroom, some twenty-five other villages in northwestern Galilee were represented. There were sizeable numbers from al-Birweh; Sha'b, Saffouri and Deir al-'Assi; other villages – Sufsaf, Amqa, Kabri, Nahaf, Beled al-Sheikh, Kweikat, Menshiyyeh – had one or more households each. Unlike most other camps in Lebanon, where sizeable village quarters were formed, Shateela's small size and fragmented composition prevented such village clustering. Even the majority Majd al-Kroomites did not form a quarter of their own.

Not all Shateela's original population were villagers. Although Abu Kamal raised no objection to the incorporation of city people, the Yaffawites at first angrily refused. Despite being reduced to the same state of penury, lower-class city Palestinians retained their sense of superiority over villagers. The idea of living in tents among *fellaheen* (peasants) was abhorrent to them. They had to be forcibly transferred, and at first they demarcated their living space from the rest of the camp with a path. Contact between them and other inhabitants was limited for the first few years. Although other urban Palestinians came to settle in Shateela, they did not affect its predominantly rural ethos and remained without foothold in its main institutions.[4]

So closely was Abed Bisher identified with Shateela camp that when, in the early 1960s, the real owner of the land set about trying to repossess it, it was against Abu Kamal that he brought a case, not against UNRWA or the government. After Abu Kamal's retirement in 1969, the directorship passed to his son Jihad, and in 1978 to a grandson.[5]

The setting

Those who first settled in Shateela, the *mu'essesseen* (founders), describe the area in 1949/50 as a 'desert'.

> At the beginning there was nothing here but sand. All these buildings that you see around us now – Sabra, the market, Dana Mosque, Hayy Gharbeh – none of this existed then. There were some old stores and barracks left by the French Army. A few houses – not many – in Hayy al-Basha and Hayy Farhat. We walked on dirt roads to get to Corniche al-Mazra'. Two kilometres beyond Shateela there were woods where no one dared to go after 6 pm for fear of robbers. (Abu Turki)

Turks as well as the French had used the area for military installations: there were old trenches and tunnels.[6] Nearby was an enclosure for a cemetery which eventually became Da'ouq 'camp' (the core of Sabra), and beyond it Beirut's first civilian airport. These were the only signs that Shateela was close to the city. The rural atmosphere of a zone that would become one of the most densely populated of Beirut's suburbs is suggested by Abu Turki's recollection that, close to Shateela's main entrance, there was a little sand-hill where Beirut families used to come on summer evenings to enjoy the cool breezes. To Palestinians a 'desert', this large area of sand dunes and pine woods south of Beirut had quite another character to Lebanese. Or rather, it had different potentialities for people with different interests. For city planners, its vocation was to be the 'lungs' of the city, an area of recreation and sports: hence the siting of Chamoun's Sports City on the ridge overlooking the camp, as well as, nearby, a horse-riding club and golf course. Basha Shateela was not the only notable to build his summer–winter residence here, conveniently close to the city; there were other, grander villas such as those of Riad al-Solh and Sabry Hammadeh. A number of politicians and merchants also saw the possibilities of the land for speculation, especially after the selection of the site of Beirut's International Airport between Khaldeh and Bourj Barajneh. Neither city planners nor grandees imagined the demographic explosion to come, the result of multiple factors that would bring waves of new settlers over the next three decades: the pull of Beirut's construction boom, the push of low wages and landlessness in the rural hinterland; later, war in the South would add to the push factors. This influx would radically change the character of the area, encouraging the growth of commerce and service institutions as well as of low-cost urban housing.

In the 1950s there was hardly a building between Shateela and Bourj Barajneh camp five kilometres to the south, and only a few houses between Shateela and tiny Da'ouq 'camp' to the north, built on land intended for a cemetery. The Ma'wah al-'Ajazeh (Old People's Home), by whose clock Shateela people used to tell the time, went up in the early 1950s, next to Da'ouq, at the heart of what would be Sabra, one of Beirut's densest commercial areas. To the east of Shateela lay the old Shi'ite settlements of Hayy Farhat and Ghobeireh. To the west, there was nothing between Shateela and the sea except a low ridge of sand-hills, where the three giant Chamoun stadiums and the Boulevarde running past them would be built. In winter the sea could be heard in the camp.

The camp as habitat

The hardships of the first years of Shateela were quite different from those that came later.

> Being low-lying in a *wadi* [river bed], Shateela was a wind-trap. The wind blew sand into our food and the winter storms carried away our tents. We suffered a lot from this in the beginning. Some people put tar on their

tents to try to keep out rain but this caused fires. UNRWA gave us tent pins but they were wrenched out by storms. We went and dug up paving stones wherever we could find them, and put them inside our tents to weight them and to lean our backs against. Later people bought wooden planks, *zinco* [corrugated iron] and flattened-out petrol cans to make huts. But it was forbidden to use stone or cement.

UNRWA bought water in lorries but there was never enough. Women used to go and fill from Lebanese neighbours. (Abu Turki)

Restrictions on housing and water were the basic means through which the state maintained the temporariness of refugee settlements around Beirut. Jihad says that his father agreed with this policy:

He wanted Shateela to be temporary, to remind people that they aren't living on their land, they aren't in their own homes, they aren't living happily. That's why he fought against the idea of building the camp like other buildings. He didn't want it to become solid, he wanted it to be a temporary place for Palestinians to gather in until they could return.

For people of the camps, constraints on housing fuelled a continual angry struggle to improve their basic life conditions, so as to 'live like other people'. It was a struggle that took the form of small individual improvements wherever there was means and scope for them. Tents were abandoned for *barakiyat*, huts of wood and tin; tin walls were replaced by stone and plaster. Poverty prevented all but minimal outlays: wood could be salvaged, tin sheeting was cheap. But even if people could have afforded it, cement was forbidden, especially for ceilings. This prohibition effectively prevented the upwards expansion of housing.

Water was similarly restricted. The Beirut Water Company was not allowed to supply Shateela residents; instead there were four public water tanks filled periodically by UNRWA lorries. Every resident had the right to draw one petrol can of water a day. A guardian was appointed for each tank – old men who could not do heavier work – to supervise distribution. Each household contributed 25 piastres a month to their salary. Quarrels over water were frequent. Sometimes the *natour* (guardian) would let a woman jump her turn or take more than her share; sometimes they sold the water. This system of water distribution remained until 1969. Abu Turki's friendship with one of the Farhat family allowed him to extend company water from Hayy Farhat to his home; this was a source that continued to supply water to Shateela during the Amal sieges.

Among the earliest UNRWA installations were the clinic, the school and two lines of public latrines, one for men and one for women: 'a disgusting situation' a founder bitterly recalls, and one that also remained until the uprising of 1969. Waste disposal and sewage were also the object of state restrictions – private cesspits were as forbidden as cement ceilings. There was nowhere to throw waste water except the public latrines; even a trickle on the street brought fines.

> There were no sewage pipes and it was forbidden to dig a hole under the house. It was also forbidden to throw water anywhere except in the public toilets. They were at the edge of the camp, beyond the last houses; you had to walk maybe 50 metres. Small children had to use a pot, and their mothers would empty it in the morning. (Abu Muhammad Farmawi)

A boy in the 1960s, Ahmad Haleemeh remembers that it was his duty to empty the household 'slops' in the public latrine. He also remembers 'problems' because boys sometimes climbed up to peep at women. Certainly these were among the most humiliating reminders of refugee status. In the 1960s many householders paid bribes to the police so that they could dig the forbidden cesspits under their houses.

Other early UNRWA installations were the Director's office (his tent) and the 'restaurant' (a supplementary feeding centre for children). Schooling began almost immediately, in three large hospital tents. There was also a workshop for repairing damaged tents, an early income-generating project which closed when tents were abandoned.

There were no restrictions on electricity except poverty; the Director and some other better-off householders were able to bring it to their homes by the time of the transition from tents to *barakiyat*. An account given by Abu Turki points to the advantage Shateela enjoyed through proximity to Beirut:

> I think it was in 1956, I went to the city and contacted the Prime Minister, Sami Solh. He gave me his card, and I took it to the Director of the Electricity Company. He said, 'We have no instructions from the authorities to supply electricity to the camp. But because you have a card from the Prime Minister I will give you a meter.'

Abu Turki was able to convince the Director to give him four meters 'unofficially', paying the deposit as well as LL750 (a large sum in those days[7]) for the cable needed to extend the current from Sabra to his home. Thus Abu Turki became the 'feudalist of electricity' of Shateela camp, renting out current to other homes. For one radio and one light bulb from 6pm to midnight, people paid him LL2½ a month. Demand was strong – people had begun to buy radios at this time and wanted light by which their children could study – so the lines were constantly overloaded.

In the 1950s few public buildings in Shateela could be called autonomous. One was the mosque, built around 1955 in the heart of the camp, at the juncture of its three main streets. It had an outer wall of stone and a tin roof; with only one floor, it was much smaller then than now; inside there was a special section curtained off for women and children. Schoolboys were mobilized to sweep out the mosque on Thursdays and before feasts. Each household gave LL2 a month as an *ikramiyyeh* (honorarium) to the *sheikh*. Ahmad Haleemeh recalls that his grandfather liked the boys to pray in Shateela Mosque, whereas his father preferred them to attend 'proper' mosques downtown.

Another important indigenous institution, then as now, was the cemetery. There were two, one in Bir Hassan near what later became Akka Hospital, the other in the Hursh (the Forest), part of which later became the Martyrs' Cemetery. Shateela, because of its proximity, had special rights and duties *vis-à-vis* the cemeteries, regarded as national territory. Women and children were responsible for cleaning the graves before the feasts and decorating them with palm fronds, flowers and ribbons. Because of their quiet, students used to use the cemeteries to study in. But no one lingered after dark, since cemeteries were believed to be the haunts of jinn, as well as of thieves and drug addicts.

Jihad Bisher recalls that his father, the Director, set up a tent opposite his own in which were placed some mats and cushions, and invited a few older men who were not working, the village notables, to meet there occasionally as a kind of consultative body, a *mejlis al-shuyyukh* (council of old men). When the Mufti visited Shateela, as he did several times during the 1950s, it was here that he was received. Some of the early settlers deny that this body had any real representative role, claiming that the Director used it to cover his own decisions or those of the authorities with the appearance of consultation. Others claim that, on the contrary, the notables were more skilled at solving social conflicts and problems than the revolutionary institutions that came later.

At the other end of the spectrum of age and status, a scout group was formed in the late 1950s in a hut adjoining the school. Patriotic teachers had encouraged this development but, by the 1960s, under Deuxième Bureau control, Shateela scouts ceased to be autonomous. One of their functions was to line the airport road to cheer visiting heads of state. No one mourned when the group was closed down by the authorities for fear that it would become a nucleus of Palestinian nationalism.

Work, income, living standards

In the 1950s, most Shateela men earned their living in daily paid manual labour, mainly in construction. There was a labour market on Corniche al-Mazra', a few kilometres north of the camp.

> They went to Barbir on foot and waited to be hired. Maybe someone would want a foreman, or a skilled worker with concrete, or a man to carry construction materials. The one who wasn't chosen returned home with his food packet. It was a market for daily workers, whose wage in those days was LL2. Palestinians worked the whole day – they carried stones and bags of sand and cement to the top of buildings – for only LL2. (Abu Turki)

The *hamal* (porters) were the lowest category of labour, one that in Lebanon is entirely occupied by non-national workers. Lebanese business and manufacturing, which was concentrated in the metropolitan area, benefited enormously from the sudden increase in the labour supply provided by the Palestinians at a moment when new markets were opening up.

Palestinians did not remain *hamal* for long, although construction work has remained until now a fall-back in time of need, and for students during summer. The next step was to become specialists in one of the building trades (plumbing, plastering, tiling, electric wiring, etc.). It was such skills that enabled most Shateela people to build their own homes, and eventually gave rise to a small group of master builders employing others. 'Free work' was preferred by many men because good money could be made, especially when the Beirut building boom got under way. But accidents were not indemnified and could lead to long periods of unemployment. Ahmad Haleemeh's father strained his back lifting a heavy stone while working as a tile-layer. His family survived his six months' disablement mainly because, living in a compound household, food could be stretched to provide for them. Heavy manual labour combined with poor housing and malnutrition took its toll on health.

Many men (especially older men and those who had been small landowners unused to manual labour) preferred to look for low-level salaried employment, however badly paid. Abul Abed Safedi, for example, who had been a *mukhtar* in Kabri, managed through connections to get a job as the guard of a Saudi school in Bourj Barajneh, at LL70 a month. Such a position brought the security of a monthly salary and a retirement indemnity.

Among the Yaffa and Haifa people were port workers whose skills were in demand to expand the port of Beirut. Later many of them migrated to Iraq or the Gulf where the oil boom produced a market for skilled workers of all kinds. Earnings were good, supporting the migration of whole families: only a few of these port-worker families remained in Shateela in the 1980s. People of village origin claim that city people spent their often higher earnings on consumer goods whereas they, the villagers, invested in the education of their children. Some of these differences could be seen in the 1980s, when many families of rural origin had adult children working as professionals. Such families often moved out of the camp but remained in close contact with it, helping poorer kin. City people who had stayed on were closer to destitution: their kin and quarter ties seemed too weak to survive migration.

UNRWA was a large employer of Palestinians in the 1950s. Literacy was usually required, which barred the majority of camp residents until the 1960s when schooling began to produce a literate generation; but there were some low-level salaried posts *in* camps that were available to inhabitants. After the directorship, the most important was Chief of Sanitation, who commanded several workers. Although most UNRWA professional staff (teachers, doctors, staff nurses) were from outside, guards, drivers, pharmacists, practical nurses, cleaners, cooks and store clerks were camp people. Such local appointments lay in the hands of Abu Kamal. Many people blamed him later because he filled most of these jobs with family and friends. Abu Isma'een explains:

> If the camp Director has two or three vacant jobs, he won't give them to people from outside if he has unemployed relatives. 'Those close to us have priority' – this is a universal rule. I am from Sufsaf. The Director can't give me a job and neglect the men from his village.
>
> Let's say one of the UNRWA employees is my friend. I catch him on the way to the distribution centre, so he takes my ration card and puts it in his pocket. You are not his friend so how could you take your rations before me? This is the way of the world.

On the other hand, the vital importance of UNRWA resources in the 1950s made the practice of *waasta* (connections) bitter to those excluded from it. It was not just steady UNRWA salaries that people needed; more important were the extra benefits: secondary school subsidies, places in UNRWA's technical and teachers' training institute, loans to set up businesses, papers to see medical specialists, and hardship allowances. Theoretically allocated according to need and merit, the scarcity of such resources inevitably subjected them to the law of *waasta*. UNRWA employees in the camp formed a relatively privileged group, self-selecting and bound to each other by mutual favours. Few alternative sources of patronage were available in the 1950s.

Closeness to Beirut meant that commerce had an earlier and stronger start in Shateela than other camps. One of the first shop-keepers was Abu Salem from Majd al-Kroom, of whom it is said that he returned to Palestine to bring his wife and her dowry on a donkey. Abu Salem first sold vegetables from his tent, and later obtained the commission to supply foodstuffs to UNRWA's feeding centre. From there he moved into wholesale vegetable trading and real estate to become Shateela's first and only millionaire. Up until 1982 he and his wife still worked in their shop near Shateela's main entrance.

Another of the earliest shop-keepers was Abu Turki, the 'feudalist of electricity', also from Majd al-Kroom. He was offered an UNRWA job but turned it down:

> In Palestine I had some land which my brother worked on, while I had a salaried job with the British Army. UNRWA asked me to work with them but I refused. I employed a worker whom I paid LL30 a month – UNRWA employees took only LL35. I preferred having a shop, it's more dignified. No one ordered me to carry things. Shop-keeping is better than a salaried job, it's free. If I sleep until mid-day, no one tells me 'Open!'. And if I open, no one tells me 'Close!'.

Abu Salem's success serves to highlight the more limited careers of other shop-keepers. Most of those who had started out in the 1950s were still there when I began visiting Shateela in 1982: Abu Muhammad Jisheh began by selling cloth 'from the shoulder', then opened the shop where most Shateela people bought their drapes, paying by instalment; Abu Hassan Serees was the first Shateela butcher who, unlike the Sabra butchers, gave honest measure; Abu Ali Da'bis was still there with his grocery shop in 1982, as well as widow Shehadeh. Some city families (notably *dar* Sakkhijha), who were skilled in making Arab cakes such as *namoora*, *sfoof* and *hareeseh*, were still selling them from trays or barrows on the street. The profits from such small enterprises might support a son through one of the state-supported universities, or buy a modest apartment in the suburbs, but they did not provide a basis for whole-family migration, as happened with some highly skilled port and technical workers.

Average daily wages in the 1950s were LL2½ to LL3 a day. But there was no shortage of work, and households with more than one worker could improve habitat, food and clothing. At the beginning, no one had watches, winter clothes or proper shoes, but a decade later most households enjoyed the basics as well as essential extras such as radios. Recalling that period, people remember the extraordinary cheapness of foodstuffs and essential commodities, praising Beirut as *Umm al-Faqeer* (Mother of the poor).

In such an economic environment, with UNRWA providing ground rent, rations and social services, all could survive; but the situation of each household varied, depending on the number of workers relative to dependents, as well as their earning capacity.

Families with several working sons could cease taking UNRWA rations and – a sign of social status – maintain a *diwan* where coffee was served to all visitors. But where there was sickness or disability a household might become dependent on the charity of kin and neighbours. Abu and Umm Isma'een give an idea of such differences:

> Abu Isma'een: There were people who had sons who were earning, those who came from Palestine already married, with adult sons, they were comfortable. They could spend one salary and save one salary. But I came as a boy from Palestine, my children were all young. There were eight of us and I was the only one earning. I was taking LL3 a day. We tried to spend LL2½ and save LL½ because the hygienic situation was bad and the children kept getting sick.

> Umm Isma'een: Everything was cheap then. A kilo of potatoes cost 1 piastre, a crate of tomatoes LL1. We lived according to our means. He didn't smoke, he didn't gamble, he didn't go to restaurants. I managed with what we had, not like some women who show off. And now, thank God, our children are married.

Like the other urban camps, Shateela promoted a far-reaching change in occupation, from those appropriate to Palestinian villages to the more complex skills of an 'ethnic proletariat' dependent on wage labour. Limits were set to occupational mobility by the work permit system, but within those limits Shateela workers developed a range of technical, entrepreneurial and service skills. However, because of its closeness to Beirut, Shateela also functioned as a 'station' where Palestinians acquired qualifications before migrating elsewhere (the Gulf, Libya or Europe). Thus at any given time, the majority of Shateela workers were and are 'blue collar', with better-qualified workers tending to migrate.

Occupational change from farming to urban wage labour and services did not produce immediate change in social relations, political consciousness or culture. A Lebanese Marxist visiting the camps in the early 1970s remarked on their peasant conservatism.[8] Among many factors inhibiting a sense of working-class identity was the scattering of workers over many small enterprises, the survival in exile of village and kin ties, and the predominantly nationalist ethos of the PLO General Union of Palestinian Workers.

Women and work

Did Shateela women work for wages in the 1950s? The question is intriguing because of a tendency to deny it. One old lady said that such a thing might have happened in other camps but not in Shateela. Closer enquiry reveals a different picture, however.

> Women went and filled [crates] with oranges and lemons. They went to
> Bourj Barajneh and the plantation owners came and took them from
> there in lorries. Some women picked the fruit, others weighed it, others
> put it in boxes. They came to take them at 4 am in winter. (Fatimeh
> Ghreiry)

Fatimeh herself helped her husband to sell vegetables on the street in front
of their home and so did not go with neighbouring women and girls to the
plantations. She also remembers that women worked on construction sites
near the camp, 'going up and down carrying earth and stones on their
heads'. The fact that only the first settlers remember women doing
construction or plantation work suggests that it stopped after the first
few years. In spite of the tendency to 'forget' such a thing, one woman told
me that, as a young girl, she had carried vegetables on her head from door to
door for wages.

The code about women differentiated between kinds of work, its site, and
a woman's marital status and economic circumstances. Work *in* the camp
was more respectable than work outside it; work in the home was best –
helping husbands in shops that were extensions of homes was always
accepted. It was recognized that widows, divorcees and women whose
husbands were sick had to work to provide for their children. Women
(*niswan*) had more freedom and mobility than *banat* (girls, unmarried
women) because of the importance attached to pre-marital virginity. It was
a flexible code, cast-iron in its basic tenets yet well provided with practical
loopholes, mainly self-enforced through fear of shame and ridicule, and
seldom transgressed.

Although the provision of schooling in camps meant that girls were better
educated than their mothers, and hence more qualified to find employment,
the sexual code prevented this except in special circumstances, for example
to educate a brother, or when there were no young men in the family. A
factor that held back the employment of *banat* was the lack of professional
training in camps. At best, girls might be apprenticed to a seamstress: this
was the case with Zohra 'Issa Khalaf, put out at eleven years of age to learn
sewing because her father had tuberculosis. But opportunities for girls in
camps to become teachers, nurses or secretaries before the 1970s, when the
Resistance movement expanded training programmes, were few. Only one
case of an unmarried woman from the camp working in the 1950s can be
recalled, a girl from Haifa who got nursing training in a Beirut hospital, later
working in the UNRWA clinic. UNRWA locations were considered
equivalent to 'home', and widows who needed to work had priority for
salaried employment as UNRWA cooks or cleaners.

Many Shateela women have traded in or near their homes when their
situation demanded or permitted it. While her husband was in a sanatorium,

Umm Mahmoud Haleemeh bought and sold vegetables (proving a sharp trader, according to her grandson Ahmad). Fatimeh Ghreiry was able to give her husband a hand selling vegetables because they had no children. When asked how she had calculated weights and prices she said, 'I worked it out. Sometimes the neighbours' daughters who were in school helped me.' Umm Salem, the millionaire's wife, is remembered as having 'stood beside her husband from 7.30 am to 10 pm', in spite of Abu Salem's prosperity. When Hajji Hafeezha's husband became too sick to push a vegetable barrow, it was she who used to buy the stock for their little sweet shop outside Galilee School, carrying it down from Sabra on her head.

Women could also add to family income by providing services within the community such as midwifery. In Nabatiyyeh camp in the 1950s, payment to unofficial midwives was LL5 per delivery, with a cake of Lifebuoy soap if it was a boy. Several Shateela women are remembered as having practised as *daya* (midwife), even though hospital deliveries were becoming common. One of them, Umm Fahd, contributed effectively to her husband's earnings as an UNRWA pharmacist, with all six sons and daughters obtaining professional training. Another such traditional medical practice sometimes undertaken by women was *jabr*, the art of bone healing.

Although such work was considered shameful, some women worked as cooks and cleaners, under the pressure of need. Most were of poor city origin, perhaps because solidarity or shaming mechanisms worked less effectively among them than among rural people. Usually such women were the wives of low-wage earners with many young children. In such families, the oldest daughter would be taken out of school to look after younger siblings.

The relation between class and gender is clearly shown in people's reluctance to talk about women who worked as domestics for others: household status and community reputation are involved. Only unconventional women, those whom people call (*q*)*awiyyeh* (strong), admit, 'Yes, for my children's sake I worked in homes.'

Neighbours

We had good and bad experiences with neighbours. In the 1950s, before water was brought to the camp, we used to go to Lebanese neighbours to get water. There were a few houses in Sabra, a few in Hayy Farhat. They were very helpful, they gave . . . But very early on, maybe it was in 1952, there was a kind of invasion of the camp by Lebanese neighbours, the Stetiyeh brothers. They were narcotics smugglers. One of their sisters was married to someone in Shateela[9] and she had a quarrel with one of the workers in the clinic. She went to her brother and they brought their people and invaded the camp with sticks and knives. This was the first time that guns came out from hidden places in Shateela. My brother Kamal shot into the air to show them that we can defend ourselves. The oldest Stetiyeh brother got a knife wound near the heart and almost died. I remember I was twelve years old, I went out with the others to keep guard. We had to keep guard all night in shifts until there was a reconciliation. That was the first time that Shateela people fought as a camp to defend themselves. People from villages, people from cities, everyone fought to drive the invaders out. (Jihad Bisher)

Apparently a trivial personal episode, the Stetiyeh battle took on importance in the perspective of Shateela's subsequent history, first because of the possible linkage between the drug smugglers and the authorities via their patron, a member of the Lebanese political elite; second, because it welded the heterogeneous population of the camp into a single defensive unit. A core element in village solidarity was the ancient practice known as *faza'a* (defensive rush), whereby if any member of a village was attacked, the whole of the population – men, women and children – would rush to their defence. The fight with the Stetiyeh gang was such an instance of *faza'a*.

Another early clash is narrated by Khaled Shehadeh, a distant kinsman and political opponent of the Director:

The people of Hayy Farhat hated barrow salesmen coming to their quarter and shouting 'Tomatoes for sale!' or 'Oil for sale!' There was someone from our village, *Allah yerhamu*,[10] Qayyed Ayoub, who sold oil. The first time they beat him . . . The second time they beat him . . . Then we beat Abu Hassan Farhat. The Director was from our village [Majd al-Kroom]. He got up and he said, 'Look, my boys! They are trying to ride on our backs. We must teach them a lesson.' There was a battle and we threw them back from the edge of the camp into their own quarter. They ran to Ghobeireh to fetch the police. Three or four policemen came and shouted at us. Abed Bisher knew their *shaweesh*.[11] He told them, 'Stop where you are! I am Abed Bisher and I'm going to Hajj Amin!' By God, not one more word was said. They went back to their houses in Hayy Farhat. .

This story is interesting not only in showing Abu Kamal in action, mobilizing the camp against outsiders, but also for the suggestion it gives of coordination between the Mufti and the higher Lebanese authorities, so that mention of his name was enough to cause both Lebanese neighbours and local police to withdraw. A second point of interest is that Hayy Farhat people were Shi'ite. In accounts of relations with Lebanese neighbours in the 1950s, one finds no sectarian consciousness on either side. Abu Isma'een's house was near to Hayy Farhat:

> When we first came they were good to us, they gave us water. Occasionally there were quarrels between children – Palestinian children are rough, they curse and throw stones – and our Lebanese neighbours would tell us we don't know how to control them. But they were good people. Of course the people of Hayy Farhat are Shi'ite and we are Sunni but in those days no one knew a Sunni from a Shia, we were all Muslims.

The only neighbour with whom Shateela continually had fights was 'Ali Handar, a man from Barja who set up a coffee house just outside the main entrance to the camp. The term 'coffee house' sounds innocent enough to Western ears but to rural Palestinians it had the connotations of 'bar' or 'cabaret'. The moral consensus did not permit the opening of a coffee house *inside* the camp and the presence of 'Ali Handar's just outside its boundaries was a provocative reminder of the evil influence of the city. Many people believed that the Handar *kahweh* was part of a sinister campaign by the authorities to undermine moral values.

In fact the Handar cafe became a place of gambling and peddling drugs, where several Shateela men are said to have ruined their families. In the 1960s it would be used by the Army Intelligence Bureau to recruit informers. Brawls between people from the camp and the coffee house owner were frequent.

> There was another battle against the coffee house at the entrance to the camp, after 'Ali Handar made a series of immoral attacks against girls on the western side of the camp. We caught him and gave him a beating along with his relatives and allies, *dar* Jammel. We beat them and we broke up the coffee house. They didn't dare to come near us again. All the families of the camp took part, from Saffouri, from Kweikat, from al-Birweh – all. (Khaled Shehadeh)

In fact there were other fights with 'Ali Handar, and camp leaders continually campaigned to keep Shateela's youth out of his clutches. In the 1970s, under the Resistance movement, orders were issued putting the cafe out of bounds. The Handar cafe represented the dark side of Shateela's closeness to Beirut, the threat of alienation and corruption, of sociocultural rupture, of loss of control over the new generation. It was partly to prevent evil outside influences from entering the camp, partly to stop Shateela's young men from going out at night, that Abu Kamal maintained a night guard on the camp's two main entrances. While 'evil influences' are customarily articulated in moral/sexual terms, Abu Kamal was surely equally concerned to limit political contacts between 'his' people and Beirut.

Internal politics

The Mufti's influence over camp populations in the early 1950s is suggested by an anecdote told by Shafiq al-Hout.[12] With some other young Palestinian radicals, al-Hout attempted soon after 1948 to organize 'Committees of the Dispersed' to represent the people of the camps. The attempt failed after a meeting called in Bourj Barajneh camp was physically broken up by the Mufti's following.

Because of the way Shateela's population had been recruited, supporters of Hajj Amin led by Abu Kamal had the upper hand throughout the 1950s. However unofficially, since his legitimacy was contested by Jordan and Egypt, the Mufti continued to play a low-key leadership role in Lebanon, maintaining discreet contacts with the people of the camps. He is remembered as having visited Shateela on several occasions, once to condole with Abu Kamal for the death of a son. The heads of respected camp families always visited the Mufti at the time of the feasts, kissing his hand and receiving gifts of money. Hajj Amin's political influence was backed up by his power to procure jobs:

> Employment in UNRWA was based on the recommendation of Hajj Amin. Even travelling to Saudi Arabia needed a letter from the Mufti for them to admit a Palestinian. Work in Saudi Arabia began before the rest of the Gulf people started going there in the 1950s. Anyone who went to the Embassy without a letter from Hajj Amin didn't get a visa. (Abu Muhammad Farmawi)

There were several points of policy agreement between the Mufti's Arab Higher Council (AHC) and the Lebanese authorities. They were equally opposed to permanent settlement of Palestinians in Lebanon, and hence against any move that could further this aim. Both sides would have liked to restrict the mass of refugees to rural areas and occupations, the Lebanese government to develop the backward farming sector, the AHC to preserve the conservative peasant base of Palestinian society. Hence a third point of consensus was to keep the conditions of the Beirut camps as miserable as possible, to inhibit permanent settlement. Shateela people remember demonstrating during the 1950s against UNRWA proposals for more solid housing. Later this policy would boomerang against the AHC, with people putting the Palestinian leadership in the same bag with the Lebanese authorities as enemies of minimally decent living conditions.

Other political currents were not slow to appear, however. Opposition to the Mufti was transferred from Palestine along with loyalty. Many people blamed him and his style of leadership for the country's loss; arguments on this burning issue broke out continually in informal social gatherings in the camps (sometimes resurfacing thirty years later).

The *shuyyukh* were in harmony with the line of Hajj Amin, the paternalist line which said, 'I am your father, Palestinians. You don't have an opinion. I decide.' The older generation was influenced by Hajj Amin and by religious thinking: 'We want the teaching of the Quran!' They feared that the generation influenced by Abdel Nasser and by nationalism would escape from their control. They tried to frighten us with talk of the state. We considered them as an obstacle to our movement. (Khaled Shehadeh)

The desperate need to find a solution to their problem made the refugees fertile ground for recruitment to the 'Opposition' parties, which were becoming stronger at this time. The appeal of these parties was mainly to younger men. Khaled Shehadeh was one of these: twenty-two at the time of the *Nekba* (Disaster, Palestinian term for the war of 1948), he had been a worker in Haifa Oil Refinery and had taken part in communal battles. Although a member of Shateela's dominant village, he became a local leader of the Arab Nationalist movement:

There began to be movements in Shateela, among them the PPS, the Ba'th, the Arab Nationalist movement and the Lebanese Communist Party. We got to know all these movements and their thinking through our discussions and relations with one another. Sometimes discussions escalated into fights – PPS against ANM, communists against nationalists. Each one stuck to his own way of thinking. We talked about how to get Palestine back. We differed, but in freedom. There weren't spies in those days. . . .

I was ready to enter any party that named Israel as the enemy. I started with the Muslim Brethren but only stayed with them two or three weeks. Their speeches disgusted me – 'The human being is nothing, the country is nothing, patriotism is nothing, only God counts.' I wanted my country. Later we formed a group; we called ourselves 'Al-Shebab al-'Arabi al-Filasteeni'.[13]

Student milieus also generated political discussion and membership in the 'Opposition' parties. Jihad Bisher recalls pressures to join the Ba'th or ANM in secondary school in Bourj Barajneh in the late 1950s: 'At first I thought their aims were right. But because my father was one of the following of Hajj Amin and we were brought up to respect our fathers, I refused to join.' Abu 'Ali Abbas, whose family moved from Ba'lbek to Shateela in 1959 when he was fifteen, recalls that it was a *buqra hizbiyyeh* (a focal point of political parties). He himself became a Ba'thist and a student leader, one of the first *shebab* (young men) from Shateela to reach the university.

Older people, however, retained a distrust of political parties that had begun in Palestine and was also probably a strand within Islamic-based Palestinian nationalism. This was one reason for party recruitment taking place in schools and workplaces rather than in the camp itself. Heated political discussion and joining in demonstrations: these were the limits of most people's political activity. The fact that Nasserist Arab nationalism was a movement rather than a party was probably an unarticulated reason for its popularity with the Palestinian masses. At the height of Nasser's popularity, in the late 1950s and early 1960s, there were hardly more than six ANM members in Shateela. Other parties had not more than one or two members each, and the Lebanese Communist Party (LCP) had none according to Abu Muhammad Farmawi.

Old-style Palestinian resistance continued. Jihad Bisher recalls carrying a letter from the Mufti to a *qa'id* in South Lebanon – as a boy of fifteen he did not risk being searched. The letter was destined to be smuggled into Israel/Palestine and distributed among Mufti supporters in Galilee. In contrast to the Arab nationalists who placed their faith in joint Arab action led by a new leadership, the Mufti's following gave priority to Palestinian action. This was the main division within diaspora politics until 1967.

Nasser's popularity among the Palestinian masses was due primarily to his speeches and actions challenging imperialism and his continual references to Palestine; also to the facilities he gave for military training, as well as his encouragement of Palestinian institutions (the PLO, the students' and workers' unions, the Sawt al-Filasteeni radio station). The growth of Nasser's popularity eroded the influence of Hajj Amin, a shift that worried the Lebanese authorities and contributed directly to the intensification of control that took place under President Chehab (1958–64). The other development that weakened the influence of the Mufti (and of Abu Kamal over Shateela) was the influx of worker-migrants that caused an overspill into the space around the camp, altering the demographic and political physiognomy of the area.

The preoccupation of the refugees with Palestinian and Arab regional issues kept them from getting involved in purely Lebanese politics. Older residents remember the hanging of a Shateela man in the Hursh, allegedly as a spy for the Kata'eb (probably during the 'Muslim revolt' of 1958); and Ahmad Haleemeh recalls that one of his uncles was briefly involved with the Najjadeh (a Beirut Sunni counterpart to the Kata'eb). But such affiliations were rare. One sign of how little camp Palestinians were interested in Lebanese politics is their lack of response to offers of nationality made by various *zu'ama'* (leaders). Although Abu Kamal failed to isolate Shateela from radical pan-Arab political currents, he succeeded in keeping it out of the 1958 civil war, the '*harb* Chamoun':

Emotionally Shateela was on the Muslim side but we tried to stay out of the fighting. We told the national Muslim parties[14] that we couldn't get involved; we didn't want disturbances in the camp. My father said, 'If anyone wants to join the fighting, he must leave the camp.' And when Sa'eb Salam[15] sent a vehicle with a gun to guard Shateela's eastern entrance, my father sent it away. He told them, '*We* are responsible for Shateela's security.' (Jihad Bisher)

By the end of the first decade of exile, however, the isolation that the Director had striven to maintain was becoming artificial. Traumatized though they were by exile and poverty, the refugees' passionate desire for a solution to their problem inevitably made them receptive to hopeful messages from their Lebanese and Arab environment.

'The educational revolution'

Schools were opened in the camps with great rapidity. The earliest years were ones of material shortage but of great enthusiasm on the part of everyone concerned: administrators, teachers, parents, students. Jihad Bisher belonged to the generation whose schooling was interrupted by fighting in Palestine. Already aged eleven in 1951, he attended Shateela school from the start:

There were three large 'hospital' tents and some very primitive chairs. We had three teachers, one for each tent; and there were two classes in each tent, so that each class had to listen to the lesson of the other. The teachers were all Palestinian, not highly educated but very good. They worked hard with us so that we could catch up.

The following year UNRWA rented classrooms in Sabra. Jihad says they moved because, when tents were blown down in storms, families moved into the school tents. The rooms were cramped; there were many students – they came from Sabra[16] as well as Shateela – Jihad remembers an average of forty per class. Girls sat in the same room with boys – 'I don't remember any parents refusing this.' Enthusiasm for education was such that even older women, for example Jihad's mother, attended UNRWA adult literacy classes. Jihad uses the term 'educational revolution' to describe the enthusiasm with which people turned to schooling, but there were in fact rather well-defined class limits to access and benefits.

A couple of years later UNRWA rented part of a Lebanese-owned apartment building on the western edge of the camp which became the Galilee School for boys and the Menshiyyeh School for girls (both were destroyed during the Amal sieges). According to several Shateela people, there was an agreement between UNRWA and the Lebanese government that UNRWA would not build schools for Palestinians, only rent them. It was only after the uprising of 1969 that a school was built, Ariha (Jericho) School on the eastern edge in Hayy Farhat, under the inspiration of its first headmaster, Sa'eed Abdallah, himself a Shateela man.

In the early years Shateela schools only had elementary classes. For other levels, students had to go into Beirut or out to Bourj Barajneh, usually on foot. Family need for income meant that most boys left school to work at the end of the elementary cycle. At most they might be apprenticed to earn a technical certificate.

Bridging the critical gap between free UNRWA schooling and the qualifications needed for white-collar employment called for tenacity and connections.

> After I got my elementary certificate my father sent me to a technical school to study carpentry or mechanics, but after four days I quit; I wanted to go on studying. By that time all the schools were full up. Without telling my father I went to see a friend of his, an UNRWA Inspector of Education, Diab Fahoum. He was a great patriot. He loved young Palestinians and wanted to get them educated. I told him my story.
>
> Fahoum took me to Bourj Barajneh school and spoke to the headmaster, Shareef Nashasheebi. He said, 'There's no room', but Fahoum told him, 'I want this boy in school.' My class was in a kitchen and there was nowhere for me to sit except in the wash basin. Eventually they brought me a small chair and I sat between the desks with my books on my knees. (Jihad Bisher)

Khaled Sarees, who later became an UNRWA teacher and headmaster, recalls peeping as a boy of four years old into the first tent school; but when he began school two years later, it was in the rented building. His account of his own career underlines the many, sometimes contradictory benefits that people hoped for from education:

> In those days people waited for their sons to grow up so they could help them financially. They wanted them to be educated but they didn't have the means to make them doctors or engineers. Besides, it was forbidden to us as Palestinians to practise as doctors or lawyers. Their biggest ambition then was to have their sons work in an office or a company.
>
> The most my family wanted for me was to be a teacher. We couldn't have higher ambitions because we knew our social circumstances. As a teacher you can work, you can help your people. We were always hearing from our families that the reason we had been thrown out of our country

was ignorance. That's why we grasped at education. It wasn't just to get jobs.

Whereas at first all Shateela teachers were urban Palestinians who lived outside the camp, by the end of the first decade this began to change. Khaled Sarees was one of the first Shateela boys to enter Sibleen (UNRWA's technical and professional training institute)[17] but there were others who taught in Shateela before him, among them Abdel Rasheed Ma'rouf from Deir al-'Assi, a village famous for the number of its teachers; Muhammad Fa'our from Sha'b, the first 'home-grown' headmaster; and Sa'eed Abdallah from Majd al-Kroom. It was Sa'eed who formed a group of 'sons of the camp' to coach younger boys to pass official examinations enabling them to go to state universities in Syria or Egypt (in Egypt under Nasser, special facilities were granted to Palestinian students). According to sociologist Bassem Sirhan, teachers came to play an important social leadership role in camps, distinct from the pre-1948 leadership of *shuyyukh* and *wujaha'* (literally 'faces', clan and villager elders).[18]

The sudden availability of free general schooling meant a disparity in literacy between younger and older generations. We may assume that schooling must have had an effect on 'mentalities', and hence on family relations, social structure and culture. Nonetheless, it is not easy to reconstruct what these effects were. Part of the difficulty lies in the many years of war and displacement which impede recollection of the early period. Another arises from the value attached to parental authority and family relations, which not only suppresses challenges to these but also suppresses consciousness of suppression. The fact that signs of respect for parents such as kissing their hands continued well into the 1960s suggests that schooling at first made little difference to parent–child relations. Among the factors diffusing sociocultural change and preventing conflict or alienation, we may count work migration, which took many younger men beyond the family circle; the similarity of cultural atmosphere between school and home; and the nature of the education provided, geared to producing general literacy with a technical orientation. Although the schooling of girls posed a threat to gender values, ways were found to contain such threats, for example through greater watchfulness and more explicit warnings.

Health: conditions, services, indigenous practices

Malnutrition, poor housing and insufficient clothing were probably the main cause of sickness in the 1950s. It is difficult to find surviving medical workers who can give an overview of that time but from many accounts it seems as if adult working men were the category most at risk. Heavy manual labour to which they were unaccustomed, wounds suffered during the war of 1948, or beatings during post-war attempts to infiltrate: all these were male-specific hazards.

Tuberculosis was fairly common in the 1950s and seems to have attacked mainly adult men. Because of its infectious character, TB sufferers received prompt treatment in Lebanese sanatoria but other kinds of respiratory disease were also common. Men also appear to have suffered a high rate of kidney and back problems.

A Shateela doctor who grew up in another camp, Dr Muhammad al-Khateeb, describes health conditions in the 1950s. Housing in Nabatiyyeh was more solid, but winter cold was more severe than in Shateela. Waste water ran off a hill instead of collecting in stagnant pools between housing. But what he says about clothing and nutrition is probably true of all camps:

> Food was not enough. In the 1950s, people were very poor. They ate a lot of potatoes because they were cheaper. If they bought meat it was mainly bones, to make soup. It was a very bad period for children. UNRWA gave us a cup of milk and a vitamin tablet every morning. Maybe the milk wasn't good, or maybe it was watered, but we always had diarrhoea.
>
> I remember that many children suffered from toothache and earache. The UNRWA clinic in Nabatiyyeh didn't have a dentist or a doctor then. Because of this I lost two of my permanent teeth. We didn't have winter clothes. Some of the children had to wear their parents' jackets to go to school. Most of us had no shoes or jerseys. No one could afford to buy *mazout* (fuel oil) to heat their houses. I remember crying from the cold.

Every few days the women of Nabatiyyeh had to travel 10 kilometres, up and down hill, to bring firewood for baking and cooking:

> Some would be carrying their babies if they were suckling. Sometimes they were delivered on the way. Many women had miscarriages because of the distance and the loads. My mother was one of them. I remember they brought her home in pain and I heard them say that she was bleeding. Later on I understood what it was.

In Shateela, women did not have to go out to gather firewood but certainly they suffered from conditions specific to the camp and to their gender. Though winter temperatures were far less severe in Beirut than in Nabatiyyeh or the Beqa', no housing was rain-proof or flood-proof. Because of this, women all tended to suffer arthritic pain. Summer heat and humidity also bore harshly on them, particularly after the change from tents

to huts with corrugated iron roofs. Umm Isma'een brought up seven
children in such a one-roomed *barakiyeh*.

> We couldn't stay at home in summer because it got so hot. When the sun
> hit the *zinco* the hut became like an oven. Maybe outside there's a breeze
> but it doesn't enter the *barakiyeh*. My head used to burn! After I'd made
> breakfast and fetched the water I'd take the children and a mat and go
> down to the Hursh, and sit with them under the trees until the evening.

Some women could not bear the hardships of the sudden change from a
normal life to camp conditions. Pakeeza Ghazaleh recounts how her
mother, a city woman, *bint nas*,[19] who came from Haifa wearing high-heeled
shoes, never got over the shock of her only son's breakdown (after being
beaten by frontier guards), and of transfer to Shateela. She could not bear the
heat in summer, nor cope with carrying water from distant taps (city women
never learnt how to carry heavy weights on their heads the way village
women did); she developed an enlarged heart, dying at the early age of
forty-eight. It was to provide medicines for her mother that Pakeeza began
working as a nurse.

Because of the pressure of immigration into Shateela, the camp rapidly
became oversettled: its houses were smaller and more crowded than in other
camps, its streets narrower. Elsewhere people could make courtyards and
garden plots but Shateela by the early 1960s seems to have had all the
features of an urban slum. In consequence, there were high rates of
gastroenteritis, respiratory infections and skin problems in young children.
Umm Isma'een attributes her children's frequent illnesses to the lack of
hygiene and the small, stuffy hut they lived in. It is interesting to find that
this family, though not well off, resorted to private Lebanese medical care
for their children. There was a children's specialist in Sabra who only
charged LL1 (half his normal fee) on Fridays.

UNRWA's free medical services were available to all Palestinian refugees
from the beginning but remained at a rather rudimentary level. Doctors
differed greatly in concern; some did not observe clinic hours and hardly
bothered to examine patients. Before the 1970s very few were Palestinian,
and none lived in camps; nurses also generally lived outside. This meant that
outside morning clinic hours there was no one on hand who could give even
simple emergency treatment. Some people say that only people on good
terms with the Director obtained referral slips to see specialists or to enter
hospital for an operation. They sum up UNRWA medical services in the
1950s as 'An aspro and *yallah*!' (Get out!). Political activists had better not
show their faces. Pakeeza Ghazaleh, who worked in the clinic, gives a
somewhat different picture:

We used to begin at 7.30 am. At 8 am the doctor came and everything would be already prepared. People would be crowding outside. I stamped their cards and gave them a place in the queue. Abu Fadl, the door-keeper, used to give them their numbers. The one who came first, entered first. That man was honest, he didn't [weaves hand to indicate deviousness]. Each according to his turn. Every sick person came to the UNRWA doctor. If he could treat him he did so. If it was beyond his capacity he sent him to the Ras al-Naba' Polyclinic. And if it was something urgent he gave him a paper for the American University Hospital. They would admit him as soon as he showed his paper.

UNRWA certainly succeeded in several of its health targets, for example the upgrading of *daya* ('Arab' midwives), the improvement in care of pregnant women and infants, and the eradication of epidemics. But basic health conditions – nutrition and housing – deteriorated sharply in Lebanon, and it is disputable whether the medical services available to refugees were much in advance over those in Palestine. When asked about this, Fatimeh Ghreiry said laconically, 'We had doctors there, we have doctors here.' She went on: 'Palestine was healthier. We treated sick people there at home and they recovered. Here you take them to twenty doctors and they don't get better.'

Given poverty, it is not surprising that indigenous medical practices survived. One of these was the practice of *jabr*, bonehealing. Umm Nafidh Awdeh from Sha'b, still in Shateela until 1985, was skilled in this ancient Arab art. Bone-setters took only a small fee, nothing at all if the patient was a neighbour or poor. Every housewife knew the use of *maramiyyeh* (sage), *na'na* (mint), *mardaquoush* (oregano) and *zoofa* (hyssop).

Religion and magic were two other sources of cure to which people continued to resort, side by side with doctors. Fatimeh Ghreiry from Safed says, 'For something mild like headache, my father-in-law read the Quran. If it was something more serious, he would make a *mowlid*'.[20] Religious *sheikhs* were believed to be able to cure infertility with *hijabs*, long strips of paper covered with Quranic verses rolled up and worn by women inside their clothing. The crucial importance of procreation keeps such magico-religious practices alive even now. As in many other parts of the world, it is mainly older women who control the secrets of sexuality, fertility, abortion and infant care.[21] Although indigenous beliefs and practices are usually ridiculed as superstition, one still finds traces of them. In Bourj Barajneh camp in the early 1970s, women still 'threw lead' as a technique for discovering who was putting the evil eye on their babies. Few women do not fasten a turquoise bead on a newborn baby's clothing to avert the evil eye. Most women still avoid visiting a newly delivered mother if they are menstruating.

UNRWA nurse Pakeeza reveals her own ambivalence when recollecting the struggle between the clinic staff and mothers in regard to certain folk practices, such as swaddling and putting *kohl* around the eyes of newborn infants:

> In UNRWA we forbade the use of *kohl*. We shouted at women who did it, we told them that it damages the eye. Yet in the *Hadeeth*[22] it says that it's OK to use *kohl*. Look at gypsies! They always put *kohl* on their eyes and they never get glaucoma.

With regard to swaddling, Pakeeza was more of a modernist: 'If I saw it, straightaway I took the scissors and cut the bands.'

If infant mortality rates went down, due in part to more hygienic delivery and better postnatal care, general health could not but suffer from camp conditions. Popular consciousness of the prevalence of sickness was one basic reason for the 'health politics' of the Resistance movement, among the earliest of whose services was the Palestine Red Crescent Society (PRCS).

Social structure

Palestine's indigenous class structure was crisscrossed by social relations of many kinds: ties of kinship, of locality (between people of the same village or city neighbourhood), of patronage, and of work or political association. As exiles in an unfamiliar system, Palestinians in Lebanon clung to all pre-1948 ties without exception. Whatever cleavages might have divided people before were temporarily submerged in a shared predicament. Among these ties, those of patronage continued to play a vital symbolic and practical role. We have already seen how the Mufti's backing put Abu Kamal in charge of Shateela camp, prolonging a social order formed in Palestine far into the 1960s; other notables from the Galilee area were also involved in the daily life of camp populations. Bassem Sirhan, who grew up in the household of his uncle Faris, a large landowner from Kabri, gives this picture:

> He [Faris Sirhan] used to come from his office at 2pm and they would be waiting inside. He would tell his wife, 'I'll talk with them for five minutes' but he would talk for three hours and forget his lunch. If you want to be a traditional leader you can't turn anyone away. They came at any time, at 6 am, at midnight. His wife used to be angry, she worried about his health. She told him to have fixed hours. But peasants can't have fixed times, it's not part of their culture.
>
> The camp people came to him with all their problems. Villagers from his own area consulted him in all matters, but a wider range came for

letters of recommendation for help with the Lebanese authorities. He held political power through the AHC and the Mufti; the Lebanese government considered them to be like the PLO today. People referred to him in masny things even though he had no phyusical or financial control over them.

No one ever married a woman from any of the villages that followed him without consulting him. He had to be there and ask for her hand. If he talked for them he would never be refused. They consulted him whenever they had clashes between families or villages. When the Lebanese government couldn't solve it, and UNRWA couldn't solve it, he would make a reconciliation. This went on up to 1965.[23]

Those who came to consult Faris Sirhan kissed his hand and called him *beg* or *effendi*. It sometimes happened that people asked for money but this was rare. His main role was as *merja'* (reference, guide, arbitrator).

Another large landowner from northern Palestine exiled in Lebanon was Kamel Hussein *effendi*[24] from Khalsa of whom it is said that 'his people' continued to offer him yearly tribute until the 1970s. Unlike Sirhan, however, he had little power to help people. Lesser notables are recorded as having helped individual clients to obtain camp sites or jobs.

Patronage survived in Lebanon because of people's need, and its survival helped in turn to sustain the pre-1948 rural social structure, particularly the authority of the *shuyyukh* and the *wujaha'*, along with the cultural values that upheld it, such as respect for seniority. ANM militant Abu Muhammad Farmawi connects such values to broader social structure:

> If someone like me spoke about politics [the *wujaha'*] would say, 'Who is this? He's only a boy, he doesn't have the right to stand up and speak in front of Hajj Amin Husseini.' They thought that politics is only for certain families – *beit* Husseini, *beit* Nashasheebi, *beit* Abdul Hadi – only they have the right to deal with politics. That's how they were brought up.

The ambivalent political role of old men, the *shuyyukh*, indicating compliance for militants like Abu Muhammad and Khaled Shehadeh, and for others a living link with Palestine, comes out clearly in disagreements about the *mejlis al-shuyyukh* that Abu Kamal set up in the early 1950s, a policy renewed during the Resistance period. To a radical like Shehadeh, the concept of *wujaha'* lost its meaning with the loss of Palestine, and any attempt to reconstitute it could only be spurious. Debates about the role of the *shuyyukh* under the regime of the Intelligence Bureau were common in the 1970s, and again after the massacre of 1982 and the 1985 battle with Amal, when some old men tried to negotiate truces: such efforts were seen by younger men as contrary to the spirit of resistance. By the end of the 1980s, however, the death of so many of the 'generation of Palestine' changed attitudes towards thenm; people began to praise their skills in solving conflicts and to mourn them as irreplaceable.

The special status and respect allotted to the *wujaha'* did not extend to their wives or lead to any special role or conditions for them. *Diwans* were a purely male affair, with the men who kept them up preparing coffee and tea for visitors. Pakeeza Ghazaleh, who lived in Shateela from 1952 to 1962, remembers that Umm Kamal, the Director's wife, carried water on her head like everyone else: 'If she were the king's wife she would live the same way.'

Village-based ties were reconstructed in camps in Lebanon through social processes of 'in-gathering' such as those used by Abu Kamal to recruit the Majd al-Kroom majority in Shateela. Such reconstructed village fragments formed a powerful defence against alienation in exile as well as a basis for the transmission of mainly village culture. People from the same village supported each other in quarrels with others. At the same time village ties underwent subtle alteration as they were put to new purposes, for example as a channel of access to jobs or educational subsidies. In Shateela, the people of the 'big four' villages – Majd al-Kroom, al-Birweh, Saffouri and Sha'b – fed their ties through the practice of *waasta* according to the rule summarized by Abu Isma'een: 'Those close to us have priority.'[25] Villagers with a head start in schooling obtained the lion's share of UNRWA's training resources, migrating ahead of others to the oil-producing countries where they formed bridgeheads for later migrants. People of the bigger villages were more likely to reproduce in exile their specific social characters accents, food preparations, reputations) and were likely to maintain mutual insurance funds.

For people from smaller villages, village-based ties had less utilitarian value, continuing as a basis for social exchange but leaving more space for other ties such as those based on neighbourhood. The presence in Shateela of several city households meant that the pre-1948 barriers between *ahel al-qariya* (village folk) and *ahel al-mudun* (city folk) were bridged here earlier than in other camps. Already by the early 1960s there was intermarriage between them. The proximity of 'strangers' forced people to invest in other relationships than those of kinship and village. A much-quoted proverb supports this shift: 'The neighbour who is near is better than the brother who is far.'

Camps became communities to be defended. This is clear from stories of *faza'a* as well as the norm of celebrating joy and mourning loss together: '*Al-farah lil kull wa al-a'za lil kull*' ('joy is for all and sorrow is for all') was the maxim for such practices. It was the custom to invite all the neighbours for a wedding; mourning visits were even more strictly inclusive. Fatimeh Ghreiry says, 'If someone died, we went to condole whether we knew them or not.' This was in spite of the fact that being a city woman, she only visited regularly three or four neighbours whom she knew well.[26] The *hayy* (neighbourhood) and open spaces within and around the camp (streets, markets) were a crucial arena of social interaction.

Kinship ties continued to be important for the refugees in Lebanon, but we need to distinguish between their continuation as a basic social value and shifts in forms and practices. The size of kin units that moved to Lebanon and the degree to which they settled together varied consierably. In certain cases, a whole camp quarter would be inhabited by a single lineage; village clusters were in any case always linked by multiple ties of consanguinity (*hasab*) and marriage (*nasab*). But in many other cases, villages and kin units were scattered between different camps and different host countries. Economic pressures also tended to split up kin clusters, as individual households followed employment opportunities and decided, say, to move from Tripoli or Ba'lbek to Beirut. Even though certain practices associated with the *hamuleh* (patrilineage) continued into exile – for example cousin marriage and 'honour' killings – yet the old clan system was dealt a fatal blow by loss of land and dispersion. The gradual emergence of socioeconomic differentiation also weakened clan ties, with wealthier members tending to dissociate themselves from poorer ones. To speak of 'nuclearization' would be a distortion, as households continued to be composed of more people than a typical Western family (old parents, widowed or divorced sisters, orphans), and married sons continued to live close to their parents, sometimes forming compound households. People still expected kin to help them (though such expectations were often disappointed); they still visited kin frequently. But exile hastened processes of change which had already begun in Palestine.

In certain cases political parties became the basis for ties that could be stronger than those of kinship, village or neighbourhood. When Abu Muhammad Farmawi had to leave Lebanon on political missions, he instructed his wife not to go to his family or hers if she needed money, but to fellow party members. Exile did not destroy pre-existing social relations but modified them and added new ones. Social exchange with Lebanese was limited in the first decade, not by deep differences of culture or identity but by the refugees' humiliation by their poverty. Nonetheless, new ties were formed, mainly within the context of work or politics, and these would expand during the 1960s.

Village customs

I remember that at A'eed al-Fitr and A'eed al-Adha' my father used to take me and my brother and go from house to house in Shateela to congratulate people on the feast. We had to go to every house to ask people if they needed anything. That used to happen in the morning. In the afternoon people used to return the visit to my father. This went on until he retired in 1969 . . . He also encouraged the social life of the villages in Palestine, the gatherings – the *mejlis* or *diwan* – and many village habits such as, for example, making tomato paste. Our women used to stay up all night boiling the tomatoes to make paste. Things like that he insisted on. It was part of his vision of the camps as gathering places for Palestinians, to be ready for the return. (Jihad Bisher)

This suggests that the conservation of village culture in the camps was to some extent the result of national leadership policy, disseminated through the social relations we have seen continuing to operate in exile, although it was surely also a spontaneous reaction to separation from Palestine. But what is striking about Jihad's description is the way in which he takes for granted the links between material culture – for example, the making of tomato paste – and quasi-sacred customs such as the visits made at the time of the religious feasts. One of the forces behind Palestinian survival in the diaspora has certainly been this welding together of moral and material values in rites which underlined consciousness of the collectivity. At the same time, we note the way that Jihad subsumes the whole camp in the homes that his father visited, a feat only possible if leading families were taken as representing others. This presupposed, implicit social structure underlay the preservation of culture; when that changed, cultural meanings changed even when forms were preserved.

Although poverty and change of occupation threatened an expressive and symbolic culture formed in rural Palestine, they did not eliminate it (any more than they eliminated pre-1948 social structure) but rather reinforced forms that had adaptive usefulness in harsh conditions, as well as those that, on the contrary, were associated with symbolic values. The effort needed to celebrate weddings, for example, with even a hint of the usual consumption of food, exchange of gifts and extravagant displays placed such celebrations in the realm of cultural struggle. We may imagine that cultural continuity became politicized to the degree that people felt it to be threatened. Abu Kamal's setting of a night guard around the camp gives an idea of the self-conscious frontiers erected against alienating urban influences. Even in conditions of rapid population growth and change, the Director's control over settlement allowed him to keep Shateela 'pure', preserving both its Palestinianness and its peasant village ethos.

Few occasions assemble the full range of Palestinian expressive, symbolic and material culture as fully as marriage, and no other has mobilized more cultural tenacity, both in the ways marriages are arranged as well as in the ways they are celebrated. Marriage has also acquired new meanings as the celebration of survival and affirmation of national identity. In Shateela in the 1950s, however, the only change was one of means. Class/cultural differences between village and city people were still clearly demarcated.

One of the first couples to marry in Shateela, in 1951, Ahmad Haleemeh's parents only had a *mowlid* (religious ritual). Instead of dishes of meat and rice, neighbours who came to congratulate the family received a few sweets and cakes. The bride wore her mother's wedding dress, and her *jihaz* (trousseau) consisted of a quilt and some sheets.

The weddings of people from larger villages are said to have been celebrated with some of the customary festivities. Sha'b and Saffouri people helped each other with wedding expenses. When his eldest son Muhammad married, Shehadeh Fa'our (from Sha'b) gave a party which is still remembered. Pakeeza recalls another early marriage:

> Right at the beginning, when we first came to the camp, we saw a wedding party. It was for villagers, maybe from Majd al-Kroom. They were dancing the *debkeh*, men and women holding hands. We said, 'Yeeh! [expression of disapproval] it is shameful for a woman to hold a man's hand and move her body in this way.'

Pakeeza goes on:

> We didn't do this. How was our wedding day? They put the bride in her father's house, they displayed her on a high chair. All the women were with her – no men! The men stayed alone in another house. The women sing and dance in the house of the bride. Then those who aren't relatives leave and the bridegroom comes.

Instead of the embroidered *thawb*, city women wore a succession of long dresses of different colours – white, pink, black, blue, red. When the groom came, the bride put on her white dress again, with the *tarha* and *kleel* (train and crown). Wedding photos of even the poorest families show how grand the bride and bridegroom's clothing had to be, even if it was borrowed or hired.

Insight into marriage practices from a very different angle comes from an unsentimental story told by Abu 'Ali, from the time of tents. How could they give a newly married couple the privacy necessary to consummate the marriage? The solution was to hire a separate tent for three nights, the maximum that most families could afford. This was not enough in the case of at least one Shateela man, still remembered thirty years later as unable to *yudkhal fiha* (enter her) in the allotted time.

Shateela expands

During the 1950s two new waves of refugees reached Shateela, one from Anjar in the Beqa', after clashes between Armenians and Palestinians there, the second from the South, as the Lebanese authorities removed Palestinians from border areas to prevent 'infiltration'. Apart from these two waves, migration to the Beirut camps was a matter of individual families, as people stopped expecting a rapid return to Palestine and sought to better their situation. As Abu Turki says, everything was more accessible in the capital:

> Work was more available and easier to find. The city was so close, you could go on foot and come back, without paying transport. It's a city, a capital! Everything was closer – schools, clinics, doctors, the UNRWA headquarters – everything.

In spite of some formalities, transfer to the Beirut camps in the 1950s was not officially impeded. The Directorate of Palestinian Refugee Affairs had to give permission; UNRWA then had to transfer the applicant's *nafoos* (registration). The Director also had his say, the power to accept or refuse new settlers being part of his job description.

Shateela's limited space rapidly filled up. The growth of the camp had a number of contradictory implications of which Abu Kamal was well aware. On the one hand, he favoured growth for nationalist and proprietary reasons. Like the other first settlers, he saw size as a means of gaining official recognition and 'imposing our existence'. His status and salary were also, people say, linked to the size of the camp's population. On the other hand, he was aware that Shateela's visibility from the Airport Boulevarde annoyed the authorities, and feared that any expansion outside its original boundaries would provoke hostile reactions from landowners and the state. Nonetheless Abu Kamal encouraged Palestinian settlement outside the camp's boundaries until, in the early 1960s, the authorities stepped in to stop the transfer of *nafoos*; by that time Hayy Gharbeh was already in existence. Such expansion enabled him to claim later, when resisting government/ UNRWA proposals to transfer Shateela, that its population had reached 15,000.

An account given by an early immigrant to Shateela, Abu Isma'een, accurately reflects the various pressures involved in migration:

> I came as a boy from Palestine. I only had an older brother in Tripoli. He sold *falafel* (fried bean patties) in an alley. He made LL10 a day, not enough for both of us, especially after I got married. We had relatives in Shateela so, in 1955, I came to them as a guest. They helped me find a hut

and told me to bring my family.

The Director was supposed to inform the police if there was anyone living here whose presence wasn't legal. But I had relatives here and they had links with the Director, so he left us alone. In the 1960s there was a decision from the Ministry of the Interior that everyone must return to their original area of registration. For example, I'm registered in Tripoli, I have to leave Shateela and return to Tripoli.

While working in a weaving factory (in Hazmieh), I got to know a man from Ba'lbek. He had a cousin who was a police officer at Nabatiyyeh, the home town of Rafeeq Shaheen who was head of the Directorate of Refugee Affairs. This friend offered to take me to Nabatiyyeh to meet his cousin if I paid the expenses. I agreed.

After a series of transactions in the *diwan* of Rafeeq Shaheen and the Directorate, Abu Isma'een received word that his *nafoos* had been transferred. He comments, 'Now I belonged officially to the residents of Shateela and the police couldn't expel me.' His account shows how Palestinians were beginning to build relations with Lebanese, through which they became a part, albeit a marginal one, of the Lebanese social and political system.

Notes

1. The official title is Camp Services Officer but Abed Bisher is remembered as '*al-Mudir*' (the Director) or as Abu Kamal.

2. One very small camp, Mar Elias (population around 600), lies within the municipal boundary. So also did Da'ouq, an unofficial 'camp' (destroyed in May 1985).

3. A *mukhtar* (village headman) from Kabri claimed that when he first pitched his tent in Shateela, Abed Bisher tried to drive him away. This may have been because he posed a threat to Abu Kamal's leadership.

4. To urbanites, Shateela people seem to have kept their village customs and ethos, but Palestinians from rural camps describe them as like city people, 'shrewd' and 'unconcerned with others'.

5. Hereditary transmission of official posts such as *mukhtar* is customary in rural Middle Eastern communities. In relation to UNRWA camp directorships it is unusual, and points to the special circumstances of Shateela's founding.

6. As a boy, Abu Ahmad 'Issa Khalaf walked through one of these tunnels to the sea. Later destroyed by building, it was probably the origin of stories about Shateela being connected by a network of tunnels to Sabra and Bourj Barajneh.

7. The value of the Lebanese pound then was about LL3 : $1.

8. See S. Franjiyeh, 'How Revolutionary is the Palestinian Resistance Movement?', *Journal of Palestine Studies*, vol. 1, no. 2, Autumn 1972.

9. Several older Shateela men, married before 1948, had Lebanese wives. This was due to the migration of Lebanese workers to Palestine.

10. 'God have mercy on him/her', a phrase always used in referring to the dead.

11. *Shaweesh*, leader of a small military or police unit (a Turkish term).

12. Originally a journalist and political activist, al-Hout became a representative of the PLO in Lebanon.

13. This was one of several small groups that merged with the ANM.

14. 'National' in this context means 'Arab nationalist', as opposed to 'Lebanese nationalist'.

15. Sa'eb Salam, a Sunni Beirut *za'eem* (leader), was one of the leaders of the uprising against President Chamoun in 1958.

16. Urban Palestinians began to rent accommodation in Sabra from the early 1950s. In 1953 the small 'camp' of Da'ouq was established for poor urban families, with its own school classes.

17. Sibleen's intake varied between 274 (1963) and 496 (1975): UNRWA–UNESCO *Statistical Yearbook* 1977–78 (no. 14).

18. B. Sirhan, 'Palestinian Refugee Camp Life in Lebanon', *Journal of Palestine Studies*, vol. IV, no. 2, Winter 1975.

19. 'The daughter of people', an expression indicating a property-owning family background.

20. The *mowlid al-nebbi* is the Prophet's birthday and a fixed feast (12th Rabia al-awal), but a *mowlid* may be held in a home, e.g. in cases of sickness, thanksgiving for a baby's birth, etc. A *sheikh* with a specially melodious voice is invited to chant.

21. For references to traditional birth control practices, see A. Bendt and J. Downing, *We Shall Return: Women of Palestine* (London: Zed Books, 1980), pp. 59–60.

22. *Hadeeth*: sayings attributed to the Prophet Muhammad.

23. B. Sirhan, interview March 1991. Sirhan also described how his uncle gave sanctuary to a young girl from a Tyre camp whose parents wanted to kill her because she had lost her virginity.

24. Turkish in origin, *effendi* is a title lower than *beg* and *basha*, often given to Christians, foreigners and urban notables.

25. See the quotation from Abu Isma'een, p. 43.

26. A couple of old ladies from Yaffa, living in Shateela in 1984, told me proudly that they had never gone outside their home.

3.   The 1960s, Rule of the Deuxième Bureau

The state moves in

Tightening of control over the camps occurred in stages. First, after the *'harb* Chamoun', at the beginning of Chehab's presidency, a police station was set up in the Hursh, near Shateela's southern exit. Abu Turki remembers this because his home was on the southern boundary, marked in those days by an UNRWA sign:

> Later the police came and opened a station in the Hursh. Their captain was called Abu Aqash. He told us that we had to register our names whenever we go to the city, and when we come back we have to tell him.

If people didn't comply, the police responded with 'harsh words and threats'. Khaled Shehadeh also underlines the sharp transition from Chamoun to Chehab:

> [At first] the police stations were far from the camp, their role was simple. If they caught a Palestinian on the border, or if he'd committed a crime, the police brought his name to the Director of the camp . . . But with the establishment of the Chehab regime they began to treat Palestinians harshly. At the time of the PPS coup[1] they killed a lot of Palestinians who were members. They put a police station inside the camp as well as a Deuxième Bureau office. One was over the Director's office, the other next to it. They started to recruit spies and collaborators and to observe all active, nationalist Palestinians.

The two branches of the state – the police and the Deuxième Bureau (see Political Glossary) – had different functions. The task of the Deuxième Bureau was to suppress any kind of political activity, that of the police to enforce all regulations concerning housing. Thus began nearly a decade of intimidation and extortion.

The primary targets of DB pursuit were the *hizbiyeen* (party members), in particular those of the ANM, viewed because of its alliance with President Nasser as the most potent threat to national security. Abu Muhammad Farmawi was an early ANM member who moved to Shateela in 1960:

Membership in the ANM meant that I had political activities, for example organizing demonstrations and distributing pamphlets. This led to my being followed by the Deuxième Bureau. I was arrested many times. There was a law of Permanent Emergency under which the police had the right to break into our homes at any time to search.

They used to come at night to listen under my window, to see who was with me. Once when my son died and people came to condole with me, they broke into my house because they thought I was holding a meeting. They blocked my passport and forbade me to leave Lebanon. Later they tried to force me to leave but they didn't succeed because there was nothing they could accuse me of that would justify deportation.

They tried many other kinds of pressure besides arrests and beatings. They contacted my friends and told them not to be seen with me – 'he's suspect'. For a period, no one dared to say '*marhaba*' (hallo) to me, no one visited me. They found out where I was working and told my boss to dismiss me. They instructed UNRWA to stop my rations on the pretext that I was out of the country.

They even came to my wife and tried to convince her to leave me: 'Tell him if he doesn't give up politics, you'll ask for a divorce.'[2] They sent people to my family, they sent people to her family.

Those arrested were usually taken to one of the army barracks or to General Security headquarters. They were interrogated, beaten, sometimes tortured. Abu Muhammad says that it was more psychological intimidation than real torture. For example, detainees were forced to sit with their necks under a wooden yoke and their feet in cold water. There were some deaths, but the DB wanted to avoid scandals that would be taken up by 'Opposition' media. Their object was to deter the *hizbiyeen* by continual harassment and threats. Another technique used against 'trouble-makers' was to summon them to the DB office and leave them sitting there all day, depriving them of a day's wages. Not only were all meetings prohibited but also the reading of proscribed newspapers such as *Al-Nahar*. Listening to 'Sawt al-Arab' (see Political Glossary) was a serious offence.

In the 1960s UNRWA appointments began to be subjected to DB scrutiny, particularly the appointment of teachers. Whereas before, Palestinian teachers had been a force for nationalist revival, during the Chehabian era a screening process took place that obliged teachers to be prudent if not to collaborate.

The state began to influence UNRWA in such a way that anyone who wanted a job there had to get the OK of the Maktab Thani [DB]. If he got it, straightaway he'd obtain a post. The state would put through a phone call to the Director of UNRWA: 'There are several applicants for this job. The one we want is so-and-so.' This began at the beginning of the 1960s. (Khaled Shehadeh)

The most destructive of the methods used by the DB was the recruitment of collaborators. In some cases these were people who feared the new political movements; some would have served any authority; others wanted UNRWA jobs or feared losing them. There were several grades: the 'big' collaborators were those who openly associated with the DB and who were present during interrogations and beatings. Another category secretly reported what people were doing and saying. There were also 'occasional agents', people who gave scraps of information as a price for obtaining permits or avoiding fines.

The *'umala* (agents) were hated but few dared to express their hatred.

People would say, 'They ought to be killed!' but if an agent approached them it was, '*Ahlan, ahlan!*' (welcome). They'd bring him tea, they'd invite him in. It's regrettable, but although they hated the agents, the majority pretended they loved them because they were afraid that if they didn't, the agent would inform against them.

But if someone's son wanted to marry the daughter of an agent most fathers would refuse. '*Marhaba*', yes, from fear or hypocrisy, but marriage – 'No! Not the daughter of the agent!' (Abu Muhammad Farmawi)

Oppression extended beyond the *hizbiyeen* minority to grip the whole camp population in an iron net of prohibitions, permits and punishments. People's first concern was with their homes: to make them rainproof, provide outlets for waste water and sewage, enlarge them to accommodate growing families or to protect their privacy with an outer wall. Such improvements were strictly forbidden. Through bribes, some households managed during the 1960s to dig cesspits or replace walls of wood and *tanak* (tin) with stone; but even bribes could not waive the rule against cement roofs. The smallest repairs, such as mending a leaking roof, required a permit. In their hunger for fines and bribes, the police hunted for a trickle of water or scrap of orange peel thrown on the street. Everyone remembers lying under leaking roofs. Abu Muhammad says, 'We had to hang blankets under the ceiling to prevent water dripping on the children.'

The system was designed to yield information as well as money; it left few loopholes.

Even if you needed to put a nail through one of the *zinco* sheets on your roof you had to get permission from the DB, from the Directorate,[3] and from the police. If you were lucky enough to get permission, this luck came first from paying money to all three parties; then from begging them; and then maybe also you might have to give certain names. They wanted the names of people working for the Palestinian cause. Some people gave false names . . . Giving names was very rare. People avoided giving names by trying not to know. Let people work underground, why should I dig and find out? (Jihad Bisher)

Another way of avoiding giving names was to give bigger bribes: 'This suited the DB and the rest; and people could manage it because life was a bit easier than before.'

The harsh methods used by the authorities to prevent political activism backfired, especially since police harrassment over house repairs affected everyone, whether they were politically active or not. Nothing did more to generate hatred against the state and to unify all political currents, as well as the less militant with the activist minority. Twenty years later even people who had not joined Resistance groups could still recount countless incidents of brutality or extortion. Everything was forbidden:

It was forbidden to listen to Sawt al-'Arab. If you wanted to sprinkle water on the path near your door, to make it cool, it was forbidden. If a young man wanted to visit a friend after 8 pm, it was forbidden. We were forbidden to leave our homes at night. If people sat up in the evening with neighbours, enjoying themselves, they'd come and knock on the door, and say, 'It's forbidden to visit after dark.' ('Nawal')

Umm Ghanem remembers worse things:

Policemen! Could a woman clean in front of her door? She didn't dare. If the tin roof flies, do you dare to nail it down? Never! They would come and arrest the owner of the house, and imprison him, and fine him LL20. If two women quarrel the police would arrest both of them, and tie their legs with belts, and beat them on the feet. Yes! On their feet! The police and the Maktab al-Thani stayed in the camp night and day. Did you dare to speak a word? They were like this at the door [imitates someone listening].

Transfer attempts

Jihad Bisher believes that from the beginning the authorities wanted to remove Shateela, although the first serious transfer proposal did not surface until the 1960s:

> They wanted to move Shateela because it's so near Beirut. Whatever happens there will be known immediately in the city, there will be reactions. Whereas if we were far away, if something happens, we can't communicate, no one will hear about it. My father and all Shateela people knew it was important to the authorities to get rid of the camp. And they knew it was important for them to keep it in its place.

While Basha Shateela was still alive, the authorities approached him to find out if it was true that he had given the land on which the camp stood to Abed Bisher. By the 1960s the Basha was dead, but the real owner returned to raise a court case against Abu Kamal, accusing him of having obtained the land by fraud. On this occasion, the Director argued that the land had been donated not to him personally but to all the camp's inhabitants (said to be 3,000 by this time). The case ended with the owner being allotted ground rent.

Soon afterwards, the authorities informed UNRWA of their desire to transfer the populations of both Shateela and Bourj Barajneh to a site near Sa'diyat, about 20 kilometres south of Beirut. Abu Turki was a member of the camp delegation that went with UNRWA officials to inspect the site:

> It was a barren area, just rocks, a hillside overlooking the sea. There wasn't even a village. I spoke for the delegation. I said to UNRWA's Director who was with us, 'Why do you bring us here? If you really wanted to help us you would spend this money on improving Shateela. We won't leave unless you bring tanks and destroy the camp.'

Abu Kamal also opposed the Sa'diyat transfer scheme, arguing that UNRWA had the right to move its installations to Sa'diyat but that it could not move the people. He hinted that transfer would be resisted bodily.[4] The seriousness of the Sa'diyat project is indicated by the protest visits made by camp delegations to an array of *zu'ama'*, including Sa'eb Salam, Sami Solh and the Lebanese Mufti. To have removed by force a population now swollen to several thousands was politically impossible, given the splits in the government and the strength of the 'Opposition' media and parties. Eventually the project was dropped.

Other sites were proposed during the 1960s but without the pressure that accompanied the Sa'diyat project. However, in the early 1960s a motorway was dug linking Sabra to the Airport Boulevarde, which cut through the western side of the camp and destroyed several homes. Although people who lost homes were compensated with space elsewhere, the road was doubtless intended to remind Shateela people of the temporariness of their settlement. At about the same time there were rumours of a project to build a high wall around the camp, to hide it from tourists. Later there was talk of a municipal project to cut a boulevard right through the centre of the camp, transforming it into a public garden.

The threat of bulldozing was thus present to Shateela people many years before bulldozers were actually used, during the September 1982 massacre, to crush housing near the massacre site. It was a threat that engendered a permanent sense of insecurity but also a determination not to be moved. Umm Majed said in 1989: 'These policemen would come and they always used to tell us, "We are going to remove this camp." But they couldn't do it. All our lives the Agency ruled. We are still here.'

Re-creation of a Palestinian 'entity'

While the establishment of the PLO in 1964 was welcomed by many Palestinians as a progressive step, it also created waves of opposition. These were mainly of two kinds: there were the Mufti loyalists, hostile to Egypt's influence, and there were organizers of clandestine networks preparing for armed struggle. Both trends were well entrenched in Lebanon, both inside and outside the camps, so that dissention over the PLO was experienced with particular acuteness in this region. However, the PLO on balance benefited from Nasser's patronage, since Nasserist Arab nationalism was probably at this time the strongest force among Palestinians of all strata.

President Chehab would have liked to continue to support Hajj Amin but did not do so because of the logic of his pro-Egyptian foreign policy (aimed to appease Lebanese Nasserists). He also realized that the Mufti's influence had been eroded by the immense popularity of the Egyptian president. Hence his rapid recognition of the PLO, ahead of most other Arab states.

Immediately after the Alexandria Summit, Shukairy made a tour of diaspora Palestinian communities to mobilize their support for the new 'entity'. His visit to Lebanon is widely remembered since the authorities allowed him to hold mass rallies, the first of their kind. Abu Muhammad Farmawi took part in the ceremonies of welcome:

> He stayed in the St. George's Hotel and I was head of the delegation from Shateela that went to greet him and offer our allegiance. We called a meeting in the Mosque to pledge support. The following of Hajj Amin began to make trouble – they considered Shukairy an appointee of the Arab League. They said, 'There ought to be elections, we should choose between Shukairy and Hajj Amin.' So there were quarrels and fighting – blows, stones, pulling hair . . . After this Hajj Amin began to dwindle.

With the waning of the influence of the Mufti, his following in the camps was also weakened. The position of Abu Kamal was made awkward and ambivalent by the placing of the DB and police around his office, as if to protect him. His earlier leadership status as founder and *qa'id* was reduced to the lesser one of an UNRWA functionary. Whereas previously, the police came to him before questioning anyone in the camp, he was now powerless even to protect 'his' own people.

> It was a very difficult time for my father. They [the DB] didn't try to harm him because they knew he was with Hajj Amin. But they tried to make him cooperate with them in one way or another. He was hurt by seeing other Palestinians hurt and not being able to do anything about it. He used to try to warn people to keep out of Shateela if he knew they were wanted. Sometimes he would go to the DB offices to beg for someone's release. After I was taken and beaten by the DB, he told me that in a period like this one mustn't show one's patriotic feelings, but try to appear like any ordinary person. (Jihad Bisher)

Although the Chehab regime recognized the legitimacy of the PLO and its unions at the level of the camps, repression of all political activity remained in force. Abu Muhammad experienced this contradiction:

> We were asked to form the [workers'] union in Lebanon after the first Arab Summit Conference in Alexandria. It held its founding conference in Gaza in 1964 and I attended it. When we returned we began to recruit members in the name of the PLO. There was opposition from the state but it wasn't open opposition because the president had attended the Alexandria Summit and agreed to everything.

Abu Muhammad was arrested along with four other General Union of Palestinian Workers' members, but could not be charged with any misdemeanour since the Union was legal. He was released but the Deuxième Bureau stepped up pressure on him as on leaders of other PLO unions to give up politics or to leave the country. He refused to do either.

The PLO did not have offices within the camps; most of its work was contacts with Lebanese political leaders and media. Even though PLO mass unions – workers', students', women's and others – were fully legal, DB control of the camps excluded their activities there. Shateela is close to the PLO's office on Corniche al-Mazra' so that its people sometimes joined demonstrations there. A woman who later joined Fateh describes how, as an enthusiastic schoolgirl, she went to the PLO to ask for volunteer work:

> I was one of those who wanted to do something. I remember going to the

PLO office; it was in the time of Shukairy; I asked about Civil Defence training. They said, 'You're too young. What else can you do?' I said, 'Let me collect contributions.' So they gave me a box, and I went from building to building collecting money. They hadn't any ideas how to mobilize the people. ('Nawal')

Arms and clandestinity

The preparations for armed struggle and the opening of military training camps for Palestinians in several Arab countries affected people in the camps in Lebanon within the limits of the strict secrecy made necessary by Deuxième Bureau surveillance. In the early 1960s, weapons began to pass through the Beirut camps on their way to the South.

The first [ANM] decision to start training was taken in 1962 and it was from this time that arms began to enter the camp. I brought guns from the Egyptian Embassy along with Umm Muhammad. They were called 'Ustab Port Sa'id'. She wrapped them like a baby and bared her breast as if feeding it. These arms were not for the camp but for the people who were undertaking armed operations against occupied Palestine.

Because Shateela is close to Beirut and the Embassy, we went and took the arms from Abdul Hameed Ghaleb[5] and put them temporarily in Shateela. Then we took them to Jiyyeh. From Jiyyeh, people took them to 'Ain Helweh, and from there to Shabreeha and Rashidiyyeh; and from there to Yareen. Yareen was the main store from where arms entered occupied Palestine. (Abu Muhammad Farmawi)

If the authorities feared political activity in the camps, they were even more concerned to prevent Palestinians from getting military training – the two were in any case closely connected. The seriousness with which the authorities viewed this development is suggested by Khaled Shehadeh's description of a visit to Shateela camp by the head of the section within the DB that dealt with Palestinians:

Joseph Kaylani came to Shateela camp and called a meeting of all the families of the camp. With him came four or five DB agents as big as mules, with their pistols, and behind them a vehicle full of soldiers. We sat on the ground in front of the Director's office – there was still space then – and they brought out stools and chairs for the *shuyyukh*.
Kaylani addressed his speech to the *shuyyukh*: 'O good old men! Maybe you don't know that some of your sons are going to an Arab

country' (he couldn't say Egypt) 'to get military training. You should know that Lebanon is your country, always ready to listen to your demands and help your sons with education. How should you treat those bad sons, trouble-makers, who seem determined to disturb you?'

I got up, 'Excellence, with your permission!' 'Sit down!' I said, 'Sir, I'm not a student in school and you are not a teacher. I want to speak about the subject you have raised.' He said, 'Speak!' I said, 'As a Palestinian I ask you to give me arms and training and lead me against Israel. This people has a country and all the Arab states are our family.'

An old man got up, Abu 'Ata Za'mout from Sufsaf, about ninety years old. 'What he's telling you is true, sir.' Then all the *shuyyukh* got up saying, 'We agree with Khaled Shehadeh!' After two days the DB came and took me and beat me all night. They nearly slaughtered me.

In 1967, during the 'Six Day' war, the Lebanese Army carried out what Shehadeh called a 'cheap deceit', taking militant nationalists like himself to a training camp in the South, in a move to defuse their enthusiasm to fight. They stayed there two months and the DB turned up to their passing-out ceremony – 'those who had killed us with their beatings'. But there was a small but steady trickle of men from Shateela and other camps going to PLA or Resistance group training courses outside. Minimal training on loading and cleaning guns was even carried out in homes in camps, under the noses of the DB.

Many small Resistance groups that later disappeared or merged with larger ones were active in the camps in Lebanon. Those with the strongest roots seem to have been the ANM (out of which was formed the PFLP in 1967), Fateh (whose leadership was not in Lebanon but in Gaza and Kuwait), and Sa'eqa, formed in 1966 from Palestinian Ba'thists. United against Lebanese state oppression, there was little internal conflict in the early days in spite of differences of strategy, Arab alliance and ideology. The ANM articulated one major trend in Palestinian thinking, that armed struggle could only be successful if carried out as part of a broader Arab effort; Fateh articulated a contrary theory, that Palestinian action was essential to trigger off events that would build Arab mass and government support. There was competition between the ANM and Fateh to be the first to begin Resistance operations. Because of their links with Nasser, ANM leaders adopted the policy of 'above zero and below provocation'. It was Fateh that carried out the first announced operation, just before 1 January 1965, an event that was enthusiastically received in the camps.

Although there was support for Palestinian armed struggle, attitudes towards early Resistance organization in the camps are difficult to reconstruct in all their variation at this distance in time, and after so many upheavals. There were undoubtedly many crosscurrents, debates and misgivings. Faith in Nasser remained widespread for much of the 1960s (even after 1967 many kept his portrait on their walls). Nevertheless there was a decline in membership of 'Opposition' parties, whether as a result of DB oppression or because of searching for a Palestinian framework; there was also widespread fear of the authorities and their informers. What emerges very clearly is that most of the support for the Resistance movement came from the generation that grew up in exile, the 'generation of the Disaster'. It is also clear that *istinhad* (readiness for insurrection) grew steadily throughout the period, especially after 1967. Hatred of DB oppression was one element in creating this mood, but anger at the Lebanese Army's actions against PRM fighters in the South was perhaps an even stronger one.

The contradiction between nationalism and fear of the authorities led to many conflicts between parents and children. The woman who speaks here was a schoolgirl in the 1960s:

> Before the 1967 war, in 1966 I think, they started First Aid courses. We had this special khaki uniform, a blouse and skirt with a tie, and the symbol of the First Aid. It was the Red Crescent [see Political Glossary] that ran the course, supervised by the Lebanese Army. Of course my parents didn't want me to come near anything like politics, not even First Aid. Not because they didn't want us to do it but because they felt that the people behind it were politicians, and they had suffered a lot [from politics] in Palestine. Also because they were worried about us.
>
> Every time I put on my uniform, my parents started in on me. When my mother didn't succeed in persuading me to give it up, she set my older brother after me. Once he hit me. But I was so stubborn. I felt this was something that I had to do. So I used to take my uniform to one of our neighbours, and put it on there. ('Fadia')

The response of younger Palestinians to calls for action is clear from the massive participation of schoolchildren in demonstrations. Although protest action escalated after 1967, demonstrations also occurred in the early 1960s. Fayrooz Isma'eel, who left school in 1964, recalls a demonstration of schoolgirls in which a classmate got caught by the police: 'Sakeena was very boyish, she ran, I hid. The police caught her. But they brought her back the same afternoon.'

Some idea of the readiness of the young for action is given by this account of a 'youth cell', self-formed and independent of any political movement or group:

> We were seven brothers and sisters; we used to get pocket money. Every week we held a session and asked ourselves who in this camp needs

money more than others. Then we put the money in an envelope and pushed it under their door, without them knowing where it came from. We did this after school, my brothers and sisters, and the children of the neighbours. Perhaps it was only LL5 or LL10 but in those days that was worth something.

From this work I got to know the people of the camp and built relations with them. We knew the woman whose husband had died, who had three or four children and was in need. We knew the woman who lived alone, and had no one to give her money. It was us alone, our parents didn't know. We never spoke about it. We were afraid that if the Deuxième Bureau got to know, they would stop us. Another way we built relations with people was by teaching their children.

We discussed things, we asked each other about the villages we came from. In this way the young men and women of the camp got to know each other and became unified. ('Nawal')

In general, old men and village notables were against the political activists, anathematizing them as 'troublemakers'. Khaled Shehadeh has a revealing recollection:

The old people were an obstructive factor to our movement. Every action we took, they'd say, 'What! Another demonstration!' If we distributed pamphlets, it was, 'What's the use of them?' When we called meetings, they said,' Look out! Abu Hanoon will come.'[6] The old people always tried to frighten and discourage us.

When her husband was arrested, Umm Muhammad Farmawi did not receive much sympathy from other women at the bakery or the water tap. Some pitied her for being married to a 'troublemaker', while others blamed her for not keeping her husband's mind fixed on providing for his family. Everyone shared the longing to return to Palestine, but not everyone believed that it was necessary to *work* for the return, especially if this meant incurring the wrath of the Lebanese state. Folk wisdom taught that it was better to appease authority than to provoke it. Not all old people were afraid to help the Resistance, however. A Fateh 'responsible' from Shateela remembers an old woman, Hajji Sara, in whose home he used to hide incriminating documents when Deuxième Bureau searches were expected.

Fateh cells were formed in Shateela in conditions of tight clandestinity. Early members contrast the solidity of Fateh in those days with the *fowda* (chaos) that came later, with mass recruitment. 'Fateh was a *tanzeem* [organization] in the real meaning of the word,' says one such Shateela man; 'It was on an international level.' An early local leader recalls:

We had to undergo six or seven months of testing. During this time we were on probation. We had to prepare demonstrations, make digests, write reports, collect information. We were only accepted as members if we passed this test.

Fateh's structure was designed to limit the contact of members with one another, to prevent infiltration. This member recalls going deep into the Hursh to discuss politics with cell-mates, *shebab* from Sabra and Shateela like himself. Each small cell was linked to the *tanzeem* through a unit leader.

Plastic sandals and certificates

How Shateela people remember living conditions in the 1960s tends to reflect differences in their economic situation and political leanings. It is clear that socioeconomic differentiation was beginning to appear, in contrast to the early 1950s when there was equality in destitution. As a house-painter who became a workers' union organizer, Abu Muhammad Farmawi emphasizes continuing hardship:

> In the beginning of the 1960s when I first came to Shateela the level of living was very low. For example, I took a wage of LL3½ daily. I had a wife and two children, we had to live on this amount. I paid LL20 for the house [i.e. rent] and LL2½ for electricity. Of course we went on taking rations. We ate meat three times a week. We drank tea. True, if a guest comes we are obliged to offer coffee, this is part of our tradition of hospitality. But we ourselves drank tea.
>
> In winter at first we used *mazout* but it makes a bad smell so we changed to charcoal. My children went to school in winter in plastic sandals without socks. I couldn't afford to buy them boots or proper winter clothing. New clothes for the feast are something basic, however. I used to start saving months before the feast to buy them clothes.
>
> When my daughter got sick, my wife was obliged to sell the watch I had given her at our wedding to take her to a specialist. UNRWA didn't cover it.

Fayrooz Isma'eel remembers as a child, in winter, carrying a *men'al* (brazier) to the public oven to get hot ashes. When stirred, they gave off heat for several hours.

Speaking for a slightly different social stratum, Jihad Bisher emphasizes an improvement in income and living standards that was certainly true of families with several wage earners:

The period immediately after 1948 was one of shock – people didn't know what to do. But by the 1960s they began to settle down, to try to improve their lives and build for the future. People of my age became old enough to start working for their family. There were many chances of work for Palestinians in the Gulf. UNRWA had a kind of employment office and hundreds of Palestinians who had graduated from secondary school, technical schools or university found salaried employment.

Jihad estimates that 5 per cent of Shateela households had sons working in the Gulf by the early 1960s, and that by the end of the decade the proportion had risen to 25 per cent. Migrants' remittances were important in enabling younger brothers to obtain professional training. With two or three sons (and occasionally daughters) working in the oil-producing countries, some families eventually succeeded in renting or even buying apartments outside the camp. Emigration did not always have such happy results, however. People tell of migrant sons who did not help their families, or who married foreign women and abandoned their Shateela wives.

One basis of socioeconomic differentiation lay in the gap in income and security between daily paid manual labour and salaried employment. Salaried employment required certificates higher than the Brevet, the stage at which free UNRWA schooling ended. It was not easy to finance the passage from the Brevet to the treasured professional certificate. UNRWA gave help with secondary school fees to a limited number of students,[7] and had its own Teacher and Technical Training Institute, Sibleen, but its yearly intake was also very limited. Most students had to find other means to finance their education. Ahmad Haleemeh's mother sold her wedding gold.

Although Shateela remained, as Abu Muhammad emphasizes, a working-class area with only a very small proportion of secondary or university students, nonetheless the drive towards higher education, which was to have its moment of expansion later with Resistance movement autonomy, began in the 1960s. The opening of the Egyptian-sponsored Arab University in Fakhany in the early 1960s made a difference. Although in Abu Muhammad's opinion there were no more than three or four families in Shateela who could forgo adult sons' earnings, we nevertheless find a small number who managed to get degrees, studying and working at the same time (this was possible at the Arab University since attending classes was not compulsory). Abu 'Ali Abbas was one of this small group. He had come to Shateela with his family in the 1950s at the age of fifteen, from Ba'lbek, where the nearest secondary school was 17 kilometres away in Zahleh. As well as being intelligent and determined, he was lucky to have five older brothers, which meant that his earnings were not needed. He went to secondary school in Beirut and then registered as an external student in the Arab University. While studying, he worked as a teacher in Lebanese private schools. Abu 'Ali was one of the group who gave evening classes to younger boys, helping them to pass the *towjihi* (official Arab school finishing) exam. Another of this group was Sa'eed Abdallah, who later became headmaster of Jericho School in Shateela.

However, the great majority of Shateela men remained in the category of manual worker, except for those who had small shops. However, they were workers who were becoming more skilled and were making more money. This came about in two ways. Adult men who had left Palestine without a *mihneh* (craft) picked one up through practice: 'With time the one who worked with tiles became a tiler, the one who worked in building carpentry became a master carpenter. So they beame *mihiniyeen* [specialized craftsmen] and their income increased' (Abu Turki). The second way was for boys to be apprenticed to a local *mu'allem* (master craftsman) for periods from three to six months, obtaining certificates in pre-industrial skills such as ironwork and car repairs. Up to the end of the 1970s, skilled manual workers as well as professionals could find jobs in the Gulf and send home part of their earnings.

Many initially 'unskilled' labourers developed themselves into master craftsmen, just as much of camp youth studied night and day to become teachers or accountants: these ideal collective stereotypes were certainly justified. However, there were certainly contrary cases which are overlooked or suppressed in the accounts most people gave. Real hardship hit the families of men who never, for one reason or another, found steady employment:

My mother kept pushing my father to work but he didn't want to listen to her – 'You want me to work for that dog!' Like many villagers he wasn't educated, he didn't have a profession. Once someone offered him a porter's job. He went there but the next day he didn't go back, he couldn't stand it. He suffered a lot until we grew old and could help. ('Fadia')

Another pattern was that of the worker who jumps from job to job without acquiring a specialized skill. This man of Haifa origin was a youth in the 1950s, and never went to school:

I moved from place to place. If someone didn't pay enough I left, if pay was higher somewhere else I left. I did a lot of different things, I worked in a carpenter's, a bakery, a garage, a tile factory. I worked for an Armenian in Bourj Hammoud, but I left him because he used to hit his workers and I feared my turn would come. (Abu Ahmad 'Issa Khalaf)

Such job mobility was feasible in the late 1950s and 1960s, years of Lebanese economic expansion. There was plenty of work, and commodities were cheap. Umm Ahmad says, 'You could get the best crepe-soled shoes for LL5 in those days. If you didn't eat meat for a week you could buy a watch.' She was one of the first housewives in Shateela to own a refrigerator and a washing machine.[8]

Professional salaried women workers began to appear in the 1960s though their numbers were few. Fayrooz Isma'eel, born in 1947, was one of them. Still remembered in Shateela for being always first in class, she was picked to go to UNRWA's Women's Training College at al-Tireh in the West Bank, graduating in June 1967, in the middle of the 'Six Day' war.

> We have relatives in Bourj Barajneh and some of them worked in Libya. We visited them after I returned from al-Tireh. They said that since I was qualified as a secretary they could find me a very good job in Libya. I said OK, I'd like to travel. My father didn't want me to go, but my mother encouraged me.

Fayrooz later found a job in Libya for her sister who had done a secretarial course at the YWCA in Beirut: these two professional women were able to make a home for their parents and younger siblings in Libya. Fayrooz continued to study as an external student, taking a BA in philosophy at Benghazi University and eventually migrating to London.[9] She recalls other Shateela working girls in her time:

> There was Nawal Ma'rouf, she left the camp before me to work in Kuwait, she had a married sister there. There were a few others from my generation. Not all were secretaries. Some were governesses, some were dressmakers, two were nurses – nursing still wasn't accepted then.

What all the accounts make clear is the crucial function of the household family as a unit of economic survival, and of socioeconomic differentiation. While such factors as rent-free land, UNRWA services, external charity and internal redistribution guaranteed that no one starved, other factors discriminated between households in terms of well-being. As we have seen, the health and capacities of the *rabb al-a'aileh* (household head) was one of these; another, discussed in Chapter 2, was village origins and *waasta*; but perhaps most important were the abilities of children. Their intelligence, zeal, gender and birth order all entered into a lottery that could bring better fortune or bitter disappointment to individuals and families. The psychological costs are suggested in this comment of Abu Muhammad's:

> There were cases where the parents were determined that their son should study. But they had to cut the cost from their daily living, from their food, from their clothes. The mother worked, the daughter worked, so

that the son should have school fees, clothes, transport, pocket money. This led to daily scenes along the lines of: 'Son, I'm paying with my blood, I'm depriving your brothers and sisters so that you can get educated, but you . . .' This would create complexes in the boy.

Even without parental pressures, anxiety could be transferred to children. Fayrooz speaks for many of the generation of the Disaster: 'From a very early age, I felt responsible, I felt I had to work to help my family. I grew old at a very early age. I never behaved like a little girl, never.'

Popular culture

The vivid recollections of the *a'yad* (feasts) by Palestinians who were young in the 1960s highlights their character as a time of play and plenty which contrasted with the hard work and poverty of daily life. Abu and Umm Ahmad Khalaf 'Issa evoke the funfair that used to be set up in Ard Jalloud, an empty space near Shateela:

Parents gave children the *a'ediyya* [money to spend on the feast] so that they could go and ride on bicycles, or swings, or go to the cinema. They ate pickles. There were donkeys, photographers . . . The men with the donkeys used to shout to attract the children, 'My donkey is best.' Those people came who pull razor blades from their mouths, eggs from their ears – magicians – it's just like the cinema. They fought. There was one who pulled scarves from his mouth, scarf after scarf. There were circus people, some rode motorbikes, others one-wheeled bicycles. And a woman dancer. In those days if you had a lira you could see all those things; each spectacle cost five piastres.

In those days there were still men who travelled from place to place carrying on their back a *sandooq al-'ajayeb* (box of wonders). Those who peeped through its eye-hole could see moving pictures of stories like 'Qays wa Leila' or travelogues. For men there might be pictures of naked women cut from magazines.[10]

Umm 'Issam Qurdah, a Shateela housewife who grew up in 'Ain Helweh, remembers outings with her father at A'eed al-Fitr that included promenades along the sea front, swings, boat trips and ice creams. New clothes were *de rigueur* even for children from the camps. Umm 'Issam's mother got upset if a spot appeared on any of her daughters' dresses during the three days of the feast. This would have meant re-washing and ironing them, with a heavy iron heated by filling it with charcoal.

Ahmad Haleemeh remembers fifty to sixty people gathering for special occasions in his family home in Shateela, a large one made up of four or five units. A religious family, they needed no other entertainment than special feast food and each other's company. In some families there might also be card-playing and mild gambling.

National occasions formed a basis for cultural manifestations in exile. Fayrooz Isma'eel was often chosen to deliver the *khutbeh* (oration) on commemoration days such as 2 November (the Balfour Declaration) or 15 May (the establishment of Israel). Sometimes the *khutbeh* was written for her by an older relative; often they were readings of well-known Palestinian poets. Parents and *wujaha'* used to attend these ceremonies, which were held in schools. Schools remained a focus of nationalist culture in spite of Deuxième Bureau surveillance.

> One of our teachers, Ustadh Hassan, used to tell us nationalist stories. We always sat quietly, we liked him, we paid attention to his stories. But we didn't understand their implications until we grew older. Teachers weren't allowed to have political activities then. (Fayrooz Isma'eel)

Cinema-going, almost unknown in Palestine, became permitted first to children in Lebanon as a part of the *a'eed* celebrations. Cinema Sharq opened in the early 1960s opposite Shateela's main entrance, near the 'Ali Handar cafe. Most of its clients came from the camp. Fayrooz Badran's father refused to go to the cinema on religious grounds[11] but he used to accompany his two small daughters to Cinema Sharq and wait for them outside. Later Fayrooz would go at feast times with a group of classmates to downtown cinemas such as the Rivoli in Sahet al-Bourj.

The cinema was only one of many new cultural media that camps close to Beirut brought within reach of the refugees. Television sets made their appearance in the early 1960s. Everyone remembers Hajj Taha's television because of the centrality of his shop for school supplies, near the Mosque, and because he rented chairs out to viewers.

> There were boys who wanted to watch TV but who didn't have a franc. So they kept watch on Hajj Taha and when he left his shop they dug a hole in the wall. As soon as it got dark they went and watched TV. When they left, they put chewing gum over the hole so that he wouldn't discover it. (Fayrooz Isma'eel)

Television and radio (cassettes would come later) had the effect of popularizing contemporary Arab singers, overlaying older Palestinian song traditions. It was mainly village women who carried on pre-1948 forms of expressive culture which would be revived, later, by the Resistance movement. The chief occasions for folk singing were gatherings for mourning or weddings; another was the departure of pilgrims on the *hajj*, at which women encouraged them with a special kind of song (*haneen*). Women would start off with familiar songs, and then improvise. Only older, unschooled village women have kept up the tradition of oral poetry and improvised singing; city women never practised this art, and younger women have lost it with schooling.

The influence of urban Arab and Lebanese culture was naturally stronger in camps like Shateela and Bourj Barajneh than in the rural camps which remained, in comparison, 'conservative' and 'backward' (terms used of them by the camp people). Perceptions of city people as 'civilized' and village people as the opposite have strong roots in Arabic culture and society. In Shateela, this cultural hierarchy was given weight by the presence of city Palestinians as well as the closeness of the city. Insights into the persistence of the city/rural boundary as well as the psycho-social processes that makes city ways superior are given by Fayrooz and Nadia Isma'eel. Their age and social situation, girls from Sufsaf living on the edge of the Jaffa quarter, give their recollections a 'strategic' interest:

In the afternoons city women always had a gathering at which they drank tea and coffee, and smoked the *argeeleh* [water pipe].[12] They wore their nicest dresses. If one of them had recently got married, she would put on one of her bridal dresses, which were always *décolleté* . . . They would put make-up on and a flower in their hair. Village women didn't do this.

We always used to laugh at our families. Now I feel sad because I missed a lot of Palestinian culture. We don't know the Palestinian *debkeh*. The older generation used to gather in a·yard in the camp, they made weddings in the open air and danced the *debkeh*. When Sufsaf people had a wedding, our city neighbours used to say '*Fellaheen!*' We were children, we didn't want to feel inferior. We felt that they were ahead of us, for instance in the way they dressed.

Nadia: We hated everything that was *fellaheen*, everything that was *moda 'adeemi* [old-fashioned].

Fayrooz: It's because we lived in an area with Yaffa people. In 'Ain Helweh, Sufsaf girls grew up in a village environment, they know the *debkeh*, they know the songs. I know a lot of proverbs but I don't know the folklore. Maybe it's because everywhere, peasants are . . . less than city people.

Nadia: But the *fellaheen* gave more attention to the education of their children. City people didn't even educate their sons. They let them take jobs or open a shop. In the end we turned out better than they.[13]

We sense here some of the effect of urban influence and education in producing cultural change. Yet peasant cultural practices persisted in spite of Shateela's closeness to Beirut. Here is Hajj Taha (the first television owner) describing his eldest son's wedding, towards the end of the 1960s. He begins by giving a detailed account of his own wedding in Sha'b, a few years before the exodus, and continues:

> I wanted to get him married because he was the first of my children, and I wanted to make a celebration for him just like the one I'd had. Just as my father had been happy in my wedding, I wanted to be happy in the weddings of my children.[14] I organized celebrations that lasted three or four nights; every night I invited all the people of the camp. There were four or five poets. And I had a slaughtering – thirty-four legs of lamb stuffed with rice and meat, and three or four more sheep for *kibbeh* (meat pie). We brought *leban* [yoghurt] from the Beqa', fresh sheeps' *leban*. We brought *bamieh* [okra] from Tripoli, and green beans. We cooked these things and everyone ate them. They were days of happiness, days of enjoyment. It was a perfect wedding party, everyone was happy. There was slaughtering and joy, and my son rode on a horse, but in those days we didn't have video cameras to record it. I'll tell you how many people I invited – 350 invitation cards went out to villages and camps!

This wedding took place twenty years after leaving Palestine and before the 1970s national cultural revival. Hajj Taha was possibly exceptional in his project to reproduce exactly the repertoire of pre-1948 village weddings. Others began to adopt elements of city weddings, for example the bridal couple on a dais, surrounded by flowers. But for Palestinians in exile, weddings became a signifier of identity, infused with collective national meaning, distinguishing Palestinians from Lebanese. The terms *hafez 'ala karameh* and *karamat al-jiwaz*[15] are used by Palestinians of the camps to evoke this identity-emphasizing character of their weddings, indicating a range of linked values, from the necessity of the virginity of the bride and the proper conduct of marriage negotiations to the exchange of gifts and lavish celebrations.

In any account of the 1960s, it should not be forgotten that In'ash al-Mukhayem (see Political Glossary), famous for its revival of traditional Palestinian peasant embroidery, began from Shateela soon after the 1967 war. It was not easy to find original dresses as models: for reasons not fully understood, such embroidery had disappeared from most of the Galilee before 1948; the few *thawab* brought to Lebanon had been sold or cut up. Revival thus required a difficult process of research, adaptation and training.[16] The In'ash also built a model kindergarten near Shateela (destroyed during the Israeli invasion of 1982), where several generations of kindergarten teachers were trained, almost all of them from camps.

The last days of the Deuxième Bureau

Palestinians later looked back to the defeat of the Arab armies in 1967 as a decisive moment that liberated them from Arab tutelage. Even though they had been supporters of Nasser, members of the ANM took the same view.

> After the defeat of 1967 the situation changed. First, the Palestinian people began to arm. This wasn't with the support of the Arab regimes but it prevented their collapse after the Jordanian, Syrian and Egyptian armies were crushed. And once Palestinians began to be armed they reacted differently to their situation. Here people were oppressed, they wanted freedom. When they got arms they felt that freedom was within reach. Everyone was pushed by this current and there began to be a widespread readiness for insurrection. (Abu Muhammad Farmawi)

In Lebanon, the Israeli commando attack against Beirut Airport in December 1968 set off a new turn in the descending spiral of political crisis. There were mass demonstrations against Lebanese Army moves to curb the *feda'yeen* in the South. In the spring of 1969 the Army, acting independently of the Karameh government, tried to encircle the resistance forces, stepping up arrests of Palestinians and Lebanese leftists, and besieging the town of Bint Jbeil which tried to protect the commandos. These clashes led to the celebrated demonstration of 23 April, in Beirut, when police opened fire on an unarmed crowd, killing twenty and wounding hundreds. In the ensuing uproar, Prime Minister Karameh resigned.[17]

Many Shateela people took part in this demonstration including this schoolgirl:

> They announced early in the morning on the radio that there was to be no demonstration. But we gathered in all the schools – I was in Haifa school then – and we went out until we reached Corniche al-Mazra'. It wasn't just Palestinians who were taking part, there were many Lebanese also – nationalists, students, people from unions. There were many girls and women. This was something that encouraged us, that the Lebanese were not against us.
>
> I had been in many demonstrations before but this was the first time that I saw blood and death. We reached the Barbir Hospital and found the Army waiting for us there. They wouldn't allow us a step further. We were trapped. Somebody started shooting and one of the demonstrators fell, shot in the head. It was the first time that I'd felt bullets that close, aimed to kill. I was worried – my younger brother Muhammad was with me and many other friends and neighbours from Shateela whom I considered as brothers. We started moving the wounded to the Maqassad

Hospital but it closed the gate in our face. Maybe they were frightened or maybe they didn't want to give treatment for free. In the end they opened. Umm 'Ali Nasrawiyya was the one who made them open the door, she shouted at them. It was like a second demonstration in front of the hospital gate.

Later in the afternoon I saw my brother coming, covered in blood. When I saw him like that . . . But he said, 'Don't worry, I'm not hurt.' He'd been carrying a friend who'd been shot in the thigh, his artery was severed. He survived by a miracle. ('Fadia')

Many stories are told about Umm 'Ali Nasrawiyya, who lived in Shateela and was famous for her nationalist spirit. Whenever fighters were killed, she took part in their funeral cortège. She also used to take food to the fighters in the Arqoub. All her sons except one were killed, and people loved her more for that than for her role in demonstrations. It is said that she once led a march of children up to Sabra, but the police stopped the march, arrested Umm 'Ali and gave her a public beating on the soles of her feet.[18]

Demonstrations around Shateela became an almost daily occurrence. The greater readiness of ordinary people to challenge the authorities can be seen in this anecdote from Abu Muhammad:

Once when I was arrested, people demonstrated outside the police station. They [the police] were about to put men in the Land Rover to take me up to Ba'bda when women surrounded it and forced the police to let me out. It was a case of *Allahu akbar*.[19]

He adds:

We began training students with sticks, at night, in the playground. then we started carrying arms at night, with covered faces. Before 1967 people were afraid; after it, they began to confront the Deuxième Bureau. If one of them hit us, we hit back.

The collaborators were especially afraid of us. We used to go out masked and attack them with sticks, the way they are doing now in occupied Palestine.

In August 1969, Abu Kamal resigned from his post as Director, handing over to his son Jihad, who had Resistance group credentials. Feeling in the camp was said to be 'boiling', and a confrontation with the forces of the state seemed only a matter of time. In some other camps there were real battles, but in Shateela the end of the Deuxième Bureau came without violence. Abu Muhammad gives this description of their last hours, on 19–20 October:

At 5 pm we gathered and decided to throw them out of the camp. We gathered some of the *shebab* and gave them guns. We had three Chinese-made Schneitzers, and I made different people walk around with them to make it seem that we had more. They got scared.

We gathered in front of their office with this show of military force. Women came out, children came out, they gathered with us in front of the police station. We threatened them, 'If you don't leave we'll destroy the office over your heads.'

They contacted their headquarters and explained the situation. At 8 pm exactly a truck came and carried them away.

A Fateh local leader gives a slightly different version which underlines uncertainties and internal divergences:

Fateh Organization wanted a battle but I was against attacking because they had packed and taken all their papers before leaving the camp. So what would we gain? At 10 pm a police patrol entered the camp from al-Hursh and reached the mosque. We could have killed them because they were surrounded by our men. But I said, 'No killing.' We didn't have the weapons for a long battle, just one Klashin with 120 bullets and seven Carlostadts with 460 rounds. When the police found everything calm, they withdrew.

The next morning, at 7 am, some organizations wanted to raise the flag. But we [Fateh] said, 'We can't raise it yet, we must be able to protect it.' We waited until 9 am, and then we raised it, without a battle. They had left in the night, everything was over.

As for the collaborators, there were two points of view: either to kill them or to throw them out. I was for the second way. Killing between Palestinians means blood, and blood is never forgotten. If we had executed 'Sa'eed' from Sha'b, all the people of Sha'b would have stayed far from the Revolution. Besides, many people were accused of being agents without real evidence. If we had allowed one execution, there would have been hundreds. The Revolution would never have recovered. (Abu Makarem)

Notes

1. On 31 December 1961, the PPS attempted a coup against Chehab, possibly supported by Jordan. See K. Salibi, *Crossroads to Civil War* (New York: Caravan Books, 1976), pp. 11–12.
2. The Deuxième Bureau also hinted at rape, to force Abu Muhammad to stay

at home to protect his wife. Undeterred, Umm Muhammad asked a neighbour's daughter to keep her company when he travelled.

3. The Directorate of Palestinian Refugee Affairs, a section of the Ministry of the Interior.

4. According to his son, Abu Kamal told the Minister of the Interior that if the government went ahead with transfer, it had better prepare '15,000 jute bags', a hint at resistance. The Director must have been including the population of areas around Shateela in this figure.

5. A. H. Ghaleb was Egypt's ambassador to Lebanon during the 1960s. Opponents of Chehab used to call him 'High Commissioner' (in reference to the French Mandate).

6. 'Abu Hanoon', 'the father of kindness', a satirical popular term for the state.

7. The number varied each year: for example, in 1959/60 it was 856.

8. When I interviewed this family in 1989, their home in Shateela had been destroyed, Abu Ahmad was disabled, Umm Ahmad's sewing business was shattered and they were 'squatting' in an unfinished building: a sad contrast with their situation in the early 1960s.

9. Since moving to London Fayrooz Isma'eel has had several short stories published. Two appear in an anthology of the writings of Black and Third World women, *Charting the Journey* (London: Sheba Feminist Publishers, 1988).

10. Information given by Mo'ataz Dajani. Shateela people remember the *sandooq al-'ajayeb* up to 1967.

11. The Quran condemns *tashkees*, the creation of human likenesses. Some pious Muslims see the cinema as doing this.

12. These *istiqbals* (receptions) used to be a feature of city women's life in all classes throughout the Arab region, as well as in Iran and Turkey.

13. Differences between rural and city people is still a favourite folk theme. See T. Alqudsi-Ghabra, 'City and Village in the Palestinian Wedding Song: The Palestinian Community in Kuwait' in S. Sabbagh and G. Tulhami (eds), *Images and Reality: Palestinian Women Under Occupation and in the Diaspora* (Washington: Institute for Arab Women's Studies, 1990).

14. The word *yifrah*, to be happy, is closely linked to marriage in popular speech, and is seldom used in other contexts.

15. 'Guarding one's dignity' and 'dignity of marriage': besides dignity the term *karameh* contains the ideas of honour and generosity.

16. When In'ash was hunting for original embroidered dresses, a young woman from Bourj Barajneh camp discovered her grandmother's, hidden deep in a cupboard. None of her generation had seen such clothes before and thought it must have come from India (Mrs Serine Shahid, personal communication).

17. Petran, *Struggle over Lebanon*, pp. 97–105, has a detailed account of this series of events.

18. For a description of Umm 'Ali Nasrawiyya, see M. Omar, 'Les gens et le siège, *Revue d'études palestiniennes*, no. 7, Spring 1983.

19. Ba'bda is the location of the military and civilian courts for the province of which Shateela is part. 'God is greatest' is shouted by crowds when in a state of *istinhad* (insurrection).

4. 'Days of the Revolution', 1969–82

Flags and euphoria

Looking back after 1982 with a feeling that few of the aims of the Resistance movement had been achieved, at least as far as they were concerned, Shateela people nonetheless remember well the joy that accompanied the liberation of the camps.

> Everybody was happy, everybody was singing, everybody wanted to join in. I remember that there were three or four nights when nobody slept. People who had been working in underground organizations revealed themselves. Young men who had had nothing to do with it felt ashamed. (Jihad Bisher)

Abu 'Ali Abbas commented ironically, 'After they put up the Palestinian flag, people felt as if they had liberated Nablus.'

There was a rush to join an organization. Although there were only three at the time of the liberation (Fateh, the PFLP, and Sa'eqa), others soon opened offices. Ahmad Haleemeh, still a schoolboy, tried to join Fateh but was reallocated to the PLA, which gave him a gun, a uniform and the job of organizing a youth section. In the first few weeks, before the arrival of a Palestinian military force, the Kifah Musellah (Armed Struggle), everyone took turns at doing guard duty, even women. There was a mood of total identification with the Resistance; fighters from outside Shateela were treated as honoured guests: 'It was felt to be shameful not to be the first to give the fighters food, water, shelter.'

> I remember old men coming to our office in Shateela, fighting for a chance to do guard duty. Three or four hours weren't enough for them – 'I haven't done guard duty today!' It didn't matter with which organization. They weren't divided between political currents, that came later. At the beginning the important thing was to join the 'Revolution'[1] and to liberate Palestine. (Abu Muhammad Farmawi)

Liberation had another instantaneous effect: it left people free to enlarge their homes, using solid materials forbidden before. In this anecdote, the ideas of 'liberation' and 'building' are practically identical:

> I had a friend called Shehadeh 'Ali Shehadeh who wanted to be the first to build his home with solid blocks. Sometime in October 1969 he asked me, 'When shall I build my house?' I told him, 'Soon *insh'allah*' – it was two or three days before the Deuxième Bureau left the camp. Sure enough Shehadeh was the first one to build, and it was as if he was celebrating a feast. (Abu Makarem)

Many problems arose from the suddenness of liberation, especially because the urge to build clashed with the lack of space.

> When the Revolution came to the camp, everyone wanted to build. This created problems between neighbours: 'You are too close to me!'; 'You shouldn't open a window here!' This was the biggest cause of quarrels. It was the role of the Kifah Musellah or the Popular Committee to solve such problems. (Abu Muhammad)

Jihad Bisher, camp Director from 1969 to 1978, says, 'We had to be on 24-hour alert for friction or problems caused by building.' The *shuyyukh*, already grouped in 'neighbourhood committees' from before the liberation, often intervened successfully in such disputes.

One of the first buildings to be rebuilt in cement was the Mosque. A committee of three old men – Abu Ahmad Sa'eed, Abu Khaled Mrad and Abu Waleed Ma'rouf – was in charge of this project, collecting money from every household and even from migrants in the Gulf.

The geography of the camp also changed in ways that left their imprint on speech long after the departure of the PRM in 1982:

> The camp was divided into *mahwar* [bases, axes] belonging to the main organizations. Wherever each organization had its office and its guards, the surrounding area belonged to it. Each had its 'square', its territory, and people get used to using these names – 'Iqleem Fateh', 'Iqleem Dimokratiyyeh', the 'Maktab Siyasi' [political office of the PFLP] and so on. (Abu Muhammad Farmawi)

The *ashbal* (lion cubs) training ground on the southern edge of the camp also became an established landmark. Streets – even the camp itself – were renamed. After his assassination, Fateh Security Chief Abu Hassan Salameh's name was given to the main street, skirting the western side of the camp, and a monument to his memory placed where it joins the Airport

Boulevarde. However, Shateela's new name – Mu'asker al-Karmel – never stuck.

Although the worst collaborators had left the camp with the Deuxième Bureau, some joined the 'Revolution', to the disgust of militants like Abu Muhammad who had suffered from them:

> One of the most notorious collaborators in Shateela – he had been present during my interrogations – was carrying a Klashin while we in the PFLP still had only two guns. Once I went to a meeting with the chief of the Kifah Musellah. Among the people there were three former agents. I refused to sit with them. The chief told me, 'Some of them we asked to be agents, to bring us information.' But it was lies.

With liberation, arms began to flow into the camp. Guns and bullets had been rarities before, treasured and hidden. Now the arms merchants came. Although the camp leadership tried to control the distribution of weapons, imposing fines on those who kept them in their homes, the building up of arsenals constituted a real danger. It was not the weapons alone, but the combination of weapons with Resistance group factionalism that was dangerous. When the Kifah Musellah arrived some weeks after the Cairo Accords to take over control of the camps, they forbade the carrying of arms. This order was contested by local organization leaders. Resistance militias were then allowed to carry arms within their *mahwar* but not outside it; only the Kifah were authorized to make armed patrols inside the camps. Again there were friction and clashes. Finally joint Kifah–Resistance group patrols were formed.

An idea of the effect of the liberation of the camps on children is given by this recollection by a young woman, now a Resistance group cadre, then a child:

> What I remember first, and most – the scene that sticks in my mind – was when the Resistance entered the camp and threw out the Deuxième Bureau. I was five or six at the time. The people were all in the streets welcoming the *feda'yeen*. They were shooting in the air and I was afraid – it was the first time I'd heard bullets. So I stayed far away, at the head of our alley. But this picture of the *feda'yeen* entering the camp in their uniforms amid the celebrations of the people is one I'll never forget. ('Leila')

The new authority

Several points of friction emerge in accounts of relations between the Kifah Musellah and the people of the camps which illuminate some of the obstacles to building a unified Palestinian people. The Kifah was a special unit drawn from the PLA, which had been formed along 'classical' lines within the armies of Iraq, Syria and Egypt. Nothing in their training qualified them to work with civilians:

> They came from the forces of 'Ain Jallout, stationed in Egypt or the Beqa' and they had a hard, rough mentality. At first they didn't mix with us. They were commanded by military officers who had no experience of solving social problems. They looked on the camp as if it was a military barracks, they expected us to stop and salute them in the street. Their only way of dealing with people was through punishments and imprisonment. This attitude doesn't work with our people, so there were problems and confrontations. (Abu Muhammad Farmawi)

That the Kifah behaved arrogantly towards the people of the camps is corroborated by others, yet there were political reasons why the PFLP in particular developed this critique. Abu Muhammad says that the Kifah was 'with the PLO, and the PLO was Fateh'. The historic rivalry between these two groups for leadership of the Resistance movement took a particularly sharp form in Lebanon. The comments on the Kifah's 'hard, rough mentality' and Gaza provenance also reminds us that most 'Lebanese' Palestinians originated in Galilee, and that regional differences persisted long after 1948.

With time, solutions to many of these problems were worked out through processes of consultation and negotiation. As a relatively autonomous camp leadership took shape, it was able to take a stronger role and to mediate between the Kifah and the people of the camp. Friction between the Kifah and the Resistance militias was at least partly solved by forming mixed patrols. With time the Kifah also began to be integrated into the locality through visits, friendship and marriage.

Later, an independent Palestinian judicial system began to emerge:

> In the middle of the 1970s, when Lebanese state institutions became very weak, a Palestinian system called the Revolutionary Courts was set up. This new judicial system was drawn up by people who had studied law, proper judges. It was independent from the Lebanese courts except in cases of problems between a Lebanese and a Palestinian; such cases had to go to the Lebanese courts. But if it was between Palestinians, the Revolutionary Court looked after it. The Kifah was the executive arm of

this new legal system, applying decisions such as arrest or fines.[2] (Abu Muhammad)

Autonomy: trial and error

Autonomy for the camps was specifically included in the Cairo Accords, which mentioned 'local committees' that would coordinate with the Kifah Musellah and the Lebanese authorities.[3] Jihad Bisher gives an idea of early trials in the search for bodies to implement autonomy:

> Things began to get more organized with periodic meetings being held between the leaders of Resistance groups, to take decisions and to avoid friction and clashes. I was camp Director at the time of the liberation, so I met with the group leaders and we formed what we called the Unified Command. Its aim was to restore peace in the camp, train young people for defence, improve public services and keep an eye on UNRWA schools and other Agency activities.

Later, in 1973, a PLO Executive Committee decision called for the formation of Popular Committees in all the camps, and laid down uniform guidelines for their composition, tasks and procedures. Members were from the camps but were appointed by Resistance groups to represent them:

> A delegate from the mass unions, from two to five independents, and one member from every Resistance group – this was how the Popular Committees were formed. According to the rule of *nuss zayd wahid* [half plus one] the chairman always had to be from Fateh – it was the same in the unions . . . Everything depended on the personality of the other members. The chairman could make them nothings. If they were weak they just followed him; if they were strong they would argue and fill their positions. (Abu Muhammad Farmawi)

The addition of 'independents' came at a later stage, to give more authority to the Popular Committee by adding respected 'elder citizens', and to give more weight to the *ahali al-mukhayem* (the families of the camp) *vis-à-vis* the Resistance groups. This method of composition produced Popular Committees of unwieldy size, and even though subcommittees were formed out of them to deal with special tasks, they remained handicapped in several ways. First, the Popular Committee had no real political or leadership role but acted rather as a mediator between the PRM leadership, where real power lay, and the people of the camp; according to a widespread formula, its role was to look after the 'social side'. Second, although the

Popular Committee's main task was to improve the environment and public services, its budget was too small and irregular to carry out major works. Abu Muhammad voices a general complaint:

> Certainly there were some achievements. The Popular Committee had a budget from the PLO and aid came from other sources. This enabled them to do certain things, mend and asphalt roads, bring water and electricity, dig wells, repair sewage pipes. But, regrettably, there was some stealing. There was no supervision or accountability. People at the top didn't care what happened, they never punished those who stole.

A third problem was that, because of their constitution, the Popular Committees did not really represent the people of the camps, nor did they develop their participation; instead, like the popular unions, they became an arena of struggle between the Resistance groups. Thus, although elections were sometimes held, they carried the danger of PRM group clashes.

A chronic point of conflict developed around financial responsibility. Fateh, as the wealthiest of the Resistance groups, and recipient of donations destined for the PLO, was accused by other groups of using funds for its own purposes; Fateh, on the other hand, saw itself as funding institutions from which all benefited equally (for example, the Institute of Social Affairs, which paid pensions to the families of martyrs and prisoners), without receiving credit.

> Our brothers in the other organizations would say, 'Let's make such-and-such a project.' They would let Fateh pay for it and then name it in the name of all the organizations jointly, though by rights it should have been in Fateh's name. (Abu Makarem)

Whatever the weaknesses of the Popular Committees, they were an improvement on the past and provided a framework for participation that could be criticized and improved. As a form closely associated with the PLO/PRM, they spread into all the neighbourhoods around Shateela. Indeed, committees and subcommittees proliferated during the 'Days of the Revolution' to the point where the terms became derided, synonymous with chaos rather than autonomy. In the favour of committees, it could be said that they provided a channel for the participation of the largest number in the 'Revolution'. Autonomy was not an end in itself but rather an element within an overall strategy of national struggle.

External attacks and internal clashes

From the early 1970s, the camps in Lebanon increasingly became the target of Israeli attacks using air, land and sea. These were to a large degree accepted by the people of the camps as a measure of the health of the Resistance movement. They were ready to accept high losses as long as Resistance attacks continued, convinced that retaliation proved that Israel was getting hurt.

No topic concerned people more than Resistance operations. News broadcasts were listened to and PRM bulletins scanned for news of the *feda'yeen*. Special pride was expressed if kin, friends or 'sons of the camp' were involved. Deep mourning was expressed for martyrs.[4] In a very real sense the Resistance movement represented the people of the camps, since most of the fighters were their sons. Equally there was concern when armed struggle stagnated. An early Fateh member looks back in bitterness at the Resistance movement's inability to develop militarily:

During the war of October 1973 the Resistance didn't carry out a single operation. It was shameful. In 1975, what happened? A thousand bullets were shot from Shateela at 'Ain al-Romaneh,[5] without causing a single casualty. Our operations were like immunization to a child, they made Israel stronger. Look at what happened after the Dalal Moghrabi operation! Israel reinforced its fleet off Lebanon.[6]

Lebanese–Palestinian clashes also continued to occur, with major episodes in May 1973, when the Lebanese Army besieged three camps for a month, attacking Shateela from positions in the Sports City and lower Hursh and strafing it from the air; and again in the Civil War of 1975/6, when Shateela was shelled and sniped at from 'Ain al-Romaneh. Several Shateela *shebab* fought against the Maronite militias in East Beirut; others drove supply trucks to the besieged camp of Tell al-Za'ter through the Lebanese Forces' lines.

Inseparable from the Palestinian struggle, fights between Resistance groups formed a third source of danger. Abu Muhammad gives a general view:

The period was divided into different stages, all of them unstable, each one marked by conflict, mobilization, accusations, confrontations. An early point of conflict was over the Kifah, because the PFLP wasn't part of it. There was also conflict over the battle in Jordan. In 1974 the issue was one of 'national authority', when the PFLP withdrew from the Executive Committee and formed the Rejection Front. Each political stage had its conflicts.

He adds:

> In some early periods we forgot that it is Israel and imperialism that are our enemies, we imagined that our enemy is another Palestinian group. There was provocation and mobilization due to lack of consciousness. Each organization pursued the others, collected information about them, and attacked them so as to gain their members.

Although in general Fateh cooperated with Sa'eqa and the DFLP against the PFLP, there were also serious clashes between Fateh and Sa'eqa in 1976/7, after Syria entered Lebanon to protect the Maronites.

Inter-Resistance group fighting was deeply disturbing to the people of the camps, first because of their attachment to national unity, and second, because such battles wasted the lives of their sons. It is possible to discern some kinds of self-defence against factional conflict worked out over long historical experience. An anecdote told by Ahmad Haleemeh's father points to one of the strongest: family solidarity. In a period of conflict between Fateh and the PLA, Abu Ahmad found himself aiming his gun at one of his sons in the other formation. Both lowered their guns and went home. It is said of mothers in camps that they bring up their sons to put fraternal ties before political ones.

Older women also spontaneously formed themselves into delegations that visited the Resistance leaders to complain of conflict or other problems. But a more usual 'interposing force' was the *shuyyukh* and *wujaha'*. Although their problem-solving role was normally confined to conflicts within the camp, it is clear from the following two accounts that, in emergencies, they also represented the families of the camp to the Resistance leadership.

> When I became Director, I kept the *wujaha'* as my father had done, to solve problems and as witnesses . . . Let's say I want to meet Abu Ammar because there's a big problem, I'd put the *wujaha'* in my car and go to the offices, and I could talk strongly because I had them with me. They are the fathers and the uncles of the *feda'yeen*. They are the owners of the camp and the reservoir of the 'Revolution'. (Jihad Bisher)

Fateh's policy towards the camps included reinforcing the 'leadership' role of the *shuyyukh*. One of the projects of Fateh's Building Committee was to reconstruct a village *diwan* where they could meet:

> We brought straw mats, mattresses and hard-backed cushions, and coffee-making equipment to make bitter coffee. The old men used to sit there every evening and talk. They talked about the problems of the camps, and if there was a quarrel between two organizations they used to go and solve it. (Abu Makarem)

Such a policy had several resonances. At a symbolic level, the *shuyyukh* incarnated continuity with historic Palestine, passing on the *shebab* stories and values from that period.[7] Furthermore, whether or not they belonged to Fateh, the *shuyyukh* were inclined to be conservative, pious and hostile to the radical ideas current in some sectors of the Resistance movement. At another level, the following testimony suggests that the *shuyyukh* sometimes represented the people of the camp in *opposition* to the Resistance leadership:

> If we wanted something from Abu Ammar we used to give a lunch for him at Nadi Beladna [Club of our Country, a sports club built by Fateh in Sabra] and let Abu Ahmad Sa'eed tell him what we wanted. He was forceful and self-confident when he spoke to the leadership. He used to say '*Willek abu Ammar!*'[8] It's not polite but that's the way he spoke. (Abu Makarem)

Abu Ahmad Sa'eed was the leading personality in Shateela after the death of Abed Bisher, and his *diwan* became, according to Abu Makarem, the political heart of the camp. In portraying Abu Ahmad as a personification of peasant straight-speaking, Abu Makarem is doubtless expressing a retrospective desire for popular forces that could have restrained the Resistance leadership from policies seen as dangerous to the 'Revolution'. (Abu Ahmad was killed in the 1982 massacre, on his way to the Israeli lines under a white flag, to tell them that there were no arms or fighters in the camp.)

Building a 'revolutionary environment'

> In 1977 the 'Revolution' established one of our most important institutions, the Building Committee. This Committee built al-Iqleem, the Fateh centre in Shateela, consisting of a head office, a library and a hall for exhibitions; and in front it built a kindergarten for 150 children.
>
> In Hayy Gharbeh there was an area of tin huts where people of mixed nationalities lived, a spot of moral corruption – hasheesh, cocaine, prostitution. So the Building Committee took the decision to bulldoze it and rebuild the houses in cement. The same year we laid two big sewage pipes from the bginning of Shateela to the end of Abu Hassan Salameh Street. In the Hursh we built a centre for the Scientific Committee for military and technical studies. Near the Sports City we built a public bakery, a school for political education, and a sports club, Nadi Beladna. It had judo, karate, boxing, two football teams – everything that could keep our youth away from drugs. Our brother Abu Hassan Salameh used to come there to train. (Abu Makarem)

The PLO/PRM was the creator of a public domain which did not exist before 1969 and which would be destroyed in 1982. Voluminous though it is, Abu Makarem's catalogue includes only a fraction of all Resistance building which, in a relatively short period, laid a grid of training grounds, workshops, cultural centres, health facilities, schools and clubs over an area that before 1969 had been nothing more than an agglomeration of low-income housing and 'waste' land. Although Resistance offices and military training schools formed a core to this public domain, Abu Makarem is right to underline its broader socio-cultural aspects and the drive to ameliorate physical conditions. Two major PRCS hospitals, Gaza and Akka, were sited within the Sabra/Shateela quadrilateral, while in nearby Bourj Barajneh and Fakhany were spread most of Samed's productive complex, which included factories, a film-making unit, a library and publishing offices.[9]

The underlying polemical context of the account is suggested by the comment that precedes it: 'I'm replying to those who say that the "Revolution" didn't do anything.' In the bitter mood that prevailed after 1982, people remembered many shortcomings. Shelters remained insufficient in spite of the likelihood of attack. The proliferation of committees and social 'projects' was not matched by the development of Resistance cadres trained in social as well as military work. Nevertheless, in spite of their competitiveness and the lack of a coherent plan of social action, the PRM was a catalyst for a habit of public action that outlived its buildings.

With the ending of Lebanese Army control, free building on 'waste' land around Shateela began in earnest. Settlers here included Palestinians displaced from other areas, such as the South and the 'Maronite enclave'; also other Arabs, non-Arabs and people denied Lebanese nationality, such as Kurds, Bedouin and gypsies. The largest component was composed of Lebanese Shi'ites, who were partly integrated into the Resistance movement as members, fighters and clients of services. Abu Makarem's remark about 'corruption' suggests a moral/social boundary between the camp and this large, heterogeneous population. Abu Muhammad gives a more positive view, saying that most were workers seeking cheap accommodation, and that some of the foreigners (especially Pakistanis and Bangladeshis) joined the PRM.

At the beginning of the 1970s, the population of the camp and close surroundings is said to have been 20,000. Towards the end of the 'Days of the Revolution' it had reached 47,000 (this was the last count made by the Popular Committee for the purpose of water distribution). Many of these were PRM fighters and cadres from outside.

The famous Sabra meat, vegetable and fruit market dates from the beginning of the Resistance period, as do the chains of small shops, some of them illegal, that fronted all the streets and alleys of the area. Sabra's bustling commerce displaced the older city centre for West Beirutis. Private schools and training institutions of every kind burgeoned to match the growing population. Two large new Sunni mosques were built, Dana beside the vegetable market and Imam 'Ali on Tareeq Jdeedeh.

The military and financial power of the PLO/PRM changed relations between Shateela and its neighbourhood, just as it changed relations between Palestinians and Lebanese generally. Conflicts which had occurred in earlier periods ended: whereas in the 1960s landowners had tried to remove squatters through lawsuits or evictions, now, as Abu Turki puts it, 'No one dared to approach us.' Physically and socially the boundaries between Shateela and its surroundings became blurred. Dense building pressed against the camp on all sides so that it seemed one mass; only UNRWA people and old inhabitants knew exactly where the boundaries were. Social boundaries were also blurred. The existence of the PLO/PRM as an overarching framework had the effect of encouraging all kinds of reciprocity. One sign of this was an increase in the number of marriages between Lebanese and Palestinians. Such marriages often crossed sectarian as well as national boundaries, and often took place through Resistance group contacts.

Only one serious clash is reported for the whole period, again with the Stetiyeh 'gang' which had attacked Shateela in the early 1950s. In its causes and its outcome, the second Stetiyeh battle, in March 1970, demonstrates the PLO/PRM's assumption of responsibility for order in its domain.

They were smugglers, they had money, and they wanted to buy Palestinian influence. I was camp Director at the time and I remember that they came to me and offered to build me a new office. They were trying to do business under the cover of the Revolution. Maybe they also had political motives, but their main purpose was selling drugs.

The Kifah Musellah surrounded them in their building, up near the Sports City. There was shooting. One of the Revolution's best officers, Sa'eed Ghawash, offered to go up and talk to them, to stop the bloodshed. They said, 'OK' but when he reached there they shot him. They were captured and taken to a [Palestinian] military court and executed. No one was sorry for them except Lebanese who were against Palestinians anyway. They knew how bad those people were.[10] (Jihad) Bisher)

Although the Palestinian Resistance had been supported by a large segment of the Lebanese people, and although Lebanese were integrated into the PRM in many ways, the power imbalance between the PLO/PRM and its Lebanese allies eventually created resentment and a growing nostalgia for the Lebanese state. On the Palestinian side the relationship was construed as one of revolutionary fusion, summarized in the slogan *sha'b wahid* (one people). But Lebanese increasingly perceived PRM authority as illegitimate, and resented Palestinians as privileged. Such resentment was strongest among ordinary citizens, outside the framework of the 'national/progressive' forces, and it increased as loss and destruction from Israeli attacks mounted and as, after the 1975/6 Civil War, hopes for reform of the Lebanese political system faded. The 'revolutionary environment' built by the PLO/PRM would come to be termed 'expansion' and even 'colonization' by some Lebanese.[11]

Changes in popular culture

In considering popular culture between 1969 and 1982, we need to discriminate between three overlapping frameworks: (i) Palestinian cultural revivalism, a mainly middle-class phenomenon linked historically to the PLO/PRM but not contained by it; (ii) popular culture in the camps, predominantly rural in origin though undergoing change; and (iii) the culture generated by the Resistance movement which combined its own militant symbols with revivalist and populist ones. Such a discrimination allows us to see disjunctures between the three frameworks in spite of their association within a broad national movement. We must not forget, either, that two basic cultural institutions continued quite outside these national frameworks: most camp children continued to be educated in UNRWA schools, whose syllabus changed little after 1969; and religion continued as an accepted element in popular culture, repressed in nationalist discourse.

The relationship between popular culture in the camps and both revivalism and Resistance culture is an interesting and complex one. On the one hand, in much Resistance-oriented writing and art, the people of the camps were presented as symbols of the misery of exile (as in the paintings of Isma'il Shammout), and of resistance and rootedness in the land (as in some of the stories of Ghassan Kanafani). Yet at the same time, the camps were perceived as areas of total deprivation, in need of social assistance and political organization. There was also a widespread Resistance view of camps as 'reservoirs of men for the Revolution'. Such perspectives suggest the class/culture gap between PRM cadres and the people of the camps. Even though the Resistance leadership adopted elements of peasant culture – the *keffiyyeh* and *agal*, the rural naming system – as mobilizing symbols and signs of 'authenticity', in its hierarchies, ethos and mentality the Resistance was nevertheless deeply urban, as much in its leftist wing as in Fateh.

Abu Makarem tells an anecdote about a leading member of a Marxist Resistance group who committed a social blunder by stepping into Abu Ahmad Sa'eed's *diwan* without taking off his shoes: the old man snapped angrily at him, 'Was your father Abu Durra?' Abu Durra was famous in pre-1948 Galilee as a tough fighter against the Mandate. In this reference, Abu Ahmad was scoring twice against the leftist cadre, first by implying that although the cadre might know all about Marxism, he did not know Palestinian history; second, since the cadre was *not* Abu Durra's son, he was only 'empty words', not like the *mujahideen*, the 'real' fighters of the past. The story indicates the barriers that the people of the camps could present to outsiders.[12]

In two other stories told about Abu Ahmad, he challenges leaders of leftist groups. Both are worth quoting because of their pungency. In one of them he addresses a leader of the PFLP: 'You say that all property is for the people, so why is your office in Shateela stealing our water and electricity?' In the second, Abu Ahmad visits a DFLP leader in his office:

> His office had air-conditioning and wall-to-wall carpeting. They talked about politics and the [Revolution's] lack of money. The leader began to curse the 'Right' – Fateh and Abu Ammar – because of their wealth. So Abu Ahmad asked him, 'And *you*, did your father leave you an oil well to furnish this room?'

Although the Resistance groups differed sharply on political issues, they shared the same fund of themes and symbols, those that were generated with the birth of the Resistance movement and those that continued to be worked on by the intellectuals and artists most closely associated with it. To capture this culture in all its diversity is difficult now, since so much of it was destroyed by the invasion of 1982, and no studies have yet been made. But a quick review suggests the centrality of four associated symbols: the flag, the gun, the fighter and the martyr. Another recurrent symbol in Resistance posters is the Palestinian woman in traditional dress carrying a Klashin. The Palestinian people – as peasants and workers, or as crowds carrying coffins – is also represented. Palestinian history as an unknown subject, to be rediscovered, was a central theme of countless consciousness-raising *nedwaat* (seminars).

Songs were undoubtedly one of the most important channels through which Resistance themes and symbols reached the camps. The habit of composing them to suit new political conjunctures, deeply rooted in popular culture, survived the destruction of 1982. Abu Makarem gives some examples of famous early Fateh songs in the context of emphasizing cultural aspects of the Resistance movement.

> Fateh invented a new artistic form, group songs, something we didn't have before. [Sings] 'I am the son of Fateh/Who never praised anyone else.' After 1965 all Palestinians began to sing these songs, and when they

sang, they carried the gun. There's another song that Abu Jamal Da'bis used to play on his *'oud* to the *ashbal* in Shateela: 'Oh gun, shout Revolution!' There was the song-writer Abdallah Haddad who used to compose political songs: [sings] 'The voice of the Security Council silences all others/But the dollar is stuck in its throat.'

We weren't just bullets and guns as people think.

Manifestations around the burial of martyrs and the care of their graves formed a focus of cultural activity where popular and Resistance culture overlapped closely. Political discourse – disseminated through a wide array of 'occasions', contacts and media – was another crucial channel of cultural influence, transmitting 'a new language, new thinking, a new identity', one that left its deepest imprint on the 'generation of the Revolution' (i.e. those who were children in the 1960s).

With the expansion of PRM programmes, the tempo of daily life in the camps changed, becoming charged with commemorations and celebrations: Resistance group birthdays, the calendar of national 'days', and international days such as 1 May and 8 March. All these were occasions for speeches by Resistance leaders, displays of handicrafts, performances of plays, songs and dances. Such events became part of, and helped people to absorb, the continual attacks and losses. 'We mourn and marry on the same day' was the way one young PRM cadre expressed this new popular culture of resistance.

Mahranajat (rallies) and *ihtafalat* (celebrations) might be held in camps or in larger spaces such as the Arab University. The following passage gives the flavour of one of these, held towards the end of the 'Days of the Revolution':

> Under the symbol of a crown of pink hollyhocks, the DFLP inaugurated a great popular festival in which one could already see the immense popular joy that would greet a Palestinian state already almost visible. Throughout the day, a vast crowd moved among the displays of Lebanese and Palestinian handicrafts, of books, cassettes, posters, toys, and between performances of songs, dances, marionette shows, films and theatre. Over everything was a memorial where a flame burned and two fighters stood motionless in front of a large panel covered with photos of martyrs. In a small room nearby, where bitter coffee was served, there was an assemblage of simple objects that recalled the usurped land – birth certificates, pre-1948 identity cards, coins, pieces of jewellery, old dresses.[13]

Some of the criticism of the Resistance movement after 1982 focused on the effect it had on schools, and on educational standards. There were people who said, 'They ruined our youth', blaming the PRM for a constellation of problems such as loss of zeal on the part of teachers, and students dropping out to 'join the Revolution'. At the beginning, people say, the Resistance groups used to send volunteers who were too young back to school. But later, with competition, they began to accept boys as young as twelve or thirteen. 'What could they become,' asked one Shateela man bitterly, 'except the bodyguards of the *abawat*?'[14]

On the other hand, the PLO and PRM did much to fill gaps that could not be covered by UNRWA schooling, providing scholarships for secondary school and university, training courses and adult literacy classes. Additionally it supplemented UNRWA's school programme with clubs for sports, recreation and cultural activities. Perhaps it was inevitable that there should be a clash between the two 'revolutions' and two sets of values, that of armed struggle on the one hand, and the older 'educational revolution' on the other.

Families and the Resistance movement

By 1969, slight changes had already taken place in Palestinian kinship and families as a result of many different factors arising from exile – the scattering of family units, schooling, occupational change, secondary migration and socioeconomic differentiation. Among these changes was a weakening of the *hamula* (clan, patrilineage), a process that had begun before 1948. At the household level, there was a shift from the compound, patriarchal form (composed of a couple, their unmarried children and married sons, with pooling of income and expenditure), towards a looser form, with parents and married sons living close together but independently. Father/son and mother/daughter-in-law relations altered in consequence, becoming less authoritarian. Although clan elders were still respected, they interfered less in the affairs of individual households.

Yet Palestinian family ties, whether between kin or household members, lost none of their importance in exile; on the contrary, they acquired new meanings: as protection against alienation, as a source of emotional or financial support, as a social value rooted in religion and national identity. Especially in the camps, people were reluctant to allow or admit to change in the family sphere. Thus change was slow as well as being masked by the ideology of non-change. Furthermore, family values were broadly the same between home, school and Lebanese society.

In one sense the separation of the Resistance movement and families implied in the above heading is distorting. The PRM developed within Palestinian Arab society. Families in the camps were similarly part of the national movement, with memories of village battles and heroes of their own. Yet, as a power structure, the PRM was largely external to the camps and to

Lebanon. In addition, although it came without any explicit aim to change social or family relations, its programme of mass mobilization was bound to have implications for the family sphere. This was not apparent at the beginning because of people's longing for action that would end exile and restore Palestine. Identification with the Resistance movement was so strong that tough dilemmas – such as that between love for sons and love of country – did not at first show up in all their harshness. Over time, however, as the *tanzeemat* (organizations) interacted with the field of family relations, many kinds of change were set in motion. That such changes have not been 'radical' is partly due to conservative counter-currents as well as political setbacks. Perhaps the most important change is that values related to the family have been raised out of the realm of the accepted and unspoken into the arena of open debate.

After 1969, with open recruitment, it often happened that most of the men in a household or family 'cluster' would join a Resistance group or the Popular Militia organized by the PLA. Ahmad Haleemeh remembers a relative taking him, his father and two uncles along to one of the PRM offices (he was a boy at a secondary school at the time). The traditional association of males with fighting meant that sometimes three generations in the same family would join up, with old men asking to be given guard duty and boys going into the *ashbal* (lion cubs; see Political Glossary). Although women in the early days did militia training with the PLA, they did not join Resistance groups, except perhaps secretly. Searching for women members to interview in the large (16,000) camp of Bourj Barajneh in 1974, I found only two.

In some cases there was conflict between sons and fathers on the issue of joining a Resistance group or going outside for military training. Young men in Bourj often gave it as a sign of the nationalist enthusiasm of their generation that their parents had been unable to prevent them joining. One recalled:

> A teacher came [to Syria] to collect students who had left home without their parents' permission, and because there was going to be a feast. But we refused to go with him. We valued the feast, but we stayed in the [training] camp. We forgot our families for the sake of our country.[15]

Such conflicts never seem to have resulted in permanent rupture. Ahmad Haleemeh recalls the case of a man in Shateela who was so angry with a son who left school to join a training session without his permission that he ordered him out of the house. But after a few months the rift was mended, and the boy returned home.[16]

Members of the same household usually joined or supported the same Resistance group, but this was not always the case. Father/son and brother/brother solidarity is a basic principle of the Arab family system, especially strong in rural areas, but it is one that generates tension. Competition between Resistance groups was linked to family rivalries, particularly those between brothers and cousins. The primacy of the eldest brother, particularly marked in the Palestinian peasant inheritance system,[17] played a role in pushing younger brothers into other groups, especially if the eldest had leader status. In many cases, the reason for members of the same family joining different groups was political/ideological disagreement. It was more usual, however, for whole families to be 'counted to' specific groups, a tendency that was encouraged by group activities for women and children. The welfare projects set up by the major groups – kindergartens, crèches, youth clubs, clinics, workshops, allowances for martyrs' and prisoners' families – tended to give priority to the families of members, thus reinforcing families as social units.

Daughters' struggles to join Resistance groups were infinitely harder than those of sons,[18] and much more productive of sociocultural change. This episode from a young Shateela woman's life story is revealing:

I left school after the end of Intermediate, because my family needed me to work at home. Afterwards I regretted giving up my education without a struggle – I felt I had capacities, that I could have become a doctor. My father is very pious, he didn't allow us to have political activities, he didn't even allow us to visit friends. My closest friend was my older sister; when she married and left Lebanon, I felt abandoned. I felt that if I didn't escape from home restrictions I would sink forever.

There was a training session at the Women's Union for adult literacy teachers. I confronted my father, I told him I'd kill myself if he didn't let me join. He relented. But he never allowed me to become a member of a group. ('Samia')

Another account of parent/daughter struggle, this time from a cadre, shows similarities and differences:

When I first entered the Jebha [Front], I was a child of ten years. I joined their guides and then their youth organization. Later, as a student, I joined their Women's Bureau.[19] My father was a comrade in the Front, this is what helped me. But in Palestine he had been a *sheikh*, and he was very fanatical. He kept on at me to wear a headscarf, I was forbidden to cut my hair, I was forbidden to wear jeans.

My mother was against me working with young men – she wanted me to marry so that she could relax.

I was still in school, but I confronted this problem with my parents. I told them, 'I don't want to marry, I want to do national work. But if anyone ever tells you that I'm not behaving correctly, then you have the right to do what you want.' ('Amal')

We notice that, while 'Amal' wins her struggle, it is only by incorporating her parents' rules into her own behaviour. As *banat* (young unmarried women) in the camps were drawn into the PRM, a great deal of scrutiny was focused on them by their families, the community and Resistance group men. Women cadres had to exercise extreme self-control – over their clothing, facial expressions, gestures and exchanges with male comrades. The Resistance groups acted pragmatically, for example putting pressure on men to let their wives or daughters join the movement, but they did not conduct campaigns aimed at change in gender values. Pre-marital virginity, marriage and childbearing remained ideologically compelling for women.

Nevertheless, one important kind of change was that people – including women themselves – became accustomed to women taking a more prominent political, economic and social role. This observation made before 1982 holds true today:

> Women working with the Resistance often saw themselves as politicizers of their families. Arriving home from work, they initiated lively discussion, bringing news and analyses of the latest political and military events, as well as information about new services and projects in the camp, thus linking the family with the larger world outside the home and their neighbourhood.[20]

Conjugal relations also changed, not so much because of PRM mobilization as women's rising levels of education and entry into professional salaried employment. With jobs and several kinds of training offered by the PLO and PRM, women increasingly worked outside the home and contributed to household income. But it was not their earnings so much as holding positions of responsibility that changed their family status. When asked about change between 1948 and 1988, one old woman laughed and said, 'Now women speak in front of men.'

Relations between couples were also modified by the decline in parentally arranged marriages and the increasing independence of individual households.[21] When marriages took place between Resistance group comrades, other changes were likely to result, such as the continuation of the wife's political activities and her stronger voice in family decisions. However, most observers agree that there was little change in the division of domestic labour, whatever women did outside the home.

A separate economy

From the late 1960s the Lebanese economy began to close towards Palestinians. Many factors contributed to this gradual process, among them the end of the Lebanese economic 'boom', reactions towards the Palestinians' increasingly high political profile, and the growth of Lebanese sectarian consciousness that affected specific localities and institutions. For example, the Maqassad, a large Sunni medical/educational complex which had encouraged Palestinians as students and given them jobs in the 1950s and 1960s, stopped doing so around 1970. Even middle-class Palestinians, accepted before, began to encounter obstacles.

This trend towards closure increased sharply with the expulsion of thousands of Palestinian workers from East Beirut in 1976. Some of these migrated to Germany, while others moved to areas controlled by the Joint Forces (see Political Glossary), mainly West Beirut, Sidon and Damour (many settled in and around Shateela). Lagging levels of industrialization in these regions made it hard for workers displaced from the 'Maronite enclave' to find jobs similar to those they had left. The escalation of Israeli and Haddad's bombardments of the South after 1976 created economic hardship in this area also.[22]

Attacks and insecurity restricted Palestinian workers' mobility and increasingly confined them to camps. During bouts of conflict, people often went to stay with relatives in safer areas. For example, during the Civil War, Abu and Umm Isma'een took their children to 'Ain Helweh; Umm Isma'een did temporary harvesting work in Sidon plantations to help out.

The PLO and PRM responded to this economic crisis with a rapid expansion of its service and productive institutions, creating jobs and helping families hit by war destruction or loss of earnings to survive. By the end of the 1980s it was estimated that around 65 per cent of the Palestinian workforce was employed by national institutions.[23] Samed increased its factories and workshops, setting them up near camps and in the war zone, adding new productive 'lines'. Social development projects in the camps – kindergartens, clinics, training schemes – also helped to create employment. One of the social consequences of this national drive was that, instead of emigrating to the oil-producing countries, more highly educated Palestinian workers now stayed in Lebanon to work with the 'Revolution' in *sha'bi* (popular, low-income) areas, as teachers, doctors, nurses and social workers. Even though the majority of the camp workforce continued to be manual workers, a significant minority became administrators of projects located in camps.

Although wages in the PLO/PRM economy were lower than in the Lebanese economy, this was partially compensated for by the national welfare system, which included compensation for war damage and pensions as well as free medical and other services. Perhaps the main weakness of the 'Palestinian economy' was the uneven distribution of employment and projects between urban and rural camps. As part of the *mantaqa ra'isiyyeh* (chief place, centre) where most PRM head offices were located, Shateela was relatively privileged in terms of PLO/PRM employment.

Individual Palestinian responses to economic crisis were varied, and demonstrated their versatility and resourcefulness. No longer able to reach the weaving factory across the 'Green Line' in Hadeth, Abu Isma'een bought a knitting machine and set up a family-based knitwear production unit. The practice of double employment was used to augment low salaries: a man might occupy a low-level salaried job, say as a guard or store clerk, and after hours do 'free work' as an electrician, house-painter or television repairman. More shops were opened, especially on the main outer streets where the number of passers-by made new kinds of merchandise profitable: travel bags, photographic equipment, cassettes, fast food. Shateela exhibited more such commercial expansion than other camps because of its closeness to Sabra market which, by the 1970s, had replaced the older, downtown markets.

Another widespread response was to invest in children's education with the hope of promoting them into the ranks of qualified professionals. PRM subsidies of secondary and university education assisted this drive, which propelled an increasingly large number of students from camps to study abroad, mainly in the USSR and Eastern Europe. Some families even managed to send their sons to study in the United States. Although it was the provision of scholarships by the PRM and friendly governments that made this trend possible, families also contributed, for example by providing living expenses and forgoing their children's earnings.

More women took jobs outside the home between 1976 and 1982. One reason for this was the rise in the number of women heads of households, widows left by war with the responsibility of bringing up their children. To them went priority in all Palestinian institutions. Another reason was the expansion in PLO/PRM social institutions which created a demand for women employees and workers. Professional training courses offered a channel to the kind of work, such as kindergarten teaching, of which families approved. The Red Crescent Society trained nurses, a profession that national struggle had made respectable. Economic pressures may also have played a role. With inflation there was a need for extra income, especially in households with many young children.

Both social background and ideology intervened in opening or blocking the way for women to work outside the home. We see the interaction of these factors in the case of Abu Muhammad Farmawi, who was from a village but who belonged to a progressive Resistance group:

When Umm Muhammad asked to work on the basis that we needed money, frankly I refused. I agreed only when she became convinced that women have to have a productive role in society. Women must work, not just in the house – children and cooking – no! And not just for money. But because they form half of society and must have an active and productive role.

Two kinds of pressure, economic and social, acted upon camp households to increase their earnings. On the one hand, there was the rising cost of living, and on the other, rising needs and expectations, higher standards of clothing, home furnishing and equipment. People of the camps wanted to live like other people, like Lebanese. Such rising living standards were more evident in urban than in rural camps, where homes remained simpler in style and people still wore 'old-fashioned' clothing. But in Shateela in the last years before the invasion, most homes had televisions, refrigerators and washing machines, and a few families had a car. Such prosperity was relative – Shateela was still in many ways a 'slum', with crowded housing and poor environmental conditions. But it was a bustling, cheerful slum where people looked optimistically to the future.

Farewell to the *feda'yeen*

Presenting a thoughtful and self-critical summing up of the period of Resistance movement autonomy in Lebanon, Abu Muhammad Farmawi notes that, in spite of the Palestinians' long history of struggle, the PRM was not prepared for the opportunity given it by the defeat in 1967 of the Arab armies. The years in Lebanon were valuable because they gave the Resistance a time and a space in which to mature and to develop a mode of internal coexistence:

The Palestinian people never had the freedom to carry arms and direct their own cause until the defeat of the Arab armies in 1967. This meant that the Revolution was not properly prepared, and this led to conflicts. In the beginning in Lebanon there were violent quarrels and confrontations; conflict took a military shape. But I consider the period in Lebanon a 'revolution within a revolution'. By 1982 almost all the Palestinian groups were in the PLO, and relations between them were better. We reached a way of dealing with political, theoretical and organizational differences without violence, through democratic dialogue. This was the best stage that the Palestinian Revolution has reached.

After Likud and Begin came to power in June 1977, Israeli/Haddad bombardments of the South intensified. Hardly a day passed without an attack from the air, sea or land; Haddad's long-range artillery could reach the outskirts of Sidon. Yet their exposure to continual attack did nothing to dent the morale of people in the camps. On a visit to Rashidiyyeh in the spring of 1981, with other journalists I watched children in a Women's Union kindergarten carry out an air-raid drill (Israeli planes had been sighted that morning), and I was impressed by the coolness of the young women teachers. We asked two young girls of about eight, walking arm in arm, what they wanted to be when they grew up: one said a doctor, the other a teacher. Nearby in Tyre was a Red Crescent hospital where we spent several nights; it was well staffed and equipped, and had its own small nursing school. Between Tyre and Nabatiyyeh a Samed factory full of mainly women workers was producing jeans to send to Yemen. It was the same scene in Bourj Shemali, 'Ain Helweh and Damour: a people – men and women, old people and children – working, producing, learning new skills, believing in the future. The PLO Unified Information man who accompanied us said that Resistance/PLO cadres liked going to the South to renew their revolutionary roots.

In that part of West Beirut where the PLO/PRM had its headquarters – Fakhany, Sabra, Shateela – everything continued in the last year before the invasion much as it had done before. Work went on in spite of air raids such as the one in July 1981 which destroyed a whole building in Fakhany, killing 200 people; or the car-bomb in October of the same year which took out the front of the building that housed the Palestine Planning Centre. Everyone expected an Israeli–Lebanese Forces 'pincer movement', and military retraining sessions were held for the whole PLO early in 1982. In spite of a good deal of grumbling, everyone recognized that this was a useful shake-up for cadres who, in the twelve years since 'Black September' (see Political Glossary), had got too used to office routines and Beirut *dolce vita*.

Looking back, I am surprised by the number of activities and new developments in this final period of Resistance movement autonomy. Among the people I was meeting at that time as I prepared a research project with Palestinian women, there was no fear or foreboding about the future. Even if there was occasional talk of corruption at higher levels, where *abawat* built personal followings to swell their budgets and importance, this was only the seamy side of a popular movement that had not lost its revolutionary credentials for the mass of Palestinians. Wherever one looked there were concrete expressions of optimism and confidence. A Fateh woman cadre interviewed in February 1982 spoke of the Revolution having reached an 'advanced defensive stage' that allowed, even necessitated, the formation of women's demands. Among other promising events, I remember that Samed started its own journal *Iqtisad* (Economy), as well as a library on Palestinian crafts; the PFLP opened a model *hadaneh* (crèche) near Shateela, where working mothers could leave small children all day; the Women's Union held a three-day training seminar for young cadres from the camps and, to mark International Women's Day, its leaders met to discuss ways to improve 'outreach'. Another initiative from that final period were 'Street Committees' in which housewives in *sha'bi* areas organized to demand basic services.

By the spring of 1981, Lebanon's potential for triggering broader conflagrations began to attract a more serious level of concern in Washington. Erupting in April, the Syrian 'missile crisis' (when Damascus moved SAM-6 air defence missiles into the Beqa' to deter Israeli overflights) prompted the Reagan Administration to send Special Envoy Habib for on-the-spot mediation efforts.[24] In July, after an intense bout of Israeli–Palestinian fighting, Habib was again involved in mediating an Israeli–PLO cease-fire. This was a political gain for PLO chairman Arafat since it constituted Washington's 'most explicit recognition to date of the necessity of involving the PLO in issues of Middle Eastern war and peace'.[25] Although Arafat demonstrated his control of the PRM by forcing antagonistic groups to observe the cease-fire, this was at the price of considerable internal dissension. King Fahd's peace proposals of 7 August further deepened divisions within Fateh's leadership, as well as in the PRM generally.

The other serious problem facing the PLO/PRM at this time was the growing alienation of its Lebanese base. The slogan *sha'b wahid* (one people) was wearing thin. Hostility from the Maronite right and parts of the Lebanese state was familiar and expected; what was new was the hostility of a large part of the Shi'ite community which had earlier supported the *feda'yeen* against the army in the South. For reasons that will be discussed later (Chapter 7), Shi'ites were becoming increasingly anti-Palestinian from 1978/9. By 1981, Harakat Amal, the leading Shi'ite political/military movement, was able to close off parts of the South to the Joint Forces and to extend its control to parts of Beirut's southern suburbs. Overshadowed by the PLO/PRM's greater military and financial weight, the LNM was losing its vigour and coherence. Ordinary Lebanese citizens living in the 'nationalist/progressive' area, terrorized by air raids and car-bombs, were increasingly angered by militia rackets and fire-fights. The PLO/PRM appeared unable to solve these problems, or unwilling to devote sufficient attention to them.[26]

In the months before the invasion there was an escalation in serious incidents: during Amal–PRM clashes in the South, the Joint Forces shelled Shi'ite villages. In January 1982, there were several days of fighting in West Beirut between Amal and the LNM after the latter proposed setting up local committees to fill the absence of state services. And in Sidon in April there were inter-militia clashes that destroyed part of the old souk.

The Israeli invasion began on 3 June with air raids on the Sports City and other known PRM locales. An UNRWA bus coming down from Sibleen was rocketed, and several students killed and wounded. Some of their bodies were brought for burial in Nahr al-Bared. I had just begun research there. The next day I travelled back to Aley via the Beqa' with a Red Crescent ambulance, whose driver ignored my suggestion that we should cover the posters of Arafat with which the ambulance was plastered: 'If they're going to hit us, they'll hit us,' he said.

By 14 June, the Israeli Army was within a few kilometres of Shateela and even closer to Bourj Barajneh, having met up with the Lebanese Forces at Ba'bda in the long-awaited 'pincer movement'. There followed the three months' siege of West Beirut, with almost continuous bombardments from air, land and sea. There were strikes all around Shateela – Fateh's military college, the Sports City, the old people's home, Gaza Hospital, the In'ash Centre – but, though damaged, the camp itself was not badly hit. Some residents even stayed on there, preferring the danger of bombardment to crowdedness and water shortage in the refugee centres. PRM cadres shook off the paralysis caused by the rapid Israeli advance and began organizing defences, water and other supplies. Emergency hospitals were equipped and staffed with amazing rapidity here and there throughout the western half of the city. People quickly became accustomed to the siege situation. It was as if the Israelis had always been there, only for the purpose of providing daily dramas to recount to friends.

It was at the height of the siege that Umm Mustafa, worried at not having heard any news of her mother in 'Ain Helweh camp, bundled all her nine children into a neighbour's taxi and drove through Israeli lines to Sidon. 'There's nothing dearer than the family,' was her simple explanation. 'Either we'd all get killed or we'd all get through.'

In mid-August the Palestinian leadership announced its decision to leave Beirut in exchange for American and Lebanese written guarantees of protection for Palestinian civilians.[27] This was included in the Habib Accords:

> Law-abiding Palestinian noncombatants left behind in Beirut, including the families of those who have departed, will be subject to Lebanese laws and regulations. The Governments of Lebanon and the United States will provide the appropriate guarantees of safety . . .[28]

On 1 September the last contingent of PRM fighters left from the port, amid extraordinary scenes of farewell caught by some of the media people who were there.[29] A small incident described by an onlooker epitomizes the relationship between the *feda'yeen* and the people of the camps who had so joyously welcomed them in 1969, and who were now being left behind:

A woman in her late thirties, wearing old torn clothes, tugging two young children behind her, broke from the crowd and ran across the street waving a placard at the departing convoy. Written in an illiterate hand in poor Arabic it read, quite simply, 'I will take your place'.[30]

Notes

1. People of the camps commonly refer to the Resistance movement as *al-Thawra* (the Revolution), *al-Muqawwimeh* (the Resistance) and *al-Awda* (the Return).

2. For a discussion of PRM attempts to set up a legal system in Lebanon, see J. Peteet, 'Socio-Political Integration and Conflict Resolution in Palestinian Camps in Lebanon', *Journal of Palestine Studies*, vol. 16, no. 2, Winter 1987.

3. The Cairo Accords legitimated Palestinian armed struggle from Lebanon and gave Palestinians rights to employment and autonomy. (For the text, see Khalidi, *Conflict and Violence*, Appendix 1, p. 185.)

4. Palestinians call those killed in the course of national struggle 'martyrs': *shaheed* (sing.), *shuhada'* (pl.). The word has religious connotations – in Islam a *shaheed* is one who sacrifices his life for the faith or the community – and is etymologically linked to the root *shahida*, to witness.

5. 'Ain al-Romaneh in the 'Maronite enclave' is only a few kilometres away from Shateela, across the 'Green Line' dividing East from West Beirut.

6. The reference is to a sea-borne commando attack in March 1978 which triggered the Israeli 'Litani Operation' (an invasion of South Lebanon) in the same month.

7. A young man from Shateela reminisces about one of these old men: 'Abu Ahmad Sa'eed, that human encyclopedia of the historic events that had taken place in Palestine . . . The man who always told the younger generation . . . about the heroism of the Palestinian fighters Izzideen al-Quassam and Abdul Qader Husseini . . .' Z. al-Shaikh, 'Sabra and Shatila 1982: Resisting the Massacres', *Journal of Palestine Studies*, vol. 14, no. 1, Fall 1984.

8. *Willa* and *willek* are terms of address that indicate anger and the authority of the speaker; usually used by fathers to sons (rural in origin, still used in camps).

9. Samed's main productive complex was near Bourj Barajneh camp, and produced garments, furniture, ironwork, leather goods and handicrafts. Workshops were set up later in Baddawi camp, the South and other parts of West Beirut.

10. K. Salibi, *Crossroads* mentions this incident (p. 545).

11. The term 'colonization' is used in a retrospective article on the camps that appeared in *L'Orient/Le Jour* on 18 April 1991, by Agence France Presse correspondent Najib Khazzakha.

12. This anecdote of Abu Ahmad Sa'eed scoring against a Marxist-group Resistance cadre has an ideological colouring. It was told to me by a local Fateh leader with strong Islamic leanings a year after the collapse of the Soviet Union.

13. Adèle Manzi, a founder of Najdeh Association, which runs a complex of workshops, training courses and kindergartens in the camps (translated from French).

14. *Abawat*, plural of *abu*, is a colloquial term for the PRM leadership with critical undertones.

15. A quotation that appears in R. Sayigh, *Palestinians: From Peasants to Revolutionaries* (London: Zed Press, 1979), p. 179.

16. Another case of father/son conflict: a Shateela boy aged about fifteen went to the Hursh with friends. One of them had a gun and 'Imad' accidentally shot himself in the leg. His father was so angry that he refused to visit him in hospital. Eventually one of the boy's uncles persuaded his father to forgive him. Such intervention is a traditional mechanism for preventing family rupture.

17. On primogeniture in Palestinian rural society, see N. Abdo-Zubi, *Family, Women and Social Change in the Middle East: The Palestinian Case* (Toronto: Canadian Scholars' Press, 1987).

18. Confrontation with the father has been described by Palestinian women militants as the hardest step a woman can take.

19. At least four of the Resistance groups had women's bureaus through which projects and campaigns for camp women were organized. Women cadres tended to be concentrated in such work.

20. From R. Sayigh and J. Peteet, 'Between Two Fires: Palestinian Women in Lebanon', in R. Ridd and H. Callaway (eds), *Caught Up in Conflict* (Basingstoke: Macmillan Education, 1986), p. 118.

21. Families continue to play an essential and elaborate role in making marriages. What has changed is the imposition on men and women of spouses chosen by their fathers. Increasingly the choice is made by the man, and women can usually refuse husbands proposed to them by their families.

22. A survey carried out in 1988 found a total of 4,468 homeless Palestinian families, of which 75 per cent had been displaced more than twice, and 19.7 per cent more than three times. The figure is said to be higher now.

23. This figure was given to me by the late N. Badran, a Palestinian researcher who took part in the TEAM study of Palestinian institutions and communities carried out at the end of the 1970s, and published in Beirut in 1983.

24. On the 'missile crisis', see Cobban, *Palestine Liberation Organization* p. 109.

25. *Ibid.*, p. 112.

26. See R. Brynen, *Sanctuary and Survival*, ch. 7, for an analysis of problems and failures of the PLO/PRM in this period.

27. See R. Khalidi, *Under Siege: PLO Decision-making in the 1982 War* (New York: Columbia University Press, 1986).

28. Quoted by Cobban, *Palestine Liberation Organization*, p. 124.

29. See for example L. Saraste's magnificent *For Palestine* (London: Zed Books, 1985).

30. From S. Banna, 'The Defence of Beirut', *Race and Class*, vol. XXIV, no. 4, Spring 1983.

5. The Massacre

According to the cease-fire negotiated by Special Envoy Habib in early August, the IDF lines were only a couple of kilometres from the south-eastern tip of the Sabra/Shateela quadrilateral. On 3 September, after the evacuation of the last PLO contingent of fighters, IDF units moved forward, establishing positions in the Henri Shehab Barracks, Jnah, the Officers' Club and the Kuwaiti Embassy, from where they were able to snipe at the camp. During this period, the Lebanese Army dismantled fortifications in the area. There was thus little distance for the Israelis to move when, early on 15 September, the invasion of West Beirut began. By midday they had encircled the area. From the Lebanese Army Officers' Club where they established their headquarters, the whole of Shateela and its surroundings were visible (see Map 2).

The next day, according to the Israeli journalist Kapeliouk who questioned Israeli soldiers as well as Palestinians and Lebanese when researching his book about the massacre:

> At 3 pm, the commander of the Israeli forces in Beirut, General Amos Yaron, along with two of his officers, met the Lebanese Forces' intelligence chief, Elias Hobeika and Fadi Ephram. With the help of aerial photographs provided by Israel, together they made arrangements for entering the camps.[1]

The targeted area was crammed with people recently returned from the places where they had taken refuge during the war, now supposedly over. Schools would soon open, everyone needed to repair their homes, clear the streets and get ready for the winter. There was fear of what the regime of Bashir Gemayel would bring, but there was also determination to rebuild. People felt some security from the fact that they were unarmed, and that all who remained were legal residents. Many of the massacre victims were found clutching their identity cards, as if trying to prove their legitimacy.

One contingent of the Special Units commanded by Hobeiqa entered the area through the sand-hills overlooking Hayy Orsan, just opposite the IDF headquarters. At this stage they were almost certainly accompanied by Israeli soldiers, since the dunes had been fortified by the Resistance. Another contingent entered through the southeastern edge of the Hursh, between Akka Hospital and Abu Hassan Salameh Street. Apart from co-planning the operation and introducing the Special Forces into the area, the IDF provided several kinds of back-up: they controlled the perimeters and prevented escape through light shelling and sniping, as well as by blocking the main exits; they also used flares to light up the narrow alleys at night.

From the sand dunes near the IDF headquarters, dirt roads led down into Hayy Orsan and Hayy Gharbeh. Umm Fady's home lay close to one of these roads:

> On Thursday afternoon we were sitting in this room when the shelling started. That's when the water-tank on the roof was hit. . . . With every explosion, dust was coming down on us.
>
> I said to Abu Fady, 'For God's sake get us out of here.' He said, 'If I could have got you out, wouldn't I have done it?' At first he couldn't get the car out because our neighbour's car had been hit, and rubble was blocking the road. But finally, somehow, he got it down the alley. He got us out, and all the while he was making the children laugh, to take their minds off the shelling. When we left, none of these houses was destroyed, that happened later. They hadn't started the killing.
>
> Once we reached my aunt's home in Sabra, I said to him 'For God's sake, Abu Fady, don't go back. Stay with us.' But he said, 'No, I must go back to get the children's clothes and their milk.' So I sat and waited for him, and I waited and I waited.[2]

In the rest of her story, Umm Fady tells how she returned alone twice to the massacre site to look for her husband: 'At first I felt lost. I couldn't recognize anything. The whole quarter had changed, what with the bulldozing and the bodies.' A foreign journalist asks her, 'Where are the dead children?' and she shouts at him angrily, 'Leave me alone! I'm looking for my husband.' Eventually she finds his body half-buried under rubble.

I recorded Umm Fady's story in the spring of 1983, after I came across her in Hayy Orsan rebuilding her home with the help of a single worker. With her were her three small children in a pram. The youngest was born a few weeks before the massacre.

The family of Umm 'Issam was luckier, although their home was in the Hursh, close to the path of the Special Units:

> We only escaped by a miracle. The Israelis were shelling and my mother

was scared that the roof of the club where we had taken shelter would collapse and we would suffocate. So we took the children and went to friends in the centre of the camp. After a while we saw people running: 'What's happening?' They said, 'Israel is slaughtering people in Gharbeh.' I went to see what was happening. On the way I met a woman crying 'Help me!' I put my hand to her stomach and found that she was bleeding. We found a car and put her in it and they took her to Gaza Hospital. As for us, we escaped to Bourj Barajneh.

Among the several accounts of the massacre that have been published, there is one by a young man who was in Shateela at the time. It conveys the confusion and horror of those two nights and three days, as well as his own conflicting feelings as he and a few other *shebab* joined in a heroic but futile attempt at resistance.[3] This insider account makes clear the camp's defencelessness – the *shebab* manage to find only two or three Klashins and one RPG; but their more basic problem is that they have no clear picture of what is going on, neither from where the attack is coming nor the lines of its approach. In such a difficult situation, there is tension between the *shebab* over what to do, whether to hit back blindly with whatever ammunition they have or to try to evacuate people up to Sabra, where some narrow alleys remain open.[4] There is a brief confrontation and one of the Palestinians is killed. Helping the wounded, listening to people's stories, searching for news of friends, the narrator almost forgets that his own family is still in the camp. Outside is scarcely more secure: Haddad's militia are said to be searching homes in nearby Shiah and Basta. Hooded informers have already made their appearance as the IDF round up and interrogate men in the Sports City.

One of the stories given in al-Shaikh's account is of the tragic 'peace attempt' of the camp's old men, the *shuyyukh*. Before anyone is aware that a massacre is beginning, they meet to discuss the situation in the house of Abu Ahmad Sa'eed. It is proposed to send out a delegation representing the major villages under a white flag, to tell the Israeli commanders that there are no arms or fighters in the camp. People say that there was heated discussion at the meeting, and that Abu Kamal Sa'd refused to go, saying, 'We were accused of selling Palestine, do we want now to be accused of surrendering Shateela?' Others at the meeting argued that if nothing was done, the Israelis would intensify their shelling and destroy the camp. In the end, a small group set out headed by Abu Ahmad Sa'eed. They were killed before ever reaching the Israeli lines. Near their bodies on the street leading up to Sabra, at a junction with an alley, people later found empty beer cans and hypodermic syringes.

Photographs of the massacre were so shocking that they shook the world and helped set in motion moves of protection, investigation and monitoring which set constraints upon anti-Palestinianism in the months to come. Yet the photographs also dehumanized the victims, locking them in a timeless moment of disfiguration. Stories people told about the massacre, though slower in their impact, tell much more of the human and social qualities of the victims, and of the survivors who tell the stories.

Abu Hussein Harb's shop for children's bicycles was on the southern end of Abu Hassan Salameh Street, opposite Hayy Orsan. Umm Hussein tells how her husband became concerned about a missing nephew when the Israelis started shelling the edges of the camp; he and their sixteen-year-old son Hussein went out to look for him and never returned. Like many other Palestinians living in the quarters surrounding Shateela camp, the Harbs were refugees from East Beirut.

Fifty metres up the street from the Harbs was the home of Umm Ahmad. Her husband and five youngest children were shot dead by the Special Units; she and three older children were wounded but managed to run away. Suad, paralysed by a bullet in the back, lay under the bodies of her younger brothers and sisters for two days until she was rescued and taken to Gaza Hospital. People say that for weeks Suad lay screaming with pain. Gradually, with the encouragement of a Scandinavian therapist and through her own courage, she worked herself back into mobility.

Still further north, in Shateela camp proper, Ahmad Haleemeh's parents and aunts were still divided between their home and the Iqleem shelter. It was not until Friday night that the Special Units began to penetrate the alleys leading off Abu Hassan Salameh Street into the camp. The men of the family decided that they should delay escape no longer, after hearing the death groans of one of their neighbours. But Umm Ahmad and her sister refused to leave Iqleem until they knew their sons were safe and willing to go to Sabra.

After the Haleemehs reached a relative's home in Sabra, Abu Ahmad remembered that he had forgotten the family's identity cards. Returning early on Saturday morning to fetch them, he was arrested by Israeli soldiers, now in full control of Sabra, and taken to the Sports City for interrogation.

Another description comes from a young woman who had returned to Shateela with her mother and younger brother and sister shortly before the assassination of Bashir Gemayel:

I was still in bed, it was early morning, and I was listening to the news. Or maybe it was women talking in the street. When I heard that Bashir had been assassinated I got up in a rush. There was a lot of noise, Israeli airplanes were flying overhead. Everyone expected that Israel or the Army would do something. My father came and asked us if we wanted to leave the camp. We told him no, if they do anything it will be to arrest *shebab*. He should leave with my brother and we will stay and look after the house.

I went out to get water, and saw some young men carrying guns to defend the camp. Later at night, around 9 pm, a man passed carrying his daughter; she was covered in blood. Talk began that Sa'd Haddad's men were carrying out a massacre, but we didn't believe it. Then a woman passed by bleeding; she said that there had been a massacre. There was a lot of talk and confusion. My mother said, 'Let's go!' but I didn't want to leave the house. What protected us was the explosion of an arms depot in Hayy Farhat.[5] Our men exploded it so as not to leave it [for the enemy]; this meant that they couldn't approach our side of the camp. We stayed two days, and then my father came and said, '*Khelas*, you've got to leave.' So we went out through the alleys to Hamed Street. We didn't go through Sabra because the Israelis were already around Gaza Hospital.

These and other stories illustrate qualities shown by the people against whom the massacre was aimed – courage, humanity: qualities conspicuously absent in the Israelis and Lebanese who planned and carried out the massacre. It is striking, too, how people carried out routine activities – going back to look for children's milk or family identity cards – as if certain that law and order existed, that some things could not happen.

From whichever route you chose into the Sabra/Shateela area following the massacre, you were immediately struck by the concentration of destruction. It was as if the place and its people had been the object of an attempt at total destruction. After the air, land and sea bombardments of the summer had come the Lebanese Special Units, programmed to slaughter and loot; and with them had come bulldozers which had cut broad swathes through housing, toppling breezeblock walls like cardboard. It was women who hunted through the ruins for bodies or scraps of possessions, screaming curses at the Arab governments, Israel and America. All along Abu Hassan Salameh Street there was a mêlée of mourning women, Western journalists and International Red Cross volunteers. Most of the bodies had been taken away by 20 September, but the stench of death was still everywhere, and all the outsiders wore gauze masks.[6]

It was not only the scale of atrocity and destruction that made the scene so catastrophic, but also its political message. Now the Resistance movement was gone: Palestinians in Lebanon and Lebanese who had supported them were at the mercy of the political forces whose character and intentions were signalled by the massacre itself. It was the beginning of a new era.

Yet to this area whose name had become internationally synonymous with horror, within days the inhabitants began to return. They started to clear rubble, patch up their homes, get children registered for school, have wounds treated. The war was over, emergency shelter and food distribution programmes were being closed down. However horrifying, Shateela was a place where Palestinians had a right to be; UNRWA services would be resumed; news of evacuated fighters and missing people would filter back here faster than outside. There was a double urgency to the rebuilding: not only was winter approaching but the Lebanese Army was now back in charge of the Beirut camps; everyone expected that building restrictions would be reimposed.

Notes

1. This passage from A. Kapeliouk's *Sabra and Shatila: Inquiry into a Massacre* (Belmont MA: AAUG, 1984) is quoted in Cobban, *Palestine Liberation Organization*, pp. 128–9.

2. Umm Fady's story is quoted in a fuller version in R. Sayigh and J. Peteet, 'Between Two Fires: Palestinian Women in Lebanon', in R. Ridd and H. Callaway (eds), *Caught Up in Conflict* (Basingstoke: Macmillan Education, 1986), pp. 123–5.

3. Z. al-Shaikh, 'Sabra and Shatila 1982: Resisting the Massacres', *Journal of Palestine Studies*, vol. 14, no. 1, Fall 1984. Other essential reading: 'Sabra and Shatila: Testimonies of the Survivors' (told to Layla Shahid Barrada) in *Race and Class*, vol. XXIV, no. 4, Spring 1983 (special issue on the invasion of Lebanon; the same issue reprints T. Friedman's award-winning report from the *New York Times*, 26 September 1982); J. Genet, 'Four Hours in Shatila', *Journal of Palestine Studies*, vol. XII, no. 3, Spring 1983.

4. This detail does not form part of al-Shaikh's published account but was given to the author in discussion.

5. Hayy Farhat is on the eastern edge of the camp.

6. It was never possible to make an accurate count of the victims: an IRC representative counted 328 bodies, but this was without the mass graves or the 'disappeared'. Kapeliouk in his book on the massacre gives an estimate of 3,000; the Kahan Commission, based on IDF intelligence, suggest from 700 to 800. A Palestinian researcher who questioned survivors listed 1,326 victims (*Democratic Palestine*, no. 51, 1992, p. 34).

Part II:
The Production of the 'Battle of the Camps'

6.   Lebanon in the Wake of the 1982 Invasion

At first sight Israel's apocalyptic invasion of Lebanon in the summer of 1982 appeared to have created a radical shift in the Lebanese and regional balance of forces. Pushing far beyond the limits of previous Israeli–Arab wars, Sharon's blitzkrieg above all demonstrated Israel's scope for using weapons of mass destruction against the Lebanese and Palestinian population without any effective international or Arab state deterrence. Although the unexpected resistance of West Beirut to three months' bombardment and siege pointed to flaws in the Sharon/Begin logic of applying maximum force, by the beginning of September some basic Israeli objectives seemed to have been achieved, while others appeared to be within reach. The Palestinian Resistance movement had been removed from those areas – Beirut and South Lebanon – whose control had enabled it to pose a political if not military threat to Israel. Even if it survived such a blow, the PRM could be expected to be thrown into crisis, a development that would encourage the emergence of 'moderate' leaderships in the Occupied Territories. The Israelis' old ambition of installing a Maronite 'ultra' as Lebanese president had been realized; Syria appeared marginalized, and with it the Steadfastness Front (opposed to Egypt and Camp David); deprived of the PRM, the Lebanese 'Opposition' appeared similarly negligible, incapable of challenging the new order that the United States, Israel and the Maronite right intended to build out of the invasion.

Yet events rapidly unravelled the 'givens' on which the three main beneficiaries of the invasion had based their calculations. Within three weeks of his election as president (on 23 August), Bashir Gemayel was assassinated, removing from the Lebanese arena the one man charismatic and ruthless enough to dominate internal political forces and possibly exclude external ones.[1] Immediately following the assassination, Sharon's invasion of West Beirut, breaking the US-brokered cease-fire and leading to the Sabra–Shateela massacres, underlined the antagonism between America's role as would-be neutral arbitrator and the Israeli one of conqueror and occupier. Israeli–US divergence was deepened during the protracted, ultimately futile negotiations for a Lebanese–Israeli agreement. The collapse of the 17 May (1983) Accords was a second watershed in the unravelling of the 'victory' of 1982, marking the failure of Israel's other main war aim of a peace treaty with Lebanon, the beginning of the end of America's intervention, the Syrian come-back, the resurrection of the Lebanese 'Opposition', and a chapter in the discrediting of the regime of President Amin Gemayel. The 'uprising' of February 1984 which expelled Gemayel's army from West Beirut marked the third and final defeat of the 1982 'victors', rapidly followed by the withdrawal of US forces from Lebanon.

This chapter examines in more detail the unfolding discomfiture and retreat of the three 'victors' of 1982. The account pays particular attention to the mistakes and excesses committed by the Maronite-controlled Lebanese Army in its moves to control areas formerly the domain of the PRM/LNM alliance; this story enfolds another, that of the revival of the Lebanese 'Opposition' and its revolt against US–Israeli–Maronite domination, culminating in the uprising of February 1984. Syria's part in the re-emergence of the 'Opposition' both served as a medium of Syria's return to the centre of Lebanese politics and enabled it to assume a role as arbitrator and controller. With Syria's plans for ending the Lebanese crisis, in conformity with its own strategic and ideological aims, came the seeds of conflict with the Palestinians in Lebanon. In a final section I look more closely at Lebanese resistance to Israeli occupation, a struggle with several distinct stages which brought together groups with very different aims and ideologies, hence containing within itself the embryos of future struggles.

The 'Pax Americana'

The Reagan Administration, which had first condoned, then restrained the Israeli invasion, used the new situation created by it to assert its influence over Lebanese and regional politics. The end of August found it solidly installed as mediator, guarantor and guide *vis-à-vis* the Lebanese state, an almost mandatory power position. Special Envoy Philip Habib's pivotal role in the negotiations leading to PRM withdrawal and an end to the war presaged an opening for the United States simultaneously to press Lebanon into peace negotiations with Israel and to protect it from too exorbitant Israeli demands, presenting itself as 'honest broker' to the Arab governments without modifying its fundamental strategic alliance with Israel. If successful in Lebanon, America's 'honest brokerage' could hopefully be extended to the more central Palestinian issue. This broader regional objective was signalled by President Reagan's announcement on 1 September of a new 'peace plan',[2] a move that echoed the regional dimensions to America's earlier (1958) intervention in Lebanon. With the installation of a pro-Western, pro-American president (first Bashir, then Amin Gemayel), the Reagan Administration looked forward to a Lebanon in which it could feel politically and economically at ease, a client certain to be responsive to US pressures and requirements, a centre of influence, an entry point.

American involvement in Lebanon rapidly took military, political and economic forms. A small (1,500) unit of US troops arrived in August to take part in the Multinational Forces that were charged with overseeing the evacuation of the PRM. Prematurely withdrawn, it was recalled after the Sabra/Shateela massacres (16–18 September) to take position between Beirut Airport and the Shouf foothills. On 2 October, a US military mission arrived to re-equip and retrain the Lebanese Army.[3] The United States also sold arms to Lebanon: arms purchases during 1983 amounted to one-eighth of the total budget and, paid for in dollars, were the main cause of depreciation of the Lebanese pound. At the same time, the Reagan Administration exhorted several UN agencies to increase their aid to Lebanon, and encouraged the World Bank to consider it for a loan. Several American business missions visited Beirut to explore investment openings.[4] But highest on the US government's agenda was getting Lebanon–Israeli peace negotiations on the road.

Philip Habib urged President Gemayel to put aside the thorny question of national reconciliation and to prioritize instead the removal of all foreign armies from Lebanon.[5] The underlying assumption was that, with Syria and the PRM out of Lebanon, an American-backed Maronite state would have no trouble in controlling the Muslim-progressive 'Opposition'. Habib assured Gemayel that these withdrawals could be brought about. Israel's readiness to withdraw was not in doubt once it had received the security guarantees that Gemayel was equally ready to provide. Once the Israelis had proclaimed their intention to withdraw, the US Administration assumed that Syria could be pressured into a parallel withdrawal. Astonishing in retrospect, the failure of US diplomacy to sound out the Syrians before concluding the 17 May Accords appears as part of its policy of excluding Syria from Lebanon, an exclusion that the Israeli invasion of 1982 was seen, mistakenly, as having practically achieved.

Both partners in the peace negotiations dragged their feet, and it was only after strenuous American diplomacy that talks finally began on 2 December 1982. Alternating between Khaldeh (Lebanon) and Kiryat Shimona (Israel), quagmired in Byzantine hassles over protocol, the slow pace of the talks gave time for Lebanese opposition to them to crystallize. Walid Jumblat was among the first to rally public opinion against the concessions being prepared. One of the early meetings was disrupted by a rocket attack, sign of the growing Lebanese Resistance movement. Full coverage of the talks in the Lebanese press underscored violations of Lebanese sovereignty. For though under US pressure, Israel gave up the fully fledged peace treaty that Sharon had promised as one of the fruits of the invasion, yet it gained from the Accords, as finally drafted, important concessions and guarantees, as well as some steps towards 'normalization'.[6] However, without Syrian compliance, the agreement finally signed on 17 May was born dead. In spite of a last-minute visit to Damascus by Secretary of State Schultz, the Syrians were obdurate.[7] Since Israel had made its withdrawal conditional on prior Syrian withdrawal, this first base of US settlement strategy was never reached.

The collapse of the 17 May Accords was the first, most serious sign of failure of the Reagan Administration's Lebanon policy, hinged as it was on the removal of all foreign armies. However, other signs of miscalculation surfaced during 1983. Unaware of its inner sectarian tensions and over-confident in its 'restructuring', US military advisers encouraged the Lebanese Army's repressive actions in West Beirut. Yet in street fighting in August, contrary to the advisers' predictions, the army showed up poorly against the Muslim militias whose reorganization it had provoked by its sectarian aggressiveness. More seriously, as fighting between the Lebanese Forces and the Progressive Socialist Party (PSP) in the Shouf intensified in early September, US troops became increasingly embroiled in the conflict, losing whatever claims to neutrality they had begun with. In mid-September part of the Sixth Fleet gathered off the Lebanese coast began to carry out heavy artillery and air strikes against Druze and Syrian positions in the mountains. On 25 September the battleship *New Jersey*'s 16-inch guns were used against PSP militias attacking the Lebanese Army redoubt at Souk al-Gharb.[8] It was at about this time that the respected and witty Lebanese Sunni leader Selim al-Hoss remarked that the American forces had become 'just another sectarian militia'.

Furthermore, massive car-bomb attacks which destroyed the American Embassy on 18 April (1983) and the Marines' headquarters on 23 October were a sign of the emergence of new groups far more anti-American and ruthlessly efficient than the 'terrorists' that the 1982 invasion had been supposed to destroy.[9] Such glaring evidence of failure could hardly be ignored. Pressure increased in Congress and the media for a recall of American troops and an end to American involvement in the 'Lebanese quagmire'. A week after reaffirming support for President Gemayel, on 7 February (1984), after the Lebanese Army finally lost control of West Beirut, President Reagan announced the decision to withdraw US forces from Lebanon. Although the United States participated as an observer in the Lausanne Conference (March 1984, a Saudi-backed attempt at national reconciliation), American interest in Lebanon was henceforth reduced to a minimal level. Gemayel was abandoned to his fate; 'even-handedness' was swept away by a new, stronger strategic alliance with Israel. The aim of removing Syria was replaced by a policy of limited approval of its role as peace-keeper and possible rescuer of Western hostages in an area of 'dangerous instability'.[10]

Domestic critics of Reagan's 'Lebanon policy' focused on 'management failures' and the glaring discrepancy between losses and gains, rather than on the errors of political judgement behind America's initial support for the Israeli invasion and its subsequent intervention. For the Administration, Sharon's invasion plan promised, first, the end of the PLO as a serious factor in Middle East politics; second, the 'restabilization' of Lebanon under a strong, pro-American president, its detachment from Syria and probable inclusion in the Camp David Accords; and finally a new opportunity for US Middle East settlement efforts based on Israeli *faits accomplis*. However, such calculations rested upon errors and oversights. It was erroneous to assume that the US government, having first given its blessing to the invasion, could subsequently dissociate itself from the aggressor and be accepted as neutral arbiter; for large segments of Lebanese and Arab opinion the United States was blackened by association with the 1982 holocaust. A second fundamental error was to assume Syria's defeat and discount its persistence and resources. A third was to believe that an ultra-Maronite president elected as a result of the invasion could be accepted by most Lebanese as legitimate. Perhaps the most basic error was to believe that military force could produce a political solution in an arena as complex and politicized as the Lebanese and Palestinian. A leading American authority on Lebanon suggests that none of those responsible for the 1982–84 intervention had any real understanding of the Lebanese scene.[11]

Israel cuts its losses

Israel's 'Lebanon policy' failed even more painfully, though less abruptly, than that of the United States. Flaws in Sharon/Begin's blitzkrieg logic appeared in the early stages of the invasion – for instance in the Syrian stand at Bhamdoun[12] – although the speed with which Israeli forces reached Beirut, joining up with the Lebanese Forces at Ba'bda on 14 June, made their victory appear ineluctable. Yet the long summer siege of West Beirut was politically costly both abroad and at home; furthermore it showed up the Israeli armed forces as dependent on sophisticated weaponry and reluctant to face lightly armed Palestinian and Lebanese fighters in street fighting.[13] The evacuation of PRM fighters from Beirut under international supervision was far from the rout that Sharon and Begin had anticipated: many Resistance units remained in Lebanon while the PLO as an entity found a new sanctuary in Tunis, from where it again demonstrated Palestinian capacity for surmounting disaster. Finally, with the assassination of Bashir Gemayel, Israel was deprived of the only figure capable of building the Maronite-dominated, cooperative Lebanon that the architects of the invasion had aimed at.

Israel's subsequent invasion of West Beirut on 15 September under the pretext of 'keeping order' and 'cleaning out' 2,000 Palestinian fighters alleged to have remained behind[14] did more to discredit Israel with formerly supportive Western governments and public opinion than the whole of the rest of the war. To this discredit was added the odium of the Sabra/Shateela massacres. Although the massacres were carried out by Lebanese forces, Israel's role in facilitating the action has never been put in doubt, while some investigators have traced the initial planning to Ariel Sharon and Bashir Gemayel.[15] US pressure forced the IDF out of West Beirut within three weeks, before it was able to complete the mass searches and arrests it had planned. But even within this short space of time it had become the target of attacks, presaging a resistance that would mount to become the most damaging ever faced by Israel in thirty-five years of war and occupation.

While at first its occupation of almost half of Lebanon seemed to place Israel in a 'no fail' bargaining position, one in which it could stay or withdraw at will, thus putting pressure on the Lebanese government to sign the peace treaty which was the invasion's second main objective, in the event the pressure failed. Even the 17 May Accords (regarded by the Israeli government as a climb-down) proved mere ink on paper, while Israel's occupation of Lebanon proved self-damaging in terms of lives, cost and domestic opposition. Mounting casualties sapped the morale of the Israeli Defence Forces, tarnishing its image of invincibility and provoking a vociferous peace lobby, the first in Israel's history.[16] The year of 'peace' following the war's end proved almost as damaging in terms of Israeli casualties as the war itself, and from then on until the IDF's final withdrawal in June 1985 the toll of dead and wounded continued to mount. Israel's losses in Lebanon were higher than that of all previous wars together.[17]

As it became obvious to the Begin government that all the original objectives of the 1982 invasion must be abandoned, the decision was taken for a unilateral withdrawal in phased stages. The first of these was from the Shouf mountains and, with Israeli–US relations strained by months of fruitless negotiation, the IDF timed its withdrawal at the end of August 1983, without giving the Lebanese Army the opportunity to take its place. This guaranteed escalation of the conflict between the home-based Druze PSP and the Lebanese Forces whom the IDF had introduced into the Shouf region.[18] This stimulation of sectarian conflict proved a pattern of Israel's post-invasion approach to Lebanon. From their earlier reliance on a single partner, the Maronite right, the Israelis switched to cultivating relations with a wide range of groups, but always within a sectarian perspective. By arming everyone, Israel fuelled conflict *between* sects: between Druze and Maronites in the Shouf, between Druze and Shi'ites in the South. In addition they encouraged conflict *within* sects, promoting Haddad's 'South Lebanon Army' against the Lebanese Forces, and trying to create a 'Shi'ite army' at the same time as encouraging Amal and private militias such as that of the Khalil family in Tyre.

In regard to the some 200,000[19] Palestinians inhabiting South Lebanon, Israeli policies were inconsistent over time and between different state institutions. Early in the invasion there were signs of intention to remove or scatter the whole civilian population, so as to prevent it again becoming a support base for resistance.[20] But although the rebuilding of 'Ain Helweh camp was prevented during the first winter, any major transfer was unfeasible politically and administratively. Eventually, rebuilding was permitted, perhaps partly to spite the Lebanese government for whom the war destruction of camp sites put pressure on Palestinians to emigrate. The IDF also recruited and armed Palestinian collaborators.

The vast concentration camp near the village of Ansar set up in the early days of the invasion remained the primary symbol of Israel's three-year occupation of South Lebanon (there was a smaller prison for women near Nabatiyyeh). Most Palestinian males above sixteen spent time in Ansar, as well as Lebanese leftists or those suspected of being pro-PRM. As the occupation continued and resistance intensified, Ansar was increasingly used for the mainly Shi'ite village population. Altogether 15,000 prisoners are estimated to have passed through it before its dismantling in June 1985, when the IDF carried out the final phase of its withdrawal.[21]

In the final stages of the occupation, frustrated in their main objectives, harassed by the Lebanese Resistance, the IDF lost its legendary cool and became vengefully bent on leaving behind the maximum conflict and destruction. This mentality is best summed up in the racist words of Lebanon Commander General Orr: 'Once the balance between the vermin, snakes and scorpions has been restored, they will turn against us again.'[22]

On withdrawal Israel resumed the 'Lebanon policy' interrupted by the 1982 invasion, that is to say artillery and air attacks against Palestinian and Lebanese targets, over-flights, a partial sea-blockade, the recruitment of agents, and maintenance of contact with the main sectarian militias. Until May 1985, the Lebanese Forces maintained an office in Israel, and the Israelis maintained one in the 'Maronite enclave'. But Israel's two predominant concerns in South Lebanon remained the 'Security Zone' and water. The size of the 'Security Zone' was increased in 1985 to include 171 villages and towns instead of a former 51, penetrating, in places, as deep as

30 miles into Lebanese territory. A 'corridor' linking the 'Security Zone' to Jezzine brought the Israeli-surrogate 'South Lebanon Army' to within a few kilometres of 'Ain Helweh camp. The heights overlooking Lake Ka'raoun also fell within the Zone, as well as 30 kilometres of the Litani River. Many Lebanese believe that Israeli bombardment and attacks have always been motivated less by security than by the aim of depopulating the South so as to appropriate its rich water resources.[23]

'At last there is a victor and a vanquished'

After the six-month civil war of 1958, the formula of reconciliation between Maronite ascendancy and Muslim rebels had been 'No victor, no vanquished': this was the maxim that had guided President Chehab and his successors. But after the Israeli invasion of 1982, the Maronite 'ultras' believed that they had emerged victorious and now enjoyed a historical opportunity to reimpose Maronite domination on the Muslim/progressive 'Opposition'. The quotation that heads this section comes from Fadi Frem, leader of the Lebanese Forces after Bashir Gemayel's death.

The first moves made by Amin Gemayel after his election in late September point to the dualism of his regime, conciliatory in its outer face but Kata'ebi in its inner structure. Building on his reputation as a 'moderate', a man of cross-sect and cross-party friendships, not a fanatic like Bashir, he responded positively to expressions of support from Muslim religious leaders such as Mufti Khaled and Sheikh Mehdi Shamsideen; and chose as Prime Minister Shafiq Wazzan, who represented Sa'eb Salam. At the same time, however, Gemayel put Maronite hardliners in key positions. Ibrahim Tannous, who had been trainer of the Lebanese Forces, was made Commander-in-Chief of the Lebanese Army. Zahi Bustani, a member of the Lebanese Forces Command Council, believed also to be linked to Mossad, was put in charge of the Department of General Security. Simon Kassis (also known for his anti-Palestinianism) was made head of the army's Deuxième Bureau, where he built a 'palace guard' and directed terrorist operations against West Beirut. The judiciary and Foreign Service were Kata'ebized, while a decree lifting the immunity of civil servants paved the way for a purge of 'obstructive elements'. This restructuring of state and army was directed not only against Muslims of doubtful loyalty but also against Chehabist Maronites.

Although the President's control over the legislature was assured through its notoriously venal speaker Kamel al-As'ad (manager of the election of Bashir), Gemayel quickly obtained from it the right of rule by decree. He also set up two new bodies outside Cabinet and Parliamentary control: a national security council appointed from men of known pro-Kata'eb sympathies and pro-American leanings; and a council for external economic affairs, to solicit Euro-American investment in Lebanon. The second council was headed by a business friend of the President's, Sami Maroun, who was also the Lebanese negotiator in the secret talks that accompanied the official Lebanese–Israeli peace negotiations.[24]

The three main bases of Gemayel's strategy in the immediate aftermath of the invasion were: (i) dependence on American support and guidance; (ii) reliance on the Lebanese Army as power base; and (iii) avoidance of efforts towards national reconciliation. The President's personal reputation as a 'moderate' won him a wait-and-see period on the part of those religious and political Muslim leaders – the traditional elite – who opposed the progressive and secular programme of the LNM.

But the repressive face of the Gemayel regime rapidly manifested itself. On 4 October, even before the formation of the Wazzan Cabinet, the Lebanese Army entered in force into West Beirut, where it behaved like a foreign army of occupation, confiscating arms, setting up checkpoints, searching homes and feeding interrogation centres in East Beirut with streams of Palestinians, Lebanese radicals and foreign migrant workers. On 5 October alone, according to official reports, arrests reached 453. In the propaganda of the Maronite right, West Beirut was a zone infested with terrorists, subversives, counterfeiters, criminals and illegal residents, and it was the Army's task to flush them out. Arrests did not touch leaders of national movement parties (several had gone underground or left the country) but concentrated on their followers and on popular quarters. The Army broke into party and militia offices, newspaper and publishing centres. Censorship regulations were reinstated, prohibiting criticism of the Army or news about the government other than that issued by the official news agency.

Conditions in the various interrogation centres and prisons used to 'process' the detainees were degrading and brutal. A foreign photo-journalist, who spent thirty-six hours in the General Security's main office near the museum in April 1983, gives this description:

> There was a medium sized room packed with layer upon layer of human bodies and frightened, exhausted faces which looked up at me. There were four or five hundred prisoners heaped over one another for lack of space. It was evident that they had been there, in that state, for days and days, without any food or anything to drink. The air was unbreathable, suffocating, a solid block of stench.[25]

By day a government department, at night the General Security office was given over to torture sessions. The photographer quoted above saw interrogators carrying steel whips, and one interrogator who wore white high-heeled boots stamping on the bare feet of detainees. The boss of the interrogators 'was like a scarecrow out of a comic strip'. This macho, sadistic style was characteristic of the unofficial prisons run by the Maronite rightist forces during the Civil War of 1975/6, and suggests that LF personnel had been drawn in to assist the forces of the state.

Cooperation between the Lebanese Army and the Lebanese Forces was evident in many areas (the Shouf, West Beirut, the southern suburbs), and took many different forms. While the Army was busy disarming the Muslim militias, the Lebanese Forces were left in control of large parts of East Beirut. Under Tannous, the Army was subjected to a thorough Kata'ebization, its officer corps sifted to promote those Maronites who had fought in the Civil War and those Muslims who had not.[26] The LF were allowed to operate freely in all areas of army control, sometimes using Army uniforms and equipment. Palestinian detainees were often handed over by the Army to the Lebanese Forces.

As a result, the number of arrested and missing persons in the 'national/progressive' area rose steeply. Already by mid-December (1982) 2,000 names had been registered in a centre set up by the victims' families. Of these, 600 were Palestinian and the rest Lebanese. Registrations undoubtedly fell short of the real figure for at least two reasons: people in outlying areas had difficulty in reaching the registration centre, and many people feared that registration would lead to retaliation against the detainees or prolong their detention.[27] Palestinians were particularly fearful, preferring to seek Kata'ebi *waasta*, and often spending large sums in vain.

Another form that Lebanese Army action took in Beirut's western and southern sectors was the bulldozing of illegal housing and evictions of war refugees from occupied buildings. While the Israeli Defence Forces were still in occupation of West Beirut, the Lebanese Army began destroying shacks on the outskirts of Shateela. Two weeks later, it went on to tear down unlicensed street markets which had grown up after the destruction of downtown shopping centres. Similar actions rapidly followed in other parts of the 'poverty belt': during 11–16 October in Ouzai, where protesters were shot at, causing three deaths; and in nearby Bourj Barajneh, where a large, mainly Shi'ite shantytown had grown up near the Palestinian camp, with one of the highest population densities in Beirut. (Shi'ites had migrated from rural areas in the late 1960s and 1970s, propelled by poverty and Israeli attack, and protected by the PRM/LNM.) These bulldozings and evictions went on through the summer and aroused Shi'ite fears that the Gemayel regime intended to drive them back to the rural areas from which they had come.[28] They were one of the reasons for the shift of Shi'ite leaders such as Sheikh Mehdi Shamsideen (head, after Imam Sadr's disappearance, of the Shi'ite Higher Council) away from support for the Gemayel regime. They also helped to give popular legitimacy to the return of the Muslim militias,

Murabitoun and Amal, which now rose again as the only protectors of the masses against the Army and the Lebanese Forces. When in mid-July (1983) the Army, backed by the LF, tried to evict refugees from Wadi Abu Jameel, an inner-city slum, an eight-hour battle flared up, leaving casualties on both sides.

The degree of threat posed by army arrest, bulldozings and evictions, combined with the aggressiveness of the Lebanese Forces in the areas of Israeli occupation (the Shouf, Iqleem al-Kharoub, the South) as well as the Army in Greater Beirut, generated a mass mood of anger that forced even moderate Muslim leaderships into criticizing the regime. The first body to express this public mood was the 'Committee of Arrested and Displaced Persons', formed in November 1982 by women whose husbands, sons or brothers had been taken. It was mainly due to their vigorous and persistent action that the fragmented and demoralized 'Opposition' revived. Kinship legitimated the Committee's action, setting it outside the suspect realm of politics; the series of sit-ins, marches and visits to political leaders which it undertook caught media and public attention. It was a sign of the power of mass anger that Mufti Khaled, a moderate Sunni figure who had supported the election of Amin Gemayel, felt obliged to offer the women's Committee the protection of his office, Dar al-Fatwa, as a site from which to organize their campaign.

Economic crisis played a part in deepening antagonism to the Gemayel regime, especially because it hit the non-Maronite regions with much greater severity. In the South, Israeli occupation almost destroyed local agricultural production, first by dumping subsidized Israeli agricultural goods, later by cutting off the South from its usual markets, and by punitive destruction of crops and plantations. As the main agricultural producers, Shi'ites were particularly hit by these measures. In Greater Beirut the historical disparity in living levels and government services between mainly Maronite and mainly Muslim areas became even more striking after 1982. All the destruction caused by the Israeli invasion was concentrated in the South, in West Beirut and the southern suburbs, yet funds for reconstruction were channelled into the 'Maronite enclave'. Government expenditure on roads, telephone lines and loans to industry and housing had always been unequal; now it became even more flagrantly so: LL100 million went to a new sewage system in North Metn (with 150,000 inhabitants), LL30 million to the southern suburbs with 700,000 inhabitants. Most of 1983's allocation for roads went to a single motorway connecting Gemayel's home town, Bikfaya, to Beirut. All state services to the war-ravaged areas – medical, educational, infrastructural – remained almost at zero. Although economic crisis hit the whole economy (partly the result of Gemayel's heavy arms purchases), unemployment levels were higher in the western sector, predominantly an area of commerce and services, than in the 'Maronite enclave where most Lebanese industry is concentrated, as well as large port, storage and electricity installations.

In addition to unemployment and inflation, a series of large car-bomb attacks hit West Beirut and the Southern suburbs throughout this period, causing destruction to commerce and habitation as well as heavy casualties. Attributed to the LF and Army's Deuxième Bureau, these attacks were seen as part of a campaign further to impoverish and crush the people of these areas. Indeed anyone crossing from West to East Beirut at that time felt as if they were entering a different country: on one side ruined buildings, shell-pocked, garbage-strewn streets, and ubiquitous refugees; on the other broad motorways, bursting supermarkets and elegant marinas.

A more directly political source of discredit of the Gemayel regime was its acceptance of infringements on Lebanese sovereignty and interests contained in the 17 May Accords. The negotiations were fully covered by the national media and tongue-lashed by Opposition leaders such as Walid Jumblat. Whereas some Muslim leaders would – however reluctantly – have accepted such concessions in the immediate aftermath of the invasion, by the spring of 1983 their mood had changed. Ultra-Maronite excesses, the Israeli occupation, the regime's Kata'ebi face, economic crisis: all these had contributed to the mood change. Another important factor was that while actions by the Lebanese Army clearly expressed its sectarian character, it proved unable to hold down the 'national/progressive' areas. Among these the first to explode was the Shouf. Quiescent during the Israeli invasion, the Druze community rallied under Jumblat/PSP leadership against Lebanese Forces depredations.

As noted earlier, it was the Israelis who introduced the LF into the Shouf during the 1982 invasion. Claiming to represent the minority Christian population, the LF immediately began setting up offices and checkpoints, as well as carrying out 'arrests' and kidnappings. Already by October 1982, clashes were so violent that Gemayel felt forced to send Army units to support the LF on the western fringes of the Shouf, though he would have preferred to let the two militias battle themselves to exhaustion. LF–PSP conflict continued all summer, with Israel allowing Israeli Druzes to reinforce the PSP. When, in spite of urgent pleas from the Reagan Administration, the IDF suddenly withdrew from the Shouf at the beginning of September 1983, PSP–LF, Druze–Maronite conflict burst into a final conflagration disfigured by reciprocal massacres worse than those of 1860/1, leading to the expulsion of the LF and thousands of Christian villagers from the Druze heartland. The Lebanese Army was dislodged from all its positions except Souk al-Gharb, which the US declared a 'red line'. As noted earlier, it was in the final stage of the Shouf battles that the US forces entered the fray, launching air and artillery attacks against Druze positions, but failing to influence the outcome. PSP victory in the strategic Shouf mountains, overlooking Beirut and linking the Syrian-controlled Beqa' to the coast, was the second serious setback for the Gemayel regime after the freezing of the 17 May Accords.

Meanwhile the Lebanese Army was also encountering increasing opposition in West Beirut and the southern suburbs, armed as well as political. Though its size and fire-power enabled it initially to disarm the Muslim militias and intimidate the Opposition, it did not have the training or homogeneity to persist in the repressive role intended for it by Gemayel, Tannous and their US advisors. Used injudiciously to impose military rule – curfew, searches, arrests, evictions – the Army only succeeded in rousing mass hostility. Anger increased when, at the end of August (1983), the Army launched a full-scale military attack on popular quarters of West Beirut. The attack was precipitated after LF elements killed four Shi'ite youths who were putting up posters commemorating Musa Sadr, provoking an irruption of Amal movement into the official television station. Intended to eliminate the reappearing Muslim militias, the attack failed in its purpose, causing widespread destruction and fury. Fearful of entering Amal's stronghold in the southern suburbs, the Army proceeded to shell this area, causing widespread damage and displacement of the civilian population. The role of Amal in defending the suburbs – organizing medical aid, water, alternative shelter – greatly enhanced its popular legitimacy.

From mid-1983, a series of meetings between the traditional leaders of the Sunni, Shi'ite and Druze communities pointed to a stiffening of opposition to the Army's actions in West Beirut. On 10 July there occurred an unprecedented event, a mass celebration of A'eed al-Fitr in the Municipal Sportsground. Normally each sect celebrates the feast separately, sometimes on different days; that year Sunni, Shi'ite and Druze representatives all attended. Amid a crowd estimated at 15,000, fiery anti-regime speeches were made while Army tank crews looked on helplessly. This was one of the earliest signs that President Gemayel was losing the support of the centrist Muslim leaderships; it pointed also to the public anger that would support the uprising of 6 February 1984. At A'eed al-Adha', on 17 September, Mufti Khaled, Sheikh Shamsideen and a Druze spiritual leader led a huge march to the Martyrs' Cemetery after praying together in the Imam 'Ali Mosque. A few days later the three religious leaders met again at Dar al-Fatwa, the Mufti's office.

There were other signs of the imminent break-up of the Gemayel regime. On 26 September (1983) Wazzan submitted his resignation, indicating withdrawal of support by Sa'eb Salam and the Sunni moderates. Another blow to Gemayel was the first National Reconciliation Conference at Geneva (30 October–4 November 1983), forced on him by the reverses in the Shouf. It was agreed at the conference, which was attended by an equal number of Maronite and 'Opposition' leaders, that the President should visit

Washington and other Western capitals to enlist support for Lebanon's rejection of the 17 May Accords. His cool reception by the once-friendly Reagan was sufficient evidence that US interest in Lebanon was running out.

The February 1984 uprising

All through the autumn and winter the Lebanese Army continued intermittently to shell the southern suburbs from positions both east and west of the 'Green Line'. Displaced Shi'ites piled into beach huts along the sea and shacks around Shateela and the Sports City. More than once Amal leader Nabih Berri gave warning of his power to shake the regime if the army persisted in destroying Shi'ite-inhabited areas. Feelings came to a head when General Tannous insisted on moving into positions vacated by a French unit of the Multinational Forces in Shiyah, right on the edge of the southern suburbs. This was a 'red line' for Berri. On 4 February he called on all Muslims in the Lebanese Army to lay down arms. Since at least 60 per cent of ordinary soldiers, as well as many officers, were Shi'ite, his call had a devastating effect. The army in West Beirut melted, leaving only hard-core Maronites to fight their way out in two days of the worst shelling the city had seen since 1982. As a result, Beirut was once again divided by the 'Green Line'; and once again the army was divided along sectarian lines into Maronite, Shi'ite and Druze battalions.[29] The uprising of 6 February effectively ended President Gemayel's hopes of extending his authority beyond the 'Maronite enclave'. It also brought a speedy end to American intervention. On 7 February, President Reagan ordered an immediate pull-out of the Marines, now dangerously surrounded by Druze and Shi'ite militias. By 15 February, the PSP had pushed the Lebanese Army out of all the Shouf except for Souk al-Gharb, and was able to join up with Amal in the southern suburbs. With these two large sectarian militias in control of the Shouf mountains, West Beirut and the southern suburbs, the President had little hope of restoring the authority of the state over all Lebanese territory. The re-emergence of the 'Opposition' enforced the lesson that the state could only be rebuilt on a basis of national reconciliation.

At the end of February, President Gemayel visited Damascus, a clear acknowledgement that Syria now held the key to the continuation of his presidency. With Syria restraining the 'Opposition', Gemayel managed to last out his term, surviving an 'uprising' against him on the part of the Lebanese Forces (12 March 1984) and several assassination attempts, to hand over authority in September 1988 to Army Commander General Aoun in default of a legally elected president.

The initial miscalculation of Amin Gemayel and the Maronite right was to believe that a strong Maronite state could be built upon US backing and the Israeli invasion, the very elements that deprived the Gemayel regime of legitimacy in the eyes of the 'Opposition'. If there had been a 'victory', as Pierre Gemayel and Fadi Frem boasted, it was not won by the Lebanese Forces, who carefully avoided any overt military action in support of the Israeli invaders. Fragmented and demoralized though they were, the forces opposed to Maronite hegemony were not crushed in 1982; the attempt of the Maronite right to reap the benefits of the invasion only succeeded, through its brutality and ineptitude, in reanimating and reuniting them. If there is any law in Lebanese politics, it is that a power disequilibrium unites all parties whose interests are threatened against the party seeking hegemony.[30]

The Syrian come-back

By February 1984, the collapse of US, Israeli and Maronite rightist plans for a new Lebanese order left Syria as the major power-broker. This was a dramatic reversal of its apparent marginalization by the end of the 1982 invasion. Both Israelis and Americans miscalculated the degree to which the invasion had weakened Syria's position in Lebanon. It had lost aircraft and missile sites but its control of territory had been only slightly modified; withdrawal from Beirut, South Beqa' and the Shouf still left Syrian armed forces in control of more than half of Lebanon. Although Syria had disregarded its defence commitments to the PLO, national honour was saved by four days of tough resistance to the IDF advance at Aley and Bhamdoun. As for its military capabilities, the USSR rapidly enhanced these by sending more sophisticated weaponry (MIGs, tanks, ultra-modern SAM-11 and SAM-13 anti-aircraft missiles as well as the famous SAM-5s), and a large force of Soviet technicians.[31] By the time of George Shultz's visit to Damascus in April (1983) in a last-minute attempt to extract Syrian agreement to the 17 May Accords, Syria was in a stronger military position *vis-à-vis* Israel than it had been on the eve of the invasion. Israel, on the contrary, was becoming increasingly conscious of the costs, political, economic and human, of continuing its occupation.

From this position, in the course of 1983, Damascus was able to demonstrate its continuing power to influence events in Lebanon, and to abort arrangements that threatened its vital interests and objectives. Of these, clearly the most threatening was the Lebanese–Israeli agreement, especially because Lebanese opposition to it was muted by the mood of defeat that gripped some leaderships in the aftermath of the invasion. But by making Israeli withdrawal from Lebanon conditional on Syrian withdrawal (in a secret letter of understanding which accompanied the official agreement), the American and Israeli negotiators handed Damascus the weapon with which to kill the Accords.[32] Syrian rejection had several practical and ideological repercussions, stiffening the Lebanese 'Opposition', signalling Syria's Arab national and confrontational stance, and underlining the futility of excluding Syria from Lebanese arrangements. It was on the basis of opposition to the 17 May Accords that the Lebanese 'Opposition' re-formed, in July 1983, as the National Salvation Front, launched by Franjiyyeh, Karameh and Jumblat. LCP, Ba'th and National Syrian Socialist Party (NSSP) leaders also attended the Zghorta meeting at which the new Front declared its aims; Berri did not attend, but kept in touch through Jumblat. Media reports of the new Front leaders' speeches sharpened public antagonism to the regime, hitting at its Maronite bias and the betrayal of Lebanon's national interests represented by the 17 May Accords, as well as its relations with the Arab world.

At the same time, from their position in the Beqa', the Syrians supplied or facilitated the supply of arms to the 'Opposition' militias in the Shouf, Beirut and the South. Syria also supported growing resistance to the Israeli occupation. At first, most resistance operations were launched by Palestinian units stationed between Syrian and Israeli lines in the Beqa', but these diminished after the Fateh mutiny in April 1983. Later, as the operations of the Lebanese National Resistance Front (LNRF) against Israeli forces in Sidon and the South increased, Syria gave arms and logistic support to all the groups involved, with little partiality; sectarian and Islamic fundamentalist groups were helped on the same basis as the LCP or NSSP. For example, the Syrians allowed Islamic Amal and Hizbollah to maintain bases in the Beqa'; Hizbollah was enabled by the Syrians to transport arms and fighters to the South and to Beirut, where it is reputed to have carried out the attacks of April and October against American and French installations. The Syrian army in the Beqa' also helped to train the young suicide volunteers (mainly from the NSSP and Hizbollah) who carried out the dramatic 'human bomb' attacks that did so much to spotlight South Lebanon as an arena of heroic, successful resistance. (More will be said about these attacks in the penultimate section of this chapter.) While encouraging the Lebanese Resistance movement, the Syrians were careful not to allow the LNRF to become too independent: in 1984 an outstanding NSSP Resistance leader in the Beqa', Muhammed Selim, was assassinated in circumstances that pointed to Syrian involvement.

Through such measured patronage, Damascus edged towards several objectives without risking violent Israeli retaliation, reducing Israel's ability to use its occupation to extract strategic concessions, increasing pressure on it to carry out a unilateral withdrawal, enhancing Syria's Arab standing as a country of confrontation, and tightening Syrian control over the Lebanese nationalist/progressive groupings.

Control over northern Lebanon and the Beqa' also enabled Syria to demonstrate its power to influence Palestinian politics. The split in Fateh that first irrupted in the mutiny of units stationed in the Beqa' in April 1983 led to the formation of the Palestine National Salvation Front (PNSF) in Damascus, challenging Arafat's leadership of the PLO; and from there to the Syrian-backed Palestinian attack on the camps of the North in November, forcing Arafat's evacuation from Tripoli, his last Lebanese foothold. Thus by the end of 1983, Syria seemed to have completed what the Israelis had not been able to do: eject the PLO from Lebanon.[33] Achieved through Palestinian proxies, the November assault demonstrated Damascus's ability to weaken the PLO while simultaneously activating its own allies in the struggle against Israel. It also pointed forward to the bloody internal Palestinian war that would be fought out in Lebanon and nowhere else in the Palestinian arena. In 1983 and later, Syria's policy towards the Palestinians in Lebanon was determined by, first, its policy towards Lebanon as a whole; second, its drive to control the PLO in line with Syrian regional strategies and objectives.

With the liberation of West Beirut in February 1984, Syria's Lebanon policy shifted back from one of destabilization to a role of measured intervention based on Arab and international consent. Damascus could rely on the new equilibrium of forces it had helped produce to paralyse Gemayel, now increasingly under attack not only from the National Salvation Front but also from the Lebanese Forces, who accused him of ruining the economy, personal corruption and political failure. Gemayel's dependence on Syria was marked by further attempts at national reconciliation (the Lausanne Conference, March 1984), and the formation of the National Unity government under Karameh in April; membership of the Cabinet included Jumblat and Berri, acknowledging the new power of the PSP and Amal. The Karameh government soon became paralysed not only by Maronite–'Opposition' conflict (expressed in rupture between Gemayel and Karameh), but also by conflict between the moderate Sunnis, who wanted dissolution of *all* the militias, and Jumblat and Berri whose leadership was militia-based. The Syrian approach to these conflicts was not one-sided. Although sponsoring the national/progressive leaders and parties, Syria also restrained the demands of Jumblat and Berri for Gemayel's resignation, while using their denunciations to keep the President in line. Muslim and Druze leaders' visits to Damascus were the most frequent, but Syria maintained contact with Maronite leaderships, including the Lebanese Forces; Pakradouni was a fairly frequent visitor.[34] Concerned to keep a balance between the main Lebanese sects and factions, Damascus appeared to prefer a continuation of unresolved crisis rather than a solution (if one were possible) that might have attenuated its role as arbitrator. While formally supporting the reform demands of the nationalist/progressive alliance (a watered-down version of those first formulated by Kamal Jumblat in 1975), Syria seems to have begun to move towards a solution of its own, based on the three main sectarian militias. Observers predicted this outcome in March 1984 when, as an agreement appeared close at the Lausanne Conference, it was Syrian protegé Suleiman Franjiyyeh (a founding member of the anti-Gemayel National Salvation Front) who voiced last minute hard-line Maronite demands.[35]

In the period between the 'liberation' of West Beirut (February 1984) and the beginning of the 'Battle of the Camps' (May 1985), Syria displayed skill and patience in its Lebanon policies, nudging Gemayel to take steps to control the Lebanese Forces; detaching the LF from their Israeli connections; propelling its own man, Elie Hobeiqa, into the LF command;[36] managing its allies on the western side of the 'Green Line'; and preventing any one group or alliance from becoming too powerful. Underlying apparent shifts or hesitations in Syria's Lebanon policy have been consistent long-term objectives stemming from Ba'thist pan-Arabism, Syrian national security interests and concern for strategic parity with Israel.[37] Put negatively, Ba'thist Syria has been consistently concerned to prevent either a Maronite rightist takeover of Lebanon in alliance with Israel, or a radical LNM/PRM takeover threatening both Israeli retaliation and destabilization of Syria. Unlike Israel, Syria does not favour a division of Lebanon into sectarian cantons, preferring a reconstructed central state and a replastering of sectarian coexistence. Unlike the LNM, the Asad regime is not ideologically opposed to Lebanon's sectarian system, and has accepted the necessity to deal with sectarian leaderships and groups. Indeed the Syrians' own plans for settling Lebanon, the Tripartite Agreement of December 1985, was based exclusively on the leaders of the three largest sectarian militias (the Lebanese Forces, the PSP and Amal). If it had gone into effect, Lebanon's state institutions and other political leaderships would have been marginalized, and the whole country and population divided up under Syrian Army and/or militia control. Lebanese observers also noted how the Tripartite Agreement cut out the Sunni community, already weakened by loss of the PRM, and politically and geographically fragmented.[38]

Though a more skilful player in the Lebanese arena than the United States or Israel, Damascus has also made miscalculations and has had its plans disrupted by the vortex of events. The border line between a manipulated instability that buttresses Syrian hegemony and a dangerous instability that threatens it is hard to maintain. Conflicts encouraged as a way of preventing local protegés from becoming too strong have had a way of getting out of control, leading to undesired outcomes.

The events of the first half of 1985 well illustrate the pitfalls of a fast-changing situation. In early January, Israel announced its final withdrawal plan, to be accomplished in two phases: first, from the Awali line and Sidon area; second, from all the rest of the South except for an enlarged 'Security Zone'. The first phase began on 15 February. The site of large Sunni and Palestinian concentrations,[39] Sidon immediately became an arena of struggle between a wide gamut of contenders; a week before the Israeli pull-out, a massive car-bomb almost killed Mustafa Sa'd, the only leader capable of holding down the Sidon situation. The day after its liberation, President Gemayel visited the city (a Lebanese Army battalion is stationed there), while popular rallies were held by Amal, Hizbollah, the Nasserist Popular Organization and other 'Opposition' groups. On 19 March LF leader Samir Geagea launched his month-long attack on 'Ain Helweh camp from Maronite villages in Iqleem al-Kharoub; his ignominious retreat in April exposed these villages to reprisal attacks by Muslim and Palestinian militias, and paved the way for the substitution of Hobeiqa as head of the Lebanese Forces on 9 May.

Geagea's replacement by Hobeiqa in turn paved the way for the Tripartite Accords and a more complete, more stable Syrian mastery of the Lebanese arena, to be achieved through an elaborate system of major and minor alliances requiring a minimum of direct intervention. Only one major grouping, the Palestinians, had no natural place in this carefully balanced system of dependencies. On the contrary, they threatened it on many levels: as a large and relatively cohesive segment of the population in spite of being geographically scattered; as part of a national liberation movement bent on continuing the struggle against Israel; as a progressive, secular movement; because of their historic ties (more Arab nationalist than sectarian) with Lebanese Sunnis; and also as a potential base of support for Arafat. The demographic distribution of the Palestinians, clustered mainly in the South, Sidon and Beirut, increased the threat posed by their militancy, especially as Syria had no forces south of the Awali River.

The remilitarization of 'Ain Helweh camp and the re-establishment of contact between it and the Beirut camps must have worried the Syrians. Unlike the situation in Beirut and the South, Amal and the Shi'ite community had little presence in the Sidon area. The second phase of Israeli withdrawal from the South, which would liberate the camps of al-Bass, Rashidiyyeh and Bourj Shemali, was timed for June. These must have been among the considerations favouring an attack upon the Beirut camps before they could become too strong. In Amal movement Damascus found a local ally whose ambitions and dilemmas, equally acute in early 1985, made it ripe for manipulation towards a move intended to prevent the re-emergence of the Palestinians as an independent force in Lebanon.

The Lebanese Resistance movement

At first a unifying framework for the forces of the 'national/progressive' alliance, resistance against the Israeli occupation of South Lebanon both enveloped and prepared the way for other struggles, strengthening sectarian formations at the expense of secular ones but in a way that challenged older, sectarian leaderships. The Lebanese National Resistance Front (LNRF) encompassed different groups whose ideological incompatibility became more pronounced as resistance developed, changing in methods and scope. It was in the later stages that it took on the character of a mass Shi'ite uprising, and it was during this later stage that Amal movement came to the fore, a shift that marked Shi'ite reappraisal of Israeli intervention as well as realignments within Amal movement. On several levels, the story of resistance to Israel in Lebanon deserves examination as a national epic; as the most serious episode of resistance to Israeli occupation before the Palestinian Intifada of 1987; as, in some of its phases, a demonstration of Lebanese–Palestinian and cross-sectarian cooperation; and finally as leading towards the 'Battle of the Camps'. Without the new stature and *élan* achieved in resisting Israeli occupation, it is doubtful whether Amal movement would have developed such a vital stake in controlling 'its' territory, nor whether it would have launched itself against the Palestinian camps.

The Lebanese National Resistance Front issued its first statement on 16 September 1982, the day after the Israeli invasion of West Beirut. Taken by surprise, the Muslim militias had put up a token resistance; but in the few weeks that the Israelis spent in the city, attacks against them became a daily and nightly occurrence, causing several casualties. The Front was launched by the LCP and OCA with immediate NSSP adhesion; PRM groups liaised with it but did not announce their actions. Although the disparity in force between the occupying army and the fledgeling LNRF appeared at this stage overwhelming, resistance eventually proved its military and political efficacy. Behind this rapid launching of a resistance front was the aim to 'deprive the occupation army of the monopoly of initiative', unleashing a dynamic of pinprick attacks, Israeli retaliation, mass mobilization and further repression, leading eventually to major confrontations – the 'ABC of activism'.[45]

Scarcely noticed at the time in the international press, Palestinian resistance continued right through the summer of 1982, carried on by armed elements that had managed to escape the Israeli dragnet. There was continued fighting around 'Ain Helweh in June, after its fall; the ambush near Damour which killed an Israeli general believed to be head of intelligence (10 June); rocket and commando attacks against Israeli offices in Sidon in July. On 4 September, four Israeli soldiers were captured by a Palestinian unit near Bhamdoun. As noted earlier, PRM units in the Beqa' continued to attack the IDF from behind Syrian lines.

Another early form of resistance was the women's demonstrations against the Israeli concentration camp of Ansar, beginning on 1 July in 'Ain Helweh, and spreading to other camps (al-Bass, Rashidiyyeh, Bourj al-

Shemali). On 5 September, the IDF fired at a stone-throwing women's demonstration, wounding four.

These summer months also saw the first manifestations of Shi'ite protest against the occupation: in Nabatiyyeh on 20 July, a meeting of notables and mayors called for an end to the occupation; on 9 August, the inhabitants of Zifta demonstrated against the Israeli takeover of a local Amal office; on 22 August, the people of Saksakiyyeh demonstrated against a pro-Israeli militia office; on 30 August, Sheikh Ragheb Harb led the villagers of Jibsheet in an anti-Israeli demonstration; and on 5 September, at a meeting in Nabatiyyeh commemorating Musa Sadr's disappearance, speakers attacked the occupation.

Significant as signs, such early and scattered incidents had no influence on the acquiescence of many traditional Muslim religious and political leaders in the Lebanese–Israeli peace negotiations. They did, however, begin to affect the popular mood, especially after the first resistance 'coup', the destruction of the Israeli headquarters in Tyre on 11 November 1982, killing eighty-nine people, claimed by the 'Organization of Armed Struggle' (probably Palestinian). LNRF operations increased in Sidon and Tyre provinces during the end of 1982 and spring of 1983.

Although, in its later stages, Lebanese resistance came to be seen as an essentially Shi'ite phenomenon, in fact the LNRF was a multi-sectarian, multi-party formation with unclaimed Palestinian participation. This 'mixed' character was clearest in the early stages and in the Sidon area. In Sidon, until Israeli withdrawal in February 1985, there was a high degree of cooperation between Lebanese and Palestinians, all religious leaderships, and Sunni, Shi'ite and Christian sectors of the population. Druze villages in the southern Beqa', Rashaya and Hasbayya, also played an important role at this stage in resisting Israeli efforts to recruit collaborating militias.

None of the sectarian militias participated in the NLRF, each acting independently and in accordance with its own situation. Hizbollah soon began its own resistance attacks against both US and Israeli targets. Engaged in a life-or-death struggle with the Lebanese Forces in the Shouf, the PSP used Israeli Druze connections to procure arms and IDF neutrality, which restricted its resistance role in the mountains to facilitating attacks by others (mainly Palestinians and NSSP). Amal hesitated for eight months before beginning resistance, also undertaken independently of, and largely in competition with, the LNRF. This hesitation had several causes internal to Amal and the Shi'ite community. As a result of Amal–PRM clashes before 1982, and growing Shi'ite anti-Palestinianism, Amal leaders in the South took widely different stands towards the Israeli invasion.[46] Variation continued to characterize the actions of local Amal leaders under the occupation, with some collaborating, others (e.g. in Zifta and Ghazziyeḥ) refusing to collaborate. Many Shi'ite villagers at first regarded the Israeli presence with 'positive indifference' and it was some months before the mass mood swung sharply against the occupation. In Beirut, Shi'ite leaderships were divided as regards the Gemayel regime and Lebanese–Israeli negotiations. Amal's situation in the southern suburbs, and Berri's, were not as assured as they became by the autumn of 1983 as a result of Army actions. Berri's contacts with local Amal leaders in the South were precarious and his control over their positions slight.

On 6 June 1983, the first anniversary of the invasion, Amal declared a day of mourning and a general strike that was observed throughout the South. This was one of the first signs of Amal's shift towards active resistance.

The Shi'ite clergy and Shi'ite religious occasions were crucial in mobilizing popular resistance. Several turning points should be noted. The commemoration of Imam Sadr at Nabatiyyeh on 5 September 1982 was an occasion for recalling this leader's anathemas against Israel. On 4 May 1983, a spokesman of the Supreme Islamic Shi'a Council, speaking in Tyre at a celebration of the birth of Imam 'Ali, called for struggle against Israel and collaborators. In October 1983, at the feast of 'Ashoura, Sheikh Mehdi Shamsideen (deputy to Imam Sadr) denounced cooperation with Israel as *haram* (a sin). During the same feast on 16 October, the first serious clashes occurred in Nabatiyyeh, when Israeli jeeps that jostled crowds mourning Hussein were overturned and burnt.

Because of the strong ties linking Shi'ite clergy to their congregations, local imams were perhaps more important than the leadership in mass mobilization, turning *Husseiniyyehs* (meeting places attached to Shi'ite mosques) into foci of resistance. The name of Sheikh Ragheb Harb of Jibsheet is particularly remembered. The first Shi'ite cleric to protest openly against the occupation (as early as August 1982), his arrest on 17 March 1983 was a turning-point in the resistance of the South, triggering strikes and protest meetings. Echoes even reached the capital where, for the first time since the entry of Gemayel's army, West Beirut was the scene of a public meeting, one held in solidarity with Sheikh Harb. When he was assassinated by collaborators the following year (February 1984), the days of mourning brought hundreds of thousand of people to Jibsheet, in spite of Israeli attempts to cut the roads off. A national strike was called, observed in all parts of Lebanon except the 'Maronite enclave'.

A number of factors contributed towards the change of mass Shi'ite attitudes towards the occupation. The initial welcome or indifference changed as the Israelis were perceived to be digging in for a long occupation (unlike the 'Litani invasion' of 1978, when they withdrew under US/UN pressure after a few weeks). Then came Israeli dumping of its subsidized agricultural products, which hit at the South's main source of livelihood. Economic hardship increased with the closing of the South in September 1983, a form of massive 'collective punishment' separating producers in the

South from their main market in the capital. But Israeli attempts to recruit and coopt members of the Shi'ite community were perhaps the principal cause of rising Shi'ite and Amal hostility, threatening as it did the community's drive towards autonomy. Arrests of young men who refused to join the National Guard was another major cause, growing as IDF searches and arrests increased.

By early 1983, mounting Israeli casualties were beginning to affect IDF morale and Israeli government decisions, leading eventually in January 1985 to the painful decision to 'disengage'. In spite of the increasingly tough punitive measures taken (searches, arrests, killings, destruction of orchards), armed resistance developed in frequency, techniques and duration of engagements. In the first six months (October 1982 to March 1983) there were 104 operations; in the second, 211. During the second year, there were 567 (a rate of 47 a month). By the autumn of 1984 the rate was 3 a day, rising still higher in the final period of withdrawal in 1985. Whereas at the beginning armed resistance mainly took the form of single attacks using mines, RPGs or dynamite, it quickly evolved towards full-scale engagements using a variety of weapons – telecommanded explosives, automatic fire, bazookas, Katioushas. Beginning on 4 November 1983, the suicide attacks heralded a new weapon with great psychological impact. The young suicide volunteers were trained in the Beqa' with Syrian assistance, many of them coming from poor Shi'ite, Christian and Druze village backgrounds. Their final messages broadcast posthumously on Lebanese television, and their poster portraits all over city walls, gave that brief epoch a stamp of self-sacrifice and military achievement which some Lebanese and Syrian leaders used to highlight opposite qualities in Palestinian military performance. The wave of 'human bomb' attacks came to a sudden end after Israeli withdrawal in June 1985 behind the 'Security Zone'.

Collaborators were the target of about one-fifth of all attacks, which were highly effective as a deterrent. In the first phase of the occupation, the IDF had some success in forming armed National Guards in southern villages, using harassment by the Lebanese Forces as a pretext; the same pretext was used to arm collaborators in 'Ain Helweh. However, Israeli pressures in early 1983 to coopt mayors and notables into a collaborative civilian structure of village leagues failed, in spite of threats of arrest. An attempt in October 1983 to form a Shi'ite army (as an alternative to Haddad's mainly Christian one) also failed.

As Israeli attempts to stifle 'Shi'ite terrorism' hit ever-wider sectors of the population, unarmed mass resistance reached a level of intensity never shown before by any Arab people confronting an Israeli army. From late 1983, the whole of the South was in a continuous state of ferment and confrontation. Dozens of villages were attacked by the IDF in battles that often continued for days. This description of an early attack against

Ma'rakeh in February (1984) is typical:

> On February 22, the Israelis penetrated (the village) en masse. The inhabitants confronted them with stones and sticks. The clashes spread rapidly to alleys where women doused the soldiers with boiling oil. Hysterical firing by the Israelis caused one death and some twenty wounded, but the occupying forces stopped UNIFIL or ambulances from bringing aid to the inhabitants. The village was cut off for several days, while the population held a sit-in inside the *husseiniyya* demanding the release of young men who had been arrested. Popular protest spread to Tyre and the surrounding villages.[47]

As both armed and unarmed resistance mounted, the IDF faced a situation unprecedented in its history, one with demoralizing and brutalizing effects. In the final months of the occupation, Israeli actions became vengeful and savage. A punitive raid against the village of Sur al-Gharbiyeh in February 1985 gives an idea of the deterioration:

> Seven young men were killed, six of them between the ages of fifteen and twenty. According to townspeople, seven were pulled out of the round-up of all the village men. They were machine-gunned in the legs; two were bayoneted in the abdomen. People told me that seventeen-year-old Yusuf Muhammad Dira', who was bleeding profusely, asked for a drink of water. The Israelis picked him up and dunked him head first into a water catchment basin until he drowned. The other six were allowed to bleed to death on the ground in front of the villagers.[48]

The importance of the resistance in the South in Lebanese politics both in the immediate aftermath of the invasion and later, with the re-emergence of the 'Opposition', can hardly be overestimated. At the beginning it stiffened opposition to the 17 May Accords and the Gemayel regime; later it had more complex effects, proving that Israeli armed force was not invincible, calling attention to the heroism of the mainly Shi'ite population of the South, and bringing to the fore competition for popularity and influence between different components of the Resistance movement.

From the time of the first serious Lebanese–Israeli clashes, those of Nabatiyyeh in October 1983, events in the South began to rival the battles in the Shouf in claiming the attention of Lebanese outside the 'Maronite enclave'. The media reflected this shift in concern, with *al-Safir* in particular devoting a large daily section to reportage from each part of the South, along with analysis of occupation and resistance strategies. Special attention was paid to Ansar (the big central Israeli concentration camp near Tyre); an exhibition of prisoners' artefacts drew huge crowds. Television coverage of events in the South had even greater impact than the press: viewers in Beirut were transfixed by the sight of women and children confronting the Israeli Army. After years of suffering Israeli attack without any other manifestation of national concern than corruptly distributed compensation, the South suddenly found itself the object of enthusiastic celebration: solidarity strikes, rallies, posters, films and monster parades. Starting from the southern suburbs, these mile-long marches wound their way through the streets of West Beirut, with hooting ambulances, bands and marchers dressed to represent the resisting people of the South (peasants, workers, fishermen, First Aid personnel, etc.). Organized by Amal, these parades symbolized the new pride and power of the Shi'ite community, and the ending of its long exclusion from the Sunni-dominated city. By virtue of its pre-1982 organizational networks in the South, which enabled it to mobilize widespread and multiform resistance, Amal became the dominant group within the loose Resistance alliance. It was logical that Amal should become the political expression and beneficiary of this new-found Shi'ite pride, encouraging it and speaking for it. The movement's influence over the media (an Amal member had become Director-General of the Ministry of Information in 1984), as well as its ability to call up massive demonstrations, enabled it to 'capture' the Resistance movement in the South to enhance its own status and eclipse other participants.

It was in the arena of national politics that Amal leaders aimed to capitalize on the enhanced prestige won through the struggle and sacrifices of the South. In early 1985, with Gemayel neutralized and Israeli withdrawal from the South a matter of months away, the moment appeared to be approaching when Amal could impose Shi'ite demands upon a Syrian-backed new Lebanese order. Its hegemony over resistance in the South was the first step towards hegemony in West Beirut, site of important institutions of the state; and from there to a new deal for the Shi'ites in national politics.

It was in this political context that the Palestinian role in resistance before 1982 had to be denigrated, and their role after 1982 stifled. The theme of Shi'ite resistance was developed *in contrast* to the PRM and as a lesson to it. This theme played a central part in Amal's anti-Palestinian propaganda just before and during the 'Battle of the Camps'. Because of his position distant from, and critical towards, both Amal and the PRM, the views of Sheikh Muhammad Hussein Fadlallah, spiritual guide of Hizbollah, are revealing. In an interview just before the 'Battle of the Camps', he underlines the *Islamic* character of the Lebanese Resistance movement.[49] A year later, while blaming Amal–Palestinian fighting on an international conspiracy, he accuses each side of 'seeking to secure political gains on the Lebanese front', an implicit criticism of Amal, seen by Hizbollah as too secular, 'Lebanist' and ready to make deals with the

Maronites. At the same time, Fadlallah repeats Shi'ite criticisms of the PRM, associating it with the 'mud of Arab politics' and contrasting it with Islamic resistance which 'was able to defeat the Israeli occupation – *for the first time* – in an effective way'.[50] By minimizing the role of the secular left and the Palestinians in Lebanese resistance, Fadlallah illustrates the process of competition for credit which robbed the resistance in the South of its broader Arab nationalist significance, reducing and provincializing it.

Convergences and re-alignments

Few local commentators predicted the prolonged and bitter conflict between Amal movement and the Palestinians that would explode on 19 May 1985, and drag on until the end of 1987. A daily welter of events – east–west artillery bombardments, the escalation of resistance in the South, militia clashes – created a screen which obscured underlying structural shifts. Of these the most important were the end of US intervention, the Israeli withdrawal and the Syrian comeback. It was only in retrospect that the effect of these broader shifts on local alignments showed up clearly, creating alliances where before there had been enmity, and making enemies out of former allies. In addition, regional and local moves to restabilize Lebanon generated their own long-term pressures towards marginalizing the Palestinians, seen as at best unconcerned, at worst a disruptive factor.

The February 1984 uprising marked the first of these structural shifts since it brought in its train the ending of the United States' military presence as well as of the Reagan Administration's support for the Gemayel regime. Removal of the Marines and the Lebanese Army from West Beirut favoured a restoration of Syrian influence over this critical area, whether through Lebanese allies or through the requests for a Syrian peace-keeping force that inter-militia fighting was bound to engender. The defeat of the 'Jaysh al-Ta'ifi', by weakening President Gemayel, opened the way to renewed negotiations towards a solution of the Lebanese crisis, a process bound to intensify conflict between all political forces with a stake in the outcome. Enfolded within a conflict traditionally viewed as one between a Maronite ascendancy and a Muslim 'Opposition' lay other, less clearly formulated conflicts – inter-sect and intra-sect, or socioeconomic – that the new situation exacerbated. Among these was the latent struggle between Sunni and Shi'a for leadership of the 'Opposition' and, more importantly, for access to the levers of the reconstructed Lebanese state.

A side-effect of the February uprising was the liberation of the Beirut camps from Lebanese Army control. Amal militiamen immediately took over army positions around the camps; yet, although this move engendered some friction (local incidents will be described in Chapter 8), it was not seen at the time as unambiguously hostile. This was because, formally, relations between the two groups remained those of allies, jointly engaged in resistance against the Israeli occupation in the South and in confronting the Lebanese Army in East Beirut (after February 1984 the east–west artillery war was resumed). Amal–Palestinian relations were cemented by the transfer of money and arms; contacts at the national and local leadership levels continued uninterruptedly. During this period between the uprising and the beginning of the battle, Amal leaders did not call for the control or disarming of the camps.

The beginning of the final stages of Israel's withdrawal from South Lebanon, starting with Sidon in February 1985, heralded a shift as far-reaching as the American withdrawal a year earlier, engendering similar realignments. Sidon's strategic importance re-emerged, as a site of Sunni and Palestinian concentration straddling the coast road linking the capital to the South, a potential obstacle to the extension of the authority of the state, and even more to Amal's line of communication between its heartland in the South and Beirut. Israeli withdrawal opened the way for movement between the camps of Beirut and those of Sidon, reuniting for the first time since the invasion the two largest concentrations of Palestinians in Lebanon. In February the people of 'Ain Helweh had refused to allow Resistance cadres and weapons into the camps, but Geagea's month-long bombardment from the hills above Sidon in March/April provoked re-arming. These developments would certainly have been viewed with misgiving by all parties opposed to Palestinians re-emerging as an independent political force in Lebanon.

Israel in particular, since its decision in favour of unilateral withdrawal, had been searching for less costly alternatives to occupation to protect its northern settlements. A variety of means were developed, first being the extension of the 'Security Zone', policed by the South Lebanon Army backed by Israeli military personnel, which now reached as far north as Jezzine and Kfar Falous, from where the SLA directly threatened 'Ain Helweh and Sidon. The Israelis could also manipulate allies such as the Lebanese Forces (Geagea's attack against 'Ain Helweh should be seen in this perspective). In addition, they could discreetly encourage independent but anti-Palestinian forces, Amal movement in particular, to protect the South against a revival of Palestinian resistance.

Early in April 1985, after the IDF withdrawal from Nabatiyyeh and Tyre but before 'final' withdrawal in June, a *de facto* cease-fire between Amal and the IDF came into effect, with all Amal resistance attacks coming to an end. As it withdrew, the IDF handed over its positions to Amal. In late April Amal set up checkpoints around Rashidiyyeh and the other Palestinian camps in the South. These were clear signs of an informal understanding concerning control of the camps, similar to those between the IDF and the

Lebanese Army in September 1982, as a condition of Israeli evacuation of West Beirut. Palestinians say that Da'oud (see Political Glossary), one of Amal's two chief commanders in the South, was Israel's channel of contact with Amal's leadership. As noted earlier, assassination of Lebanese leftists in the South had gone on under Israeli occupation, with the probable double aim of facilitating Amal hegemony and weakening groups likely to support the Palestinian Resistance. Throughout the period before and during the first 'Battle of the Camps', Israel also released batches of Lebanese Shi'ite prisoners (e.g. on 2 April, 13 June, 24 June, 3 July); it was likely that many would join (or rejoin) Amal.

After February 1984 Syria, its return to the heart of Lebanese politics favoured by both US and Israeli withdrawals, intensified its contacts and consultations with all Lebanese groups and leaders, excluding none. The failure of Geagea's attack against 'Ain Helweh opened the way for Elie Hobeiqa's takeover of the command of the Lebanese Forces on 12 May, tipping the Lebanese Forces away from the 'Israeli option' represented by Geagea and towards the Syrians. This shift greatly enhanced the feasibility of a Syrian-brokered settlement of the Lebanese crisis which, as the Tripartite Accords of December (1985) showed, would be based on the Maronite, Shi'ite and Druze militia leaders, marginalizing the other sects and the secular political parties. Among the excluded groups the largest was the Sunni community, the most militant the Palestinians: the opposition of both to the Syrian settlement could be assumed. Any re-emergence of the Resistance movement would automatically add to the weight of Sunni protest while, on the contrary, suppression of the Palestinians would make it easier to diminish Sunnis within the newly emerging sectarian 'equilibrium'. Such considerations added to other Syrian strategic objectives based in national security and avoidance of pretexts for Israeli attack.

As Syria's man in the Lebanese Forces, Hobeiqa's actions before and during the first 'Battle of the Camps' are significant: the Lebanese Forces' office in Jerusalem was closed, thereby removing an obstacle to LF–Syrian *rapprochement*. LF units were withdrawn from the South, eliminating any danger of clashes with Amal militiamen. After the beginning of the battle, Hobeiqa was the first Lebanese leader openly to support Amal's action, condemning 'Palestinian terrorism' and calling for Syrian intervention to restore security.

The question of Syria sending a military force to Beirut arose again in the period after the February uprising since this event had brought not only liberation from Lebanese Army oppression but also a return of *fowda* (chaos), that mix of artillery bombardments, car-bombs, militia clashes, kidnappings and assassinations that characterized the war in Lebanon. Responsibility for security in West Beirut after the expulsion of the army had been undertaken by the mainly Shi'ite 6th Brigade, but it was unable to prevent the militias engaging in extortion, rackets and fights with each other. Calls for Syrian intervention were renewed by all the 'Opposition' leaderships as well as the pro-Syrian parties. However, Damascus let it be known that a precondition for sending a peace-keeping force to Beirut was the prior disarmament of all the militias.[51]

It was in this context that, on the night of 14/15 April, Amal attacked and disarmed the Murabitoun. This small militia was not a real threat to the security of West Beirut but its reputation for break-ins and looting helped to justify Amal's action. In addition, Amal accused the Murabitoun of giving cover to returning Fateh loyalists (more will be said about this in Chapter 7). In the course of an all-night battle, the PSP militia came to Amal's assistance, an on-the-spot decision that the leadership later regretted.[52] Essentially the attack was a pre-emptive one, aimed at eliminating a force that, whatever its weaknesses, presented a potential obstacle to Amal's hegemony over West Beirut, and hence to Syrian pressures towards the Tripartite Accords. This was so because, revitalised, the Murabitoun could act as a vehicle for Sunni resistance to Amal's domination of a city they regarded as historically theirs.[53] Furthermore, the Murabitoun was the only force in West Beirut likely to give active support to the Palestinian camps in case they were attacked. Of all the events in the period preceding the 'Battle of the Camps', this was the one that pointed most clearly forwards.

Notes

1. There were two main theories of responsibility for the assassination: (i) that it was the Israelis', angered by Bashir's independence at his first meeting with Begin (at Nahariyyeh, on 1 September), and to provide a pretext for the invasion of West Beirut (see 'Who Killed Bashir?', *Middle East International*, no. 184, 1 Oct 1982); (ii) that it was the Syrians', given Bashir's history of resistance to their presence in Lebanon. The Lebanese Forces accused a PPS man, Habib Shartouni, owner of an apartment in the building where the explosion took place; but although they brought him to trial, he was never executed.

2. The Reagan 'peace plan' basically called for implementation of the Camp David Accords (complete text in Aruri, Moughrabi and Stork, *Reagan*, Appendix A, p. 79.

3. Details in Petran, *Struggle over Lebanon*, pp. 297–8.

4. An-Nahar, *Report and Record*, January 1983.

5. Cobban, *The Making of Modern Lebanon*, p. 193.

6. Details in Petran, *Struggle over Lebanon*, pp. 310–11.

7. Syrian refusal to leave Lebanon or recognize the 17 May Accords only gradually became apparent during April (1983) in a series of statements made by Assad, Khaddam and Tlass (see A. Yaniv, *Dilemmas of Security*, pp. 208–11).

8. See Cobban, *The Making of Modern Lebanon*, for a good account of this eventful period, pp. 197f.

9. Even after its transfer to the 'Maronite enclave', the US Embassy was again the target of a car-bomb attack.

10. E. Picard, 'Could Salvation come from Syria?', paper presented at a conference on 'Contemporary Lebanon' at SOAS (London), March 1988.

11. See M. Hudson, 'The United States' Involvement in Lebanon' in Barakat, *Toward a Viable Lebanon*.

12. See Z. Schiff and E. Ya'ari, *Israel's Lebanon War* (London: Allen & Unwin, 1985), pp. 203–4.

13. Schiff and Ya'ari, (*Israel's Lebanon War*) in their account of the last week of the siege of Beirut, emphasize US pressures and Israeli Cabinet splits as hampering Israeli advance into West Beirut. But the defenders told stories of Israeli troops, imprisoned in their tanks, as easy targets for RPG-lobbing militia fighters.

14. Assertions by Israeli leaders in August that '2,000 terrorists' remained in West Beirut after PRM evacuation was interpreted by Palestinians as a sign of their intention to make a final push into the city.

15. Schiff and Ya'ari say that Sharon and Bashir met in East Beirut on 12 September to discuss two subjects – 'the purge of West Beirut and official negotiations with Israel – and understanding was achieved on both. Sharon wanted to be sure that the Lebanese Army would move into Beirut's refugee camps quickly and demanded that Phalangist units be sent in alongside . . . . "By October 15" Bashir promised merrily, "there won't be a single terrorist in Beirut!"' (*Israel's Lebanon War*, p. 246).

16. See M. Jansen, *Dissonance in Zion* (London: Zed Books, 1987).

17. Schiff and Ya'ari give Israeli war dead as 500 (p. 301) but this figure does not include the losses suffered during the occupation. A more inclusive estimate is 700.

18. Christian inhabitants of the Shouf were traditionally represented by Chamoun, who remained on relatively good terms with the Jumblats.

19. Yaniv (*Dilemmas of Security*, p. 231), presumably reflecting official Israeli estimates, gives a figure of 80,000 (between the Israeli border and the Awali River). H. Sharif, 'South Lebanon: Its History and Geopolitics', in E. Hagopian and S. Farsoun (eds), *South Lebanon* (Detroit: AAUG, 1978) gives approximately 135,000 for 1977.

20. 'One of the original, albeit unpublished, aims of Operation Peace for Galilee was to rid South Lebanon of the PLO so that the PLO would not have a base of operation should it ever attempt to infiltrate the area again.' Destruction of the camps during and after the invasion was part of this aim; subsequent orders not to allow their rebuilding had the intention of transferring their inhabitants north of the Awali; the Meridor Plan proposed dividing Palestinians up among several small, scattered camps, but American support was not forthcoming (Schiff and Ya'ari, *Israel's Lebanon War*, pp. 240–41).

21. J. Schechla, *The Iron Fist: Israel's Occupation of South Lebanon* (Washington: American Arab Anti-Discrimination Committee, 1985) p. 22.

22. Quoted by Yaniv, *Dilemmas of Security*, p. 284.

23. R. Selman, 'Azamat Isra'eel al-ma'iya wa al-miya Lubnan' (The Israeli Water Crisis and Lebanon's Water), *Majellat al-Dirasat al-Filastiniyya*, no. 3, Summer 1990.

24. Yaniv, *Dilemmas of Security*, p. 165.

25. Quoted by L. Rokach, 'Eyewitness Report of Torture in Lebanon', *Al-Fajr* (Jerusalem), 6 May 1983.

26. See 'Rebondissement de la guerre civil au Liban', Le Monde diplomatique, October 1983.

27. Fédération Internationale des Droits de l'Homme, *Report on Lebanon* (Paris, 27 January 1984).

28. S. Nasr, 'Roots of the Shi'i Movement', *MERIP Reports*, no. 133, June 1985.

29. See Petran, *Struggle over Lebanon*, p. 369, for details on the sectarian affiliations of the various brigades of the Lebanese Army.

30. See R. Khalidi, 'External Intervention and Domestic Conflict in Lebanon, 1975–1985', Wilson Center Working Paper no. 65, June 1985.

31. Y. Sayigh, 'Serious Commitment', *Middle East International*, no. 194, 18 February 1983.

32. See Schiff and Ya'ari, *Israel's Lebanon War*, pp. 292–7; Yaniv has a more detailed discussion, *Dilemmas of Security*, pp. 159–82.

33. For details of the Fateh split, see Y. Sayigh, 'Struggle Within, Struggle Without: The Transformation of PLO Politics since 1982', *International Affairs*, vol. 65, no. 2, Spring 1989.

34. Pakradouni liaised between President Sarkis (1976–82) and the Syrian government, and later became spokesman for the Lebanese Forces; he was closely associated with Bashir Gemayel and, after 1982, with Samir Geagea (see Political Glossary).

35. Petran, *Struggle over Lebanon*, p. 356.

36. Pakradouni gives a flattering portrait of Elie Hobeiqa in *Le Piège: de la malédiction libanaise à la guerre du Golfe* (Paris: Grasset; Beirut: FMA, 1991), p. 128, as well as details of Syria's imposition of Hobeiqa on the Lebanese Forces, Gemayel and his Tripartite Accord partners Jumblat and Berri.

37. E. Picard, 'La politique de la Syrie au Liban', *Maghreb-Machrek*, no. 116, Spring 1987.

38. On the fragmentation of the Lebanese Sunni community, see A. AbuKhalil, 'Druze, Sunni and Shi'ite Political Leaderships in Present-day Lebanon', *Arab Studies Quarterly*, vol. 7, no. 4, Fall 1985.

39. The majority of Sidon city's inhabitants are Sunni, as is 'Ain Helweh camp's large (approx. 35,000) population. One city quarter and several villages to the east of Sidon are Shi'ite, while the villages to the north and east are mainly Maronite. A small percentage of the city's population is Christian. As in Tyre, Sidon's Muslims and Christians have a long tradition of good relations.

40. G. Jada deals with this issue in 'The Role of Sectarian Consciousness in the Ideology and Organization of the Lebanese Ultra-Left (1975–1976)', MA thesis, American University of Beirut, 1985.

41. For a discussion of this concept, see E. Picard, 'De la "communauté-classe" à la résistance nationale'.

42. The PSP began its life with a cross-sectarian membership but became with time increasingly identified as Druze. Amal at first also included non-Shi'ites among its members, but Amal's stand towards the sectarian system has always been ambivalent, denouncing it, yet claiming to represent the Shi'ite community.

43. Attacks against Lebanese communists were carried out by Amal in West Beirut and the southern suburbs just before the Israeli invasion; in the South

under Israeli occupation; and in West Beirut between 1984 and 1987.

44. This conclusion is supported by the refusal of the 'national progressive' alliance to include even those PRM groups opposed to, or critical of, Arafat. (Interview with Salah Salah, member of the PFLP Political Bureau, 8 July 1986.)

45. Most of this section is based on 'Chronique de la lutte populaire', *Revue d'études palestiniennes*, no. 16, Summer 1985; and on S. Kassir, 'La Resistance nationale libanaise: quelques propositions' in the same issue.

46. Yaniv reports that at a meeting of *mukhtars* in the South in mid-June, an Amal leader expressed 'his movement's determination to fight alongside Christians and Israelis until the PLO in south Lebanon is totally emasculated' (*Dilemmas of Security*, p. 236).

47. 'Chronique de la lutte populaire', p. 36 (author's translation).

48. Interview with Jim Yamin, 'Eyewitness to the Iron Fist', *MERIP Reports*, no. 133, June 1985. For this period see also R. Fisk, *Pity the Nation: Lebanon at War* (London: Andre Deutsch, 1990), pp. 537f; Jim Muir in *Middle East International*, and Julie Flint in *The Guardian*.

49. *Revue d'études palestiniennes*, no. 16, Summer 1985.

50. Interview in *Journal of Palestine Studies*, vol. 17, no. 2, Winter 1987.

51. Berri visited Damascus in the week preceding the first Amal attack. On his return (16 May) he announced that Syria was willing to undertake a peace-keeping role in West Beirut after the disarming of the militias. Palestinians believe that it was during this visit that the decision to attack the camps was taken.

52. Interview with M. Hamadeh, March 1990.

53. Although the Murabitoun was disbanded after 14 April, with Koleilat fleeing to France, some of its elements remained and took part in the night attacks against Amal and the 6th Brigade that went on in the margin of the 'Battles of the Camps'. Later, in February 1987, a combination of leftist, PSP and ex-Murabitoun militiamen rose against Amal and almost crushed it.

7. Amal Movement and the Shi'i Awakening

To a Lebanese journalist who asked him why Amal movement had launched its attack against the Palestinian camps, Nabih Berri replied, 'To avenge ancient battles.'[1] Without taking this remark as literal truth, we can nonetheless see how it illuminates the historic grievances of the Shi'i sect, as well as the way history is invoked to justify – indeed to produce – actions taken in the present. There are at least two dimensions to the grievances of Lebanon's Shi'i community: first, those suffered by the sect as a whole, defeated in the struggle for succession after Muhammad's death, a defeat kept alive in the rites of 'Ashoura;[2] and second, those suffered by Lebanese Shi'ites in particular, in earlier periods as well as in the setup of the modern state, where they were marginalized by the Maronite/Sunni condominium embodied in the National Pact. Berri speaks here as leader of a movement that had risen to prominence by articulating the claims of Lebanese Shi'ites. Furthermore, he speaks at a moment when Amal's leadership felt it was riding the crest of a wave, within sight of achieving the aims put forward between 1969 and 1975 by the movement's founder, Imam Musa Sadr. As (Shi'ite) Mufti Qabalan said in a *khutbeh* (Friday sermon), re-telling an argument he had had with (Sunni) Mufti Hassan Khaled after the first camps' battle, 'The Shi'a have come out of the bottle and there's no force that can make them go back.'

This chapter will begin with a historical explanation of the political marginality of the Shi'a in modern Lebanon (the 'bottle' of Mufti Qabalan's metaphor), with indicators of the economic, social and cultural 'backwardness' that both accounted for, and perpetuated, Shi'i subordination in the structures of the state. It will point to the way that social relations within the sect, more polarized than in the case of Lebanon's other communities, made the mass of Shi'ites responsive to the appeals of radical parties such as the LCP and Ba'th. It was precisely in a conjuncture of growing protest and escalating Israeli attacks that a charismatic Shi'ite figure, Imam Musa Sadr, launched his Movement of the Deprived through which, by powerfully articulating Shi'ite grievances in historico-religious terms, he drew the

Shi'ite masses into sectarian frameworks, among them Amal movement. The last part of the chapter will place Amal in a rapidly changing regional, national and local (southern) environment, examining its 'revision' after the Civil War of 1975/6, and the new leadership that took over following Imam Sadr's disappearance in 1979. Amal's fluctuating relations with Syria and with the Palestinian Resistance movement are examined for clues of the alignments that led towards the Amal–Palestinian battles of 1985–87. A closer look at the struggle between different Shi'ite 'poles' for leadership of the sect, which became more intense in the aftermath of 1982, is shown also to be a factor in pushing Amal into this battle. A final section points to the preparations – political, ideological and military – made by Amal's leadership in the period before the battles began.

Historical background

The Shi'a were not latecomers to Lebanon. On the contrary, before the migration of the Maronites from Syria in the eighth century, Shi'i tribes were spread through Kisrwan, the North and the Shouf as well as in the two outlying regions associated with them today, Jabal 'Amil (South Lebanon) and the Beqa'. During the tenth and eleventh centuries, a Shi'i dynasty ruled in Tripoli, under the protection of Fatimid Cairo. But towards the end of the Crusades (*c.*1290) the Mamluks attacked the Shi'a for allegedly cooperating with the Crusaders, driving them out of Central Lebanon.[3]

Lebanese Shi'a belong to the main Twelver or Imami sub-sect of Shi'ism, and it is this common doctrine that links them to the Shi'a of southern Iraq and to Iran where Twelver Shi'ism was adopted as state religion after the Savafid conquest in the sixteenth century. The role of the Lebanese *'ulema* (men of religious learning) in instructing the Persians in Shi'ite doctrine has justly been a cause of Lebanese Shi'ite pride. Jabal 'Amil still forms part of a single cultural circuit with Kerbala, Najf and Qom. Possession of an ancient tradition of learning made the exclusion of the Shi'a from modern Lebanon's political, economic and cultural centres the more humiliating.

How did such exclusion come about? The Beqa' and Jabal 'Amil have not always been as impoverished and peripheral as in modern times. Until the late eighteenth century, South Lebanon was part of a production and trade circuit centred on the port of Akka and including northern Galilee, while Beqa' Shi'ites sold pastoral produce in Syria and took part in entrepôt trade between the coast and the inland cities. But punitive raids in 1771 by the Ottoman governor of Acre, Jazzar ('the Butcher'), destroyed agricultural stock and libraries alike, a blow from which Jabal 'Amil never recovered. More serious, because more permanent, were the new frontiers drawn up by the European powers after the defeat of Turkey in World War I.

Under late Ottoman administrative arrangements, the Beqa' and Jabal 'Amil both formed part of the *wilayat* (province) of Damascus; the Shi'ite *zu'ama'* (lords) took little part in the politics of Mount Lebanon during the late Ottoman period, nor in the structures – the Qaymakamate of 1842, and the Mutasarrifiya of 1860 – upon which the modern Lebanese state was built. Similarly, Shi'ites took little part in the flow of migrants to Beirut that, beginning in the early nineteenth century, built it up to become the leading port and trade centre of the eastern Mediterranean. But the political and economic peripherality of Shi'ite regions did not become fixed until 1920, when the Great Powers at Versailles drew the frontiers between French and British zones of influence, allocating Syria and Lebanon to France. By taking four formerly Syrian provinces and adding them to Mount Lebanon to create a more economically viable state ('Greater Lebanon'), France severed both Shi'ite regions from their habitual economic and political ties: 'From a zone destined to be no less flourishing than their neighbouring harbours south and north, Haifa and Beirut, the South of Lebanon had overnight moved to the periphery.'[4]

Shi'ite discontent with French Mandate arrangements persisted but, unlike the Druze, did not take the form of armed revolt.[5] In general the French were seen to favour, beside the Maronites, the non-Sunni sects. In 1926 they recognized the Shi'a as a millet (see Political Glossary) with their own Ja'fari rite and courts, possibly as a reward for Shi'ite non-participation in the Druze revolt of 1925.[6] The French also circumvented Shi'ite discontent by coopting the lordly families, granting them licences to grow tobacco and channelling all political favours through them.

French appeasement of the Shi'ite *zu'ama'* needs to be seen in relation to the active opposition of Lebanese Sunnis to separation from Syria, as well as to the Maronite hegemony that the French Mandate helped to establish within the embryonic structures of the state. Strongly entrenched in commerce and in the three largest coastal cities (Sidon, Beirut and Tripoli), the Sunnis posed a more serious threat to the existence of 'Great Lebanon' than did the formerly dominant Druze community, now an impoverished and mountain-bound 6.5 per cent of the population. In 1936 Sunni calls for union with Syria took a more organized form in the 'Conference of the Coast', an event that precipitated the formation of the Kata'eb party. Although Shi'ites from the South and the Beqa' attended the conference, most Shi'ite leaders did not support the pro-Syrian movement.[7] In this pre-independence period, Shi'ites were scattered across the Lebanese political spectrum, some supporting Emile Eddeh's pro-French National Bloc, others Bishara al-Khoury's Constitutional Bloc. A fairly substantial number of Shi'ites joined the Kata'eb party, some others the LCP and PPS. The Ba'lbek leader Sabry Hamadeh was associated with al-Khoury and Riad al-Solh, architects of the National Pact of 1943. The Shi'ite *za'eem* of

Tyre, Kazhem al-Khaleel, was a life-long member of Camille Chamoun's post-independence National Liberal Party. Dispersed and secondary within Lebanon's ruling elite, Shi'ite parliamentarians did not act together to voice the demands of their community.

In spite of the conflict between Maronites and Sunnis that had punctuated the Mandate period, it was between these two rival communities, the former heirs to the French, the latter heirs to the Ottoman Empire, that the National Pact of 1943, blueprint for independent Lebanon, was made. The underlying rationale is suggested by Petran: 'This compromise smoothed the way for the bourgeoisie, Christian and Muslim, to develop lucrative commercial and financial relations with the oil states.'[8] Among the most important of the Pact's provisions was the allocation of the top political offices on a sectarian basis, with the presidency going to the Maronites, the premiership to the Sunnis and speakership of Parliament to the Shi'a. It needs to be noted in relation to the National Pact, first, that the prerogatives and length of tenure (six years) of the presidency made this post in itself a guarantee of Maronite ascendancy; second, the distribution of offices was made without reference to the actual size of the communities. No census had been taken since 1932; because of its explosive potential, none has been taken since.[9]

Shi'ite parliamentarians such as Sabry Hamadeh, Kamel al-As'ad and Adel Osseiran were key players in the oligarchic political system. Hamadeh and al-As'ad between them formed a powerful electoral axis that practically controlled the Parliament, including presidential elections. Yet the legislature as a whole had little weight in comparison with the executive power of the presidency and, as already noted, the Shi'ite *zu'ama'* and deputies cared even less than other leaderships to increase state expenditures in the rural regions or the share of their sect in the offices of the state. When they exercised patronage, it was generally limited to members of their own families: at one time Speaker Sabry Hamadeh was rumoured to have more than sixty relatives on Parliament's payroll. At the same time, the economic, social and cultural development of the Shi'a lagged far behind that of the rest of the country. It was this flagrant gap that eroded the legitimacy of the Shi'te leadership, and formed the basis of the appeal of the various radical movements, secular and sectarian, that emerged in the 1960s and 1970s. It is to this gap, of which one manifestation was the class polarization that characterized the Shi'a more than other communities, that we now turn.

'A people oppressed in their own country'

Shi'ite political subordination in post-independence Lebanon has economic, social and cultural roots that feed into and reinforce one another, and account for the forms their political mobilization has taken. At the beginning of independence (1943), 85 per cent of Shi'ites lived in outlying rural areas engaged in agricultural or rural production. Land ownership was polarized into very large and very small holdings, with large landowners estimated to own three-quarters of the best land. For example, in the South four powerful families each owned around 4,500 acres, while in Ba'lbek-Hermel five families owned more than half the land.[10] A high proportion of Shi'ites were peasants who worked as share-croppers or wage-labourers on large estates, using their own unirrigated, less fertile plots for subsistence production. Although the South is rich in water sources, state projects to distribute water equitably have been held back by political corruption. Established as a cash crop since the late nineteenth century, tobacco production has been a focus of Shi'ite discontent. With crop size and prices fixed by a monopoly (established under the Mandate) which systematically favoured the larger producers, small tobacco planters had no alternative outlet; and as tobacco factory workers they suffered low wages and refusal of union rights. In the Beqa' a similar cartel controlled the production of sugar beet.

With independence, modern capitalist agriculture began to penetrate Lebanon's outlying provinces, bringing water pumps, chemical fertilizers, tractors, usury and debt. Peasants were increasingly forced off the land as both subsistence agriculture and share-cropping declined. State neglect and economic non-development of the outlying areas meant that there were few alternatives to agricultural labour, intensifying the poverty of peasant households. The development of a Shi'ite middle class was held back by low levels of commerce, services, and private and public construction. After 1948, southerners also suffered from wage cuts caused by the availability of Palestinian refugee labour.

An idea of the poverty of the Shi'ite community is given by income estimates made by demographer J. Chamie. He gives the average Shi'ite family income (*c.* 1970) as LL4,532 (US$1,500) compared to the national average of LL6,247 (US$2,082). More significantly, Shi'ites constituted the highest percentage of families with less than LL1,500 (US$500) a year. It must be remembered that average Shi'ite family size is higher than the national average.[11]

Low rural incomes were exacerbated by the low level (or absence) of state services to the outlying provinces compared with those of Mount Lebanon. In the early 1960s half the villages of the South had no running water and were not linked to roads; in the Beqa' the proportion was even higher. None had electricity. More serious was the lack of schools. More than half the children of the South were reckoned to be without schooling in the early 1960s; in the Beqa', again, the situation was worse. Medical services were primitive: three clinics in the South, one hospital for the whole Beqa'. Such low levels of state expenditure were primarily the result of Lebanon's liberal economic system, which meant low taxes and corrupt practices of public tender and inspection. One study estimates that the South, with 20 per cent of the country's population, received less than 0.7 per cent of the state budget.[12]

Shi'ite educational levels reflected this state neglect. One reliable source gives a figure for Shi'ite illiteracy in 1943 as 68.9 per cent compared with 31.5 per cent for Catholic Christians; other figures show that by the early 1970s, 50 per cent of Shi'ites were unschooled compared with a national average of 30 per cent; and that only 6.6 per cent of Shi'ites had university education compared with 15 per cent of Sunnis and 17 per cent of Christians.[13] Their educational deprivation formed a basis for other Lebanese to stereotype Shi'ites as primitives and peasants, and as a reason for excluding them from high-level posts in government. A Lebanese scholar recalls that in the 1950s, Beirutis spoke slightingly of Shi'ites without fear that there would be any present to take offence: 'They were porters, boot-blacks, street-cleaners – non-persons.'[14]

The poverty of the Shi'a also held them back from setting up the sectarian sociocultural institutions – schools, orphanages, clinics, charities – developed by other sects to compensate for lack of public services. Leading Sunnis had begun to found such institutions in the late 1930s, perceiving the critical role they played in the social advancement and political hegemony of the Maronite sect. Philanthropy is a product of a modern business bourgeoisie, and only began among the Shi'ites in the early 1940s when a returning migrant from Africa, Rashid Beydoun, founded the 'Amiliyeh School for boys. An anecdote told by the above-quoted scholar tellingly indicates the vast gap between Shi'ite rich and poor. In the mid-1960s he accompanied a boy from a remote Beqa' village to be interviewed for a scholarship by the board of directors of the 'Amiliyeh School. The board members were all wearing diamond rings; the Shi'ite boy had managed to attend school by riding an hour by donkey from his village home.

Ruralism and 'backwardness' blocked Shi'ites from improving their economic situation by moving into urban-based occupations such as commerce or state employment. Banking and import/export trade, the two dominant sectors of the Lebanese economy, were mainly in the hands of Greek Catholics and Sunnis, with growing Maronite and Orthodox participation by the early 1940s. Sunnis controlled the market for grain, meat, fruit and vegetables. The non-participation of Shi'ites in these sectors was both linked to, and expressed in, the slightness of their settlement in Beirut, the city whose importance as port and commercial centre for the whole eastern Mediterranean had been growing throughout the nineteenth century. In 1943, only 3.5 per cent of Beirut's commercial centre was Shi'ite.

and only 6.8 per cent of the city's population as a whole. The few Shi'ite businessmen who tried to break into sectarian-based business networks had a hard time of it.[15] The slightness of their demographic/economic foothold in Beirut constituted a serious obstacle to the advancement of the Shi'ite community in proportion to the concentration of economic activity in the capital.[16] Another source of blockage to Shi'ite social mobility arose from the tightness with which their most influential *zu'ama'* exercised their traditional prerogatives of patronage. Where most other sectarian leaders sought state employment and promotion for members of their electorate or sect, Shi'ite *zu'ama'* either restricted such favours to their own families, or refused them altogether.[17]

Shi'ite absence from the higher levels of the Lebanese state is exemplified by the fact that, in 1962, they occupied only two out of seventy senior civil service positions; as late as 1984, only one in twelve Lebanese ambassadors was Shi'ite.[18] Full sectarian breakdowns for the various sectors of the state are unobtainable, but it is generally accepted that Shi'ites form the majority of the lower levels of all sectors of the state apparatus, including the army and police. In this respect, Shi'ites differ from most other Lebanese communities, whose members are not drawn by state employment, given low public-sector salaries and more favourable opportunities in the private sector. The situation of the Shi'a as a large but oppressed sector within the 'bureaucratic class' helps to explain their ambivalent stand towards the state, oppositional and yet 'Lebanist'.

Under President Chehab (1958–64), the state began to bring water, roads, electricity and schools to remote rural areas. Although this point is contested, Chehab is also said to have increased the access of Muslims to higher-level state positions. Chehab's reforms did little to create employment in the rural hinterland, or to stem the mass exodus of landless villagers, but they are seen as important for the Shi'a in bringing about two kinds of change: (i) the expansion of schooling raised literacy levels and, with the establishment in the 1960s of low-cost universities, helped to enlarge the Shi'ite intellectual stratum, while the presence of teachers in villages provided an alternative leadership to that of the lordly families and *'ulema*; (ii) the expansion of local government bodies under Chehab was beneficial to Shi'ites by increasing their access to state employment, extending contact points and lessening people's dependence on the *zu'ama'* and deputies.[19]

Migration, urbanization, politicization

Shi'ite emigration – a result of their economic blockage – began later than that of Maronites and Druzes, moved in another direction and touched a different class. Beginning in the late nineteenth century, the educated sons of small shopkeepers and artisans in provincial towns such as Tyre and Nabatiyyeh began to seek their fortune in West Africa. Their loss was deeply felt by the community, who blamed the *zu'ama'* for failing to find employment for 'the flower of our youth' in the capital. In Africa Shi'ite migrants occupied a middleman position, with many becoming extremely wealthy, for example in the diamond trade. However, Shi'ite emigration was also more temporary than that of other communities, with growing African economic nationalism as well as new investment openings in Lebanon causing high rates of return of migrants and of capital. Back in Lebanon Shi'ite *mughtaribeen* (returned migrants) formed an active new business stratum interested in gaining a share in Beirut banking, trade and real estate, as well as in developing the South, e.g. through agrobusiness and tourism. The emergence of this class was crucial in providing impetus and financial backing for Amal movement.

Mass rural-to-urban movement, beginning in the late 1950s, involved all Lebanon's outlying rural areas, with Shi'ites forming the largest sectarian component. By 1975, it is estimated that as much as 40 per cent of Lebanon's rural population had left the land, and an even higher proportion (60 per cent) from the South, where Israeli aggression from the late 1960s added a new source of migratory pressure. Most Shi'ite settlement took place in the suburbs around Beirut and by 1975 is estimated to have reached a figure of 315,000, about one-third of the population of Greater Beirut. At first the authorities were not particularly worried by Shi'ite settlement close to Palestinian camps.[20] But by the mid-1960s the build-up of Shi'ite settlement began to have its own disturbing social and political implications: the erection of illegal housing on privately owned land, confrontations with the army, and the encirclement of Beirut by the *hizam al-bu'us* ('misery belt') that extended into the Christian eastern sector of Beirut as well as the mainly Muslim western one. The radical shift in the sectarian balance among the inhabitants of the capital, in addition to the poverty of the newcomers, posed a threat as much to Sunnis as to Maronites.

The effects of urbanization on Shi'ite life and politics were not unidirectional. If anything, displacement seems to have strengthened local and community ties, while at the same time introducing new sources of social and ideological differentiation. The suburbs were a place where Shi'ites from South Lebanon mixed with Shi'ites from the Beqa'; where many were radicalized and joined the 'Opposition' parties or Palestinian Resistance groups, but where also Shi'ite rites such as 'Ashoura were reaffirmed, thus becoming fertile ground for sectarian mobilization.[21] Although ties with the *zu'ama'* were weakened, they were not altogether cut: at election times people were bussed back to their natal villages to vote for the 'bek'.

By 1975 (the eve of the Civil War), the Shi'ite community is estimated to have grown to 750,000, forming probably 30 per cent of the Lebanese population, the largest single sectarian community. Their former ruralism was now radically reversed, with two-thirds of Shi'ites urban in residence, and more than half living in or near the capital. Their class profile has also been greatly modified, with intermediate strata emerging to fill the wide income and status gap that used to divide the *zu'ama'* from the peasants and tribesmen. Among these new strata were three of particular political significance: (i) a bourgeoisie based on returning migrants, who aspired to convert their wealth into a stronger role in Lebanese politics; (ii) an expanding stratum of salaried urban workers; and (iii) an industrial proletariat (including migrant workers in the Arab Gulf). Similarly to the Palestinians (and unlike the Lebanese Sunnis), Shi'ites have also entered the intellectual professions in relatively large numbers; as school and university teachers, lawyers, political thinkers, publishers and film-makers. Nasr describes them as an 'amibitious and radicalized intelligentsia' intent on challenging the poverty of their community.[22]

Such rapid economic and sociocultural displacements could not but have effects on Shi'ite politics, pressing intellectuals, workers, students and indebted peasants into the 'Opposition' parties: the LCP (established in the South from the early 1940s), as well as the Ba'th (particularly strong among students), the ANM, the PPS and, at the end of the 1960s, the Organization of Communist Action and the Arab Socialist Action Party. By the early 1970s Shi'ites are said by several sources to have formed the majority of the progressive, secular parties, although, contrary to what later sectarian movement leaders often alleged, they were not just the 'cannon fodder' of the progressive parties, but also leaders and ideologues.[23] Shi'ites also joined the Palestinian Resistance movement from the time when operations from Lebanon first began. Most of those who joined were students, but there was also support from the villagers which was critical in allowing the *feda'yeen* freedom of movement. Most of the 'Opposition' parties formed clandestine militias in the border villages as Israeli attacks intensified; Shi'ite villagers supported *feda'yeen* action in early confrontations between the PRM and the Lebanese Army. Without such support the PRM would not have been able to wrest from the Lebanese government the right to launch military operations against Israel from South Lebanon, embodied in the Cairo Accords of 1969.

The movement of Shi'ites into the progressive parties and Resistance groups was as disturbing for the Shi'ite leadership as for the Lebanese authorities, but at first aroused no adequate response. The *zu'ama'* were too firmly entrenched in their fiefdoms and oligarchic alliances to feel personally threatened. The Shi'ite clergy, unworldly and anti-political, were helpless in the face of leftist arguments. The threat posed by the left to Shi'ite solidarity as well as to the Lebanese system was felt most acutely by a still embryonic alternative leadership, educated younger men, deputies, lawyers and businessmen who rejected the limited mentality and corrupt methods of the *zu'ama'*, but who were anti-leftist, suspicious of Arab nationalism and did not want to get rid of the Lebanese sectarian system, only to make it fairer. Such men had nowhere to go politically. As one of these 'new men' said of Shi'ite politics before the arrival of Musa Sadr, 'It was the politics of polarities: feudalism, *al-iqta*, on one side, extremism, *al-tatruf*, on the other. A new way had to be found.'[24]

While the radical displacements of the Shi'ite community arose from a specific situation of poverty and marginality, they were yet part of broader upheavals taking place in Lebanese society as a whole, more worrying to the authorities only because of the former quietism of the community and its growing demographic weight. Picard points to the many economic, social and cultural transformations of the 1960s that provoked alarm among those with most to lose by radical change: rapid income growth with increasing polarization of wealth; growth of industry, a working class and union organizing; strikes by farmers, workers, teachers, students, fishermen; mass protests and demonstrations; calls for restructuring the army, reforming electoral law, and – most alarming of all – for deconfessionalization. The country's political and religious leadership was also disturbed by a loosening of family and religious ties, and the spreading of class consciousness and secularism.[25]

Musa Sadr and Shi'ite sectarian mobilization

The arrival of Musa Sadr as Mufti of Tyre in 1959 introduced to Shi'ite and Lebanese politics a leader who combined the attributes and skills needed to mobilize the mass of Shi'ites on a sectarian basis; and by doing this, to shake the Lebanese political system. He was a cleric, and profoundly Shi'ite Muslim in orientation, but he was also widely read, understood the appeal of modern ideas and could handle their challenge. His unusual qualities and the timing of his arrival – at the beginning of Chehab's presidency, just after the Muslim uprising of 1958 (during which the Beqa' Shi'ites had taken up arms against the government) – combined to ensure that he 'immediately found his way into the Lebanese establishment'.[26]

Concerned to curb the rise of Nasserism and the left, as well as to strengthen the Lebanese state and weaken the *zu'ama'*, Chehab was on the lookout for 'new men'. Musa Sadr fitted this description well and Chehab rapidly legitimated the newcomer by granting him Lebanese nationality. Later he donated state funds to the boys' vocational school that Sadr set up in Bourj al-Shemali, near Tyre.

There is no doubt, either, of the ready welcome given to Sadr by 'political Maronitism'. Michel al-Asmar, Maronite intellectual and founder of the Cénacle Libanaise, 'believed that the Shi'a and the Maronites were the two principal communities of Lebanon, that bridges ought to be built between them as a way of offering an ideological alternative to the Sunni–Pan Arab conception of Lebanon'.[27] Al-Asmar championed Musa Sadr from the beginning, inviting him to speak at the Cénacle, introducing him into other circles and speaking of him as 'the coming man'. Maronite leaders such as Chamoun and Gemayel supported moves to set up the Higher Shi'ite Council which would be Sadr's vehicle to formal leadership of the community.

Musa Sadr's intelligence, dynamism and powers of oratory put him in a class of his own, overshadowing the usual run of Lebanese politicians. Such outsize qualities naturally polarized Lebanese reactions toward him: on one side admiration verging on hero-worship; on the other, deep suspicion. Shi'ite reactions were equally ambivalent even though coloured by pride that one of their own should have achieved such eminence; Sadr's championing of the poor was dismissed by many of his co-religionists as simply a means to power. Though Lebanese in origin, Sadr was born and brought up in Iran and viewed by many Lebanese Shi'ites as too Iranian. Uncertainty as to his ultimate purposes disturbed even his closest Lebanese associates.[28]

Sadr's first decade in Lebanon (1959–69) was spent in energetic social institutional work which established him as foremost Shi'ite and a national figure. Much of this work was inconspicuous: establishing youth clubs in villages; visiting Shi'ite communities in Beirut, the Beqa' and Africa; arbitrating between feuding clans in Hermel; and discussing the problems of the sect with men who would become the inner circle of his movement. But in addition he undertook a series of actions that brought him into the centre of national politics and gave the Shi'a a visibility in Beirut that they had lacked before. These actions drew attention to Sadr's readiness to cross sectarian boundaries, and to his breadth of vision: he spoke from a church pulpit, in the Cénacle, at the American University, and was also closely associated with the Greek Catholic social reformer Bishop Gregoire Haddad.[29] In addition, Sadr was as much a hit in Beirut salons (a centre of oligarchic politics) as in public meetings, a living challenge to the stereotype of Shi'ites as primitives and peasants.[30]

His election as first president of the Supreme Islamic Shi'a Council (SISC) in 1969 was a turning point in Sadr's career, crowning ten years of untiring preparation, and launching a new period of open sectarian mobilization. The SISC was in itself an important landmark for Lebanese Shi'ites. Up to this time they had not had a separate representation, but had been represented by the Sunni-dominated Higher Muslim Council. The idea of a

Shi'ite institution had long been supported by the Maronites for obvious divide-and-rule reasons, but there had been opposition to it from Shi'ites who feared that it would not only cause Sunni–Shi'ite tension but also, more seriously, intra-Shi'ite divisions.

Musa Sadr used the SISC as a legitimate position from which to articulate Shi'ite demands, to represent the community to the government and to the outside world, and to activate the Shi'ite masses. The many actions undertaken by Sadr as SISC president fall into four main 'lines': (i) in June 1973, the SISC presented the Lebanese government with a list of sixteen Shi'ite demands for which Sadr continued to campaign;[31] what was novel about these demands was that they were accompanied by the threat of the resignation of all thirteen Shi'ite ministers and deputies if there was no response; (ii) Sadr also received a flow of visitors (diplomats, journalists, Lebanese politicians) at the SISC office in Hadeth, overlooking Beirut, where he expounded his views on Lebanese, regional and world politics;[32] (iii) as a religious/state official, Sadr was able to render an important service to President Asad's regime by issuing a *fatwa* (a religious decree) clearing the Syrian 'Alawi sect of the charge of heresy (although an offshoot of Shi'ism, the 'Alawis had adopted so many pre-Islamic elements into their faith that it had always been questionable whether they could be called Muslims); (iv) Sadr also embarked on the series of religious/political mass rallies that took the name of the Movement of the Deprived (MOD). Without the legitimacy conferred by the SISC, it is doubtful if such a campaign would have been possible.

Sadr was a frequent visitor to Arab leaders and capitals, dramatizing the story of South Lebanon as it increasingly became a target of Israeli attack, and enhancing the representation of the Shi'a at the regional level. Among Arab leaders, his closest relationship was with President Asad of Syria.

What was the political/ideological colouring of the Movement of the Deprived? In a detailed analysis, Nasr points to both universalist and specifically Shi'ite themes in Sadr's discourse, fused by stressing Shi'ism's history as a movement of the oppressed against usurpers and tyrants.[33] In many of his speeches Sadr claimed to speak for all the oppressed: 'The Movement of the Deprived works to obtain justice for citizens deprived of their rights, whatever category they belong to.' Yet that Sadr was primarily addressing fellow Shi'ites is clear from the occasion of his speeches and rallies (Shi'ite commemoration days), their sites (Nabatiyyeh, Ba'lbek, Tyre), and, above all, his choice of a language saturated with Shi'ite themes and symbols.[34] He spoke to Lebanese Shi'ites most specifically in appeals to their pride and militancy: 'Our name is not Metwalis [see Political Glossary] but those who refuse, revolutionaries, insurgents against tyranny even if we have to pay with our blood.'

Like the Lebanese National movement, Sadr called for militant action to achieve a more just social, economic and political order. His denunciations of the ruling class (although he did not use the term 'class') were virulent: 'usurpers', 'profiteers', 'exploiters', 'those who suck the blood of the people'. He accused the Lebanese state (*al-sulta*) of criminal negligence in failing to defend the people and land of the South against Israeli aggression; and of systematically depriving the Shi'ite community of resources for development. Sadr called for a more just distribution of state employment and expenditures, but he was much less clear about reforming the political system than the LNM. He did not attack the confessional system in itself but called for adjustments to make it less discriminatory. Even when the Movement of the Deprived took part in labour strikes, it slogans remained 'socially general', avoiding targeting employers or the economic system.

Like the PRM and LNM, Sadr identified Israel as the primary enemy, but whereas they defined Israel as the enemy of the Arab nation, as aggressive in its structure and as an organic part of American imperialism, Sadr expressed Israel in Islamic terms – as Evil, as the enemy of Islam, or as coveting Lebanese land and water.

Again in contrast to the LNM, which based its discourse on Arab nationalist ideology, Sadr expressed a firm Lebanese patriotism and associated the Shi'a with Lebanon's existence: 'It is Shi'ites who guard Lebanon's frontiers, it is Shi'ites who work the Lebanese soil.' Sadr also took care to avoid including the Army in his criticisms of the Lebanese state: 'Whenever it was given orders, the Army defended [the country] with tooth and nail.'[35] This was an important nuance since the majority of lower-income Shi'ites had a son in the Army.

Up to 1975, Sadr's movement was closely associated with the LNM, joining in the same strikes and demonstrations, raising similar demands. Sadr in his speeches supported not only the Palestinian cause but also the Resistance movement and its right to struggle against Israel from South Lebanon. Like the LNM and PRM, he called for mass armed struggle, saying in a much-remarked speech at a rally in the Beqa' in March 1974, 'Weapons are the decoration of men', presaging the formation of Amal, initially the military wing of the Movement of the Deprived. Jaber suggests that Sadr's support for the PRM was tactical: in 1969, the *feda'yeen* were so strongly implanted in the South that to have access to Jabal 'Amil, Sadr needed Palestinian goodwill.[36] At the same time the alliance with the PRM gave Sadr's movement respectability in the Arab world. But relations between Musa Sadr and the PRM leadership were not close. Pakradouni quotes one of Sadr's criticisms: 'The Palestinian Resistance movement is not a revolution because it doesn't have a sense of martyrdom.'[37] He was no closer to LNM leaders than to those of the PRM. Pakradouni says that he was 'anti-communist but above all anti-Jumblatist', accusing Kamal Jumblat of responsibility for the prolongation of the Civil War of 1975/6, and of wanting to 'fight the Christians to the last Shi'ite'.[38]

At the end of 1973, when it became clear the government was not going to respond positively to the SISC demands, Musa Sadr increased the momentum of his mass rallies and heightened his verbal attacks against the state. During 1974, the crowds attending his rallies were the largest in Lebanese history, and their fervour sent shivers down oligarchic backs. This was the peak phase of the Movement of the Deprived, when the Imam (as his followers titled him) succeeded in three basic aims: drawing Shi'ite deputies and Cabinet members into a single bloc supporting SISC demands; demonstrating his capacity to shake the state; and sapping the influence of his primary antagonist, Speaker Kamel al-As'ad, both inside Parliament and in his fiefdom in the South. In December 1974, in a by-election at Nabatiyyeh, Sadr's candidate Rafeeq Shaheen defeated the candidate of al-As'ad by 20,000 votes to 7,000; both the leftist candidates (LCP and Ba'th) were also defeated. The Imam had taken up the causes of the left but expressed them in a religious language that had greater resonance for most Shi'ites. Sicking and Khairallah put the difference well: 'the leftist currents are those of intellectuals who are attempting to mobilize the masses, while the Shi'a movement is a mass movement joined by intellectuals.'[39]

Elections held that year for the SISC's leading committee showed al-As'ad without a single supporter, while the leftists had moved closer to Sadr: 'Five or six years after its emergence, Imam Sadr's Movement has largely succeeded in providing the Shi'ite community with a strong and unified politico-ideological leadership.'[40]

Amal Movement and the Civil War of 1975/6

Amal's existence was accidentally revealed by an explosion during a military training session near Ba'lbek in July 1985, in which some thirty trainees were killed. This event forced the announcement of the formation of a new militia, the Afwaj al-Muqawwimeh al-Lubnaniyyeh (Amal), a hitherto secret Shi'ite commando group formed probably in 1974, to defend the South against Israeli attacks.

Since the establishment of his movement Imam Sadr had called on the Lebanese state to defend the South or, failing that, to give the people arms to defend themselves. During his great rallies of 1974 the theme of armed struggle became a central element in the Imam's speeches, linked not only to Israeli attacks but to the Shi'ites' historic struggle against oppression and the injustice of their situation in Lebanon. At Ba'lbek (17 March) and Tyre (5 May), the Imam called on the crowds to take a sacred oath to carry arms against tyranny. An analyst of Sadr's discourse remarks:

The threat of using force against the state is continually present in [his] public interventions: calls to arms, encouragement to carry arms 'the decoration of men', and the veiled threat of destroying the Lebanese system: 'The whole Shi'ite community has openly declared its position: either it is justly represented at the centre of the Lebanese political system, or this system will fall without any regrets.'[41]

It was thus entirely logical that the Movement of the Deprived should form its own militia wing. Furthermore, by 1975, most other Lebanese political parties and movements had militias, a trend encouraged by the growing tension and clashes that preceded the Civil War. Of Amal's early history little has been written, even in studies of the movement.[42] It has been taken for granted that Amal issued from the Imam himself and the small inner group that surrounded him; yet our knowledge of the politics of this group remains shadowy. The Imam's earliest military adviser was an Iranian, Mustafa Shamran, who was a leading element in the Khomeynist revolution; and even though Amal's political leadership remained formally in the hands of men like Husseini and Berri, it seems possible that the conflict between 'Lebanist' and 'Iranist' tendencies within the Shi'ite movement (later to irrupt in the Amal–Hizbollah battles of 1985–90) already existed in embryo in Amal.

It is of interest to note that the first group to help Amal with training and arms supplies was Fateh. This was a relationship that continued despite mutual recriminations, suspension of relations and open conflict right up to (and after) the 'Battle of the Camps'. The Imam's movement was never part of the PRM/LNM coalition but there was close cooperation between them in the demonstrations and strikes that preceded the Civil War. Personal as well as political differences separated Sadr from both Jumblat and Arafat.

Formed mainly of unpaid or poorly paid 'volunteers', Amal's size has fluctuated from 800 in 1975, a few score in late 1982 and 14,000 in 1985.[43] Political decision within Amal has remained firmly in the hands of a politburo supposedly elected by party members (mainly urban middle class), while the militia is formed of youths from the poorest strata, without voting rights; this reproduction of class structure within party hierarchy is characteristic of all Lebanese and Palestinian party/militia formations, and explains the remarkable stability of their leaderships.

The disclosure of Amal's existence came three months after the 'Ain al-Romaneh 'bus massacre' from which most historians date the beginning of the Civil War.[44] The second round of heavy fighting started at the end of August. In his study of the Civil War, Salibi suggests that it was the threat of mass Shi'ite militarization that tipped the Maronite rightist decision to prepare an all-out attack.[45] Yet however large Amal's potential size, it was too newly formed to play a significant part in the Civil War; Khalidi hardly mentions it in his review of fighting forces.[46]

However, the main factor that weakened Amal's role during the Civil War (as well as putting an end to the MOD) was the vacillations of Imam Sadr. Having contributed as much as anyone to the collapse of the state and the militancy of the ultra-Maronites, Sadr drew back on the brink of war. It is possible that he had not intended to shake the state as effectively as he did; possibly also he underestimated the readiness of the Maronite militias for pre-emptive action. Although using the language of war for political ends, the Imam was not prepared for the reality of the Lebanese Civil War, with its large-scale destruction and sectarian killings. As the clashes escalated, Sadr embarked on a series of actions – sit-ins, hunger strikes, calls to end the fighting, meetings with leaders on both sides – that appeared to backtrack on everything he had said and done over the past three years. Gone were the calls for social justice and Shi'ite militancy in claiming their rights.[47]

A more fundamental divergence between Sadr and the LNM/PRM appeared, however, with Syrian intervention in March 1976 to save the Maronite rightist forces from defeat, thus restoring the sectarian/political equilibrium that Damascus judged vital to Syrian security and interests. Imam Sadr supported Syrian intervention, joining the short-lived pro-Syrian Front of Patriotic and National Parties, formed to weaken the LNM/PRM.[48] In retaliation, the Joint Forces closed down all Amal's offices in West Beirut.

One particular phase of the Civil War concerns us since it left a legacy of suspicion and bad feeling between Amal and the PRM. This was the campaign carried out by the rightist militias between January and August 1976, to 'clean out' all Palestinians and Muslim Lebanese (most of whom were Shi'ite) from the 'Maronite enclave'. Beginning with the mixed Palestinian/Lebanese shantytown of Qaranteena (19 January), the Lebanese Front forces besieged and attacked one low-income settlement after another, expelling the survivors into West Beirut. Although Palestinians and Lebanese Shi'ites were equally victims of this fascist demographic purge, as often happens in defeats there was mutual recrimination. At a critical moment in the siege of Tell al-Za'ter, on 6 August, the neighbouring Shi'ite shantytown of Naba' ceded, facilitating the final assault and storming of the camp on 12 August. Palestinians blamed a follower of Imam Sadr, Sheikh Muhammad Yaqoub, for making a deal with the Maronite forces that saved the inhabitants of Naba' at the expense of the Palestinians.

Shi'ites were equally bitter about the scale of their losses, with Imam Sadr accusing LNM leader Kamal Jumblat of being ready to carry on the Civil War 'until the last Shi'ite'. Shi'ite families expelled from the 'Maronite enclave' mainly settled in the southern suburbs, which later became Amal movement's principal demographic base outside the South. Much of Amal's appeal as a Shi'ite-led movement working for Shi'ite goals grew out of the Civil War experience in which Shi'ites were killed fighting (as they came to see it) for 'others'.

Imam Sadr emerged from the Civil War discredited with all parties: the state, the Maronite right, the LNM/PRM coalition, and even with many of his own followers. In Lebanon's post-1976 geopolitical space he had nowhere to go except to the South, the Shi'ite heartland from which he had begun his meteoric rise only sixteen years before. Little is known about his activities between the end of the Civil War and his disappearance in 1978; his English-language biographer passes this period over in a few pages.[49] It is reasonable to suppose that, together with his inner circle, he reviewed the history and current situation of the movement, identifying mistakes and making plans for the future. From his post-war conversations with Pakradouni, in which he blamed the Maronite right, but even more sharply the LNM/PRM alliance, for the disasters of the Civil War, one can discern the germ of Amal movement's ambition to form a 'third force', allied neither to right nor left but pursuing Shi'ite and Lebanese interests.

In eclipse between 1976 and 1978, the figure of Imam Sadr was resuscitated and endowed with new iconic power through his mysterious disappearance on a visit to Libya in August 1978. Responsibility was never finally established, although the Qadhafi regime remained the primary suspect; rumours and accusations continued to reverberate. Whatever really happened, it is certain that the Imam became an even more powerful mobilizing symbol in his absence than he had been in his life. As the 'vanished Imam', he recalled Shi'ite religious tradition, while the manner of his disappearance seemed to repeat the Shi'ite history of persecution and betrayal at the hands of Sunni despots. Many Lebanese Shi'ites continued to believe in his eventual return, and until now the annual commemoration of his disappearance serves as an occasion to unify and mobilize the community.

Amal Movement from 1978 to 1985

One effect of Imam Sadr's dramatic disappearance was to bring the movement he had founded back from decline to a renewed vigour and popularity. The post-Sadr Amal differed in many respects from the parent movement: in leadership, policies, structure and, perhaps most importantly, in the Lebanese and regional framework surrounding it. The early 1970s had been a time of LNM/PRM popularity, supported at least verbally by an array of Arab governments. In spite of many setbacks, the Arab nationalist tide still appeared the dominant one. But with Sadat's visit to Jerusalem (November 1977) and separate peace with Israel (March 1979), disarray and division deepened in the Arab world. By the end of 1979, with the overthrow of the Shah, Iran emerged as a Shi'ite Muslim power centre, a model and inspiration for Lebanese Shi'ites and a counterweight to Arab Sunni regimes increasingly associated with capitulation and corruption. In those parts of Lebanon controlled by the LNM/PRM there was a loss of revolutionary momentum, the result of many factors: political stagnation, external attacks, internal conflicts, infrastructural breakdown, the loss of Kamal Jumblat. But the most serious development was the escalation of Israeli aggression against the South. A foothold for attacks from Lebanese territory had been created after the Civil War by the establishment of a border strip manned by Lebanese Army and militia forces under the command of Major Sa'd Haddad. Haddad not only implemented Israeli policy against PRM forces, restricting their operations, but also directed heavy artillery bombardments against Palestinian and Lebanese residential areas throughout the South. The election victory of Likud and Menachem Begin in May 1977 brought about an instant escalation in both Haddad and Israeli attacks.

In March 1978 occurred the first full-scale Israeli invasion of South Lebanon, the 'Litani Operation'. Although ostensibly in retaliation for a PRM operation that reached Haifa,[50] Israeli spokesmen admitted that their real objective was to expand the strip commanded by Major Haddad into a 'Security Zone'. During the 1978 invasion, around 1,000 civilians were killed (IRC estimates), many in atrocious ways. Eleven villages in the Tyre province were completely destroyed and altogether about 250,000 people were displaced, many permanently. The Chamber of Commerce and Industry for the South estimated losses to the agricultural sector at LL165 million.[51] Although Palestinians were also killed and their homes destroyed during the invasion, Lebanese human and economic losses were higher. That Palestinian Resistance groups acted in classic guerrilla manner, withdrawing before superior force, fuelled Lebanese resentment. Israeli air, naval and artillery attacks became a daily feature of life in the South; although they often took PRM operations as pretext, as in the case of the March 1978 invasion, the scale of Israeli attacks was grossly out of proportion to PRM attacks, which were reduced after 1976 in an effort to accommodate Syrian interests in avoiding a major confrontation.

Subjected since the late 1960s to Israeli attacks, by 1978 the inhabitants of the South had had enough. Their earlier anger against the Lebanese state and Army for not defending them had by the end of the 1970s been transformed into anger against the Resistance movement whose presence was ostensibly the cause of Israeli aggression, and against the Arab states for failing to help to defend them. Just before his disappearance Imam Sadr had been engaged in yet one more mission to solicit Arab aid for the martyred South. Thus the post-1978 Amal movement took off from a basis of growing

Shi'ite regional power and growing local Shi'ite anger.

Amal's new leadership inherited much from the movement's founder, including his aura and the veneration created among the masses by the circumstances of his disappearance, his image and his speeches. But, freed from his overpowering presence, Sadr's successors could set Amal movement on a more pragmatic, more parochial course. Although Amal benefited from the new prestige of Iran's Islamic Revolution, in fact the new leadership distanced itself from Sadr's Iranian connections. (This was one reason for the subsequent emergence of a pro-Iranian Shi'ite movement antagonistic to Amal: Sadr himself bridged this latent rift.) The new Amal chose to stress its primordial commitment to Lebanese sovereignty and territory, identifying itself with the Lebanese nation. In his study of Amal movement, Norton underlines the ideological and practical aspects of this Amal/Shi'a/Lebanon identification, pointing out that 'the Shi'a must preserve Lebanon in order to preserve the social and political integrity of their community.' He also quotes from Berri: 'If the partitioning of Lebanon and the settlement of people [i.e. Palestinian refugees in Lebanon] cause significant damage to some, they would absolutely annihilate Harakat Amal.'[52]

In other respects Amal's ideology remained deliberately vague and all-embracing, allowing the movement to 'swing with the Shi'ite wind' (to quote AbuKhalil) and to avoid the danger – ever-present in Lebanese politics – of being left behind by sharp turns of events or the popular mood. The new leadership were all secular men (Sadr had few followers among the local Shi'ite clergy) and they lacked the Imam's Islamic beliefs and references. Not only were they less religious, but their Shi'ism differed from his. He had believed in, and expressed, a Shi'ite interpretation of world history; they were focused on the political and material interests of a specific Shi'ite community. They went even further, fusing the meanings of 'Shi'a' and 'Lebanon' in a way parallel to the earlier Maronite identification of their community with Lebanon. This again contrasts with the way Sadr identified Lebanese Shi'a with the 'oppressed' at large, claiming social justice for all the deprived, whatever their sect. The discourse of the new leadership was and is populist in style, but focused on the defence of the Shi'ite community rather than on the rights of all Lebanese workers and poor peasants.

Although Amal's charter attacks 'loathsome sectarianism', in its membership and actions the movement has nevertheless been almost entirely Shi'ite. Furthermore, the charter contains no specific proposals for reforming Lebanon's sectarian system and although, as the majority of the Lebanese population, Shi'ites have nothing to lose through deconfessionalization, Amal leaders have only occasionally called for this. Towards the Lebanese crisis, Amal has developed that aspect of Imam Sadr's policy that emphasized dialogue, keeping a foot in both camps. Sadr was ready to accept Franjiyyeh's National Charter of 1975 even though this would have transformed the Maronite right to the presidency into a constitutional principle instead of a mere 'understanding'. Since 1978, Amal's leadership has repeatedly underlined its support for a strong state capable of defending Lebanese territory and interests. It has frequently appealed for a return of the Lebanese Army 'even if 100 per cent Maronite' to the South.[53]

Although constrained by Shi'ite memories of their brutal expulsion from East Beirut in 1976, there is no doubt that Amal leaders would be ready to come to terms with the Maronite right if a suitable occasion arises (as indeed happened in Damascus in December 1985, when Amal, the LF and the PSP signed the Tripartite Agreement). Amal's objections to 'Maronite–Sunni dualism' are not so much directed against the principle of a sectarian regime, as against Sunni monopoly of Muslim representation.

For Amal after 1978, defence of the South becomes fundamental. Sadr always evoked the sufferings of the South as a symbol of oppression and injustice, but for the new leadership the South assumed a more concrete meaning as a specific territory where 80 per cent of the population is Shi'ite and which, along with Beirut's southern suburbs, forms the main demographic basis of the movement. That a special relationship exists between Amal and South Lebanon is clear from the movement's charter, where it is said that 'the motherland cannot survive without the South, and there can be no true patriotism without fidelity to the South.'[54] References to the South are obligatory in Amal leaders' speeches, and Amal actions have similarly underlined the connection. For example, in September 1980 the movement took over the office of the Mejlis al-Janoub (Council of the South), a fund set up by the government supposedly to compensate victims of Israeli attack, but said to give money only to homes adorned by portraits of Kamel al-As'ad. In April 1984, when Berri was invited to join Karameh's 'National Unity' cabinet, he insisted that a ministry of state for the South should be established and that he should be put in charge of it.

Ideological emphasis on the South reflected the shift that took place after 1976 in Amal's base and representativeness. Imam Sadr had been equally popular among the semi-tribal Shi'a of the Beqa' as with the villagers and businessmen of the South; and Amal's first fighters had come mainly from the Beqa'. After the Civil War, the movement's centre of gravity shifted definitely southwards. Even though Amal continued to recruit among the displaced of the southern suburbs and in the Beqa', the more important local commanders were in the South. This shift was also reflected in Amal's leading committees where, with the exception of Akef Haidar, most members were southerners. (This was one reason for Islamic Amal and Hizbollah's relative strength among Beqa' Shi'ites.)

In terms of regional alliances, Amal has been particularly careful to underline its political and financial independence. Not to take 'foreign money', not to play outsiders' political games – these have been a basic element in Amal's ideological appeal to Shi'ites, as well as supporting its 'Lebanist' image. Contributions mainly from wealthy Shi'ite migrants have enabled Amal to claim to be the only political force in Lebanon that does not depend on outside support. As noted earlier, relations with Iran were attenuated. Amal's much closer relationship to Syria, which will be discussed later, has been subject to real fluctuations as well as to a policy of de-emphasis.

As to other political forces in the Lebanese arena, Amal has also marked its distance from them, even while joining the various short-lived pro-Syrian fronts. Amal's aloofness is based both on its 'Lebanism' and on Shi'ite demographic superiority which guarantees its primacy, as long as it succeeds in capturing representation of the sect. Whereas the small groupings of the LNM were forced to coalesce by the difficulty of their project, Amal's mass support and pragmatism make it both possible and desirable to avoid any but short-term alliances. Amal's radically different stand towards the PRM, which became clearer after 1978, has been a main line of demarcation between it and its pre-1976 allies for whom, on the contrary, support for the PRM was a binding element.

In structure, Amal movement changed in several ways. While retaining the image of spontaneity and volunteerism that had characterized its predecessor, the Movement of the Deprived, the new Amal built a nucleus of 'responsibles', leaders of functional sections such as security or military affairs, as well as leaders of specific localities. Local leaders and cadres doubled between military and political functions: most Amal militiamen carried on civilian lives after taking basic military training, only fighting in times of conflict. This was one reason for the fluctuating size of Amal militia forces, and for their frequently poor military performance. The control of the civilian leadership over the military (a sensitive point in all such formations) has been maintained in Amal's case by keeping the head of the military section a relatively subordinate post, as well as by a system of checks and balances which prevents any one leadership level from becoming too strong. As already noted, militiamen are not part of the voting group that elects Amal's two controlling bodies, the Politburo and the Executive Committee. In this way Amal has so far succeeded in avoiding the kind of rebellion of youthful fighters against aging politicians that, in the 'Maronite enclave', produced the split between the Lebanese Forces and the Kata'eb (Geagea's *intifada* of 12 March 1985).

Because it is a movement and not a party, Amal remains far less centralized and hierarchical than, say, the Kata'eb, the PPS or LCP. It is characteristic of a movement that local leaders who join it bring with them personal followings, thereby retaining a measure of political and ideological independence, and subscribing only to the broadest of the movement's aims. As Norton notes in the case of Amal, its regional and local representatives retain a large measure of autonomy (indeed to call them 'representatives' is somewhat misleading).[55] This structural looseness allows Amal to incorporate members with often contradictory orientations, and enables it to claim to represent a circle of supporters much larger than its actual membership. The disadvantages appear during crises in the form of internal dissension, or sudden, sharp drops in popularity. Amal's ideological heterogeneity and structural looseness have been very visible during two recent crises: first the Israeli invasion of 1982, when some southern leaders welcomed the invaders while others resisted; and again during the 'Battle of the Camps', when many members disapproved and many fighters dropped out.

With Amal, as with most other Lebanese political formations, organigrams, charters and internal regulations give little key as to what forces keep particular leaderships in place, or how political decisions are actually arrived at. Memberships are usually little more than democratic façades to hidden structures; leadership elections are usually influenced by external factors. Particularly influential in Amal's case has been the group of wealthy backers who help finance the movement. There have been accusations that Amal militiamen have been used in the interests of this group, both in particular incidents such as driving out refugee squatters from a beach where a tourist hotel was planned, and in a more general way in the battles against the Palestinians, whose operations endanger the economic development of the South.

Amal and the Palestinians

What caused the sharp deterioration in Shi'ite–Palestinian relations between 1976 and 1982? This subject has never been examined carefully, most writers contenting themselves with repeating a stock list of Shi'ite accusations against the Palestinians and leaving it at that. The situation was obviously more complex. Without minimizing the seriousness of the mistakes committed by the Palestinians, we should at least attempt to look at all the factors at work.

Unquestionably the most important factor was Israel's calculated policy of raising the cost to the inhabitants of the South of the PRM's presence. Although Palestinian bases and camps were also targeted, the Lebanese suffered greater economic loss and disruption. The scale of Israeli retaliation was out of all proportion to PRM attacks. An unpublished study giving details of frequency and type of Israeli attacks against the South, carried out before 1982, shows the disparity between Palestinian and Israeli attacks; for example, in a single day (16 May 1974), Israel air-raided six Lebanese villages as well as 'Ain Helweh and Nabatiyyeh camps, causing more than 300 dead and wounded and immense destruction; more raids were carried out the following day. This was in retaliation for the PRM attack on a paramilitary youth training school at Maalot in which between 21 and 28 Israelis were killed. In relation to Israeli attacks against South Lebanon, it needs also to be noted that the PRM on several occasions halted its operations: in June 1972; after the October 1973 war; after the Shtoura Accords of 1977; after the March 1978 invasion. In July 1981 it accepted and abided by a total freeze. In contrast, reductions of PRM activity were met with Israeli escalation.[56] Given the low frequency of PRM attacks, it is clear that, short of ending resistance altogether, there was little more the PRM could have done to reduce damage to the South.

State compensation to Lebanese victims of war damage was so corruptly distributed that the name of the responsible body, the Mejlis al-Janoub, was changed to the Mejlis al-Jayoub (Council of Pockets). The conditions in which refugees from war in the South lived in Beirut were worse than those of Palestinian camps.[57] With no hope in sight of ending Israeli attacks or the flow of refugees, shantytown conditions increased resentment against the Palestinians, increasingly seen as the cause of southerners' sufferings.

Then there was the problem of PRM fighters' behaviour in the South. Palestinians admit that a sharp step downward was taken after 1971, when PRM fighters began to carry weapons openly in villages, a practice that had been strictly prohibited before. The number of fighters increased at about the same time, as a result of the transfer from Jordan. Their visibility drew Israeli retaliation against the villages, while their behaviour began to approximate to that of an occupying army. There were stories of petty theft, requisitioning property, whistling at girls and treating village elders without respect.

However, the accusations are more serious than that. A typical list includes 'ugly acts of theft, rape, crimes, extortion and oppression'.[58] A villager told Norton, 'We gave the Palestinians everything and they gave us back insults, corpses, and a lesson in corruption.'[59] Mafia-like rackets thrived throughout all the militia-controlled areas, pointing to the gap between the high-sounding slogans pronounced by LNM/PRM leaders and the actual practices of their men on the ground.

Could such Mafia-like behaviour have been controlled? Answers to this question vary. Some people say that the PRM did punish offenders but that people forgot the punishment and only remembered the crime. Others say that small incidents became exaggerated through talk; others that these were the faults of a 'popular army', the faults of the people themselves. It is probably also fair to say that there was no real concept of revolutionary discipline within the PRM leadership. If Fateh's own security apparatus, Corps 17, was one of the most disreputable of PRM institutions, how could it be expected to instil order?

Another source of problems was the proliferation of fighting groups in the South. Whereas in the early days there had been only Fateh and the ANM (later PFLP), by the mid-1970s there were some nine different Resistance organizations as well as several Lebanese militias. Clashes between them were inevitable, sometimes over petty issues such as territory or supplies, sometimes over differences of ideology or because of conflicts between the governments that funded them. Thus there were clashes between Sa'eqa and the pro-Iraq ALF (see Political Glossary) and, after the beginning of the Iraq–Iran war in 1981, between the ALF and Amal. Tension was also growing between Marxist/secular groups (such as the DFLP, the LCP and OCA) and the Muslim militias (at that time mainly Amal). Such a situation made it easy for third parties to spark off clashes that caused civilian losses and resentment. A certain Sidon strongman, Abu Arida, said to have shelled the Sidon souk in April 1982, causing extensive damage which was blamed on the PRM, turned out to be an Israeli agent who was later implicated in the car-bomb attack against Mustafa Sa'd in February 1985.

Thus, a third factor that cannot be discounted is the presence of Israeli and other agents, who worked in various ways and disguises to deepen the rift between the people of the South and the PRM. The looseness of recruitment practices in all but a few of the groups made it easy for agents to infiltrate them. For example, a Fateh commander particularly notorious for Mafia-like behaviour, 'Azmi Sgheyer, disappeared in the mêlée of the Israeli invasion of 1982, confirming suspicions that he was an Israeli agent. There is also little doubt that several Amal cadres doubled as Israeli and/or Deuxième Bureau agents.[60]

One of the functions of agents was to spread hostile propaganda against the PRM. Small incidents were immediately blown up and spread around. More serious than this, however, was the campaign to convince the southerners that the real purpose of the PRM in their land was not to liberate Palestine but to set up a substitute state. This accusation, made credible by the amassing by the PRM of heavy weapons combined with reduction of Resistance operations, did more than anything else to arouse Shi'ite hostility. While corrupt elements in the PRM, racketeers like Abu Za'eem, might have been content to stay forever in Lebanon, this was not true of the mass of Palestinians for whom this country had meant little but loss. Yet the historic Shi'ite experience of oppression made it easy for them to believe that the PRM intended to lord it over them forever.

Given the vital importance of the South to the Resistance movement, the question arises whether the leadership knew to what point the situation was deteriorating; and if it did, why was so little effort made to stop the downward slide? A Shi'ite friend who was a member of a Resistance group from 1968 to 1975 says that he first saw mistakes being made in 1970/1, but that 'no one would listen'. At no level of the Resistance movement was the question of PRM relations with the Shi'a taken seriously. The core of the problem as he saw it was, 'They used the South as if it was a piece of land with no people on it. As long as it could put them on the political map, they didn't care what happened. I know, because that's the way I used to think myself.'[61] The speaker identified the indifference of the PRM leadership to the sufferings of the people of the South as Sunni arrogance towards Shi'ite 'underdogs'. Yet the issue could equally be defined in other terms, for example the problem of lack of revolutionary discipline, or of the status of military men in Arab societies. That it was defined primarily in sectarian terms can only be explained by Shi'ite sectarian mobilization in the late 1970s.

Thus a fourth factor is the crystallization of a perspective separating out Lebanese Shi'ite interests from those of Palestinians and setting them in opposition. While many historical and contemporary factors contributed to the rise of Shi'ite sectarian consciousness (including PRM mistakes), Amal movement was the party that, to a great extent, made this its primary goal and *raison d'être*. Given Amal's Lebanist orientation, its sense of proprietary rights over the South, its drive to reconstruct the Lebanese state and gain stronger representation within it for the Shi'a, it could not but contest the PRM presence. Even if the PRM had been better disciplined, the conflict was inevitable.

In the last eighteen months before the 1982 invasion, confrontations between Amal and sections of the PRM/LNM grew in frequency and seriousness. At the beginning Fateh tried to stay out of these clashes so as to preserve the role of arbiter in what it saw as squabbles between leftist and Islamic, or pro-Iraqi and pro-Iranian, groups. However, as Amal's new military capacity to challenge the PRM became evident in greater tactical skill and the closing off of parts of the South to PRM access, Fateh began to use heavy artillery against Amal positions, causing serious damage which of course further intensified Shi'ite hostility. For example, in one such clash, the Joint Forces shelled the village of Hanawayy, near Tyre, causing heavy damage.

In February 1982, Amal–PRM clashes spread for the first time to Beirut. The issue was an LNM proposal to form neighbourhood Popular Committees to deal with everyday problems caused by absence of the state. The PRM backed this proposal, which responded to mass needs and went no further than forms of self-administration already established by the Lebanese Forces and the PSP. Amal opposed it on the grounds that such a move would encourage partition. The ensuing clashes demonstrated that Amal movement was now a force to be reckoned with in Beirut itself.

During and after the siege of Beirut in 1982, Amal–Palestinian relations returned once again to alliance. A Palestinian-supported Amal unit based near Aramoun effectively held back an Israeli landing near Ouzai. Though few in numbers, Amal fighters in the southern suburbs fought beside the PRM and Murabitoun in defending West Beirut. After the war, Amal was re-armed mainly from PRM sources in the Beqa'. Fateh also helped Amal financially, on the basis of their common antagonism to Israeli occupation of the South and to the Gemayel regime. According to a Palestinian source, the last such payment was made only a week before the beginning of the 'Battle of the Camps'.

Amal within Shi'ite politics

In explaining Amal's decision to attack the Palestinian camps in mid-1965, we need also to take into account the state of Shi'ite politics. This is because, in common with the other sectarian militias, Amal's legitimacy ultimately rests on its ability to capture and hold the representation of the Shi'ite community. This logic has held on both sides of the 'Green Line', producing violent confrontations between groups seeking to monopolize the representation of one or other of the main sectarian communities.

The disappearance of Imam Sadr removed from Lebanese Shi'ite politics the only figure able, even if incompletely, to hold together its divisive tendencies. Amal's new leaders aspired to continue his centralizing policies but, though supported by important social strata, they have not been able to prevent the emergence of several challenges to their leadership.

The least serious, so far, has been that of the *za'eem* stratum. The most powerful of these, Kamel al-As'ad, has remained in national politics. He was Speaker of the National Assembly from 1972 to 1984, and was instrumental in the election of Bashir Gemayel as President in 1982. But he has been forced to live in the 'Maronite enclave' and is unable to visit his domain.

Whereas Sadr combined in himself both official Shi'ite representation (as head of the SISC) and popular representation (as leader of the Movement of the Deprived), now these two functions are split and potentially in conflict. Presided over by Sheikh Mehdi Shamsideen, a cleric and jurist, the SISC has become a rival centre of influence, with greater appeal than Amal for most of the *'ulema* and for others favouring a reconstruction of the Lebanese state with minimal reforms. After his election as Speaker in October 1984, Hussein Husseini became another pole of Shi'ite influence, allied with Shamsideen. This 'centrist' group does not have a mass base and therefore cannot challenge Amal directly, but it can erode support for its leadership through informally expressed criticism. The thrust of this group's criticisms against Amal is its illegitimacy as a militia. Militia politics, they argue, have brought nothing but chaos, gangsterism and civilian suffering. Whatever Amal's claims to defend the community and the nation, by eroding legality and state institutions it is dangerous to both. (At the same time, 'centrists' are thankful that Amal is there to confront Hizbollah, a group that they view as far more dangerous.) 'Centrist' critiques certainly formed one of many pressures upon the Amal leadership to undertake decisive action against the Palestinians, since by doing so Amal would be seen as acting on behalf of the state, and as representing legality. Berri, in his speeches during the battles, constantly underlined the theme that Amal was making sacrifices for the sake of all Lebanese.

At the same time, by furthering Syria's aims at a Lebanese settlement based on the three main sectarian militias (the Tripartite Accords), Amal's leadership could hope to ensure itself against the threat of dissolution of its militia base, making it far less vulnerable to 'centrist' campaigns.

Although this charge could not be made openly, Berri was also accused by the 'centrists' of being too close to Syria. All Shi'ite leaders in West Beirut (like other 'Opposition' leaders) publicly supported Syria's special role in Lebanon, but to 'centrists' Berri's lack of any power base in Shi'ite or Lebanese politics outside Amal made him dangerously dependent on Syrian backing to maintain his leadership position.

Thus in 1985 the other, possibly more serious, challenge to Amal arose from the more Islamic, more anti-Israel and anti-Western groups supported by Iran. Two such militant Shi'ite groups, Islamic Amal and Hizbollah, had demarcated themselves from Berri and Amal movement during the invasion of 1982, setting up bases in the Beqa' with tacit Syrian approval. In 1982/3 both these groups accused Berri of being too ready to cooperate with an American-backed Kata'ebi regime. The speed with which Hizbollah commenced attacks against the Israeli occupation (and against US bases) was an implicit criticism of Amal's slowness to embark on resistance. Militant Shi'ite propaganda against Berri at this time focused on the fact that he had an American 'green card' and owned petrol stations in the United States.

Hizbollah contrasted with Amal in many ways. As in Iran, its fighters were closely supervised by clerics; they also received more rigorous military training than Amal fighters, and were much better paid. Financed by Iran, Hizbollah also set up an impressive complex of social institutions – schools, religious study circles, orphanages – which disseminated its ideology and brought in recruits. Such sociocultural support was particularly attractive to war-displaced and rural migrant Shi'ites because of their poverty and the absence of state services in their areas. Amal did not have the means or will to set up similar services, terming them in its charter as 'entice(ment) with charity organizations'. Although Hizbollah later lost much of its esteem and popularity,[62] in the period preceding the 'Battle of the Camps' its star was still rising. Its support by some of the most respected Shi'ite *'ulema*, in particular Sheikh Muhammad Hussein Fadlallah, highest Shi'ite reference in Lebanon, also exposed Amal on its weakest side, that is its reputation for religious laxity and political opportunism.

These challenges from within the sect formed one kind of pressure upon the Amal leadership in the period from February 1984 to May 1985. The movement had reached a peak of mass support, prestige and power as a result of its role in the February uprising, as well as in the escalation of mass resistance in the South. At the same time there was nothing stable about this ascendancy, which was challenged from within the sect as well as by all the other political forces now free to act again in West Beirut. Berri's dilemma was to consolidate Amal's gains and avoid becoming trapped in the dangerously fluid situation in West Beirut, where the February uprising had been followed by a sharp deterioration in security, with kidnappings and assassinations becoming almost daily events. As the group that had guaranteed public order after the expulsion of Gemayel's army, Amal stood to lose most from this return to chaos. In this situation, its leadership may well have calculated that a decisive pre-emptive blow against the Palestinian camps would not only remove the latent Palestinian threat to Amal's complete hegemony over West Beirut and the South, but it would also increase the movement's popularity with the Shi'ite masses, and once and for all establish its paramountcy within Shi'ite politics, giving it an uncontested right to negotiate any eventual Lebanese settlement in their name. Disciplining the Palestinians would also show Amal acting in a quasi-governmental role, underlining its support for Lebanese sovereignty and winning it credit with other anti-Palestinian forces, especially the Lebanese Forces and most of the Lebanese Army.

Amal's relations with Syria

The relationship between Amal movement and the Syrian regime did not have a clear beginning, nor has it ever been explicitly defined or acknowledged beyond the same general affirmation of Syria's special role in Lebanon made by all the nationalist/progressive groups. Rather like quasars in the universe, one has to infer Syrian–Amal relations from events rather than from formal declarations. If the relationship can be called an alliance, it is one that has not followed a straight, undeviating line, but has gone through periods of dissonance as well as convergence. Furthermore, the question of Syria is one that has caused dissension within Amal as well as within political Shi'ism (though far less intense than the dissension caused by relations with Iran).

Musa Sadr's friendship with President Hafez Asad may be taken as a starting point. The basis of their *entente* is said to have been their shared opposition to the Shah and support for the Khomeynist revolutionaries: Sadr was the architect of the Syrian–Iranian alliance of the 1980s.[63] It is safe to assume that the two men shared the same hostile view of the leadership of the PRM. (It will be recalled that Asad's 'corrective' coup in November 1970 ousted the leftist wing of the Ba'th leadership which attempted to intervene in the clashes in Jordan in support of the Palestinians.) The service done to Asad by Imam Sadr's *fatwa* concerning 'Alawi orthodoxy has already been referred to (p. 168), and suggests that Amal's founder was concerned to secure Syrian sponsorship for his budding movement. His support for Syria's intervention in the Lebanese Civil War in 1976 is an even clearer sign. As Seale notes, 'In the difficult summer of 1976, a crucially delicate moment of Asad's career, [Sadr] did him an important service by keeping the Lebanese Shi'a community out of Kamal Jumblatt's leftist coalition which Syria was at the time trying to rein in.'[64]

That alignment between Amal and Syria was a fundamental aspect of the reconstructed Amal which emerged after the Civil War is suggested by the fact that Syria now became Amal's main source of arms and training. Between 1976 and 1982, the Syrian presence in Lebanon took the form of participation in a joint Arab peace-keeping force, the Quwwat al-Reda', which was prevented by an informal American/Israeli 'red line' from deploying south of the 'Awali River. Norton suggests that Syria found it useful to have an ally in this critical area.[65]

It would be a mistake, however, to view Amal's leadership as unconditionally pro-Syrian in this or any other period. Their potential divergence is illustrated most clearly by an event in 1979 when a meeting of the Front of Steadfastness (opposed to Camp David) was held in Damascus. At the end of the meeting, Colonel Qadhafi announced his intention of visiting Beirut, and received an official invitation from the Lebanese government. The fury of Lebanese Shi'ites was expressed by Amal movement which, led at that time by Hussein Husseini, called out massive demonstrations in the Beqa' and Beirut which effectively blocked the Libyan leader's visit. 'It was the first time,' a Shi'ite informant says, 'that there was a demonstration in Lebanon on *a Lebanese issue*. It was an explosion against everyone: against Qadhafi, against Sarkis [President of Lebanon], and against Syria.[66] As the Libyan leader's host, the Syrian leadership was blamed by Lebanese Shi'ites for extending hospitality to the man they held responsible for the disappearance of Imam Sadr. On this occasion, the Syrian regime was the target of mass Shi'ite anger expressed and directed by Amal.

In 1980 Nabih Berri replaced Husseini as chairman of Amal's Politburo. It was said at the time that Berri's election was influenced by Arafat (Husseini's hostility to the PRM was well known, sharpened by incidents such as a rocket attack on his home). If Arafat indeed intervened, it could have been partly to please the Syrians. PRM–Syrian relations were in a benign phase at this point, with Syrian military forces in Lebanon facing a revival of Maronite hostility activated by Bashir Gemayel, and Arafat eager to strengthen the anti-Sadat Front of Steadfastness. Berri had been a member of the Ba'th before becoming one of Musa Sadr's inner circle during the launching of the Movement of the Deprived. Unlike Husseini, he did not have a basis of leadership outside Amal (Husseini was a deputy and member of a noted family of *'ulema*), nor close links with other influential Shi'ite figures, and therefore had little potentiality for welding Amal into an independent force.

Syrian/Amal divergence reappeared during and after the Israeli invasion of 1982. From Damascus, Berri may have been viewed as too ready to take part in an American-sponsored Kata'ebi regime. Bashir Gemayel had begun campaigning for the presidency at least a year before the invasion and among his moves had been the sending of emissaries to Amal, as well as hints that his regime would be built on a Maronite–Shi'ite alliance.

From the end of the war, Amal's stand towards President Amin Gemayel and to the US 'protectorate' was one of equivocation and wait-and-see. As noted earlier, Amal did not join the Lebanese National Resistance Front; neither did it denounce peace negotiations with Israel nor the presence of US troops in Lebanon. There were many reasons behind Berri's hesitation: the shock of the invasion; weakness and division within Amal movement; the collapse of the LNM which, although Amal was not a member, nevertheless had been a partner in opposing Maronite rightist projects of partition; and renewed challenges for leadership of the Shi'ite community from Speaker Kamel al-As'ad and Sheikh Mehdi Shamsideen. From the perspective of Damascus, Berri must have seemed insufficiently militant in opposition to the post-invasion order. That relations between Amal and Syria went through a latent phase between September 1982 and February 1984 is further suggested by Berri's non-attendance at the meeting that launched the National Salvation Front in July 1983 (see p. 140), giving as his reason a wish not to be seen to be too close to the Syrians.

The February 1984 uprising was a major turning point in Amal–Syrian relations. It changed the balance of forces not only between the Maronite right and the national/progressive forces, but also between the groupings within the 'Opposition'. Berri emerged from the uprising confirmed as Amal and Shi'ite leader, paramount among the array of parties and militias who would in the coming period vie for control over West Beirut. It was not the size or quality of Amal as a fighting force that seemed to promise it hegemony (although its potential size was certainly greater than that of any other party), rather it was three other factors: first, as the first Shi'ite leader to call on Shi'ite soldiers in the Lebanese Army to lay down their arms rather than kill co-religionists, Berri reaped the political advantage of reminding all Lebanese that this central national institution rested on a Shi'ite base; second, he had demonstrated that Shi'ite demographic strength in the southern suburbs could be translated into effective action in the capital; finally, Amal's mass base in the South, coupled with the swing in Shi'ite feeling against the Israeli occupation, gave it the potentiality for leading a *jihad* (holy struggle) against the occupying forces, with the reasonable hope that after eventual IDF withdrawal Amal's control over the South would be uncontested. All that would then remain would be to connect hegemony in the South with hegemony in West Beirut to make of Amal the most powerful actor in the coalition facing political Maronitism. For the first time since the launching of the Shi'ite movement, some of its objectives appeared within reach.[67] One cannot doubt that this sudden change of status affected Syrian perceptions of Amal.

On the national level, Berri's enhanced status as Shi'ite leader was quickly acknowledged as Premier Karameh invited him to join the post-Lausanne 'national unity' government (the first time that Amal was represented at Cabinet level). The protracted negotiations that went on over his participation (dubbed at the time the 'Shi'ite knot') were a clear sign of Berri's new power as Amal and Shi'ite leader. Karameh offered him the Ministry of Water and Electricity but Berri refused, saying that the sectarian balance had changed, the Shi'a were more powerful than before and this must be recognized by offering him a more important, more political portfolio. Eventually the Ministry of State for the South was created for him. In addition, Berri claimed the right to countersign all payments made by the Council for Development and Construction (CDC).[68] These moves were signals to the community that he was determined to champion Shi'ite rights; to some observers they were also steps towards achieving the Maronite/Shi'a 'dualism' that was, Amal leaders believed, destined to replace the old Maronite/Sunni dualism.

It is difficult to determine exactly when the interests of both the Syrian government and Amal movement in preventing the re-emergence of the Palestinians as an independent factor in Lebanese politics converged to the point of a decision to attack in force. Consultations in Damascus between Khaddam and all the 'Opposition' leaders including Berri intensified between the February uprising and the beginning of the camps' battle. Many Palestinians believe that it was at Berri's 15 May visit to Damascus that the final plans were laid; others say that the decision to ignite the conflict was not Berri's but came from other quarters within Amal. There are also Shi'ites who believe that the camps' battle was designed by the Syrians to break *both* Amal and the Palestinians. All that can be said with certainty is that Syria gave Amal discreet logistical and political support during the first round of fighting, and afterwards it resupplied Amal with arms (including fifty T-54 tanks), as well as greatly improving its military training.

Drawing the battle lines

Among the preparations for subjugating the camps, ideological and political mobilization played a more important role than military planning. Those concerned to prepare public opinion to support or accept such a move had to work on several different levels. First, Amal militiamen had to be prepared to attack the camps; second, the Shi'ite community as a whole had to be prepared to support the battle; third, Lebanese public opinion needed to be convinced that disarming the camps was necessary and the attack justified. The first task was perhaps the easiest for, even though Amal contained an Arab nationalist, pro-Resistance current, the movement as a whole was already strongly mobilized on a sectarian basis and was the spearhead of Shi'ite anti-Palestinianism. Existing ideological trends also made it likely that the Shi'ite community in its majority would support the subjugation of the camps since not only would this reduce the likelihood of future Israeli attack, but it would also make it easier to control the large number of Palestinians living in mainly Shi'ite areas.

As to broader Lebanese public opinion, existing trends also to some extent favoured Amal's project. While all the parties that had formed the LNM still supported the Resistance in principle, most were now more or less closely linked to Syria. Beyond the nationalist/progressive circle was a large segment who believed in the absolute priority of the reconstruction of the state and who saw the Palestinians as threatening this aim. In spite of their hostility to Syria and to Syria's Lebanese allies, Maronite opinion also remained anti-Palestinian, albeit less fiercely so than before 1982. Yet even so, Lebanese support for the disarming of the camps by force had to be produced rather than assumed. This was so because of the high level of politicization in Lebanon, a polity where public opinion is neither apathetic nor easily deceived. True, a move to pacify the camps in 1985 would not provoke the massive demonstrations that supported *feda'yeen* freedom of action in 1969. Yet outside a limited circle, such a move would be an unpopular one, the more so because the group executing it (Amal) enjoyed little support outside its own sectarian/regional clientele. Even though Amal leaders would argue that, in moving to disarm the camps, they were acting on behalf of legitimate authority and in the name of all Lebanese, few outside a segment of the political class would be convinced by such arguments. Others would look for the particular calculations and interests that prompted this move. Inevitably, too, they would ask which external power was behind it (the eternal question of Lebanese politics).

Furthermore, although by 1985 probably the majority of Lebanese no longer supported the right of the Palestinian camps to autonomy and self-defence, for all except an anti-Palestinian minority the opinion was that disarmament of the camps should be undertaken by a legitimate authority and should not precede the disarmament of all the unofficial militias.[69]

It was in the context of the need to win the support of Lebanese beyond the circles of the Shi'a, the ultra-Maronites and the centrists (strong state

supporters) that the campaign against the 'return of Arafat' found its rationale. By 1985 memories of the 'excesses and deviations' of the Resistance movement had faded under the weight of more recent hardships such as those caused by the Israeli occupation, renewal of the civil war, economic crisis and Lebanese militia battles. The spectre of the 'return of Arafat' served as a reminder of the ills of an earlier period, and of the devastation the country had suffered as a result of Israeli retaliation against the Resistance movement, resurrecting dormant fears and resentments.

The anti-Arafat campaign served also to deepen already existing divisions within the Palestinian community, encouraging Amal's expectations that the pro-Syrian Resistance groups would either support their move or stand aside. Although in fact the camps' battle at first brought about a reunification of Palestinian ranks, this did not heal the rift over Arafat's leadership, which continued throughout and after the sieges, sparking internal battles. The issue of Arafat similarly divided the one-time LNM groups, offering the more pro-Syrian elements a justification for standing on the sidelines, and weakening support for the camps.

The campaign against the 'return of Arafat' began early in 1985 and took several forms: speeches by Amal leaders, newspaper articles, news items and 'events'. As an example of the latter, at a much-publicized meeting with Ibrahim Koleilat (leader of the Murabitoun) the Fateh dissident leader Abu Saleh, on a visit from Damascus in March, declared that Palestinians would soon be returning to Beirut in large numbers. A few weeks later came the Amal–Murabitoun battle, with the Sunni militia accused of integrating 'Arafatists'. During this period unsubstantiated news stories appeared, claiming that Fateh safe houses and arms caches had been found in West Beirut. A Lebanese journalist comments:

> There isn't any doubt that there were political, ideological and informational preparations. 'No to return to the situation before 1982!' – Amal created this slogan and it was taken up by circles close to Amal or to Syria. For example, during that period weekly articles appeared in *al-Safir* by Abdullah al-Amin – he liaised between Amal and the Syrians during the 'Battle of the Camps' and later became Secretary General of the Ba'th Party in Lebanon. The gist of what he said . . . was that the men with covered faces, the hooligans and gangs of Arafat are preparing to come back and sabotage the situation in Lebanon.[70]

Speeches made by Amal leaders before and during the Amal–Palestinian battles combined the theme of a return of 'Arafatist' fighters with evocations of Shi'ite resistance and liberation of the South. For example, at a rally in the South on 12 May, only days before the first attack, according to Abukhalil, Da'oud 'stressed that Palestinians would not be forgiven for their "crimes", and publicly pledged not to allow the return of Palestinian fighters to Lebanon. He said, "We want them to return, but only to subject them to punishment." [71]

At the same rally, Mufti Qabalan contrasted the success of Lebanese Shi'ite resistance against Israel with the failures of the PRM and the Arab regimes. These themes were taken up by Amal leaders after the beginning of the battle. For example: 'Those who have liberated the land at the cost of their blood have the right of decision.' [72] Nabih Berri at his press conference of 21 May said: 'A return of the Palestinian masquerade to the South is strictly forbidden . . . It's no longer permitted to anyone to fight until the last southerner . . . There's no question of a return to the situation that prevailed before 1982.' [73]

Whatever Arafat's real intentions towards Lebanon, [74] there is no independent evidence of the return of large numbers of Fateh loyalists before the 'Battle of the Camps'. After the conflict had started, many fighters returned to help defend the camps, in spite of Israeli attempts to prevent this by a sea-blockade. But before the Amal attack, return of Palestinians was limited to a small number who had left with the PLO in 1982 and whose homes were in Lebanon; furthermore, of those who returned, many belonged to the pro-Syrian Resistance groups. Moreover, the situation in Lebanon in 1985 differed radically from the situation before 1982. Even supposing that Arafat had enjoyed total support in all the camps (a questionable assumption), by 1985 the essential Lebanese support basis offered before by the LNM was absent. Without Lebanese support there was no realistic basis for a return of the PLO. The idea was a chimera, invented for purposes of mobilizing public opinion.

Another kind of preparation indirectly linked to the 'Battle of the Camps' was demographic. For reasons discussed earlier in this chapter, Shi'is were not strongly represented in the population of Beirut city. When in February 1984 Amal became the largest military force in West Beirut, the leadership saw that, to support this military presence and translate it into stable political influence, a more substantial population basis was needed. Immediately after the uprising, Amal began transferring Shi'ite families from the southern suburbs to West Beirut, forcing open empty homes to install them. Much of this organized Shi'ite transfer took place in areas of earlier Palestinian settlement. A similar project to settle Shi'ite families in Sidon was mooted but failed to take effect.

In contrast to political and ideological preparation, Amal's military planning appears to have been confined to the accumulation of arms and equipment. In part this is accounted for by expectations of quick, easy victory; a close observer reveals a second factor:

The political and military structure of Amal at that time was already on a war footing. Militancy within Amal was already high because of the political project [i.e. Shi'ite hegemony] that was being promoted at the time. There was a sense of victory, Amal was in control of Beirut . . . at the rally commemorating Musa Sadr's disappearance [August 1984] West Beirut shook with fear because of the very heavy and visible presence of Amal militiamen. This was why Amal entered the battle so suddenly and violently.

The same observer adds:

[But] Amal fighters had very little training, the movement took any Shi'ite young man who knew how to shoot. That's why they had such heavy losses and had to call in help from the 6th Brigade . . . In so far as there was a plan of battle, it was directed from outside. In fact Nabih Berri found himself in a quandary. Many times he tried to stop the fighting but he couldn't.

The length and bitterness of the actual conflict underlines both the lack of military preparation and the underlying calculations – or gamble – leading to the attack, that since the camps were (as was well known) lightly armed and had few trained fighters, resistance could not last longer than hours, at most a few days, and that as long as the attack met with rapid success it would be supported by a majority of political leaders and public opinion, while leaving those opposed too weakened effectively to protest. The main force of the attack would be directed against Shateela because of its small size, in the expectation that its fall would have a demoralizing effect on the other camps. Amal's absolute certainty of victory is conveyed in this quotation, recorded by a journalist who asked a member of its 'kitchen cabinet' during the first week of the battle why the Movement had risked the same odium as the perpetrators of the Sabra/Shateela massacre:

History is written according the balance of power. The balance of power in this region has changed in favour of our interests, and we expect this new balance to last for decades. Thus we are working with history.

It was on the altar of this Hegelian certainty that the lives of an estimated 2,500 Shi'ite and Palestinian *mahrumeen* (oppressed) were sacrificed.[82]

Notes

1. Interview with A.A., May 1990.

2. Readers interested in the Shi'a will find a rich literature available in English, much of it focused on Iran. See N. Keddie and J. Cole's 'Introduction' to their *Shi'ism and Social Protest* (Newhaven: Yale University Press, 1986) for guidance to further reading.

3. K. Salibi, *The Modern History of Lebanon* (London: Weidenfeld and Nicolson, 1965) p. xv.

4. S. Mallat, *Shi'i Thought from the South of Lebanon* (Oxford: Centre for Lebanese Studies, 1988).

5. An uprising in 1920 led by Kamel al-As'ad (grandfather of the present politician of the same name) was quickly crushed by the French. French soldiers also ransacked the home of a cleric of Tyre, Abdul Hussein Sharaf al-Deen, who led a delegation to Damascus to urge the unity of South Lebanon with Syria. (It was this cleric who encouraged Musa Sadr to visit Lebanon.)

6. S. H. Longrigg, *Syria and Lebanon under French Mandate* (London: OUP, 1958), p. 162.

7. Longrigg, *Syria and Lebanon*, p. 219.

8. Petran, *Struggle over Lebanon*, p. 33.

9. A. Hourani, *Minorities in the Arab World* (London: Royal Institute for International Affairs, 1947) gives a table showing sectarian breakdowns of Lebanon's population at the end of 1944. The percentage of the five leading sects are as follows: Maronites 29 per cent, Sunnis 21 per cent, Shi'a 18 per cent, Greek Orthodox 9.7 per cent, and Druze 6.6 per cent (p. 63).

10. Petran, *Struggle over Lebanon*, p. 135.

11. A. Norton, *Amal and the Shi'a: Struggle for the Soul of Lebanon* (Austin: University of Texas Press, 1987), p. 17.

12. H. Sharif, 'South Lebanon' in E. Hagopian and S. Farsoun (eds).

13. Norton, *Amal and the Shi'a*, p. 18. See also H. Barakat, *Lebanon in Strife: Student Preludes to Civil War* (Austin: University of Texas Press, 1977) who estimates that in the early 1970s Shi'ites formed only 8 per cent of university students (p. 36).

14. Interview with K. Salibi, September 1985.

15. F. Ajami, *The Vanished Imam: Musa al-Sadr and the Shi'a of Lebanon* (London: Tauris, 1986) has interesting reminiscences from Shi'ite businessmen (pp. 105–7).

16. Much of the information in this section comes from probably the best study of the Lebanese Shi'a: S. Nasr, 'La transition des chiites vers Beyrouth: mutuation sociale et mobilisation communautaire à la veille de 1975' in CERMOC, *Mouvements communautaires au Machreq* (Paris: Sindbad, 1985). A shorter English version appeared in *MERIP Reports*, no. 133, June 1985 ('Roots of the Shi'i Movement').

17. Ajami, *Vanished Imam*, gives several anecdotes (pp. 64–72).

18. A. Norton, 'Shi'ism and Social Protest in Lebanon' in Keddie and Cole, *Shi'ism*.

19. Nasr, 'La transition des chiites', p. 90.

20. K. Salibi, *Crossroads*: 'the authorities noted with satisfaction the rapid growth of the Shi'ite element among the Muslim slum-dwellers, with the deluded

idea that the Shi'ite Lebanese were the natural ally to the Christians of the country' (p. 10).

21. F. Khuri has data on the revival of Shi'ite rites among urban migrants to the southern suburbs of Beirut in his *From Village to Suburb* (Chicago: University of Chicago Press, 1975).

22. Nasr, 'La transition des chiites', p. 95.

23. Ajami, *Vanished Imam*, quotes a Shi'ite financier and Amal backer saying that Shi'ite youth were the 'tails' of the leftist parties: 'We had to get our young people back' (p. 73). The Amal image of Shi'ite subordination is exaggerated: LCP leaders Hussein Mroueh and Hassan Hamdan were Shi'ites; so also is Muhsin Ibrahim, leader of the OCA; Kamal Kheir Bek was prominent in the PPS; the Arab Socialist Action Party is mainly Shi'ite in leadership and membership.

24. Ajami, *Vanished Imam*, p. 73.

25. Picard, 'De la "communauté-classe"'.

26. Salibi, *Crossroads*, p. 63. See Ajami, *Vanished Imam*, for biographical details.

27. Ajami, *Vanished Imam*, p. 91.

28. Ajami well expresses this ambivalence: it is clearly his subject's multiple identities that fascinate him.

29. From the beginning Sadr's public appearances and activities received extensive coverage in the Lebanese press, especially in the Shi'ite-owned *al-Hayat* and pro-Western *al-Nahar*.

30. Ajami, *Vanished Imam*, p. 48, well describes Lebanese attention to the physical appearance of their politicians.

31. A useful analysis of Sadr's actions and speeches, with a chronology covering 1973 and 1974 and a translation of the SISC's list of Shi'ite demands, is given by T. Sicking and S. Khairallah, 'The Shi'a Awakening in Lebanon: A Search for Radical Change in a Traditional Way', in *Vision and Revision in Arab Society, 1974*, CEMAM Reports (Beirut: Dar el-Mashreq, 1974).

32. Ajami quotes from an American diplomat's report on a visit to Sadr in April 1974: 'He dwelt at some length on his admiration for our country's attachment to the rights of man and the books he had read on Washington, Lincoln and our other leaders. He then discussed the Communist menace' (*Vanished Imam*, pp. 48–9).

33. Nasr, 'La transition des chiites', p. 98.

34. Another good analysis of Sadr's speeches is given by T. Jaber, 'Le discours shi'ite sur le pouvoir', *Peuples méditerranéens*, no. 20, July/September 1982.

35. Nasr, 'La transition des chiites', p. 100.

36. Jaber, 'Le discours shi'ite', p. 87.

37. K. Pakradouni, *La Paix manquée: Le mandat d'Elias Sarkis (1976–1982)* (Beirut: Editions Fiches du Monde Arabe, 1984), pp. 106–7.

38. Pakradouni, *ibid.*, p. 106.

39. Sicking and Khairallah, 'Shi'a Awakening', p. 111.

40. *Ibid.*, p. 104.

41. Jaber, 'Le discours shi'ite', p. 86; the quotation from Sadr is from his Ba'lbek rally speech of 17 March 1974.

42. Ajami describes who joined the movement, and why, but gives little about its actual origins (*Vanished Imam*, pp. 168–70); Norton (*Amal and the Shi'a*)

writes on every aspect of Amal except this. Pakradouni quotes the Imam's close counsellor Ahmad Kobeissi as saying that Amal was formed 'to struggle against not only the Israeli aggressor but "against any aggressor whoever it is"' (*La Paix manquée*, p. 106).

43. The figure for 1975 is taken from the table of forces involved in the Civil War of 1975/6 in B. Odeh, *Lebanon: Dynamics of Conflict* (London: Zed Books, 1985), p. 215, that for 1985 from Petran, *Struggle over Lebanon*, p. 358.

44. This was the machine-gunning on 13 April 1975 of a bus load of Palestinians as they passed through a Kata'eb-controlled area, followed by the first round of heavy fighting.

45. Salibi, *Crossroads*, p. 119.

46. W. Khalidi, *Conflict and Violence*, gives approximate sizes of the Maronite militias (p. 70) and those of the 'Opposition' (pp. 75–82).

47. See Ajami, *Vanished Imam*, on the ambivalence of Sadr's attitude to war.

48. See Odeh, *Lebanon*, pp. 213–18.

49. Ajami, *Vanished Imam*, pp. 175–80: pages that contain more about Sadr's speeches than his actions.

50. This was the sea-borne operation led by Dalal Moghrabi; the Palestinians captured a civilian bus which was stormed by an Israeli anti-terrorist unit, causing many deaths and casualties.

51. These and other figures are given in *The Ordeal of South Lebanon*, (Beirut: Arab League Information Committee, 1980).

52. Norton, *Amal and the Shi'a*, p. 74.

53. See Norton, *ibid.*, pp. 80–82, on the contradictions in Amal's position towards confessionalism.

54. Norton, *ibid.*, gives the full text of Amal's charter, pp. 144–66.

55. Norton, *ibid.*, pp. 61–4.

56. Yezid Sayigh has compiled figures from various sources on the approximate number of PRM attacks from Lebanon: 1967: 2; 1968: 29; 1969: 150; 1970: 390; 1971: 103; 1972: 45; 1973; 6 (not counting attacks claimed during the October War); 1974: 17; 1975: 61; 1977: 1; 1978: 2; 1979: few; 1980: several. (Artillery attacks are not included.) These figures show a clear decline after 1971.

57. A study of refugees from Khiyam living in Beirut gives an idea of housing conditions: 45 per cent were living in two rooms, 18 per cent in one room. 30 per cent of families consisted of eight persons or more, 10.5 per cent of ten persons or more, and 38 per cent of five to seven persons (A. Fa'our, 'Migration from South Lebanon', *ECWA Population Bulletin*, 1981).

58. AbuKhalil, 'Palestinian–Shi'ite War'.

59. Norton, *Amal and Shi'a*, p. 60.

60. Norton, *ibid.*, p. 67.

61. Interview with M.M., November 1990.

62. The main factors eroding Hizbollah's popularity were the battles with Amal (1987–89) which tore many Shi'ite families apart. Most Shi'ites also condemned Hizbollah's kidnapping of foreigners which, like other Lebanese, they saw as harmful to Lebanon's reputation and economy.

63. See P. Seale in his *Asad* (London: Tauris, 1988), p. 352.

64. Seale, *ibid.*, p. 352.

65. Norton, *Amal and the Shi'a*, p. 68.

66. M.M., November 1990.

67. A good perspective on Amal's ambitions on the eve of the 'Battle of the Camps' is given by C. Mansour, 'Au-delà des sièges des camps palestiniens de Beyrouth: la montée en puissance du mouvement Amal et ses limites, *Maghreb-Machrek*, no. 109, July–September 1985.

68. The Council was one of several autonomous institutions set up by President Chehab to bypass bureaucratic delays and corruption. Enabled to solicit funds independently, the CDC has been wealthier than government ministries. Until recently its chairman was Malek Salam (a brother of Sa'eb). Salam refused Berri's conditions and later resigned.

69. This position was taken by the Sunni leader Dr Selim al-Hoss in a statement made soon after the beginning of the conflict.

70. This and subsequent quotations come from a Lebanese journalist who followed closely the developments leading up to the Amal–Palestinian conflict (Interview with A.A., May 1990).

71. A. AbuKhalil, 'Palestinian–Shi'ite War'. The author dates the real beginning of the 'Battle of the Camps' from Da'oud's 12 May speech.

72. Quoted by a correspondent in *Le Monde*, 21 May 1985.

73. *L'Orient/Le Jour*, 22 May 1985.

74. On several occasions, PLO officials did indeed promise (or threaten) to return to Lebanon. This was mainly in the period immediately after evacuation and was probably aimed at reminding the Lebanese government of the Palestinian agenda in the 'frozen' PLO–Lebanese negotiations.

8. Endangered Species: Palestinians in Lebanon after 1982

You see they destroy us and we rebuild. They chase us away and we come back. That's how it's been since 1948. I don't know if I'll be allowed to stay here. It doesn't matter. If they move us to the Beqa', to the South, to heaven, I'll take my wheelbarrow and my tools and I'll build a decent home for my family.[1]

From the end of the massacre until the February 1984 uprising, Lebanese Army units surrounded Shateela camp and patrolled inside it. They made life difficult for Shateela people but at the beginning they did not bother foreigners. There were several of these, most of them medical workers who had come to help during the invasion and stayed on afterwards, opening a clinic and a therapy centre to replace those of the Red Crescent. Like me, the foreign medics felt that the presence of foreign witnesses in the camps might help deter further massacre attempts; members of the Maronite rightist militias could now circulate freely in areas formerly protected by the Joint Forces. I wanted to continue a study of Palestinian women that I had begun just before the invasion.

There was a double urgency to rebuilding homes damaged during the war. Winter was approaching, and the Lebanese Army was expected to reimpose the restrictions that had been the most hated aspect of Deuxième Bureau rule. French and Italian units of the MNF stationed around the camp gave some reassurance; but no one knew how long they would stay.

Clearing away rubble and repairing homes had hardly started when the winter storms began, earlier and heavier than usual. Drenched, without winter clothing, women waited day after day outside distribution centres for a share of building materials; in most cases their husbands had been evacuated with the Resistance movement, or were missing or dead. Wherever it was rumoured that there was to be a distribution – milk powder, used clothes, kitchen utensils – crowds of desperate people would form, frenziedly waving shreds of paper authenticating their claims. It was like a replay of 1948/9, only thirty-five years later. Outside the building that housed UNRWA's rations store, a black lake of sewage-tainted water half-covered people's legs as they stood waiting for emergency rations.

Physical entry into Shateela was not so difficult then as it became later, after the sieges, when first Amal and then the Syrians established checkpoints near the entrance. But social entry was something else. People were traumatized and fearful. I was neither a nurse nor a doctor nor a social worker, and my presence there must have seemed inexplicable, arousing suspicion. I anchored myself at first in the UNRWA clinic, accompanying Staff Nurse Nazira on her visits to pregnant women and underweight babies. Nazira had been one of the first UNRWA workers to return to work after the massacre; she said she was afraid of only one thing – rape. I also used to spend time at the newly opened 'Austrian Clinic' (formerly a PFLP crèche), which functioned as a medical/social/cultural centre, with a kindergarten, adult literacy classes and a children's library, until it was destroyed during the 'Battle of the Camps'.

But my main friend and protector was Umm Mustafa. A colleague had taken me to meet her a few months before the invasion; now she vouched for me to her circle, telling them that I was not a spy for any of the many possible enemies, but the wife of a Palestinian and, better still, the mother of Palestinian children. Without Umm Mustafa I should never have gained acceptance. After a while my regular visits to *beit* Mi'ary (Umm Mustafa's household) gave me an acceptable social identity as her friend. As a consequence of personal history, my presence required no further explanation; I was 'naturalized'.

The Mi'ary family had lived in Shateela since 1970 and had a reputation for nationalist commitment and personal integrity. Abu Mustafa had been a member of the Popular Committee and was to be so again. He had been badly wounded during the Civil War of 1975/6 while doing guard duty in the Hursh, losing part of both feet. This handicap had not weakened his nationalism but had left him rather taciturn. Jobless now – the organization to which he belonged had given him three months' salary as severance pay – he spent most of the first winter after the war in bed, daily expecting Army arrest.

Umm Mustafa loved to visit. It gave her scope to exercise her remarkable social gifts as well as offering an escape from the dark apartment where she spent most of every day crouched over great bowls of washing or of bread dough, amid the din of nine children. These, the heaviest jobs, she always did herself, as well as the shopping and cooking. Washing floors and dishes, carrying up buckets of water, shaking out beds and floor mats were the share of her five daughters, allocated after protracted arguments. By 3 pm the main meal of the day would have been eaten and cleared away; Umm Mustafa would wash, comb her hair, put on a clean dress, take her bag from a hook near the door and, leaving the baby screaming in one of his sisters' arms, we would set out.

Umm Mustafa's social network was extensive, taking in most of Shateela and penetrating into the surrounding neighbourhoods: Hursh, Gharbeh, Sabra, Hayy Farhat. Her visits leapt over national, ethnic, sectarian, class and Resistance group boundaries.[2] Many friends were, or had been, neighbours; others were members of her adult literacy class (she had trained as a teacher just before the invasion); some were in, or close to, her husband's group; a few were distantly related. Not herself a Resistance group member, Umm Mustafa nonetheless carried on a wide range of informal, self-assumed political activities (morale-raising, reading news-sheets to illiterate women, analysing the latest events). Being a Palestinian and politically conscious gave her implacable domestic labour the character of national struggle; pride in being part of a vanguard against Israel and imperialism kept her doggedly on her feet through a seventeen-hour day. Probably she was the only woman in Shateela who used to read *al-Safir* (a radical daily) while suckling her baby.

Although Umm Mustafa took me visiting with her, I learned very little from her about the people we visited. Among her many qualities was a resolute discretion which encompassed not only political aspects of her friends' lives but also anything remotely approaching gossip. Her usual formula about the people she took me to meet was '*Nas ikteer qweyeseen*' ('they are very good people'). She never told me, and I never asked, their family names, learning them only as 'Abu someone' or 'Umm someone'. Sometimes she would tell me how she had first got to know whomever it was we were visiting. As a result, my sense of Shateela as a structured community remained extremely vague even though the number of people with whom I exchanged greetings on the street grew daily. In some ways my view was like a child's, made up of a few familiar, concrete 'cases' without any social or temporal background in which to set them.

My entry to Shateela took place at a time when the Lebanese Army was carrying out arrest campaigns and breaking down newly built walls. Some of the arrests were being made at night, selectively, on the basis of 'information'. The mood was consequently one of fear and extreme caution. I tried to deal with this by never asking people their names and never taking notes (this was also a precaution against Army searches). Even the simplest question, for example 'When did you come to Shateela?', was likely to be met with the response, 'Why do you want to know?' Anthropology's most basic method, asking questions, appeared unusable in this context, so I mainly watched and listened. On bad days the whole idea of doing research in such a place, at such a time, seemed like a parody of the irrelevance of the privileged outsider, and I felt terribly guilty at not possessing useful skills like those of my medical and social-worker friends. Passing money hidden in bags of fruit to needy families, or trying to find jobs for unemployed young men, did something to ease my conscience and helped a few individuals, but it did not advance my work at all, nor did it help the community to develop.

One of the staples of conversation in the homes that Umm Mustafa took me to in that first winter was the massacre. Many families from Tell al-Za'ter had settled in and around Shateela. Talk in their homes often took the form of comparing the two massacres, a catalogue of atrocities that was sometimes rounded off by predictions that worse was to come. These massacre story sessions were more disturbing because of the presence of young children, listening silent and wide-eyed. My first, English, reaction was that children should be protected from this kind of talk. But then I noticed that the stories did not only dwell on horrors, although this was their most conspicuous feature, but they also recalled the names and idiosyncracies of the victims, where they came from and who their relatives were. They also told about the lucky ones who had miraculous escapes, who had slipped out of the window as the killers were breaking down the door, or who had left the camp before the massacre because of a dream or a presentiment. I came to feel that, however gruesome, the massacre stories were a way of dealing with horror by turning it into narrative, absorbing it in all its detail rather than suppressing it, unassimilated and unshared, into the unconscious.

Massacre panic resurfaced several times that first winter after the war. Although, when the real massacre was taking place, people had been slow to understand and react, protected perhaps by an inability to imagine that such a thing could happen, now a mere whisper could empty the camp in minutes. After one of these stampedes, someone's two-year-old daughter was found wandering alone in an alley: in the rush to get away her father had left without her, thinking she was with her mother, and vice versa. Another day there was talk that sewage workers had found three children's bodies blocking the drains. Mothers told Nurse Nazira that their children were sleeping poorly, wetting their beds, waking often at night and crying.

Politics were carefully edited out of everyone's speech. Conversations were studded with pauses, as people mentally assessed the implications of what they had been about to say. Even Umm Mustafa often reminded me that she was not a member of her husband's organization, as if to disconnect herself from our first, pre-invasion meeting, when an interview with her had been published in a party magazine in celebration of International Women's Day. Silence extended to almost every aspect of the pre-1982 past. The graphic popular phrase used to express this cautious mode was *hayt al-hayt* which can be roughly translated as 'keep to the wall', suggesting the way a person walks when trying to avoid being seen. I fell in with this mode half-consciously by avoiding all references to politics, as if the 'Days of the Revolution' had never existed. It was not until later, after the 'Battle of the Camps', that I felt sufficiently an insider to ask people political questions.

Shateela was a good place from which to observe the Palestinian situation in Lebanon as it unfolded after the invasion of 1982. Although conditions varied slightly between the zones controlled by the Israeli, Lebanese and Syrian armies, insecurity and hardship were common to all three. Not only were these conditions forcibly present in Shateela, but the camp also formed a gathering and relay centre of news from other places. Family ties and movement – mainly women's – formed the circuit through which news travelled. Everyone had kin in other camps: Nazira had a sister in Miyeh-Miyeh whose husband was in Ansar; Umm Mustafa had family in 'Ain Helweh and Rashidiyyeh; daily conversation in the clinics and in homes reflected events in camps all over Lebanon as well as on the checkpoint-studded roads between them.

There were no days without bad news. One of the phrases people used to express the situation was 'We're back to zero' or 'back to 1948'. But this was perhaps to underestimate the gravity of the situation. In 1948 Palestinians were only refugees whom Lebanese pitied or despised according to their political/sectarian orientation. But after 1982, they were the remnants of a national movement which had dominated a large part of Lebanon for twelve years, and which many Lebanese blamed for having 'ruined our country'. The Palestinians had been powerful in Lebanese terms; now they were weak. As the Arabic saying goes, 'When the cow falls, the knives come out.'

Piecemeal pogrom

Shortly before I began regular visits to Shateela, in November 1982, the press reported the killing of a Shateela man, Fu'ad Husary, in the course of a night arrest supposedly carried out by the police. Later I got to know Fu'ad's sister, who worked in the Red Crescent. She said that the men who came to arrest her brother were armed but had no warrant. He had managed to run away; the men followed, shooting at and wounding him. Neighbours had helped carry him to Gaza Hospital; but later the armed men had returned there, pulled him off the operating table and killed him. The police denied all knowledge of the 'arrest'.

There was a stream of similarly intimidating incidents: one day a fire-bomb was tossed through an open window; another day, threatening leaflets were scattered along Abu Hassan Salameh Street. There were graffiti on walls such as, 'Your time is over, alien Palestinians!' Dynamite was thrown at night from passing cars. More worrying, explosives were twice found in Jericho School playground. Apart from the stream of Army arrests, people were kidnapped. Sometimes their bodies were found, sometimes they just disappeared.

A Shateela man, whose widow and children I met later in a refugee shelter during the battles with Amal, used to run a taxi service. One day he was flagged down near the camp by a woman with a child who asked him to take her to Mar Mikhael, an area close to the 'Green Line'. His body was found later close to his car; from the accounts of passers-by it appeared that he had been the victim of a Lebanese Forces ambush. (At that time the LF were re-establishing offices in Shiyah and other parts of the southern suburbs from which they had been expelled in 1976). The aim of such assassinations, which occurred in other areas as well, seems to have been to stop Palestinians from going outside the camps to work, thereby increasing pressure on them to emigrate.

What made the situation so precarious was the number of groups attacking Palestinians, and the latter's lack of protection. A Resistance leader who remained in Lebanon, Salah Salah of the PFLP, described Palestinians at that time as *mustabaheen*, a term with hunting connotations, best translated as 'a species or group from which protection has been lifted'.[3] Besides the Lebanese Army there was the Deuxième Bureau, the Mukafaha (a commando unit of the army formed for 'special tasks') and the various extremist militias grouped in the Lebanese Forces. There was close coordination between Israeli Intelligence and the Deuxième Bureau headed by Simon Kassis, as well as with the Department of General Security whose chief, Zahi Bustani, was alleged to be on Mossad's payroll. Israeli agents are said to have accompanied Deuxième Bureau and Security night searches in West Beirut, during which killings and kidnappings occurred. Though not accused at the time, Amal movement is believed to have carried out the assassination of a Resistance cadre in Bourj Barajneh in 1983.

Palestinians had no recourse, legal or otherwise, against this piecemeal pogram. In spite of its pledges of protection, the Lebanese government was one of the sources of aggression. Lebanese leaders of the 'Opposition', a traditional source of support, told people who went to them for help, 'We can't even protect ourselves.' The PLO outside was going through difficult days and had little attention to spare for the community in Lebanon. But as Abu Mujahed said, 'We owed what little security we had to the blood of the massacre victims.' (Abu Mujahed reappears in these pages as the first Popular Committee Chairman of Shateela after the February 1984 uprising.) As a result of world media attention to the massacre, the US embassy in Beirut and heads of the MNF showed some concern. After reports of deaths in Lebanese army prisons, pressure was brought on the government to permit inspection. But such moves had no influence over the militias, nor was there any attempt made to inspect the General Security or Army interrogation centres where the worst excesses were carried out.

Within two weeks of the massacre, and only days after its entry into West Beirut, the Lebanese Army launched a massive sweep through Bourj Barajneh camp, carried out on the first night of A'eed al-Adha', 27

September, so as to catch men at home. Around 600 men were detained. Detainees were beaten to persuade them to mount Army vehicles, and only the intervention of an Italian unit of the MNF prevented a summary execution.[4]

An estimate of the number of Palestinians in army prisons in October/ November, when arrests were at their peak, was 5,000.[5] Released detainees reported that prisons were overflowing, with extra housing requisitioned to take the surplus, and men sleeping in corridors. The government gave as a pretext for the arrests the need to clean out 'illegals' (those without residence permits) and bring fugitives from justice to trial. Rightist propaganda before 1982 had represented West Beirut under the PRM as a nest of criminals and subversives. In fact, only Palestinians who could prove their residence rights dared stay on in Beirut after PRM evacuation, and few of those arrested by the Army were charged with crimes. The real aim of the arrests – intimidation – was shown by their massive scale. More specific purposes were to identify Resistance group cadres, discourage future membership and recruit informers. In some cases, release was promised if detainees agreed to leave Lebanon. Another purpose of the arrests is said to have been to bring pressure on the PRM to evacuate from the rest of Lebanon.

Although Palestinians – connoisseurs of prisons – always discriminate between the Lebanese Army and the rightist militias, qualifying the former as 'more correct', there was evidence of brutality in army prisons. Beatings and torture were used in the three main army detention centres, Yarzeh, Badaro and the Military Tribunal. A new method of beating was used which left no traces on the body surface but did great damage to internal organs. The names of four Palestinian detainees who died under torture were given to the commanders of the MNF. One of them was from Sabra and people said that when the Army returned his body, they threatened the family with reprisals if they talked to journalists.

Army arrest was seen by Palestinians as relatively benign because the Army published lists of prisoners, family visiting rights were recognized, and most Army prisoners eventually came out alive. In contrast, people kidnapped by the Lebanese Forces were either summarily executed or transferred to prisons to which no access was allowed, and from which they rarely re-emerged. This gave rise to a gruesome trade which reached its peak between 1982 and 1985: Palestinian families known to have a missing member would be contacted by a self-proposed *waasta* (mediator) who would offer release in return for a large sum of money. Usually such deals were followed by attempts to grab the ransom without delivering the prisoner.

Though on a lesser scale, Army arrests continued through 1983: at roadblocks, during house searches or in occasional sweeps through the camps. In areas near the camps, arrest could take place haphazardly on the street. The Coordination Committee member quoted before, described an incident he had just witnessed: 'Three days ago in Sabra, some youths were waiting outside a school to enter classes. A Lebanese Army vehicle passed by, and arrested fifteen students. Whenever they see a group, they arrest them.'

Many Shateela women were without their husbands that winter; the arrests took a high proportion of adult men and youths. For no clear reason, Abu 'Mustafa was not arrested, although he and his family lived in daily expectation. Once when I was staying overnight, Shi'ite neighbours sent word that an Army search of the building was to take place that night. (Most low-income Shi'ite families have at least one son in the Army or police.) Aida, the oldest of the Mi'ary children (aged sixteen years), suggested that her father should sleep somewhere else. All the family calmly joined in the discussion which ended with Abu Mustafa deciding to stay home; to hide would suggest guilt, he said. Besides, there were not many places where he could hide. Everyone slept as usual, and in the morning he was still there.

Women did not sit at home weeping when their menfolk were arrested as they had a vital role to play. Particularly in the case of young men, as soon as word of arrest reached their mothers, they would hurry to the nearest Army post, in the Arab University. Detainees were held there before being transferred to East Beirut. If the officer in charge was an *ibn halal* (decent fellow), there was a chance that a mother could persuade him to release her son by swearing to his innocence of politics. Once men were in army prisons, women would visit them with food, cigarettes and clothing, even though this meant crossing over into LF-controlled territory. After veiled threats of rape to women being transported up to Yarzeh in an army lorry, the men in prison sent messages to them not to visit any more. So deeply enforced is this strand in women's role, however, that many persisted, in some cases trying to engage Kata'ebi lawyers or *waastas* to obtain release.

Although it was mostly men who were arrested, a few Shateela women were arrested also, as well as others elsewhere, accused of bringing money or arms from the Beqa', or of distributing the PLO indemnities that kept martyrs' families alive. Such arrests pointed not only to women's vital role in communicating between Palestinians in different regions, but also to the authorities' willingness to use hunger as pressure on Palestinians to leave Lebanon.

Palestinians in the camps suffered and survived together, their number offering a minimum protection. Palestinians scattered throughout West Beirut, many of them refugees from camps in the eastern sector (expelled in 1976), were more vulnerable to harassment, from kidnapping and arrest to rent-raising or eviction. When owners began to use Army help to repossess buildings occupied by the homeless (many were also Lebanese from the

South), some 20,000 Palestinians in West Beirut were threatened with homelessness. Several evictions were carried out in the Rawsheh and Ramel al-Baidha areas, but the campaign declined as the Army increasingly faced protest and tension.

Anti-Palestinian groups based in East Beirut did not dare enter camps (unless in army uniform), but occasionally carried out raids against Palestinians living in occupied buildings. On 15 March 1983, Samia Ahmad and Yusra Akel were taken at night from the Jammal building in Rawsheh by armed men claiming to be police. Both were Tell al-Za'ter widows living alone with their children. A week later Samia's brother and another man were taken from the same building. In July, a third man, a teacher, was taken. None of them reappeared.

Transit between one zone and another was particularly dangerous. Detected at a Lebanese Forces checkpoint, Palestinians were likely to disappear. In late September 1982, four students from Bourj Barajneh disappeared somewhere on the Damascus highway, on their way back to university in the Soviet Union. The husband of a worker at Najdeh's Shateela embroidery workshop was taken from a 'service' taxi near Bikfaya; in spite of his Jordanian passport, he never reappeared. There were many cases of women kidnapped at checkpoints, some of them involving rape. (The number of reported rape cases was probably less than the actual number since families are reluctant to publicize such news.) In spite of the danger, women continued to use the roads, compelled by financial need or family obligation. A young married woman from Rashidiyyeh camp was forced by her family to visit her husband in Damascus for fear that otherwise he might divorce her. She was stopped at an LF checkpoint at A'rbaniyyeh, and released a few days later with cigarette burns all over her body. Other women were kidnapped on their way back from Damascus after collecting family allowances or pensions. Such women often carried money for neighbours or kinswomen unable to travel; if searched, they were accused of distributing funds for the Resistance movement and taken to the LF prison in Qaranteena. Many women imprisoned by the Israelis were also charged with this 'crime'.[6]

Security in South Lebanon

Security conditions under Israeli occupation were certainly harsher than in the zones controlled by the Lebanese and Syrian armies, involving mass and selective arrests, searches, retaliation for resistance, the licensing of rightist militias and the recruitment and arming of collaborators.[7] Conditions were especially brutal in the interrogation centres set up around Sidon during the war, through which were passed a large part of the adult male population before transfer to the concentration camp of Ansar, or (in defiance of the Geneva Conventions) to prisons in Israel.

Ansar was estimated to hold 9,500 prisoners at its peak, including a large number of Lebanese suspected of belonging to Resistance groups or progressive parties. Deaths from torture and beatings occurred in Ansar, especially at the beginning, before regular IRC inspection began.

Life in Ansar was in some ways less dangerous and demoralizing than in 'Ain Helweh and its sister camps. There women with their children and old people faced the winter without men, proper housing or sources of income. They also faced the rightist militias that preyed upon smaller camps such as Miyeh-Miyeh, and on individual families in predominantly Lebanese areas such as Sidon or Na'imeh, terrorizing, evicting, killing. Intra-Palestinian suspicion and assassinations were fostered by Israel's recruitment of collaborators and National guards. A quotation from *The Economist* conveys the complex relationship between the IDF and their Lebanese allies:

> The ambivalence in southern, Israeli-occupied, Lebanon is all pervading. The Palestinians are in need and in danger because of Israel's assault upon them, yet it is to Israel that they now have to look for protection. Although the Israelis are providing some of the protection, they are also suspected of being behind some of the perils against which the protection is needed.[8]

The IDF benefited politically from acts of brutality carried out by the rightist militias, first, as the above quotation points out, because it forced Palestinians to turn to them as a source of protection; second, it made the IDF appear disciplined and humane in contrast to their Lebanese allies. The foreign media tended to underline the contrast without similarly stressing the essential connection: that it was the Israelis who had to a large extent armed, trained and paid or subsidized the Maronite rightist militias; that it was they who had brought them back to the South; and that even after Israeli policy towards the militias shifted, they continued to use them as auxiliaries.

From its high point in August 1982, rightist militia aggression against Palestinians continued well into 1983. Incidents included the slaughter of a whole family in Na'imeh, harassment of Miyeh-Miyeh culminating in the burning and looting of part of the camp in February 1983, and a series of assassinations of workers from 'Ain Helweh in April. Whole areas of Sidon and its outlying suburbs became unsafe; Palestinian families were evicted from rented accommodation and home-owners forced to sell at rock-bottom prices. In Iqleem al-Kharoub, Lebanese employers of Palestinian agricultural workers were forced to dismiss them and, in Sidon city, leaflets signed by the 'Revolutionaries of the Cedars' called on the Lebanese to 'drive all Palestinians first into the camps and then out of Lebanon altogether'. Given the post-invasion political set-up, such threats were not far-fetched.

Conditions in the other camps of the South – al-Bass, Rashidiyyeh, Bourj Shemaleh – were similar to those in 'Ain Helweh. Most males above fifteen were taken to Ansar; rebuilding was not allowed before the spring of 1983 (by which time the Israelis had exhausted the possibilities of relocation). Collaborators were recruited for 'dirty jobs' such as informing, delivering threats, carrying out arrests, and sometimes assassinations; recruitment was facilitated by the lack of employment within camps, and by fear of the Lebanese Forces or Haddad's militias preventing men from looking outside for work.

Women came and went between Shateela and the South, carrying news or bringing embroidery to be sold in Beirut. There were daily stories: how the Israelis were empowering the collaborators by making them channels for the granting of building permits, or for obtaining the release of men from Ansar; how an UNRWA employee in Sidon who refused to cooperate with the Fikry Fa'our 'committee' was beaten up by his henchmen; how Myriam, the director of Najdeh's workshop in Bourj Shemali, had been arrested by the Israelis and transferred to Israel (she was released through IRC intervention a few months later, traumatized and anorexic). Increasingly we heard the news of women's demonstrations. One of Umm Mustafa's sisters-in-law was arrested as a leader of a demonstration demanding the release of men from Ansar. However slowly, kindergartens and embroidery workshops were re-established. International organizations such as Oxfam and the Mennonites helped camp people recommence the small crafts and trades that were the backbone of camp economies. In March 1983, an LF-oriented magazine carried a cover photo of women and children rebuilding homes in 'Ain Helweh under the banner headline: 'The Palestinians are back!'

The official Lebanese 'Palestinian policy'

Official Lebanese policy towards the Palestinians in the wake of the invasion had two distinct levels: one open and declared, the other diffused throughout the machinery of the state through unofficial directives and alternative channels such as party or sectarian links. Official policy was one of protection of civilians within a framework of strict application of existing regulations, meaning the removal of all those not properly registered, and restoration of Lebanese control over the camps.[9] The government also announced its intention of reforming the Directorate of Refugee Affairs, target of rightist attacks for leniency and corruption in dealing with Palestinians.

At another level, however, declarations of protection were negated by directives to all departments dealing with Palestinians that countermanded even those modest rights granted in the past. This policy was clearest in the refusal of the Ministry of Labour to issue work permits; another move was a decree issued by the Social Affairs Ministry which greatly extended the kinds of employment from which non-Lebanese (Palestinians) were excluded. There were also long delays and difficulties over travel documents; when granted, they were often found to be stamped 'Not valid for return.' Thousands of Lebanese Palestinians abroad were refused renewal of their *laissez passer* by Lebanese embassies, and refused entry to Lebanon without valid travel documents. *L'Orient/Le Jour* (26 February 1983) gives the number of Palestinians affected in this way as 100,000. A story circulating at this time told of a Palestinian expelled from Abu Dhabi and refused entry to Lebanon, sent back and forth between the two countries like a ping-pong ball. The government also unofficially requested UNRWA not to reissue ID cards that had been lost or destroyed; without ID cards, Palestinians were liable to be arrested. Government departments always insisted that the original card, not a copy, be submitted with applications.

Uncertainty about the future added its weight to harassment and hardship. There were many ways that Palestinians could be reminded of their vulnerability. Only two weeks after the Sabra/Shateela massacre, a semi-official plan was floated in the press, aimed at reducing the number of Palestinians in Lebanon from 500,000 to 50,000.[10] Said to be the work of the University of Kaslik (directed by the Maronite Order of Monks), the 'reduction plan' was revived now in the context of discussions between President Gemayel and US Special Envoy Habib on how to regulate the Palestinian presence in Lebanon, presented by the Lebanese as a 'factor of disequilibrium'. That none of the Arab League states would accept a redistribution of Palestinians was little guarantee that attempts would not be made to implement it using a variety of unofficial means.

Another way of understanding Lebanese/Palestinian policy at this time is to see it as a variation within the regime between a maximalist position represented by Bashir Gemayel and his successors in the Lebanese Forces, and a minimalist one represented by Amin Gemayel and the Kata'eb Party. At this, the moderate pole of the Maronite right, it was accepted that the Arab states would not accept a violent transfer of Palestinians from Lebanon: the methods advocated by Bashir Gemayel and Sharon must be renounced. However, the Arab world and international community must be continually reminded of Lebanon's unfair burden, and the danger posed to Lebanese and regional stability by the Palestinian presence. In the end, of course, the minimalists and maximalists cooperated in practice, while differing in slogans and methods. Fear aroused by the militias meshed with the administrative and economic constraints applied by the government to propel many Palestinians into migration, a solution which avoided the international outcry precipitated by the Sabra/Shateela massacre.

The Lebanese government did not allow the PLO office on Corniche al-Mazra' to continue to function. While the Israelis were still in Beirut, Lebanese Army tanks surrounded it and remained there until February 1984. Even then it stayed closed (in April 1991 its reopening was still the subject of PLO–Lebanese government discussions). PLO social institutions faced varying degrees of harassment but most survived, as we shall see in more detail later. A Coordination Committee was set up by the Palestinians to act in place of the PLO office *vis-à-vis* the government. At first it was ignored, then eliminated when, in April 1983, all its members were arrested and/or deported.

The PLO after 1982

Even though managed with skill, the evacuation of the PLO/PRM from Beirut had a number of negative consequences, both for the national movement as a whole and for the Palestinian community in Lebanon. The Resistance movement's fighting forces and political cadres were rescattered over a new, wider diaspora, and although a considerable fraction remained in North Lebanon and the Beqa', they passed under Syrian control. Loss of the quasi-autonomy enjoyed in Lebanon made the PLO increasingly vulnerable, on the one side to external pressures (especially from the Arab states and the United States), on the other to internal dissension of which the most serious manifestation was the split in Fateh that irrupted within eight months of the evacuation.

While PLO structures continued, remarkably, to function – witness the 16th PNC meeting held in Algiers in February 1983 – the next five years were to be the most challenging in its stormy history. The Palestinian community in Lebanon suffered in this period in at least three specific ways: as those left behind, they bore the brunt of Lebanese anger against the PRM; because unprotected both physically and legally, they were targets of the attacks and harassment described in the first part of this chapter; third, they suffered most from the Fateh split, becoming the principal, indeed only, arena in which this struggle was fought out.

The policies of Chairman Arafat after 1982 can be summed up as pursuing three main lines: (i) *rapprochement* with Egypt and Jordan in order to form a counterweight to Syrian pressures; (ii) efforts to reinforce PLO and Fateh connections with the Occupied Territories; and (iii) efforts to enhance the PLO's status on the Arab and international levels (e.g. through visits to the USSR, Iraq, etc.).[11] Arafat's regional policies, while seeking to maintain a minimal independence (or margin of manoeuvre) for the PLO, were unpopular with Palestinians in Lebanon and created some support for Syrian-backed groups calling for the continuation of armed struggle until total liberation. PLO negotiations with Jordan, begun in October 1982 and leading eventually to the Amman Accords of February 1985, were difficult for Fateh loyalists in Lebanon to defend. Arafat's meeting with President Mubarak on 22 December 1983, the first high-level Palestinian–Egyptian meeting since Camp David, was similarly unpopular.

It was not accidental that a major phase of conflict between Syria and the PLO, first clearly manifested in the Fateh 'rebellion',[12] should have exploded in the aftermath of the 1982 invasion. The Fateh rebels had formulated criticisms of the PLO and Fateh leadership before 1982, accusing it of abandoning armed struggle, readiness to compromise, subservience to Saudi and US pressures, corruption and mismanagement. Such critiques and threats of revolt were relatively easy for Arafat to contain in Lebanon; but after 1982, with Fateh radicals such as Abu Saleh and Abu Musa relocated in Damascus along with most other Resistance group leaders (who chose to stay near Lebanon rather than follow Abu Ammar to Tunis), such containment was no longer possible.[13] All the moves made by Arafat to counteract Syrian influence in the months before the rebellion merely served to reinforce Syrian and Fateh rebels' accusations.

To understand the Syrian–PLO conflict (personalized in Arab thinking as rivalry between Asad and Arafat), one has to return to 1970, perhaps even earlier. In the early 1960s, Ba'thist Syria gave Fateh facilities for military training and organization; at the same time, there were Syrian attempts to infiltrate Fateh's leadership.[14] In the late 1970s, after the Jordanian–PRM battles, Asad led his 'corrective movement' coup against the radical governing wing of the Ba'th party which had attempted to intervene in Jordan on the side of the Resistance. As airforce commander, Asad had played a key role in aborting this attempt.

Syria under Asad tightened security on the Syrian–Israeli border, effectively barring all Resistance operations from Syria (this was one reason for the rise in PRM attacks from Lebanon in the early 1970s). Unlike his predecessors, President Asad made Syrian national security a fundamental policy principle and, through skilfully calibrated international, regional and domestic policies, succeeded in enhancing Syria's stability and regional influence. Control of the 'Palestinian factor' was a part of this strategy, perhaps less for ideological reasons such as visions of a 'Greater Syria' than because an independent Resistance movement within the Syrian zone of influence was incompatible with Asad's drive for total control. This fundamental incompatibility took a clearer shape as Syria began to extend its influence into Lebanon. Extension took place in stages, responding both to particular phases of the Lebanese crisis as well as to various international and Arab 'green lights'. Syria's interventions in Lebanon also occurred in the context of its declared goal of strategic parity with Israel, an undeclared one of avoiding confrontations in which Israel might emerge the victor.

In some phases of this gradual process, for example in 1976, the PLO/PRM presence in Lebanon appeared to Damascus as a dangerous factor outside Syrian control; but at others, for instance between 1976 and 1982, as a result of the rising challenge to Syrian influence posed by Bashir Gemayel as commander of the Lebanese Forces, the PLO/PRM appeared as a quasi-ally, and the Syrian–Palestinian conflict went through a latent phase. What differed after 1982 was less the situation in Lebanon than the opportunity offered to Damascus by the dispersal of Fateh cadres and post-evacuation critiques, to weaken Arafat and exclude him from any foothold in Lebanon. By May 1983 Syria was far along the road to building alliances in Lebanon more impressive than the short-lived Front of Patriotic and National Parties of 1976.

The Fateh rebellion came into the open in the Beqa' on 10 May 1983, when Fateh units were ordered by Colonel Abu Musa not to obey orders from Arafat.[15] Skirmishes broke out, with Palestinians in the area trying on more than one occasion to separate the factions. On 24 June Arafat was expelled from Damascus, where he had flown to try to resolve the split. A new stage was reached in September when the Syrian Army ordered all Fateh loyalist units out of the Beqa'. With their withdrawal to the North and Arafat's arrival in Tripoli in September, the lines were drawn for a decisive confrontation. Early in November, an attack force composed of PFLP-General Command (PFLP-GC), Sa'eqa and PLA units backed by the Syrian Army made heavy artillery assaults on Nahr al-Bared and Baddawi camps, causing an estimated 350 dead and 800 wounded. After the fall of the two camps the battle shifted to Tripoli from where, on 20 December, Arafat departed with all remaining loyalist Fateh forces.[16] This episode of intra-Palestinian fighting was taken by the community as an ominous sign of future battles, many judging the Fateh split as a more serious blow to the national struggle than the Israeli invasion or the evacuation of Beirut.

The Fateh split produced a threefold realignment of PRM groups: the National Alliance, formed of the Fateh dissidents, Sa'eqa, PFLP-GC and Palestine Struggle Front (PSF), based in Damascus; Arafat's Fateh and the ALF, based in Tunis; and the Democratic Alliance (DA) formed by PFLP, DFLP, Palestine Liberation Front (PLF) and the Palestine Communist Party (PCP). The Democratic Alliance joined the National Alliance in some of their critiques and positions, opposing *rapprochement* with Jordan and Egypt, as well as PLO–US dialogue; yet the DA groups stood against any moves that would weaken the PLO, such as the campaign to depose Arafat, or to establish an alternative PLO in Damascus. With the signing of the Amman Accords (February 1985), the PFLP and PLF left the Democratic Alliance to join the pro-Syrian groups in the Palestine National Salvation Front (PNSF).[17]

These issues, debates and shifts of alignment were reflected among Palestinians in Lebanon, however repressed by Israeli, Lebanese militia or

Syrian control. The Fateh dissidents had some support in the camps, particularly on issues such as mismanagement of the war of 1982 (in the South) and the decision to leave Beirut; fears that an eventual 'mini-state solution' would leave Palestinians in Lebanon marginalized were another factor. Arafat's regional and international policies were also hard for Fateh loyalists in Lebanon to defend. On the other hand, Syria's backing for the PNSF groups made them suspect to people in the camps, who had not forgotten the Syrian role in the Civil War of 1975/6 and the fall of Tell al-Za'ter. It was the 'Battle of the Camps' that swung mass feeling firmly back in favour of Arafat, and against the Syrian-backed PNSF (even though the attack caused a reunification of ranks, with the PNSF groups joining in the defence of the camps).

At another, less conspicuous level, PLO–Lebanese government negotiations continued after 1982, although contacts were rare and unproductive. The main issues were the future of the remaining Palestinian fighting forces: the government demanded their unconditional departure from Lebanon, while the PLO called for a token PLA unit under Lebanese Army control, as in several other Arab countries. The other main issue was the status and future of the Palestinian community in Lebanon: the government insisted that the camps should be relocated and brought fully under Lebanese control, while only Palestinians from 1948 should remain in Lebanon. The PLO called for the rebuilding of the camps, the reopening of the PLO office and a new PLO–Lebanese agreement.[18] During the early period (September 1982 to December 1983) the Lebanese government is thought to have used harassment of the civilian population (e.g. deportations, mass arrests) as pressure on the PLO to withdraw its fighters from Lebanon. After February 1984, President Gemayel's growing weakness and isolation prompted his meeting with Arafat in Tunis in November 1986, leading to a slight easing in official harassment, for example in the matter of Palestinian travel documents. However, the question of PLO representation and Palestinian civic rights remained in abeyance. In May 1987, the Lebanese government abrogated the Cairo Accords without any 'Opposition' voices being raised in protest.

Khanq!

Khanq means strangulation, and was the vivid term used by Palestinians of the camps to described the economic squeeze put on them in Lebanon after the 1982 invasion. Like Abu Mustafa, most Shateela men were out of work that winter and for most of 1983. A very small number kept jobs with Lebanese companies or institutions; for example, Ahmad Haleemeh's father, who had begun working with the Maqassad Hospital long ago, before it stopped employing Palestinians, was kept on until his retirement. A larger group of UNRWA employees also kept their jobs. A third contingent, the largest, started out again as self-employed craftsmen or tradesmen, after rebuilding workshops, buying or borrowing new equipment, and restocking small shops. Fear of arrest or kidnapping kept most men from going beyond Sabra to look for work. A small study by an UNRWA schoolteacher, based on children's reports of their family situation, indicated that in 1983, 88 per cent of male household heads were unemployed.[19]

Destruction of homes, workplaces and the means of production caused by the war was estimated at around 80 per cent according to an UNRWA survey of the Beirut camps. Most families had used up savings during the three months of war and unemployment. Many had lost wage earners. Openings for Palestinian workers in the oil-producing countries were also being cut back, partly as a result of recession, partly for political reasons. New restrictions in several of the Gulf countries prevented workers changing jobs once in the country; a new job meant a new application and entry visa. Only men with kin already there could obtain one. Such cutbacks reduced the flow of remittances as well as new workers.

Some older Shateela men were convinced that the 'good old days' would return and that, once the army had re-established its authority, the Palestinians would once again occupy the economic niche they had had before 1969, as an ethnic proletariat ready to work for lower wages than Lebanese workers, or self-employed within an expanding informal sector. 'You'll see, they will need us again once things have calmed down', they would reassure sceptics. But instead of an economic upturn, the crisis deepened. West Beirut had benefited most from the presence of the PRM, as consumer of goods and services and generator of employment; now it was harder hit than East Beirut by the general malaise. Not only was East Beirut spared by the war of 1982, but post-war government expenditures were biased in its favour. A series of car-bombs, thought to be the work of the Deuxième Bureau, also caused much damage to commercial and productive establishments in West Beirut. With high rates of Lebanese unemployment and work migration, Palestinians had little hope of finding work. Economic crisis was deepened by the increase in national and sectarian consciousness, which had the effect of further constricting the narrow labour market. Even co-religionist Sunni Lebanese were no longer likely to employ Palestinians.

Mass unemployment was seen by most camp people as part of a deliberate policy to make them leave Lebanon. Official policy was certainly central in creating *khanq*, especially the refusal of work permits and threats to employers who gave jobs to Palestinians. But there were contributory factors: first, the continuing crisis in the Lebanese economy; second, the degree of destruction, far exceeding all earlier wars; third, the collapse of the Palestinian economy brought about by the evacuation of the PRM.

In earlier rounds of fighting, the PLO/PRM had paid generous indemnities for human and material losses, but after 1982 there were few channels through which such help could reach people. The PLO/PRM had also been a large employer of labour of many kinds. An unofficial estimate, based on a survey just before 1982, put the number of Palestinians employed by the PLO/PRM as 65 per cent of the total workforce.[20] (Many Lebanese were also employed by the PLO/PRM.) Another important economic contribution made by the mini-state took the form of free medical services and subsidies to education. Infrastructural services to camps – shelters, repairs to sewage, water pipes, roads, etc. – had generated jobs and income as well as improving the quality of life.

After twelve years of full employment and relative prosperity, during which consumption and savings rose to levels comparable to those of urban lower-middle-class Lebanese, people of the camps were now once more dependent on UNRWA emergency rations. The painfulness of readjustment was symbolized by the numbers of young unemployed university graduates. Sent abroad before the war to study on PRM scholarships, they represented the ambitions of their families and community for a better future. Now they sat at home without hope of jobs that fitted their qualifications.

How did people manage to hold out? Abu Shady, a tile polisher, occasionally got work but had to rent a machine; on other days he sold fruit from a rented barrow. Abu Fayad, nearing sixty, carried loads of building materials. Abu Khaled used his car as a taxi, but only for local people: 'Most days I don't work but I'm still alive!' Abu Kassem made shirts and sold them from a tiny shop near the 'Ali Handar coffee house. Abul Abed, doorkeeper at the UNRWA clinic in the morning, worked as a freelance electricity repairman in the afternoons. New technical training courses were thronged with young men who had done nothing before but fight or hang about Resistance offices. A business school was opened, giving training in typing, accountancy and English. But whatever their qualifications, it was very hard for Palestinians to find employment in the Lebanese economy.

People also managed by going back to the practices of the refugee period (one reason that those who had lived through it managed better and complained less bitterly than younger people who had only known the prosperity of the Days of the Revolution). Belts were tightened: people went back to collecting UNRWA rations, baking their own bread, eating meat only occasionally and buying used clothes. The UNRWA feeding centre for children, spurned in the days of the Resistance movement, was now filled again. Women's domestic skills and thriftiness again became vital elements in sustaining household economies, manifested in careful purchase and storage of foodstuffs, making do with old, defective equipment (or none at all), sewing and knitting clothes, recycling everything.

There was also, however, a change to the economic structure: a substantial number of women had professional, salaried jobs, in several cases earning more than their husbands. Now there were young, unmarried women working as nurses or teachers, a change that had only become possible with the development of Palestinian institutions. These self-confident professional women stood out against older or uneducated ones who made money in more conventional ways, tailoring, trading, cleaning offices or producing food to be sold on the street.

Another change from the refugee period was the degree to which needy families were helped by local institutions rather than international charity. Many more hardship cases existed as a result of fifteen years of war and displacement, but part of the Resistance movement had been the development of a social services sector to help the casualties. Although at first such services were administered by educated, middle-class Palestinians, by 1983 an important minority of camp inhabitants was engaged in the services sector, whether as teachers, medical workers, administrators or social workers. Loss of the PRM cut back this development but did not terminate it, sustained as it was both by economic need and nationalist ideology. PRM institutions had planted the concept and practices of rehabilitation and self-help: SAMED had trained craft and industrial workers; the Red Crescent had taught the blind to weave straw, and amputees to make artificial limbs. Even after the financing that had sustained such projects was reduced, the pattern continued as part of the Palestinian way of reacting to adversity.

National institutions: repression and survival

The first impression on entry to Shateela after the 1982 war was one of total effacement of the Resistance movement. PRM offices, military training grounds, clinics, clubs, crèches, workshops, all were either destroyed, closed down or occupied by homeless families. They seemed to survive only in people's memories, in photo albums, or as markers of different parts of the camp. The second impression was one of tenacious survival of national structures and practices produced before 1982. The popular culture openly expressed in the 1970s, encouraged and fed by the many cultural institutions attached to the PRM, showed itself able to survive in conditions of repression and clandestinity, helped by its rootedness in family life, social relations and religious traditions.

Within weeks of the massacre, a march of mourning and protest was held in Sabra/Shateela to commemorate the *arba'een*[21] of the victims led by women from the Shateela branch of the General Union of Palestinian Women (GUPW). A GUPW centre remained open in Shateela even after the closure of all other PLO/PRM offices. Here a corps of active members distributed relief to the homeless and, under the noses of army tanks, made lists of missing people. By March 1983, they had succeeded in repairing their kindergarten, and celebrated its reopening on International Women's Day with a *hafleh* (party), the first of its kind since the war, with Palestinian songs and *debkeh*.

Other outstanding national events continued to be commemorated. On 1 January 1983 (Fateh's birthday), another march wound out of Shateela down to the mass graves which, neatly fenced in, had become yet one more symbol of Palestinian struggle. Again on 30 March there were marches in Shateela and Bourj Barajneh to celebrate Day of the Land. Lebanese Army units accompanied these demonstrations and there were struggles as the Army tried to force down the Palestinian flag. Most of the marchers were housewives and children, their readiness to confront the *Jaysh* (Army) heightened by the arrest campaign. Accounts of these marches circulated in the camp, arousing a mixture of enthusiasm and fear.

The flag remained the most fundamental of national symbols, one around which individual and community struggles could focus in the absence of all other kinds. In the wake of the massacre, flags, trophies, photos, posters, membership pins and political books were hidden away or removed from the camp. Sometimes, to show both their patriotism and trust in me, the women I visited would show me a flag or pennant pinned inside a cupboard door. To exhibit such symbols openly was to court aggression. Yet young women went up to Sabra wearing necklace pendants shaped like the map of Palestine in spite of threats and insults. When teachers in Galilee school wanted to slip a flag into a science exhibition, they had to smuggle it into the camp in someone's bag. In most homes, political posters and photos of leaders were taken off the walls; but the photos of martyrs, powerful symbols of struggle, remained in their place. Several homes had video cassettes featuring national rallies.

Popular marches were difficult for the Lebanese Army to repress without a degree of force that would have created unfavourable reactions in the aftermath of the massacre. But Palestinian national institutions, both PLO and independent, were another thing. People who worked in them had little protection while premises, stocks and equipment suffered thefts and dynamite attacks. Conditions were worse in the Israeli-occupied South where only non-PLO institutions were permitted to operate; but even in the Lebanese Army-controlled zone there was little security. Conditions were worst in the first year after the invasion, before the escalation of fighting in the Shouf and the beginning of Army–militia clashes in West Beirut. Attacks also varied between institutions, those most closely associated with the PLO being the targets of the worst attacks.

The struggle of PLO institutions such as the Research Centre, the Red Crescent, SAMED, the workers' and women's unions and the Institute of

Social Affairs to stay in operation was vital not only because of the services they rendered but also because of the historic advance they symbolized, one paid for in blood and suffering – the transformation of Palestinians from anonymous refugees to a recognized national liberation movement. Though not closed, they now faced official harassment and unofficial violence. The most heinous attack was the blowing up of the Palestine Research Centre (PRC) on 5 February 1983, attributed by Palestinians to Israeli Intelligence acting through Zahi Bustani, head of General Security. The bomb blast killed twenty-four people, of whom eight were PRC employees and sixteen local residents; there was no official investigation.[22] The explosion missed only by days the crowds of women who gathered there each month to collect war widows' pensions.

After the blowing up of the PRC, neighbours of the secretariat of the women's union begged them to close it; the GUPW survived this loss, however, operating from members' homes and through informal networks, in a mode already established before 1948 in Palestine.

Other PLO institutions took risks to remain in operation. In spite of dynamite attacks, SAMED kept its sales outlet in Fakhany, as well as its large productive complex in Bourj Barajneh, giving employment to several hundred workers. The Red Crescent continued to offer medical care at its three main hospitals (Ghazzeh, Akka and Haifa), though facing Army confiscations of its stores, entry of its premises, and harassment of personnel. Another essential institution continued to function: the Institute of Social Affairs (ISA), responsible for supporting the families of victims of struggle; difficulties were met in the transfer and distribution of funds, personnel were investigated (one was arrested) and the central office was closed, but the ISA stubbornly persisted.

Apart from the PLO, there were a few independent associations active in the camps, such as In'ash al-Mukhayem, the Kanafani Cultural Association and Najdeh. These had taken steps to legalize themselves before the invasion, and were able to keep their kindergartens, workshops and training programmes going in all the camps, in the Occupied South as well as in Beirut and the Syrian zone. In offering services, generating jobs and income, and raising educational levels, these autonomous institutions played a vital role in the partial restoration of normality. Although their premises and accounts were inspected by the authorities, they were not the targets of attack in the way that PLO institutions were. However, the work of these associations was much harder in the Occupied South, where personnel were detained, imprisoned or threatened, and premises searched. Yet staff members (mostly women) continued to make the long, difficult journey between Beirut and the South.

Two new institutions underlined Palestinian capacity to develop even in bad times: Beit Atfal al-Sumood (established in 1977 to look after Tell al-Za'ter orphans) returned to Lebanon from Damascus in 1984 with changes of outlook and method. A new set-up, the Vocational and Social Development Association, was created in early 1983 to raise the technical skills of camp youth after so many years of fighting, teaching building trades, architectural drafting, and business and office practices. Later still, in 1989, a craft centre was opened, teaching school art teachers to use traditional Arabic art forms.

The vital importance of these old and new institutions was clearly visible in Shateela after the war of 1982, where projects grew up out of the ruins. During the course of 1983, with war devastation still everywhere, an UNRWA teacher searched for rooms in which to set up a science library and laboratory; a training and productive carpentry workshop was started; the GUPW launched a women's library in its underground Sabra centre; and in the shelter of the Austrian Clinic a lending library for children was opened. With no Lebanese or Arab institution to train social workers, Palestinians organized their own three-week training course in Shateela in the summer of 1983. The struggle for sociocultural development was not viewed as an alternative to armed struggle but as an essential part of a national liberation movement.

Caution, clandestinity, collaboration

'There was practically no politics after 1982. It was hard enough just to survive. We had to work to change the bad situation of our masses.' This recollection comes from a PRM cadre who escaped arrest only by changing the place he slept every few nights. Most known PRM cadres were imprisoned and deported even though they had residence rights; others left the country when they sensed that they were being followed, fearing assassination. One high PLO official went away after threatening leaflets were stuck on his door. In such an atmosphere, political work as it had been understood before 1982, open and legal under the Cairo Agreement, was out of the question.

In Shateela the predominant mood was one of extreme caution. With the national leadership inaccessibly outside and local leaders in prison or in hiding, there was no figure or body to turn to, whether for protection or advice. There was no longer a clear Resistance 'line' to follow; suspension of all PRM publications cut people off from news, analysis, guidance. The Popular Committee did not dare to meet. People discussed the situation in small, familiar groups: What could be done? Was there any Lebanese group that might be invited into the camp to help defend it against the Army? Could the government be persuaded to put the *darak* (police) around the camp instead of the *Jaysh*? The Army arrest campaign aroused fear that informers would be recruited, leading (as indeed happened) to more selective arrests. Fear became routinized through small, practical steps. This mind-set is summed up for me by the image of Abu Mustafa standing in front of his bookcase full of revolutionary literature and saying: 'There are a few books here that will have to disappear.' Hiding things was second nature. A close reserve was also practised in talking about oneself and other people.

Among many topics censored out of conversation at that time were people's feelings towards the Resistance leadership, particularly towards the decision to evacuate the fighters from West Beirut. *Dashsharoona!* (They abandoned us!) was a phrase that women sometimes let escape when talking about the massacre. It was the massacre that turned what would have been a reproach into an accusation of betrayal. 'Some of us began to say that the Revolution had sold us,' recalls a Shateela man who later took the side of the Fateh dissidents. Many people did not accept that the PRM had had no choice but to evacuate Beirut under the pressure of its Lebanese allies; the decision should have been to stay and fight. In the atmosphere bred by defeat and anger, old internal Palestinian 'localisms' were resuscitated. 'Don't forget that most of the leadership came from outside', someone said in a moment of postmortem. The reference was not merely to the coming of the Resistance to Lebanon in 1971, after expulsion from Jordan; it was also to the fact that Fateh's leadership originated mainly in Gaza and the West Bank. Related accusations were that the leadership had neglected the camps, as well as interfered ineptly in Lebanese politics. PRM 'mistakes' were blamed for current Lebanese hostility towards Palestinians: 'We didn't do anything bad to our Lebanese neighbours, it was *they* wh owere to blame.'

Sometimes it happened that a particular frustration would release a flow of anger. A widow who had just been refused a job in one of the national institutions told me, 'The Revolution took our blood and our sacrifice but it gave us nothing solid in return. It was all *hafliyat wa mahrajanat*' (parties and rallies). But such outbursts were rare.

There were many counter-currents to the mood of accusation. Housewives whom Nurse Nazira visited, remembering that she had worked in a Resistance clinic, often expressed to her their nostalgia for the 'golden days' of the PRM. Many were enthusiasts for Abu Ammar, and would bring out photos of him kissing their children. 'God willing, they will return!' was a frequent ritual of parting. Faith in the return of the PRM was kept alive by Lebanon's unsettled state, and by occasional pledges made by the leadership outside.

The split in Fateh was taken as a danger signal in Shateela; people feared correctly that it would spread to the whole Palestinian community in Lebanon. A politicized woman, director of a kindergarten, told me, 'There's a campaign now to exaggerate the *tajawuzat wa inhiraf* (excesses and deviations) of the Revolution, and to make people forget the many good things it did.' Women were more freely able to circulate in homes, and the more politicized ones worked to counteract the tide of anger, reminding people who their real enemies were and who had caused their present suffering. Many members of groups that had previously opposed or criticized Fateh argued against such criticisms now, in a time of danger and weakness. Whatever had been the mistakes of the Revolution, all the groups were responsible.

Women as a category (especially housewives) showed greatest loyalty to Arafat, either by remaining silent or by taking up the defence. From Palestine days, women had always put national unity above factional politics, and they often intervened to stop fights between Resistance groups before 1982. (The same thing had happened during early intra-Fateh clashes in the Beqa'.) For the majority of women – apart from the few mainly younger ones who were members of 'Opposition' groups – Yasser Arafat's leadership symbolized national unity. As the crisis within Fateh deepened in the course of 1983, women's gatherings reflected their intense anxiety. The worst moments came in November/December 1983, with the shelling of the camps of Nahr al-Bared and Baddawi. That Palestinians should kill Palestinians was unforgivable in women's eyes.

The problem of collaborators never took the shape in Shateela that it did in 'Ain Helweh, under Israeli occupation. In Shateela, those who had collaborated with the Deuxième Bureau before 1969 returned to their old habit; but they were known and easily avoided. With their help, the Lebanese Army succeeded in finding several PRM arms caches, but not individual ones hidden in people's homes. In a time of fear and uncertainty, it was inevitable that some people should try to gain the favour of the Army by passing on bits of information. But this was never done on a scale to make it possible to uproot Resistance group networks completely. Through well-established mechanisms of social control, all informal contacts between the Army and Shateela people were discouraged. When it was reported that a young widow living on the edge of the camp had received visits from soldiers, her paternal uncle was asked to make her leave.

Clandestine political work went on; Resistance group networks stayed in place, even if members avoided each other's eyes on the streets and stopped exchanging visits. It was a time of testing for local 'responsibles' to whom people still turned for help. Now they were torn between honour and fear, shame and self-preservation. Umm Mustafa received several visits from widows of men who had belonged to her husband's group; though worried, she never turned them away. But the wife of another local leader shamefully shut the door in visitors' faces. Actions on this level were never seen as 'not political' or 'unimportant' by the community or the Resistance movement.

In time Umm Mustafa received word that her behaviour had been appreciated by the leadership outside.

Elsewhere, *shebab* from Shateela took part in fighting on all of Lebanon's many fronts: with the Lebanese National Resistance Front against the Israelis; with the PSP against the Lebanese Forces in the Shouf; and with Amal against the Lebanese Army in West Beirut. Palestinians fought and fell in all these battles, but without publicity. Afterwards I would hear that so-and-so's son had fought in Bhamdoun, or been martyred in Tyre. Discretion even operated retrospectively – it was two years after I first started visiting Shateela that someone told me that the 'Munich incident' had been carried out by Shateela *shebab*, as well as the assassination of Wasfi Tell.

After the departure of the PRM, a new local leadership began to form, composed of younger men, 'Lebanese' Palestinians. Some came from groups like PFLP that had opposed Fateh before 1982, others from the newly formed PNSF, the Jebhat al-Inqadh. Its key members had met in Lebanese Army prisons, where they had the opportunity to forge their new political line and programme: continuation of armed struggle, cooperation with Lebanese national/progressive forces, and priority given to improving conditions in the camps. A greater degree of autonomy for local leaderships as true representatives of the people was a central element in this programme. As one member expressed it succinctly, 'This time *we* wanted to be the ones to rule.' To some extent this ambition was realized, through intense efforts deployed throughout the 'Battle of the Camps' to sustain the besieged population. Yet, ultimately, it was frustrated by regional forces in whose planning the goal of autonomous development for Palestinian camps played no part at all.

After February 1984, several Jebhat al-Inqadh (Salvation Front) cadres returned to Lebanon from Damascus, renting homes in Shateela and using them as offices. There was, however, no Fateh loyalist representative until after the first siege (May–June 1985). Once the dominant group within the PRM constellation, Fateh was now excluded from formal representation, and its supporters led an existence similar to that of a persecuted minority. This irony was forcibly presented to me the day I stumbled upon their music and *debkeh* group practising in a cellar.

Apart from clandestine PRM–Amal contacts, Shateela people took little military part in the uprising of February 1984. Only a few weeks before, Lebanese Army units around the camp had shelled Amal militia positions further east, damaging Shateela homes in the process. During this period, Amal militiamen used to enter the camp at night, as friends and allies. Nurses from Shateela helped to look after wounded Amal militia. No one thought then that, fifteen months later, Amal would be attacking Shateela and Palestinians at large with much more ferocity than the Army had done.

Shi'ite neighbours

About half the inhabitants of the large apartment building where Abu and Umm Mustafa lived, just outside the boundaries of the camp, were Shi'ites. Umm Mustafa received daily visits from her Shi'ite neighbour Umm 'Imad. There were many strands to their friendship: cooperation over water (with tap water cut off, they shared a tank which had to be replenished daily from a distant main); loans of kitchen implements or food items; exchange of building gossip; morale-raising and sympathy. They accompanied each other on marketing expeditions; Umm 'Imad, was also a member of Umm Mustafa's adult literacy class. From Umm 'Imad, Umm Mustafa heard each latest episode of the bitter quarrel that rent the Shi'ite families inhabiting the building, a quarrel from which Umm Mustafa carefully kept aloof, since such affairs were apt to turn violent, or political.

Once when Umm Mustafa had not heard from her family in 'Ain Helweh for a long time, and could not go there because of an Israeli clamp-down on the transit of Palestinians, Umm 'Imad's mother went instead, stayed overnight, and brought back news of everyone, including a sister-in-law who had been wounded demonstrating against the Occupation. Relations between the two women could hardly have been warmer if they had been mother and daughter, or aunt and niece.

Shi'ites had started moving into the neighbourhoods around Shateela in the early 1970s, as Israeli attacks against South Lebanon escalated. Relations had been good at first. Palestinians and Lebanese Shi'ites shared common enemies (Israel, the rightist militias), and a common situation of poverty and oppression. In addition there were shared cultural elements: Islam, Arabism and the radical/populist ideas which characterized that period. Shi'ites had been attracted in large numbers into the Resistance movement, and were scattered across the different groups just as Palestinians were. Shi'ite households had benefited from PRM services and efforts to ameliorate material conditions, and Shi'ites became members of the Popular Committees set up in the outer neighbourhoods on the model of Shateela's. On the surface, the PRM slogan of *sha'b wahid* (one people) had concrete, daily-life reality. There were Palestinian–Shi'ite marriages (Shateela had quite a few such mixed households).

Relations began to deteriorate after 1978, when Amal movement began its campaign for hegemony over the Shi'ite masses. Between 1978 and 1982, the southern suburbs gradually became prohibited territory to secular leftist and PRM formations, while some Shi'ite members of Resistance groups around Shateela withdrew from membership. Amal influence altered Shi'ite perceptions of Palestinians, emphasizing national and sectarian boundaries that had not been salient in the early 1970s.

Sectarianism apart, Shi'ite–Palestinian relations were made antagonistic by a set of national/civic and economic asymmetries that transversed each other. It was not just the simple paradox, noted by a prominent Shi'ite intellectual after the first Amal attack,[23] that this was a conflict between a people deprived of their country and a people oppressed in their own country. It was that oppressed Shi'ites, nonetheless, had rights and interests as Lebanese nationals that Palestinians did not have. Amal mobilization played up the discrepancy between Shi'ite subordination within the structures of the PRM and their rights as 'sons of a government'; rather than struggling to weaken the Lebanese state for the benefit of non-Lebanese, Amal said that Shi'ites should struggle to build up the state while asserting their rights to its benefits. What this could mean in everyday terms became clear after 1982, when Shi'ites around Shateela began to use their connections with the Army and police to occupy houses or evict tenants, asserting their superiority over Palestinians as citizens against non-citizens.

The economic asymmetry also worked in the other direction, a skew that added bitterness to the national/civic issue. To outsiders, Shi'ites and Palestinians in the southern suburbs appeared to belong to the same broad socioeconomic stratum, that mass of small shop-keepers, functionaries, semi-industrial and sub-proletarian workers that Arabic amalgamates in the term *sha'b* (people), resonant with implications of shared oppositional interests. However, their common membership in the *sha'bi* stratum only concealed a sub-class differentiation which gained significance in conditions of worsening economic crisis. There are shades within poverty. Shi'ite households in the southern suburbs were, in general, poorer and larger than Palestinian camp families, had lower levels of education and were less likely to have members in the professions. Shi'ites were less well established in the oil-producing countries (their migration there started much later than the Palestinians'), and were less likely to receive remittances to invest in small businesses or children's education. Their homes were less well furnished and equipped. To Shi'ites, these material advantages were unfair privilege, the result of free UNRWA schooling and services, Arab and international aid and media attention from which they were excluded. Such perceptions accumulated as a kind of underclass resentment. The bitterness of seeing Palestinians better themselves made Shi'ites of the southern suburbs more receptive to messages of Lebanese nationalism projecting Palestinians as aliens, intruders and 'destroyers of our country'. Extensive Shi'ite employment in the Army, police and government administration helps explain how Maronite rightist stereotypes of Palestinians could be transferred to a community that still claimed to be contesting Maronite hegemony. Oppressed by their state, Shi'ites could nonetheless direct their resentment against Palestinian neighbours as an economically privileged but non-national, non-citizen group.

While Shi'ite attitudes towards Palestinians were becoming more hostile and more sectarian, Palestinian perceptions of Shi'ites remained stable up to the first Amal attack. Men like Abu Mustafa and Abu Mujahed, members of radical Resistance groups, living with Shi'ite neighbours and working with Shi'ite colleagues, continued to categorize Amal as 'sons of the same road' and 'strategic allies'. They still believed in the 'one people' slogan. Alliance with Lebanese national/progressive forces was an important component in leftist Palestinian ideology, one that differentiated radicals from Fateh; and it was radicals who now dominated camp politics. Palestinians less influenced by ideology may have had more discriminatory perceptions, tinged with a superiority derived from belonging to an older and, in local terms, more powerful political movement. But even they perceived Shi'ites as Muslims (like us) rather than as Shi'ites (different, other). In spite of the pre-1982 Amal–Palestinian clashes (seen as no more serious than intra-Palestinian clashes), nothing in their history had prepared Palestinians to classify Shi'ites as enemies. This helps to explain the unexpectedness and shock of the first Amal attack on 19 May, as well as why the incidents preceding the attack were not interpreted as pointing to a major showdown.

Once, soon after the February uprising, Umm Mustafa said to me in a low voice, so that Abu Mustafa wouldn't hear, '*Khayifeen*' (we are afraid). I was surprised. Only a few weeks before, at night, the army had taken away two young men, sons of neighbours. And Umm Mustafa herself had complained of the breakneck speed with which Army jeeps drove on the street outside the building, endangering children. Hadn't the Army deliberately fired into the camp during the fight with Amal in December? Surely it was better to have Amal militia round the camp than the 'Jaysh al-Ta'ifi'? Much later I wondered if women, les influenced by ideology than men, had a sharper nose for danger. But Umm Mustafa was unwilling to explain her remark, and I never discovered what particular happening had triggered it.

There were even signs of *infiraj* (relief from tension, end of a crisis) after the February uprising: the women's and workers' unions expanded their projects; three cultural clubs for young men were opened (they did not carry Resistance group names but corresponded with the three main Resistance parties); the Popular Committee emerged from hiding. Its chairman, Abu Mujahed, could often be seen on the road between Shateela and the Hursh, talking with Amal people about water and electricity supplies. The Movement was helping homeless Shi'ite families to settle in vacant lots around Shateela. With Nabih Berri now a Cabinet minister, Abu Mujahed hoped that state funds might become available to deal with problems such as flooding and sewage seepage, from which Lebanese and Palestinians in the area suffered alike.

There were also less visible signs of underlying tension. Change in Amal's attitude towards Palestinians in fact manifested itself immediately after the February uprising, when Amal commanders on the 'Green Line' disarmed and sent away Palestinian fighters. Around Shateela there was a rise in cases of Shi'ite house-owners either evicting Palestinian tenants or raising rents, using Amal's presence to back up their demands. (Even before 1984, there had been cases of Shi'ite families with Army or police connections moving into Palestinian property. Amal militiamen also conducted searches inside the camp, giving security as a pretext and in some cases taking protection money. Palestinians seen carrying guns outside the camp were stopped and disarmed (after the uprising camp people again began to carry individual weapons). Sometimes Amal militiamen pursued Palestinians into the camp in order to disarm them. Such actions were the cause of most of the quarrels and clashes that punctuated this period.

Yet such incidents were not taken by Shateela people as a sign of intolerable tension that was bound to lead to an all-out confrontation. On the one hand, people who were afraid were inhibited from expressing their fears. Besides, they had few practical alternatives to staying in the camp. On the other hand, camp people are accustomed to living among armed men, liable at any moment to shoot out their political or personal differences. Further, such incidents were invariably solved through higher-level contacts between the Popular Committee and Amal leaders. Perhaps the most important reason was that Palestinians regarded Amal as merely a people's militia, with neither the authority nor the power to disarm them.

The first serious clash between Amal and Shateela occurred in June 1984. It came to be known as the 'Nimrud problem'. Nimrud was a local Amal unit leader, whose nickname had been given him because of his quarrelsome, domineering character. His family lived in the Hursh and early on he set out deliberately to provoke the people of the camp. Abu Imad describes him:

Although he was only about twenty years old, Nimrud was a unit commander. He had a bullet-proof vest and never went anywhere without armed bodyguards. He used to drive his car into the narrow roads of the camp, ordering other drivers out of the way. If he saw a pretty girl he would hoot his car horn at her. Kids who came near him he hit with his gun butt.

On a February day when people in Shateela were mourning the death by shelling of a man from the Sa'd family, Nimrud drove into the camp and turned up the volume of his radio under the mosque so that it drowned out the mourning chant. The provocation was too much. Nimrud was killed by two *shebab* who immediately escaped. Amal units stayed for two hours inside Shateela, hunting for the assassins. They broke into houses and manhandled inhabitants, they broke up the youth clubs, they insulted and beat people, they even entered the Mosque without taking off their shoes.

After this incident, to calm everyone's anger, local Amal commander Khalil Hamdan spoke in Shateela Mosque, invoking Shi'ite–Palestinian solidarity and telling his audience, 'We are both *mahrumeen* (oppressed).' Yet from the time of the Nimrud incident the mood of Amal militiamen around the camp became more aggressive. In April, Ahmad Haleemeh's father was struck by an Amal jeep, although he was walking well to the side of the road. The jeep, which must have swerved to hit him, left him lying on the street with his thigh bone shattered. Condemned as hooliganism, such incidents were not given political significance. Even Amal's attack on the Murabitoun on 14 April was not interpreted as the prelude to an attack against Shateela. If they had expected the attack on 19 May, the camp would not have been packed with all 8,000 residents,[24] and there would have been more arms and ammunition.

It was only just before the incident that triggered the attack of 19 May that the camp leadership became aware that Amal militiamen were fortifying their offices outside the camp. A little earlier the Movement had requested that *shebab* from Shateela should be sent to the 'Green Line'. At the same time Amal sent orders that no one should move within the camp after dark. A leader of one of the pro-Syrian Resistance groups went out to ask the meaning of these happenings and was told that they were precautions against suspected Deuxième Bureau movements. With Ramadan beginning on 19 May, no one imagined that fellow Muslims could be planning an attack.

There were many versions of the incident that triggered the attack. An official Amal spokesman said that one of their jeeps had been fired on near Da'ouq (the small, unofficial camp at the heart of Sabra), killing some of its occupants and wounding others. The assailants, whom Amal accused of being 'Arafatists' had escaped into the alleys of Da'ouq. Some Palestinians said that Amal militiamen had followed a young man into Da'ouq to disarm him, and that a quarrel had broken out during which shots were fired; others said that Amal demanded the handing over of a number of young men. It seemed an incident like so many others. What was different this time was that Amal immediately massed large numbers of men, military vehicles and heavy artillery around the area, and began shelling both Shateela and Da'ouq. The 'Battle of the Camps' had begun.

After the siege, I asked Abu Mustafa if their Shi'ite neighbour and friend Umm 'Imad hadn't forewarned them. He said, 'They were as surprised as we were.' He added that this showed how artificial the conflict was, a product not of Shi'ite–Palestinian hostility but of 'orders from above'. He said that Umm 'Imad and her mother had asked about Umm Mustafa during the siege and visited her afterwards to say '*hamdillah al-salameh*' (thank God for your safety).

Notes

1. From an AFP report by S. Yasseen, published in *L'Orient/Le Jour*, 31 August 1982.

2. The neighbourhoods around Shateela – Hursh, Hayy Farhat, Gharbeh, the Sports City – were extremely heterogeneous. As well as Palestinians and Lebanese Shi'ites, they included people of several Arab and non-Arab nationalities and stateless residents of Lebanon (Kurds, gypsies, Bedouin).

3. Interview with Salah Salah, 4 November 1982.

4. From testimonies taken in Bourj Barajneh on 4 October 1982 by the author.

5. S. Salah, 4 November.

6. For testimony on the Israeli prison for women in Lebanon (Ansariyya), see R. Sayigh, 'The Mukhabarat State: Testimony of a Palestinian Woman Prisoner', *Race and Class*, vol. 26, no. 2, Autumn 1984.

7. There is a substantial literature on Israel and South Lebanon, including the following: Sean MacBride Commission, *Israel in Lebanon* (London: Ithaca Press, 1983); Reports of the National Emergency Committee on Lebanon (US); J. Fine, 'Human Rights and the IVth Geneva Convention in Israeli-occupied South Lebanon: An Initial Inquiry', August 1982. See also Fédération Internationale des Droits de l'Homme, 'Liban: le problème des disparus', 27 January 1984; and Amnesty International's *Concerns in Lebanon*, December 1985.

8. From *The Economist*, 16 April 1983 ('Southern Cross', p. 24).

9. Among rightist Maronite charges against Palestinians was that many of them were not lawfully resident in Lebanon. Some on the right wanted to exclude all those who had not come in 1948 and were not registered by UNRWA. (UNRWA registration lists were closed in 1953.)

10. *L'Orient/Le Jour*, 27 September 1982.

11. For the PLO after 1982, see E. Sahlieh, *The PLO after the Lebanon War* (Boulder: Westview, 1986); Y. Sayigh, 'Politics of Palestinian Exile'; R. Brynen, *Sanctuary and Survival*.

12. Different terms have been used for this: its authors termed it an *intifada* (uprising, rebellion), while Fateh loyalists called it a 'mutiny'. Popular terms used by those against the rebellion were *manshaqeen* (those who cause a split), and *jama'a* Abu Musa (Abu Musa's following), while Fateh loyalists continued to call themselves Fateh. Organizationally, the two are differentiated as Fateh–Provisional Council (Damascus) and Fateh–Central Council (Tunis).

13. See E. Rouleau, 'The Mutiny against Yasser Arafat', and R. Khalidi, 'Behind the Fateh Rebellion', both in *MERIP Reports*, no. 119, November–December 1983.

14. Y. Sayigh, 'Politics of Palestinian Exile', p. 61 n. 76.

15. The precipitating incident was Arafat's appointment, as commanders, of two men discredited during the 1982 war, Abu Hajeem and Hajj Isma'il (Brynen, *Sanctuary and Survival*, p. 185).

16. For details, see the *MERIP Report* special issue, 'The PLO Split', no. 119, November–December 1983.

17. See Brynen, *Sanctuary and Survival*, p. 187.

18. Brynen, *ibid.*, p. 228 n. 11. The same PLO demands were made when negotiations with the Lebanese government recommenced in April 1991, in the

context of post-Ta'ef pacification.

19. M. al-Ali, 'Education in Shateela Camp', MA thesis, Lebanese University, 1983 (Arabic).

20. This estimate was given by someone who worked with the survey carried out between 1978 and 1982 by TEAM for ECWA.

21. According to a pre-Islamic custom, condolence visits are paid on the fortieth day after death. Such occasions may be used to honour the deceased or to make a political demonstration.

22. PRC staff continued to work after the 5 February car-bomb, even though the building was judged unsafe. Harassment continued: on 5 April, Lebanese Army tanks surrounded the Centre, soldiers entered, forced employees to stand against a wall and searched the premises; on 5 June, one of the staff was refused entry at the airport; later in June two employees were detained, then deported; on 18 June, the car of an employee blew up, killing its owner; on 19 June, the Centre's director, Sabry Jiryis, was told to report to the Prosecutor General; the next day, the Centre was sealed off and all its equipment, furniture and archives were taken away in Army trucks; on 4 July the director was deported.

23. At the time, this paradox was attributed to the writer and journalist Wadah Sharara. He denies authorship.

24. The figure of 8,000 was given to me by the camp director in late 1983. It applies only to the population within the exact boundaries of the camp.

Part III:
Living the Sieges

9. The Siege of Ramadan
(19 May to 22 June 1985)

Each of the three main sieges of Shateela had its own particular characteristics. The first, because of the unexpectedness of the attack, was the most dramatic and heroic, the one that tested Shateela people's combativeness and resourcefulness to the utmost, the one with the most extraordinary stories of individual courage. The discrepancy between the attackers and defenders in terms of type and quantity of weapons was at its greatest, medical conditions inside the camp at their worst. This was the only siege when the attackers succeeded in penetrating the perimeter of the camp; forcing the defenders back into a small circle of families and fighters huddled around the Mosque (most of the ground lost was regained before the end of the siege). Amal's certainty of victory was so great that it repeatedly announced that Shateela had fallen, and that it had achieved total control of the Sabra/Shateela area. The first siege was notable also in being accompanied by a pogrom against Palestinians outside the besieged camps, in Hursh, Sabra, Fakhany and in West Beirut generally. This was the result of sectarian mobilization, as well as anger at heavy Amal losses and at the shelling of Shi'ite residential areas by Palestinian forces in the Shouf. Even after the siege was lifted on 22 June, in compliance with the first Damascus Agreement, people going out of and into the camp had to brave lines of angry Shi'ite families and Amal fighters.

'It was a war of annihilation!'

I give Umm Mustafa's account first because she expresses the feelings of a mother with young children: seven were with her inside Shateela; two were outside, unable to get back. It was also the first I recorded, on 23 June, the day the first UNRWA food lorry got in. Interrupted by tears of exhaustion, by children's demands for money to buy sweets, and by a visit to glimpse their rocket-shattered home, Umm Mustafa's story fully reflects the ordeal that was only now, and only partially, ending.

We thought it would all be over in two or three hours, like other incidents, but it lasted nearly five weeks. When I said, 'Let's leave', he'd say, 'It isn't serious, by tomorrow it will be over.' It was a war of annihilation. Machine-gun bullets don't worry us, it was the tank shells and rockets that drove us crazy. Every day they poured at least 500 shells on us, all heavy calibre. By the end they were using 60mm tank shells that come along the ground and contain a lot of shrapnel – they're worse than cannon. It was direct firing from close range. Every second we were saying, '*Allahu akbar*, here's one coming!' None of us expected to stay alive.

The invasion of 1982 wasn't like this. Then there were lulls between bombardments when you could go out, get water, buy things you needed. This time it was non-stop shelling. You didn't dare move outside the house. If a child wanted to drink, willy-nilly you had to go out and fill the jerrycan. Every second you expected a shell to fall.

We had to leave our home on the third day when Amal launched an attack on the southern entrance. Shells were crashing around the building, we couldn't use the streets. The *shebab* broke a passage through the walls and helped carry the children into the camp.

At first we were in one of the shelters. But then the wounded came from the Mosque – some could walk, others couldn't. They said they'd stay until there was a lull in the shelling, but we told them, 'You stay here, we'll find somewhere else.' So we came to this house, and we've been here ever since. We've been living on tinned things, rice, *burghul* [crushed wheat] and macaroni. People took supplies from any home whose owners had fled.

We had 160 wounded and 49 martyrs. Most of the dead wouldn't have died if we had had an operating theatre and proper medicine. At first they put the wounded in the Mosque but Amal concentrated their fire on it, and many were wounded a second time. Then they moved them somewhere else, but the same thing happened. Many were in a critical condition. There was Imad, they had to cut his foot off with a knife; he died the same night. There was a *shabb* called Rashid whose hand went black and shrunken. God be praised, at last the Red Cross came and took out the most seriously wounded.[1]

We were all afraid. The young were afraid and the old were afraid. Muhammad [the youngest, a year old] would come to my lap and put his arms around my neck as soon as he heard a shell. The little ones didn't leave my side. It felt like thirty years, not thirty days. We didn't dare to wash our clothes.

People told me that my daughter Aida came from Sidon to see us. She got as far as Da'ouq, then she went back. I went out yesterday to try to see her, as soon as they opened the road, with other women. It's five weeks and the children haven't had fruit or vegetables. But Amal was still outside the camp near the 'Ali Handar cafe. They were stopping people from bringing in supplies. I had to insist 500 times before they would let me back in.

'What luck to have the chance to kill a Palestinian!'

The first attack caused total confusion, with masses of people fleeing to areas they believed safer, leaving around 1,500 people inside Shateela, compared to the normal population of around 8,000. Palestinians of the surrounding neighbourhoods also left or were turned out of their homes. After Amal 'cleaned out' Sabra and Fakhany, most of the displaced gathered in Wata Museitbeh, protected by the PSP. Others scattered throughout West Beirut, in underground garages, schools and unfinished buildings.

The traffic was not all one way. Some people entered Shateela to help defend it, for example Fahd, a Lebanese young man who wanted to fight with the Palestinians; Fedwa, a nurse, to help the wounded; and Amal, a woman cadre, to give leadership to other women inside the camp.

Abu Bilal left Shateela at dawn on the morning of 20 May after his home was hit, taking his wife, children, mother and younger brothers and sisters to their relative's house near Gaza Hospital.

A few hours after we reached my kinsman's house, Amal militia swarmed into the building, breaking into all the apartments and asking for Palestinians. They arrested me along with my uncle, after shooting in the air to frighten the women into the kitchen. My son Bilal clung to me but they kicked him aside.

We were taken to an empty room in a nearby building, our hands were tied behind our back with wire, and our eyes blindfolded. They made us crouch on the floor. We were searched and our pockets emptied – later they returned my things to me.

They accused us of being fighters. I said, 'No, I am a teacher, here is my ID card.' The Amal guy conducting the interrogation began to curse Palestinians for having schools and being educated. He said, 'I'll tear up your card, then you'll be a fighter.' He asked me questions, such as how many fighters there were in the camp and how many in Gaza Hospital.

All through the interrogation they cursed, insulted and threatened us. They said, 'We are going to step on you Palestinians and Sunnis!' They cursed Abu Ammar, they kicked us in our faces, back and shoulders. They pointed their guns at our heads. One of them said, 'What luck to have the chance to kill a Palestinian!'

They asked me again how many fighters there were in Gaza Hospital. I said I thought there weren't any. Then they forced me to stand in the street outside the hospital, to see if anyone inside would shoot at me. No one shot. Then one of their snipers shot between my feet, forcing me back into the entrance of the building where they had arrested me. Five or six militia set upon me, kicking and punching me, cursing Palestinians, calling me 'Pig!' and saying that all Palestinians must die.

From there I was taken to another room where I saw four other prisoners, all civilians. The leader gave orders for these men to be killed on the grounds that they were fighters. He told me, 'If you don't talk, you'll be killed like them.' From where I sat I could see the prisoners being executed on the edge of the playing field behind the hospital. After shooting them, the militiamen threw the bodies behind a wall, and removed the traces of blood from the ground.

One of the Amal guys in the room with me again pointed a gun at my head. He pulled the trigger, but the cartridge must have been empty. One of them who seemed like a leader said, 'Don't kill anyone. We shall need them.' Later on one of them took me back to my kinsman's home. He told me not to leave and set a guard on the door.

Soon after this Amal began their assault on the hospital. They attacked it from all sides, bringing up tanks through the playing field. There was some resistance – maybe there were three or four fighters inside. The fighting lasted about an hour. I could see some of what happened because the building where I was, is right opposite the hospital, but I couldn't get close to the windows because of the shooting. I saw Amal bringing out a large group of the wounded who could walk, together with several nurses. It was between 5 and 6 pm. They made them walk through the passage that connects the courtyard of the hospital with the playing field. A few minutes later I heard a volley of shots. I didn't see the shooting but there's a woman in the building overlooking the playing field who says she did.

After the storming of the hospital, Amal came back to the apartment to look for me, but my family had hidden me well and they were unable to find me. They took away my uncle and kept him for four days in a building near Summerland, where he was beaten up. I was able to escape during the night with my family to a safer part of Beirut.

'My son still hasn't reappeared'

Rabiha is a PRCS employee, a widow, who had one child, a boy of eleven. Their home was in Shateela. I recorded her in October 1986, sixteen months after the end of the first siege.

On Wednesday 22 May I was outside the camp. I had an only son inside and I went to take him out. It was about 10 am. I brought him and we reached Gaza Hospital together. There were many people taking shelter in it. Amal militia were all around the hospital and they looked as if they were about to break in. I took my son and we ran towards Fakhany. On the way we met a girl. She told us that Amal and the 6th Brigade were near the Municipal Sportsground. 'Go back' she said, 'They are shooting everyone Palestinian.' My son was frightened. He ran off towards Da'ouq. I ran after him but lost him. So I went back to Gaza Hospital. I thought he was bound to come to Gaza, he couldn't go back to Shateela. So I sat and waited.

We were all sitting in the entrance of the hospital when the shelling started. We went down to the basement. There were many wounded people and civilians there. Some of us went to the operations room in the basement, but a doctor advised us not to stay there. He said Amal would go straight to the basement and start shooting, we should go up to the first floor. By the time they reached there they would have calmed down a bit.

It was about 5 pm. We went to the operations room on the first floor, I and twenty male and female nurses, and the doctor. We were afraid, and fasting. There was a lot of noise of tanks and shelling, and the shouting of militia. After a while the accent of the fighters outside changed from Palestinian to Lebanese. The Army entered the hospital. One of the wounded was lying almost dead in the room where we make plaster casts. They came and set fire to him. I didn't see it, but people who were there saw the fire lit on the body. We could hear women and children's voices screaming '*Allahu akbar*!' There were bullets flying everywhere in the basement. They shot with B7s at the refrigerator where they keep the dead. They took some of the wounded away, and they still haven't reappeared.

Finally they reached the first floor. They wanted to shoot us, but the doctor said to them, 'Wait, I'm a doctor, let's talk.' They put the men in one room and started checking their ID cards. They took us to another room and shut us in, and said, 'Give us the keys to the cupboards. We want to search them for arms.' We told them we didn't have the keys. They began to curse us and use dirty words, and to shoot at our feet.

After they had broken into the cupboards and taken what they wanted, they let us out. We couldn't find the doctor and the male nurses; we were afraid that they had killed them and now they would kill us. But the director of the hospital came and took us to stay with some people he knew from Amal Movement.

Outside the hospital there was a crowd of people – women and children – all trying to run away. As for the wounded, some were killed downstairs, and some were taken away by their relatives. Anyone who could save a wounded person did so; we didn't see what happened after we left. There were people who saw them shoot people behind Dana Mosque. There are some people who showed up again afterwards. But of the wounded and civilians that were led out of Gaza, none was ever seen again.

I heard from people that my son was in Da'ouq until it surrendered. He wasn't wounded, he was OK. They said that when Da'ouq fell, he was taken with a group of civilians from the Old People's Home. That was a year and a half ago, and he still hasn't reappeared.

'It was like the Paris Commune'

The speaker here is Abu Mustafa, one of two Popular Committee members to stay in Shateela. This gives his narrative an official tone. He played an important role in organizing bread and food supplies.

First we have to acknowledge the importance of positions taken by those who 'understood': Iran, Libya, the USSR, Hizbollah and the National Democratic Front (Jumblat).[2] Some Lebanese leaders, such as al-Hoss, took good stands. This helped us a lot.

Amal and the Palestinians shed blood together defending the South and our relations with them are those of a strategic and historic merger. We never expected that Amal would allow itself to be pulled by certain parties into confrontation with us. We are against the Amman Agreement and the line of capitulation. We are with the Salvation Front, Syria and the national forces in Lebanon. When, in the middle of the fighting, we heard that the US Navy was approaching, even in that difficult moment when they were shelling us, our young men wanted to fight with Amal against the Sixth Fleet. We had no readiness at all for a confrontation with Amal. But they imagined that after two or three days we would be finished. As 'the Doctor'[3] said, Syria gave Amal the green light to hit us.

We fought to defend ourselves, from inside our homes, we didn't go out and attack anyone. We fought from house to house, because if we hadn't, they would have exterminated us. That's what made our young men able to carry on a continuous defence. All our fighters were sons of the camp, young men who hadn't been trained in the time of the Resistance, 80 per cent schoolboys who hadn't held a Klashin in their hands before, the reserves of the reserves. There were no fighters from outside and there were very few who had had real military training. This is because we had no plan to fight. We salute the steadfastness of these young men fighting for the first time. They proved their worth. A new revolution has been born with them.

Most of the arms we used we took from the enemy. They shelled us with 120mm artillery shells. Some didn't explode. The *shebab* would take out the detonator and use them against the attackers. We didn't have artillery; instead we used liquid-gas containers with home made devices for exploding them. We didn't have these before the siege: they were produced during the battle, from necessity. Of course we had simple weapons, Klashins, B7s, individual arms, and things we could fabricate such as in the beginning of the Resistance movement. With these simple arms we resisted the tanks that came to shell us.

The battle was continual, non-stop. The fighters never left the bases. We formed something that we called the Rapid Intervention Committee – the way the Americans have an Emergency Task Force, we had this committee. Wherever there was an attack, this force would rush to the defence.

The battle succeeded in unifying our ranks in the camp. There was no son of Fateh, no son of the Popular Front or Democratic Front. Everyone was fighting for himself and his camp. The Resistance groups were all present and they fought jointly. The fighting was for all, the food was for all, the medical supplies we had were for all.

From the first day we had wounded. In this respect, too, we were unprepared for battle. We didn't have a hospital or clinic in the camp – there was no operating theatre, no medical supplies. We had two doctors, a man and a woman, and they gave first aid to the wounded. First aid materials were gathered from every home in the camp – cotton, aspirin – everyone gave what they had.

I asked the doctor about one of the wounded. He said, 'He can't live.' Four days later I was amazed to see him back at his base. We had young men who were wounded three or four times, and yet returned to their bases. Many of the wounded fought, even with one arm or one leg. They came back to fight even though they knew that there were no medical supplies, no proper medical treatment.

We thank the International Red Cross for their many attempts to enter the camp, but we must record for history that half our martyrs died because there was no proper treatment. For thirty days there was no kind of break in the siege. Shelling on our field hospital was so heavy that it had to be moved three times. We couldn't bury our dead at first because we had no cemetery. It's the greatest disgrace for the whole Muslim community that we were not able to take our dead out and bury them properly in a cemetery. And we couldn't take our wounded out for treatment. But our Mosque will remain for coming generations as a symbol of the steadfastness of Shateela.

Our experience was a rich one. We weren't expecting this confrontation, we lacked many of the most necessary things. This forced us to invent new ways of struggle. We used bedspreads and pillow covers to make sandbags. We needed cotton for wounds, so we took it from pillows. When we couldn't take our martyrs out for burial, we used the Mosque as a cemetery. It's true that it was a painful experience because it was a battle between allies. But out of our steadfastness we could open a school in Shateela for all the liberation movements of the world on how to manage a siege, and how to win a victory with small means. It was like the Paris Commune.

'We didn't let the *shebab* lack anything'

The next speaker, Leila, was active with the women's union. She had been through the siege of Tell al-Za'ter and was now engaged to be married. Later, during the third siege, she gave birth to a baby boy.

On the first day there was heavy shelling. We women helped the wounded. If they had light wounds we treated them, and if they needed further treatment we evacuated them up through the alleys. None of the roads was safe. We took them out of the camp on stretchers, towards the road that leads to the Sports City, but using back alleys. From there, at the beginning, an ambulance took them.

Then we started working on food. The *shebab* were fighting, and there was nothing for them to eat. The first day we made them sandwiches – bread, mortadella, *halaweh*[4] – we wrapped them up and sent them to the fighters. The bases still hadn't been established.

The second day we worked with the wounded again, and again we made sandwiches and took them to the fighters in spite of heavy shelling. On Tuesday the shelling got heavier. We began cooking for the *shebab* because sandwiches weren't enough for them. We cooked the food in saucepans and carried it to them. It encouraged the fighters a lot when they saw us bringing them food under bombardment, it helped their morale. We also helped them fill their stores with ammunition. We didn't let them lack anything. Whenever there was a lull we visited them to see how they were.

The Mosque was shelled so heavily that we had to move the wounded to another place a bit beyond it. We cooked for the wounded and for the fighters. We used to cook seven large saucepans of food every day. We took them this for lunch; for supper and breakfast we went on making them sandwiches of mortadella or cheese or jam. With Comrade Amal we went round to all the shops in the camp and bought all the goods that were in them. If the owners weren't there, we made an inventory so that we could pay them later. Some of the fighters were fasting – we made them *iftar*.[5] Those who were fasting came at night to get *suhoor*[6] – we didn't give them cooked food, only bread and cheese.

At the beginning we had supplies of tea and coffee. We distributed tea to the bases and they made it for themselves. Each base had a room which they fixed up so that they could relax in it. Families living near the base helped them too, for example by giving them tea in the morning. Every two or three days we made them *mena'eesh*.[7] That was before the bakery was hit.

Once Comrade Amal and some of the *banat* helped to stop an attack. It was at the PFLP base, on the street nearest the main entrance. We refilled their ammunition stock and confronted the attack with them. Snipers from high buildings outside controlled both the main alleys. We had wounded in one room; in the other was the kitchen. The sniping was so bad that we couldn't take food from the kitchen to the wounded. We would run with the food in our hands and jump across the alley that was exposed to sniping. It was as dangerous at night as in the day.[8] They hit the centre many times while we were in it. We had to move several times.

On the day they shelled for sixteen hours running, the house where we were cooking was hit. Rubble came down on us, and dust and smoke. And this centre where we are now was hit several times and sniped at, and its windows were broken. They didn't manage to occupy the Military College but sometimes they infiltrated it and hit us from there. They hit the windows and the walls and the cupboards. They used grenades a lot.

There was never any lack of volunteers. Several women were martyred. Sheikha Sa'eed was taking food to the *shebab* when a shell hit her. She was killed, and Nawal who was with her lost a leg.

Medical supplies were scarce and there was a shortage of things needed to clean wounds. When bandages completely gave out, in the middle of the siege, the *shebab* opened a path to the UNRWA clinic which is outside the camp. Comrade Amal went out with two other *banat* and brought everything that was there.

'We had no medical station'

Virtually the most dramatic aspect of the first siege of Shateela was the lack of medical facilities. Together with a newly qualified woman doctor and a male nurse, Dr Muhammad al-Khateeb organized medical care from scratch, under heavy shelling. His home was in the camp, although his professional work was outside it.

We were working in unusual conditions – in the middle of a battle, besieged, no medical station, no place to carry out examinations, no equipment, almost no medicines, and we couldn't move the wounded out of the battle area. On top of all this, I'm a general practitioner, not a surgeon.

We made a medical centre out of an ordinary home, after moving several times. There were many problems, for example ensuring cleanliness, training helpers, procuring food. Everything had to be done under continual shelling. We were forced to move the centre three times when shelling got too close or too heavy. Several patients were wounded a second time in the centre. It was hard moving the patients who couldn't or weren't supposed to walk; we used doors as stretchers to carry them. We decided to move patients out of the Mosque after ten days – this probably saved thirty lives – Amal knew that we were using it as a hospital by questioning women who left the camp.

The wounded had to sleep on the floor, on mattresses that we collected from houses. It wasn't ideal but we had no other choice. In our third centre we had two rooms for the wounded, and a small treatment room. There was no electricity so we had to work by candlelight. The windows were sandbagged to protect us from snipers. We put twelve patients in each room measuring 4 x 4 metres. In each room there were three or four attendants.

Our medical team consisted of two doctors, both general practitioners, and a qualified staff nurse who was able to take over a doctor's duties. We had seven girls permanently helping us as nursing assistants, to clean simple wounds, talk to the patients, help them, wash and cook. None of them was trained. I had some difficulties with them at the beginning. They would start dressing wounds themselves, thinking they were doing it just like me. I had to teach them that not all wounds are treated alike. Some I had to send away because they wouldn't follow orders. I had to shout a lot at the beginning, but by the end they were an excellent team.

We needed water and food for the wounded. We used to send girls to bring cooked food from people's homes. Luckily there was a young man, an Egyptian worker living in the camp, who volunteered to bring water for us and clean the floors and wash the bedclothes – there was always lots of blood. He also helped with burials. He did the work of six people.

We had no medical supplies, so I asked everyone who had medicines to bring them whatever they were: aspirin, cotton, bandages, antiseptics, syringes. We found a few bags of saline drip. We had no real painkillers, only aspirin, Anacin, Panadol and some Doloxene. Of course in a war you need morphine and pethidine. What we did was to give people aspirin and tell them it was something stronger, such as Valium. The patient would believe us and feel better. In a shop we found some alcohol and ten bottles of Dettol which we used to clean wounds and wash floors. We used eau de Cologne to wash our hands.

If a patient had pain at night we brought a girl volunteer to sit by the bed. Not one of the nurses, but an ordinary girl. When a girl is there, talking to him, putting her hand on his shoulder, it calms a patient and lessens his pain. Pain is subjective. What the patient needs is affection, sympathy. Another factor we counted on is a man's pride. He can't allow himself to show weakness in front of a girl.

There was another method: intimidation. We had to forbid those with stomach wounds to drink water because it can cause death through haemorrhage or infection. Of course it's difficult in summer to go without water. One patient in particular kept begging for a drink. I'd tell him, 'If you drink we'll have to take you to the cemetery. But if you last an hour without water, you'll be alright.' He'd bear it for an hour, then two, and so on for a week. It was a mixture of carrot and stick. He lived.

Another patient with a stomach wound died. We gave him the same treatment as the first young man: complete immobility, no food, no drink. His condition remained stable for five days. Then a girl gave him water without my knowledge – I found the cup beside his bed. The same night he died. I can't be sure that the water caused his death – it may only have speeded it up. But probably it seeped out of his perforated intestines, causing infection and thus death.

We tried to keep the atmosphere in our 'hospital' calm. During the shelling we didn't allow any visitors. We sat with the patients then, because if they see doctors and nurses calm, they feel better psychologically. We weren't happy about the families staying with the wounded because of the confusion and noise. It has a bad effect on other patients if they see the family of a dying patient crying. I would invite one relative, usually a father or brother, to stay with the patient, and we would ask him not to make any noise. We never let anyone who was shouting or in a state of panic enter the patients' rooms.

We received 257 casualties altogether, of whom 47 died. We sent out 57 patients with the Red Cross, the rest we treated in the camp. Around 40 of the wounded were children. It's amazing how well they bore pain.

Dr Muhammad used coins and Elastoplast to stop air escaping from perforated lungs; splints for fractures were made from doors; internal wounds were treated by immobility and prohibition of smoking, drinking and eating. But such treatment was hard to enforce: one patient died of wet gangrene after standing up on a fractured foot. Little could be done for head-wound cases: all except one died. Of a case with massive haemorrhage, Dr Muhammad said, 'Perhaps I could have saved him using an ordinary needle and thread but the stitches would probably have caused infection.'

'The gun is written on our foreheads'

Several Fateh *shebab* took part in this recording, which was carried out in their base soon after the end of the siege. They give more military details and political analysis than most of the other speakers. The mother of one of them is Shi'ite and told how Amal militia had torn her dress as she entered the camp.

First *shabb*: The story begins with the provocations that Amal movement began a month before the battle. From the time of the battle between them and the Murabitoun, they began to mobilize against the Palestinians. Da'oud Da'oud attacked us in his speeches. Nabih Berri also. They denied that the Palestinians had had any role in the liberation of the South. They put all the victories in their bag. They tried to pretend that all the blood, all the martyrs were from Amal.

The aim behind the attack on the camp – of course this was with the agreement of Syria – was the elimination of all Palestinians from Beirut and South Lebanon. The camps would be removed to the region of Mount Hirmil, an empty, isolated region where they would be under the Syrian sledgehammer. In exchange, Amal would take charge of security between Jezzine and the southern border instead of Lahd's army. This was the deal. If it had succeeded it would have meant the end of the Palestinian struggle in Lebanon. The Revolution would have been finished. That was their aim.

The confrontation was triggered by an argument over a gun between someone from the Fateh dissidents and someone from Amal. It was near Da'ouq. They took this as a pretext; suddenly we saw them massing with vehicles carrying Dotschkas and 14.5s and 106s. They began hitting Da'ouq; and another section began firing into Shateela. The shelling began at about 11 pm on the night of Sunday 19 May and continued for several hours. The battle was planned.

As in earlier incidents, the Popular Committee tried to avoid battle through mediation. But as soon as the delegation went out of the camp, Amal began firing. At dawn on Monday, the battle took a stronger dimension, with shells of 106mm and 155mm. Our young men brought out the guns they had hidden. By the third day, we realized that there wasn't going to be a cease-fire, they were determined to go on to the end.

During the first two days we occupied Amal's office on Sabra Street and controlled the area around Gaza Hospital and up to the Sports City. On the third day there was a cease-fire agreement according to which the Lebanese Army's 6th Brigade would enter to separate the two parties. But the Army brought in Amal forces wearing Army uniforms to recover their positions that we had taken. They brought in tanks and cut the road linking Shateela to Sabra and Da'ouq. Then they took control of Gaza Hospital where we had put our wounded.

Now the battle became more violent. The twelfth day was a terribly hard one. They hit the camp with tanks, with 82mm and 120mm cannon, with 60mm artillery shells, with 75mm direct MD anti-tank missiles and B10s. It was a bombardment to destroy. They continued from 5 am to 5 pm at a rate of ten shells a minute. It was a terrible day, especially for the civilians, because the shelling was targeted on shelters and homes. Many houses fell on the heads of their occupants.

After the bombardment they began an assault with tanks and infantry. The main thrust of the attack was on the entrance to the camp from the direction of the mass graves and from Cinema Sharq. In addition they had tanks in fixed positions which shelled the camp continously during the assault. Our fighters were fantastic. They blew up seven tanks and half-tracks in the first attack, which lasted about three-quarters of an hour. It failed and they withdrew. They made a second attack the same night, also a motorized one, and we destroyed five vehicles, making a total of twelve, using RPGs only. We didn't have heavy arms, only Klashins and RPGs.

After this, attack followed attack, continual shelling, night and day. There were long stretches when we couldn't sleep. We snatched a few hours only when there were enough comrades to hold the defence. By this time we had established fixed positions in every part of the camp; these stayed continually alert to ward off attack. The fighters rested in their bases. Exhaustion was greatest in the first week, when people thought the battle would finish quickly, so they didn't sleep at all. Later we made a schedule so that some rested while others fought. As the battle went on we became more organized.

Some of the sisters here cut up blankets and bed-covers and sewed them to make sandbags. We got the sand for them by digging under the floors of houses. We used these to protect the fighters from sniping and shelling. I won't describe all the ways we found to protect our fighters, but the results were very positive, and helped cut down our losses.

Around the twenty-first day we began to feel that the enemy was no longer ready to make large-scale assaults. But they continued shelling and made a few limited attempts to infiltrate which failed. At the same time, although our means were small, we began to infiltrate their area and to attack them inside their positions. The last thing they did, two days before the cease-fire, was to bring a Katiousha multiple-rocket launcher (107mm), and position it near the Sports City. One of our fighters went out and hit the battery from the roof of a nearby building and destroyed it. It had only fired four rockets. Although it was 12 noon he was able to infiltrate their base. He also destroyed two of their vehicles that had stayed hidden in the alleys there. After that they removed their tanks to safe positions near the Kuwait Embassy.

Two or three days before the Damascus Agreement they launched a desperate last attack on the side of the Military College. It began with heavy shelling of the camp. Our fighters confronted the attack, destroying three half-tracks and causing them very heavy casualties. When they made another attempt to regain the Military College, we destroyed another two half-tracks and two military Land Rovers. This was their last attempt. After this came the cease-fire and the Damascus Agreement.

Some of the methods the attackers used were similar to those of the Israeli Army in South Lebanon. One of these methods was to use land mines which they would roll into the camp after fixing an explosive head and fuse on them. They did this at night, destroying houses on the edge of the camp, so as to prevent families from returning to them.

Second *shabb*: In the name of God, the merciful, the compassionate. At the beginning we were ordered not to shoot to kill, but to aim at their legs to immobilize them. Then we heard about the killing of the wounded in Gaza and how the people who had left the camp were being slaughtered. We became like wild beasts. The one who begins the battle is to blame.[9]

Those people who were shooting at us, who taught them to fight? They forgot on whose shoulder they became strong. It was we who brought them up out of oppression.

We say OK, now there is a solution, we'll go along with it. If they tell us to give up the gun, we will refuse. This gun is written on our foreheads, it has to remain with us, no one can take it from us. Because we paid blood for it. Only when we get back to Palestine will we put the gun down.

The people of Shateela stayed steadfast for the sake of the fighters, because the fighters are their own children. They didn't come from outside. Every fighter's family was here.

In the past they kept telling us, 'You are cowards and hooligans, you can't stand up to us.' They wanted to provoke us into a battle. Our leaders would calm us down, they would tell us, 'No, we are in the same trench. We share the same blood.' We proved to the world that our blood isn't cheap.

Third *shabb*: We aren't against Shi'ites as a sect. But the attack they launched against us was one of blind hatred. They bulldozed houses, they shelled without discrimination between fighter and child, or between Palestinian and Lebanese. They accuse Israel of blowing up houses and displacing people, yet this is what they are doing here. Their slogans are lies. Israel causes this conflict between brothers so as to have a policeman on its borders to protect it after its army withdraws. Lahd's army can't do everything that Israel wants, so they found another instrument ready to destroy and kill. The massacre of Sabra and Shateela was no uglier than what Amal has done. They arrested hundreds, they killed without mercy.

We aren't against coexistence with them. We have lived side by side for thirty-five years. There's kinship between us, they have married from us, we have married from them. We aren't nationals of this country, we came here against our will. But we have some rights here. They say they are oppressed; by what right do they oppress us?

We esteem the Shi'ite *'ulema*, the honest ones, who didn't agree to what Amal did. They represent the Shi'ite silent majority, not Amal. We Palestinians don't even like to use the words 'Shi'a' and 'Sunni'. We understand 'Muslim' and 'Christian', although in Palestine we didn't even differentiate between Muslim and Christian. Muslims used to keep Christian feasts and Christians kept Muslim feasts. As for Hassan and Hussein, it wasn't us who killed them. We are against the slogans that they wrote on walls around the camp, such as 'We have to take revenge for the murder of Hassan and Hussein' and 'He who kills a Palestinian will enter Paradise.' We are against sectarian hatred. We honour their *'ulema*, for example Sheikh Muhammad Fadlallah and Sheikh Muhammad Mehdi Shamsideen, because they condemned the ugly things that Amal did.

'I didn't accept being the "woman in the base"'

The next speaker, a young woman of eighteen years, a member of one of the small Marxist Resistance groups, convinced the *shebab* to accept her as a fellow fighter. Though of Shateela, her family were not present during the siege; their home was just outside the camp. This recording was carried out much later than the siege, in October 1986.

At the beginning of the first battle of the camps it was night, we were at home, I and my family, we didn't know what was happening. Then Amal militia broke into the house and arrested my brother.[10] My mother broke down, so we took her to Gaza Hospital because she has a heart problem. My sister stayed with her and I went back to the camp alone.

I felt I had to do something. I could have worked in the Mosque giving first aid to the wounded, except that I saw that there were lots of other girls helping there. I noticed that there were no young women in the bases. At first I wasn't confident; it was a long time since I had handled weapons. But I made a test shot, firing a whole magazine into the air. That made me feel better, and I decided to stay with the comrades in the base.

I believe that women should share in fighting with men, they shouldn't just sweep and cook. This war was aimed at all of us.

In our society, people find it strange to see a girl in a base, they don't accept it. In the beginning there were difficulties. The *shebab* couldn't grasp my reasons for being there. But I made them understand that I had to be there, because it was my base as much as it was theirs. They found it hard. They said I should do first aid, I should cook, but not do guard duty or fight. But after a lot of argument they gave in.

I gave them many reasons. At the beginning of the first siege there were some young men who were not fighting. I said that if they saw a girl in a base it would be bound to affect them, they couldn't go on just sitting around. Second, the presence of a woman encourages the others in the base, and makes them fight more courageously. Third, my presence would demonstrate women's true role and encourage other girls. If I had been martyred I might have achieved something great for the Palestinian cause. People would say that this girl fought and was martyred. It would prove our role.

At first there weren't any girls in the bases. But after a while they began to visit us, and there were some who began to fight. And in the second siege there were more women fighters. The families of the camp were very encouraging, they all supported me. I'm a daughter of the camp, can I sit and watch the young men fighting alone?

A big problem at the beginning was guard duty. The comrades refused to let me do guard duty like the others, for six-hour stretches. They said, 'Do three hours, four hours.' They tried to lighten my load. It's true I got tired. But I said, 'No, I'm like you. I'm trained, I have experience of fighting. I'm strong – why shouldn't I do it?' Whenever there was an attack I felt them all watching me to make sure I was firing correctly. I pretended not to notice. At the beginning they had doubts about me, but after the first attack they were convinced that I was serious, I'd really come to fight. They saw that I didn't run away. Gradually their viewpoint changed. It was very important to convince them. They asked me many questions. I was patient, I gave them all the reasons for my presence there.

At the beginning I was very frightened but it was a hidden fear. I didn't let it show because I didn't want them to say to me, go back (to safety). I really wanted to take some steps forward. When I was afraid of something but managed to do it, this increased my confidence. I got new experience and proved to everyone that woman has a role.

I took part in several attacks. But first I sat with the comrades to learn from them the things you have to know, for example how to creep near the ground, when to fire, what to do if the enemy surprises you, the noise an artillery shell makes when it comes down, how long it takes . . . The *shebab* were better informed than I was about such things. I asked a lot of questions, because if you know what to expect you'll be less afraid, and less likely to be hit.

There were many difficulties in my personal life. I hadn't any clothes in the camp, just my blouse and jeans. I had to borrow clothes from my friends, and change in their homes. It was hard to wash. My stomach hurt all through the siege but I wrapped my scarf around it and wore a jacket all the time. I also brought some *maramiyyeh* to the base and drank it until the end. When my period came, it was very difficult. I had to go to the 'hospital' to get some painkillers. A friend brought me Kotex and I rested in her home for a day. I told the comrades I had a headache, and they brought me lemon juice! I missed my home, and felt like crying.

At the beginning I tried not to kill – I don't like the idea of killing. I shot at their legs, to force them to run away. But when a friend was martyred near me, I killed the one who killed him. If someone from our group was killed, we fought harder from anger. If we didn't kill them, they would kill us.

I took two military training courses before 1982. I know how to use a Klashin, the B7 and the BKC. The BKC stops attacks because it fires so quickly. The comrades in the base taught me how to use it. I have a firm grip and a good eye. I don't easily get nervous. Perhaps I'm anxious inside me but I don't lose my calm.

Once one of our comrades was hit in the head. We were panicked. I felt like crying, but I called to the others to help me carry him to hospital. We had to control our fear and help him in spite of the blood and the ugliness. He died; he was our friend, he was very dear to us. It affected us a lot. But we controlled ourselves because, in the end, we had a duty before us. If we had given in to our feelings, the base could have fallen.

I noticed that young men react impulsively. Particular incidents such as a friend's death affect them a lot. Women also are affected, but they control themselves more. We were in a difficult situation, we had to think about every move. If one of us got killed, we couldn't allow another comrade to dash out in a revenge attack, carried away by his feelings. Maybe we'll die but we shouldn't die for nothing.

We didn't have a leader in the base. There was a leadership in the camp as a whole; they took the decisions, we were under orders. If we carried out an attack, it was in consultation with the general command, because they had more information than us. Also, because of the shortage of ammunition, we had to cut down attacks to the minimum. There was also the danger that if we made an attack and incurred heavy losses, the enemy could have overrun the camp.

They made many attempts to overrun us, sometimes as many as three in one day. Our base was near the Military College and it got many attacks. It was called the 'Water Tank' base. Along with Cinema Sharq and Doukhi, our base was considered the most dangerous. The fall of any of these bases could have endangered the whole camp. The sniping there was very heavy. We had to knock holes in the walls of the houses so that we could get back into the camp without being hit.

It was from our base that a group of Fateh fighters entered the camp.[11] We knew they were coming because we got a radio message. We were happy to see them but were also worried that maybe it was a trick, maybe they would turn out to be Amal. There were twenty-two of them, not a small number. If they had been Amal, the camp would have fallen.

Because it was so dangerous, food didn't reach our base regularly. One day it would come, ten days no. Of course I knew more about cooking than the *shebab*, so sometimes I cooked for them. But I refused to do it alone; all those who didn't have guard duty had to help me. I didn't accept being 'the woman in the base'. Some would peel potatoes, some would chop onions, and all would wash the plates. This way we enjoyed it more. It made us feel very close, like a family. If anything happened to one of us, we all felt it. We talked to each other, we encouraged each other. We were all young, under twenty-five, and we had little experience of fighting. Sometimes in the evenings we used to sit drinking tea, telling stories and jokes. We discussed our problems. Those who had good voices sang revolutionary songs. From the beginning of the siege we stayed more or less the same group of people. Four of the group were martyred and three were wounded.

I don't believe that women should work alone or organize alone. I don't like institutions that proclaim 'We are women.' Of course I'm not against the [Palestinian] women's union, but why a special union for women? Fighters should be men and women, everything should be men and women. Our women have fantastic abilities, they can work at anything, they should be in the middle of every action. That's my view.

'Their plan was to reach the Mosque and cut Shateela in half'

This group of fighters had defended one of the most critical bases in the camp, beside the Mosque, which took the brunt of Amal attacks. The base commander (on crutches) is the first to speak. Another speaker is from Da'ouq and describes how it fell (30 May). One of the fighters holds his five-month-old baby on his knee.

At the beginning of the battle there were many people who didn't want to fight against Amal movement, so at first we refrained from shooting at them. But then there was a cease-fire, and the Army brought in its tanks with Amal behind them. We were angered by their deceit. The leading tank reached Cinema Sharq and began to shell the entrance to the camp in preparation for the entry of Amal militiamen. We confronted them. We were too close to use B7s – they need at least 50 metres to explode. So the *shebab* went up to the tops of houses and threw Molotov cocktails and hand-bombs. The tank caught fire and withdrew.

They made several attacks every day. They would begin by throwing grenades, mortars, 500s, everything they had at us. We built defences, a wall of sandbags, and stayed steadfast behind them. Every day they shelled them, they'd break and we would repair them just so as to stay put.

The next week they mounted an attack with around 400 fighters. This was when they started the operation of blowing up houses on the edge of the camp. They started at 4 am, using Chinese tank mines; there were Army experts with them. At every entrance to the camp they brought down any high building that got in the way of their fire. They were creeping in, throwing grenades. Our means were few, we had almost no arms except Klashins and B7s. Hand-grenades would have helped our defence but they were very scarce. We used Molotovs and liquid-gas containers. We couldn't just sit with our hands crossed!

They had many casualties that day, and we had seven martyrs and fourteen wounded. After that first attack they went on for a week, creeping up and throwing grenades and mines. During this time they controlled the buildings on the edge of the camp, and were able to close the road to the Mosque by sniper fire. All of that road and the alleys leading off it were exposed to their snipers. We couldn't move on the roads so we broke through the walls between the houses.

Their plan was to concentrate on the entrance near Cinema Sharq by reaching the mosque to cut Shateela in half. Our *shebab* gave the maximum of courage and endurance because they knew that if this base fell, the whole camp would probably fall, and the attackers would have no mercy on our children and old people. Many fighters who had been wounded came back to fight again. I came back on crutches. The enemy had many dead and wounded during these attacks.

We didn't have many fighters, between 100 and 200. Some of our fighters got shut outside, after they went out to help in Sabra and Da'ouq. And we had many martyrs. Right at the beginning we sent a seriously wounded fighter up to Gaza Hospital, but half-way there they left him and he bled to death. In the first week there were the bodies of seven martyrs lying in the same place as the wounded. We expected that someone would come and move the bodies out, but no car or ambulance was allowed to enter. We moved them to the UNRWA feeding centre. But the cats went in and ate the bodies. After that we decided to bury them in the Mosque, and moved the wounded somewhere else.

Our base was near the Mosque. They believed that if our base fell, the camp would fall, so they concentrated their shelling on the Mosque. Also they knew that people were using it for shelter and for the wounded. One day they announced through their loudspeaker, 'Anyone who goes into the Mosque will be safe.' So no one went in. Half an hour later they began to shell the Mosque. They used deceit and trickery.

We believe that it's *haram* to kill other Muslims. The blessed Quran says that the blood of a Muslim is *haram* for a Muslim; his blood, his honour and his property. But it also says, fight those who fight you. The battle was imposed on us, that's why we fought. We didn't want to spill their blood.

The fall of Da'ouq

Another of the *shebab* at the base near the Mosque was from Da'ouq, the small unofficial camp in Sabra that fell on 30 May.

It was Sunday, the first night in Ramadan, and we were sitting normally in our homes. Amal movement moved in to Da'ouq to arrest some Palestinian young men. We tried to get them released. We said, 'You don't have the right to arrest Palestinians without a warrant. If they have done something wrong, we will judge them.' But Amal insisted. A bit later one of their leaders collected his forces round Gaza Hospital and began shelling Da'ouq.

Only a week before this, the Movement had asked us to send fighters to fight beside them on the 'Green Line'. We set conditions, to try to avoid what happens in every battle, that Palestinians get put in the front line and come out of it with nothing. Later we realized that this was an Amal ruse to move our fighters from the Sabra/Shateela area, so as to give them the chance to enter the camp without a battle.

The first day there were negotiations, but they failed because it was clear that Amal only wanted our submission. Their position was simple: 'We are the ones who decide. There's no such thing as Palestinian autonomy.' On Tuesday there was an agreement on a cease-fire. A little later we were surprised to find them renewing their attack, supported by the 6th Brigade from their bases in the Arab University, Ard Jalloul, the Sports City and the Kuwaiti embassy. Between Amal and the 6th Brigade they amassed maybe 3,000 fighters, supported by tanks, light and heavy artillery, mortars, howitzers. As they entered areas where Palestinians lived – Fakhany, Mela'b al-Beladi, Hamed Street – they began arresting and executing people. In Da'ouq I saw them with my own eyes carrying people away on the scoop of a bulldozer.

Da'ouq resisted siege for eleven days. It's a small camp, not more than two alleys. They reached its entrance coming from the Sabra vegetable market, advancing under cover of tank artillery. There at the entrance they shot at families trying to escape, three children in their mothers' arms, a man and a woman. Their bodies lay there in the entrance. Seeing this sight, a young woman who was there, Ilham al-Hajj, picked up a B7 and fired it at a tank. They killed her with a bullet. She was one of our courageous martyrs.

Da'ouq's situation was desperate. It is very small, with between fifty and sixty families. There were no more than sixty fighters defending it, perhaps 100 if you include the *ashbal*. There was no water, no medical supplies – those who were wounded had to stay as they were. Food gave out completely. Children died in their mothers' arms. There were no shelters, no high buildings. After eleven days of continuous shelling, Amal advanced into Da'ouq. The fighters who were there withdrew after receiving guarantees for the safety of the civilians. Some of us managed to creep out and enter Shateela camp in spite of the siege. Others were taken prisoner or killed on the way.

They gathered the civilians in the Old People's Home and then took them to the Sports City where they examined their ID cards. Then they told them they were free to leave. They let them get near to the stadium steps, where there is no escape, and opened fire on them with machine guns, killing about eighty-three, including women and children.

Another *shabb*: Amal movement forbade arms to enter the camp. Just before the siege their statements sounded like the Kata'eb: 'We don't want the Palestinian camps. We don't want the Palestinian gun.' So why did they accept the Palestinian fighter in the South, and in the Shouf and in the southern suburbs? Some Amal people allowed guns into the camp, but it was for money, not for the sake of the Palestinian cause.

As for the Lebanese Army, it always complained of lack of arms – 'We don't have this, we don't have that' – this was the excuse they gave for not defending the South. So how come this flood of arms against us, as if sent by God? They lost thirteen half-tracks in the first battle of Sabra alone. They had Hauser 155s, machine guns mounted on armoured vehicles, cannon of 106mm, SP9s, American rockets . . . they had more than fifty pieces of heavy artillery (150mm) positioned in the suburbs and parts of West Beirut. And much of this material was new.

Fighters and non-fighters

In the accounts of the *shebab*, morale is always high and everyone is always ready to take part in the battle. In reality, things were somewhat different. This non-combatant talks about some of the difficulties of mobilizing people, especially during the first week, and of fluctuations in morale. He also tells stories of individual courage.

The first week was the hardest because there weren't enough helpers. It was hard to mobilize people, they expected the battle to finish quickly. It wasn't until they saw the Mosque being shelled, the day we had to move the wounded out, that everyone began to realize the seriousness of the situation. Then they began to volunteer to help. The heavier the bombardment was, the more people volunteered. Anger made people readier to fight. When Amal used to shout over the microphone, 'Surrender or we'll kill you!', people's reaction was to say, 'If they talk like this now, how will they be when they have control over us!' They stopped believing we could negotiate.

Not all men in the camp fought. Some gave religion as a reason. They said, 'It's *haram* to kill another Muslim. If I kill an Amal fighter, I'll go to Hell. If I am killed, I'll go to Heaven. So it's better to die.' Some of those who didn't fight agreed to help with the wounded.

Some men began to fight after losing a family member, like the man whose seventeen-year-old son was killed. Another man whose leg had been broken began to fight in the last week. A few spent all the siege in the shelters with the women and children. No one said anything to them.

There were fluctuations in the fighting force. Sometimes fighters got tired and went home. Others who hadn't fought would feel ashamed and take their place. If the number of men in a base got dangerously low, they would send to homes to mobilize people. But they never went to the homes of men who were known not to want to fight. We have a saying in Arabic: 'If the dog has to be forced to hunt, we don't want him or what he catches.'

The young men you see around the camp now showing off their guns are mostly not the ones who fought. The real fighters don't carry their guns. You can tell the non-fighters because they don't look you in the eye.

A few of the fighters were married men but the majority were young, some still in school. Some of the most spectacular acts of courage were carried out by boys in their teens. If we wanted to get anything done, we went to the young people. Between the ages of eighteen and twenty-five they are absolutely fearless. And at that age they're more concerned with the public good. Women and even men, once they're married, become more concerned with their own families.

There were two bad moments, when morale was at a very low point. The worst time was in the first week, around Thursday or Friday.[12] The shelling was very heavy, homes were being destroyed, we felt they were about to overrun the camps. Some fighters left their bases and went home, or came to the 'hospital' to hide. Even the leaders were afraid. At that dangerous moment I saw a young man of about twenty jump on a chair and threaten to shoot everyone if they didn't return to their bases. The tide of fear was reversed, immediately everyone went back to the front line. That boy had the qualities of a leader.

Another time, panic started because of a rumour that Amal had penetrated the camp and reached the buildings next to the 'hospital'. A young wounded fighter changed the mood by shouting, 'Yallah! In five minutes we'll push them back up to Sabra!'

There was a critical situation on the northern edge of the camp when Amal began blowing up the houses there. It went on for three or four nights and it got very dangerous. The leader of the base on that side of the camp couldn't come up with a solution. Then a young man of about eighteen came and told the leadership, 'Give me two volunteers and I'll put an end to this.' The three of them went over to that side of the camp and stayed there for forty-eight hours. I don't know what they did but from that time Amal stopped dynamiting houses.

Another time a young man came to the leadership and said, 'Give me a grenade.' They said, 'There aren't any.' He said, 'I can see twelve Amal militiamen sitting in a room, eating. I have to hit them.' It was night. As there were no grenades, he took a stone and threw it into the room. The Amal men thought it was a grenade and ran away. The young man entered the building and brought out all their guns.

Towards the end of the siege there was a very heavy bombardment and tanks tried to enter the camp near the Military College. The *shebab* didn't have orders, they just surged out spontaneously, confronting the tanks on open ground and knocking out three of them.

Another key battle was near Cinema Sharq. There were three tanks. The first two were hit and destroyed. A soldier in the third tank called out, 'In God's name don't shoot!' They could have killed him but because he used the name of God they didn't. This gave a boost to everyone's morale.

People felt better when they heard of scoring against tanks or half-tracks or fighters; of successful counter-attacks; or of Palestinian shelling from the mountains on Amal positions. Morale dropped when there were casualties, or when there was heavy shelling without any response from the mountains, or when there was a lot of bad news at once.

Morale sank in the last ten days. The truce talks were going on in Damascus; every hour brought news of a different 'solution'. Food stocks were getting low and more important, ammunition was short again. In those ten days everyone expected to die, we were waiting for death from moment to moment. But no one thought of surrender. On the contrary, we were planning a suicidal last stand. There were two ideas: one was to collect altogether and storm out of the camp; the other was to tell the artillery in the mountains to destroy the camp and us with it.

Organizing daily life

In a siege like this one there was no front line and no rear line, and little difference between fighters and civilians. Every part of the camp was dangerous, every kind of work was essential. Many people helped spontaneously, for example by making tea or food for the fighters; but there was also organization, particularly in the matter of providing bread. The speaker is Abu Mustafa.

How did we manage everyday problems? This was very important in sustaining morale and steadfastness. From the first day of the siege, all the institutions of the camp, public or private, were collectivized. I told you how we gathered medical supplies from every home. It was the same with food and flour, everything became collective. We collected all the flour from the homes, baked bread in the public bakery and distributed bread equally to everyone, in shelters, in homes and in the bases. There were many young women who shared in the job of making bread; in fact they directed the bakery. Women also ran the operation of cooking and distributed food to the fighters; there was a communal kitchen as well as a bakery which worked for everyone, civilians and fighters alike. Bread was free. Some women in their homes who had flour continued to bake bread for their families, and they would also give to their neighbours and to fighters near them.

From the homes of those who fled we took food supplies – oil, olives, grains, pulses – and we used them for the general good. Money had no value during the siege, there was no buying and selling. Defence was for all and homes were for all. Fighters in a base near any shop would open it and register whatever they took. In our Co-op we registered what people took so that when things returned to normal we could settle accounts. Stocks in the small shops soon gave out but our Co-op is large. And we did something new: we had several big cartons containing canned food, so we gave them to the central kitchen, and they distributed them to homes and to the bases. On top of this we guaranteed to stay open for two hours every day, however bad the shelling, so that people could come and take what they needed. Those who had money paid, the others we registered. There was no discrimination between man and woman, student and worker, fighter and civilian. All were equal.

Cigarettes gave out after the first two weeks, there was a 'cigarette crisis'. Whoever had 'one passed it round to four or five other people. Many people smoked tea, others smoked dried grasses, or filters, or cigarette ends that they picked up off the ground. Smokeable, unsmokeable, they smoked it.

For more than a month our children saw no vegetables or fruit. But there was no real hunger. Bread, rice and other foodstuffs we had in plenty. There was enough rice and sugar in the Co-op to feed the whole camp for another month if the siege had lasted.

Water? Amal hit the water tanks on the first day, and our wells are outside the camp. That left the water of the Company. There is very little of this water but it kept on coming. There are just two public taps but they are right on the edge of the camp. We managed to extend them through pipes further into the camp, close to the shelters. But after two or three days they discovered that people were coming and going with water. So they began to fire at the water tap near Iqleem Fateh, and many women and children were martyred there. We also extended water to the second shelter, the one near Abu 'Atef's bakery. Here also many civilians were killed. Later we found other means to bring the people water. It was scarce but it was enough.

Every home was on the front line. The camp is small in size, less than one square kilometre. Sometimes as many as 6,000 shells fell in one day on this one restricted space.

'I cooked for all the *shebab*!'

Umm Muhammad, a widow, sent her three daughters and grandson out of the siege, but stayed herself to look after her three fighter sons. One of them was wounded and had been evacuated to a Beirut hospital. A friend who is visiting takes part in the discussion.

Friend: Umm Muhammad refused to leave Shateela because she has two sons here, fighters. She couldn't leave them.

Umm Muhammad: Two! I have three! *Shebab!* Am I afraid for myself? I'm afraid for my sons. Their father died during the 'events'.[13] I had six children, all young, I worked hard to bring them up. Now they are men. Am I going to leave them now? Impossible! But I didn't feed just my sons, I cooked for all the *shebab*, so that God will protect my sons. I cooked in my own house and I distributed it. Every Resistance office would bring me a saucepan and I'd fill it. Whereever there's a base I ran to it. My legs got so swollen! The doctors kept telling me, Umm Muhammad, take it easy! But no, I'm hot-blooded.

At first I cooked from my own supplies, but after ten days they were finished. The young men had got used to me cooking for them: 'Where's Umm Muhammad?' I told them, 'There's nothing left.' So they broke down walls, wherever there was a house that had lentils and rice, and they brought them. 'Take! Cook!' They brought saucepans and I took them to fill them. They ran after me on the street: 'Food! Food!' If there was anything left in the pan, I'd give it to them. If not, '*Wallah*, there is nothing left!' I even cooked them *mloukhia*.[14] Houses, shops, they opened them all, they brought me Maggi, tomato sauce, pulses – there were no vegetables. . . .

The girls stayed in Shateela nine days, and after that I got them out. The oldest one was wounded, here in the house, shrapnel wounds in her head, chest and shoulder. She lost a lot of blood. I told her, 'Go out! Perhaps you'll find treatment outside.' At the beginning the siege wasn't complete, people could come and go. If Amal saw people afraid, like my daughter, they would let them go out. Two of my daughters got out, but this one, the youngest, had a lot of trouble. She got stopped and left behind. She began to cry. An Amal fighter drew his gun on her. She told him, 'I've lost my sisters.' 'Then go back and find them!' Women stopped and told him, 'She's an orphan, she hasn't got anybody, she's going to her uncle's home.' '*Yallah*! Take her and get out!'

Now there are girls who go out to buy vegetables and who hide ammunition underneath. And old women like me. I wanted to go but they said, 'Not you, you limp.' Some made it into a belt, and wore it under a wide dress.

At the beginning my daughter's son was very frightened, he cried. He'd hear the shelling and wouldn't go to sleep. We would tell him, 'Don't be afraid!' and feed him, and he'd be quiet. That's why I told my daughter to leave.

Amal knew the names of all those who fought and used to call them out over the microphone. They used to call on the fighters to surrender. That's what the Israelis used to do, they'd say on the microphone, 'Palestinian terrorists surrender!' The Movement didn't say 'fighter', they said 'terrorist'.

Every girl that used to help the wounded is wanted by Amal. Nawal, In'am – all are wanted. They have a list, and everyone who worked, who was here, they have their names. When people went out, the Movement asked them who was inside, and they told them.

Friend: Once we were sitting here drinking coffee. There was a crash, and suddenly everything stopped. We ran downstairs and found people lying bleeding on the street. The young men had been drinking coffee, here, at the door of their base, and a mortar came down on them. Several were dead, one of them was my cousin, Jamal. Four of them were wounded, and their sister, all from the same family. One died and God had mercy on the rest. I couldn't do anything because of my cousin lying there. But Umm Muhammad ran and got sheets and tore them up.

Umm Muhammad: I've done first-aid training and I used to have a kit. It's gone now, but if I see anyone wounded I can't stop myself, I run to him at once. They say to me, 'Umm Muhammad, you don't know what to do.' But I do. Can one stand there and watch a young man bleeding like a tap and not do anything to help him? I ask the sister what disinfectant or ointment we should put on them. We give them first aid, and thank God.

Friend: The Red Crescent are thinking now of putting a hospital in the camp, with an underground operation room. They've sent four doctors. And the other clinics will be repaired. We will have social institutions again, and a Popular Committee to offer services and work for the people. Before, these were all forbidden. From the government there was prohibition and from Amal harassment. This is what we have gained from *sumood*.

After the siege

After the Damascus Agreement and formal cease-fire came psychological distress as people realized that the siege had not really ended. Amal and the 6th Brigade were still around the camps, unreconciled to defeat. There were daily incidents; men were afraid to go outside the camp.

The first speaker, Umm Amal,[15] is one of those who cooked for the *shebab*. She describes what happened when she and other union women went out to buy foodstuffs soon after the siege was lifted.

Sabra is far and there's a lot of rubble on the road. Cars still can't come in. So we went to a market in their [i.e. the Shi'ite] area. It happened yesterday. They knew we wouldn't be buying such large quantities for a family. There was a woman – perhaps she'd lost a son in the fighting – who got very upset as soon as she saw us. She and another woman who was with her said to some Amal militia that were there, 'Why do you let them buy their food from here? We don't want to see them.'

The man we buy from is very decent. He said to me, 'You'd better go before they do something to you. I can't help you.'

Since the siege ended we've been going out to get supplies daily, sometimes twice. We don't have a fridge, there's no electricity, water is scarce. It's a problem. Last night we told the Follow-up Committee[16] that they should manage to bring cars into the camp so that we can provide the *shebab* with the quantity of food they need.

I shan't go to that area any more. I was frightened to death yesterday. There was a patrol of about twenty of them, armed to the teeth, wandering around. This woman who first spotted us said to them, 'Don't bother, I'll fix them for you!' Meaning what? When we heard that, we left everything that we were going to buy and returned. We brought these beans and some eggs, but we weren't able to bring the quantity of tomatoes we needed. When we saw them like that, mobilized and angry, we left without buying. And on top of everything the ISF[17] stationed at the entrance to the camp insisted on searching the beans. They thought we were hiding arms.

'There are many enemies'

Abu Wasseem also expresses a post-siege sense of insecurity and frustration. He had helped in the communal bakery during the siege, and had been wounded twice.

It's like a play. We've seen the first two parts and now we're waiting for the third. The time of the siege was easier. There was shelling, sniping, destruction, but now there's a psychological siege, no one has the power to move, we don't know what is really going on politically. We don't know our friend from our enemy within the current political set-up. Palestinians in the camps must see everyone around them as enemies, and must be on their guard with all of them. We don't know who is our friend. There is a common enemy, that's Israel; but there are many other enemies, and all are masked.

During the siege there were no committees. Any person who could carry out a task, did it spontaneously. There were people who had been on committees in the past, but they couldn't cope with this situation, they only speak about 'organization' and 'tactics'. Only two members of the Popular Committee stayed in the camp, the rest were outside. After such a siege there should be a popular vote to see whom this people wants to represent it. They have diverted people's attention with material aid because they know that we are in need. But the people need representatives who aren't just counters to be moved as some power centres wish, but who know their interests and will defend their rights.

It's regrettable that the PRCS didn't have the word 'Shateela' in its dictionary. Bourj Barajneh has a hospital; it's true that it's empty of equipment and medical supplies, but at least it's a hospital; it could be equipped in a few days. But Shateela didn't even have a clinic. We thank the doctors who worked during the siege, but they worked because they live in the camp, not under PRCS orders. They should have given us a clinic after the Sabra/Shateela massacre. Gaza Hospital is no use to us, if a single bullet is fired it's cut off.

'And now what?'

Medical workers as well as fighters were 'wanted' by Amal, so Dr Muhammad stayed in Shateela for several months after the first siege ended. From him come these observations on post-siege trauma, recorded in November 1985.

Much of the stress that had been suppressed while the battle was raging burst out once the guns were silent. Fear that death might come at any moment gave way to a generalized anxiety. People began to realize the full extent of the damage, and the implications of what had happened. Everyone began to ask, 'And now what?'

Those who had accepted the loss of sons or kin during the battle began to express their grief. Before, they had felt sorrow, but had accepted the death as a duty and as a natural result of fighting. They had accepted that all the martyrs should be buried together in the Mosque, without names. But after the battle, parents began to ask exactly where their son was, so as to decorate the grave.[18]

Young people mourned less for the dead. They felt they had died in a good cause, to protect the camp and the national struggle. Their lives had not been wasted. The young have got used to the idea of death, of their own death, more than the old have. What is harder for the younger people, particularly the young men, is that they can't go out of the camp. It isn't safe. Many of their names are known to Amal. So for them, the siege goes on. It's another kind of war. Many of them get nervous and irritable. They come to the clinic not in a friendly way, as before, but to quarrel and shout. New problems began for the medical workers, which hadn't existed during the siege. For example, some of the fighters, particularly those who were wounded, have begun to take drugs, mainly sedatives, but also hashish and heroin.

Once two of them came to the clinic with a companion who had lost consciousness. One of the two demanded drugs from the doctor, and when the doctor refused, he shot at him, wounding a nurse. The one who shot had been wounded in Da'ouq. This was about two months after the end of the siege. Today, five months after the end of the war, there are still many men who haven't dared to leave the camp. They feel that the place is a prison. And there's no telling when it will end. It's hard on them.

This is why last month, when there was the eight-hour battle,[19] the *shebab* reacted instantly, carrying the attack right up to Sabra, far outside the camp. This was their chance to move. Anger, anxiety and boredom were behind this aggressiveness. Some of the leaders tried to stop them, but they wouldn't come back.

Several of those who were wounded during the one-month battle really need specialized treatment, but they can't be moved outside the camp.

Another group that has suffered more than others are the young widows. They show more severe anxiety symptoms than older people. They feel sick, tired, and have difficulty sleeping. The best cure for them is work, if they are educated, and can find employment. This gets them out of the house and helps them to meet other people. It all depends on their family, what social and religious ideas they have, whether they allow them to work or not.

Depression has not been a problem as much as anxiety. But anxiety is not so serious, it can be a stimulant. On the whole the psychological situation is stable now, people have adapted to the facts of continuing insecurity. Most people are proud at having won the battle, and at having stopped Amal from entering the camp. Probably it is this pride that prevents more severe symptoms such as depression.

Notes

1. Negotiations to evacuate the wounded went on all through the siege. At last on 13/14 June, Amal allowed the IRC to enter.
2. This was one of a series of fronts replacing the LNM, of which Jumblat's PSP was a member.
3. Leader of the PFLP, Dr George Habash.
4. *Halaweh* is a sweet paste made with sugar, sesame seeds, oil and nuts.
5. *Iftar* is the meal that breaks the fast during Ramadan.
6. *Suhoor* is the last meal eaten before dawn during Ramadan.
7. *Mena'eesh* are pizza-like rounds of bread spread with oil and *za'ter*, eaten hot.
8. Amal snipers had specially illuminated sights for night sniping.
9. *Al-badi azlum*: 'The beginner is more in the wrong', a popular saying.
10. An only son, he had just returned from Germany to get married. He was one of those who never showed up again.
11. Twice during the siege, Resistance groups outside were able to send in small units carrying arms and ammunition.

12. The attack started on the night of Sunday 19 May.

13. The Lebanese Civil War of 1975/6.

14. Jews' mallow, a green vegetable used widely throughout the Middle East. It can be dried.

15. Besides being the name of a political movement, Amal is a girl's name. Though not customary, women without sons are sometimes called after their oldest daughter.

16. The 'Follow-up Committee' was a joint force (Palestinian and Lebanese) formed as part of the Damascus Agreement to prevent incidents in the post-siege period.

17. The ISF (Internal Security Forces) is a police force. Considered more neutral than the 6th Brigade, it was stationed outside Shateela at the end of the first siege.

18. Every day the graves became more ornate as families brought flowers, photographs and decorated Quranic texts. Portraits of the martyrs were printed on banners and hung outside the mosque, which acquired a shrine-like character.

19. On 7 October. This was one of several smaller attacks, lasting a few hours or days, between the first and second sieges.

10. The One-Month Siege (29 May to 27 June 1986)

Coming almost exactly a year after the first one, as if to commemorate it, the one-month siege was different in every other respect. The element of surprise was entirely lacking, since the intervening year had been filled with Amal–Palestinian clashes, with these spreading to the South and to the roads connecting the South to Beirut. Around Shateela there had been a series of attacks on the camp and on individuals outside the camp.[1] From the end of the first siege the Resistance groups had reopened their offices, so that there were now more trained fighters, arms and ammunition inside the camp. This enabled the Palestinians during the second siege to control areas outside the camp's periphery, pushing back Amal and Army gun positions so that damage was less concentrated and sniping less often fatal; there were no attempts this time to storm Shateela. Casualties were lower than the year before (twenty-one killed, thirty-five wounded).[2] A Red Crescent field hospital had been installed with an underground operating room in the charge of an orthopaedic surgeon experienced in war injuries.[3] Supplies of food and fuel were adequate, even though there were more people (the first speaker tells how people fled *into* the camp this time instead of out of it, fearing atrocities like the year before). Helping the Popular Committee to organize social services such as distribution of supplies, help and hygiene to the shelters, were cadres from the women's union and Beit Atfal al-Sumood (a national institution that cares for war orphans). In spite of the presence of both PNSF and Fateh loyalist fighters, internal tensions were at a minimum. As a result, this was the siege that, in retrospect, Shateela people would call a 'picnic'. Nonetheless it had its own tragedies and stories. It also shows the way Palestinians develop national work – such as the collecting of statistics – even under war conditions.

'We began the operation of statistics'

People in camps usually experience (and create) chaos in the distribution of relief. Now, under siege, there was an attempt to improve methods of distribution, based on accurate head counts, assessing the needs of different population sectors and taking supplies to people instead of having them crowd outside distribution centres. The speaker is a school teacher born in the camp.

The real siege began during the second week. Shelling was heavy, and families living on the edge of the camp or outside it took refuge inside. This was different from the first siege when many people fled to safer areas. This meant that there were more people, many of them homeless; so there began to be food shortages.

We began the operation of statistics, to enumerate every family inside the camp: the name of the household head, how many members of the family were actually present, how many children and their ages. In distributing milk powder we needed to give priority to particular categories, for example infants just weaned and mothers who were suckling.

We also located old people living alone, who couldn't manage to get supplies or cook their own food, so that they could be supplied from the kitchens of the organizations.

To collect the statistics we formed a team of three members of the Popular Committee and ten young women volunteers. This was called the Committee of Social Services. It also worked in distributing supplies. It worked for everyone, without discrimination between this organization or that. Our basic line was that the camp is one family. If any member is neglected, the family as a whole will be lost.

Collecting the statistics took three days. We divided the camp into eight squares relative to the density of the population, and went through them house by house. The first day we worked non-stop for twelve hours, with breaks only for sandwiches. The second day we worked six hours. Then we put time into analysing the results, dividing the families into three main categories depending on their size and the number and ages of their children. Older children can manage on one meal a day, like adults, and they can eat tinned food. Younger children need more milk, rice, lentils and *burghul*.

It came out that we had 455 families inside Shateela as well as 15 families in the Hursh. This was another difference from the last siege. We had fighters in the Hursh, and there were families living with them. This gave the fighters a motive for staying put, that they weren't just defending blank walls, but families and children.

It took us another three days to divide up the supplies into shares for each family.[4] It took this long because we weighed carefully. Two kilos had to be two kilos. Second, we divided up all shares before starting to distribute them, so that no family would see others getting supplies and feel left out. One of the [Resistance] groups distributed supplies to some families but not to others. Our Committee decided that if we were going to do this job, we must distribute to everyone at once.

Distribution was quite dangerous because the store where the supplies were kept is in one of the most dangerous parts of the camps. We called it the *halaqat al-mowt* (circle of death) because six people were killed there, four *shebab* and two girls. They aim at it because there are several Resistance offices there. But we had no choice. If we had tried to move the supplies we would have been more exposed. Inside the store room it was relatively safe.

The operation of distribution took about 48 hours, to all the 470 families. There were 10 girls and each one carried 2 shares. If they were strong they could manage 3 or 4. We worked quarter by quarter, gathering all the shares in one house, so many large, medium and small depending on the number and size of families. From there we distributed the shares to all the homes in the quarter. The operation went smoothly, and no family came to ask where their share was.

To the fighters we distributed dried *mloukhia*, a kilo to each organization. They were happy to get such a thing in a siege.

When we took supplies to the Hursh we had to cross an open road controlled by snipers. The *shebab* had put up a defensive earth wall but the enemy saw us and aimed mortars at the wall. One of the girls was wounded, but it was only a scratch, so we continued on our way. When they saw us coming with food, the families clapped and the women trilled. We went three times to the Hursh.

During the siege people lost their egoism. There's a family near the entrance to the camp, the father is called Abu Musa. It's a very large, needy family, because there are two married daughters living with them who also have children. Yet Abu Musa served bitter coffee to the *shebab* all through the siege; and when we gave him his family's share he said, 'I have a lot of beans and lentils. Take them. Maybe there's a family more in need.' There were others who said the same. This impressed me a lot.

This speaker describes other kinds of work carried out by the Committee of Social Services, such as supervising hygiene in the shelters, organizing activities for children, garbage-burning and repairs. These are covered in some of the other narratives. The teacher also discusses the importance of celebrating A'eed al-Fitr (at the end of Ramadan) under siege.

It's our tradition that, at the feasts, families give their children sweet things such as *ma'moul* [cake filled with dates or nuts] and *mlebbes* [sugared almonds]. We also offer them to people who come to wish us happiness. This time, of course, there were no such visits. But Beit al-Atfal had enough sweets and sugared almonds to distribute to all the children in the camp, not just to the families registered with them. They also offered *sharab al-wared*[5] to the children in shelters.

We also have the custom of decorating the cemetery for the feast. Everyone who has a dead relative decorates his grave. We did this in the siege; we let the children do it, on the day before the feast. Our martyrs must feel that their death has helped life to continue.

When our fighters established a base in Hayy al-Gharbeh we had to think how to give them protection, because the road there is exposed to sniping. Several *shebab* were killed crossing that road. We tried to dig a trench, but we couldn't manage it because of the sewage pipes. Then we thought of making walls of earth. But we had to protect the *shebab* while they were making them. So we took a number of old blood-stained blankets from the Red Crescent, and we brought girls to sew them together, end to end. We tied them to a thick rope and threw the end of the rope to the *shebab* in Hayy al-Gharbeh on the other side of the road. They tied it up. It was almost dark and Amal couldn't see what we were doing. So they set up light projectors and directed them at the blankets, and began to fire at them. This left the *shebab* free to work on earth walls. When Amal woke in the morning and saw that it was nothing but a string of blankets, they threw everything they had at it.

In this siege we tried to regain every building outside the camp that is related to us, such as the Jaysh al-Tahrir building and the Khalalati building.[6] We could have occupied Amal's office but we didn't try because it is theirs.

'Our mothers are strugglers'

Amneh Jibreel speaks about the role of the women's union in Shateela's defence: how younger women ('sisters') worked in fortification, and older ones ('mothers') worked in the bakery and the hospital. Amneh stayed besieged in Shateela from April 1986 to June 1988.

Just as the fighters had a role in the defence of the camp, so did women. At the beginning, there was an urgent need for women to dig fortifications and strengthen the bases. As the GUPW, we divided the sisters into groups and sent each group to a base. This was at a time of heavy shelling, but we moved around like the *shebab*. We dug earth and filled sandbags and carried them to make fortifications. These helped to diminish the number of casualties.

We have a group of mothers; some of them we sent to the bakery to make bread. They worked up to six or eight hours a day there. We also helped in the Red Crescent Hospital. The shelling began suddenly, and many of their workers were cut off outside the camp. We sent about ten sisters to help with cleaning, nursing and preparing food for the wounded. Some of the mothers also went to the hospital, working ten hours a day washing sheets. We had a lot of wounded and there weren't enough cleaning workers.

The union took part in the Social Emergency Committee formed at the beginning of the siege to provide foodstuffs, fuel and things children need such as milk powder. People in the shelters were in need of attention. We provided them with fuel and sometimes we worked a generator to give them ventilation. We knew that because of the pressure of people, sicknesses were bound to appear, such as scabies, diarrhoea and vomiting, as well as fleas and lice. So we formed a group to help the Preventive Medicine section of the Red Crescent. It visited homes and shelters, examined people and distributed vitamins to pregnant women.

We tried to deal with problems as they arose. For example, when we saw cases of scabies in the shelters we immediately informed Preventive Medicine. We helped them to distribute the treatment and to advise people how it should be used.

We had about fifteen older women who could be counted on to help us daily. All were volunteers. They'd manage their housework so as to be free from an early hour. There was also a group of older sisters who worked all through the siege on the fortifications.

Our mothers are strugglers. Most of them had at least one son fighting. There's one mother who had all six sons fighting in this siege. Naturally she was moving all the time between the bases, asking about them and the other *shebab*. She helped us in the bakery and in cooking and washing in the hospital. She is a model for all the other mothers in the camp.

One of this mother's sons was seriously wounded. While the doctors were treating him she lived moments of death. I stayed all night with her. I'd go into the room where the doctors were trying to save him, to find out how he was. His heart stopped beating several times and they resuscitated him; but his blood pressure was low, and at dawn he died. When his mother knew, she thought I had been lying to her. She came and held me and said, 'Why didn't you tell me?' Then his brother came who is also a fighter. He said to her, 'Why are you crying? Jalal died a hero and a martyr, defending his honour, his family, and his camp. We mustn't weep for him.'

Now we have many families who are without homes. There has been a lot of destruction in Hayy al-Gharbeh and the Hursh. Even after the cease-fire, Amal movement is preventing building materials from coming into the camp. At first they even forbade women from bringing in foodstuffs. But we insisted, because the *shebab* couldn't go outside. We carried in supplies in our arms, without cars or barrows. Several women suffered blows and arrest. At times, Amal took their bread and vegetables and trod them under their feet. They confiscated coffee, cigarettes, medicines and batteries. They even stopped fruit.

'I didn't tell them anything'

Atrocities on the scale of the first siege did not recur, but there were many 'arrests' like the one described below. Riad was living in Rawsheh, a quarter full of displaced Palestinians. I first heard his story from his mother, who was working inside Shateela.

The day I was arrested was a Monday, the third day of A'eed al-Fitr. I had sent my wife and child to the South, and was going to work as usual. It was 8 am. Two young men were sitting on the edge of a wall; they weren't wearing uniforms, they looked like civilians. If I'd realized they were militia I would have avoided them. As I got close, they called me over. I thought it was to ask me the time. I wasn't expecting arrest, I'm not on their list, there's nothing against me.

'Where are you from?' I didn't know whether to say Palestine or Lebanon, but since my ID card was in my pocket I told them I'm Palestinian. One of them got out a gun that I hadn't seen because it was hidden behind some plants. He put it to my head and ordered me into a building.

They sat me down and gave me a cigarette. I smoked it as if nothing was happening. After five minutes, someone they called Hanash came in. Hanash is from the following of Akel Hamiyeh.[7] He was responsible for the massacre of Haret Hreik.[8]

They began to interrogate me but I didn't tell them anything. They blindfolded me and began to beat me. Beating, beating, until I was almost dead from beating. They they brought a chair and sat me on it. They tied my hands around it, and someone put his feet on my neck. My legs were straight out and they beat me on the soles of my feet. I didn't tell them anything.

They asked me, 'Whom do you know? What organization do you belong to?' They asked a lot about the tunnels under the camps.[9] Also about the names of the leaders, and who was in Mar Elias.[10] I told them I know nothing, I don't belong to any organization. I don't live in the camps. I have nothing to say. Whenever I said that, they'd beat me more.

After the beating on my feet, they took me into a bathroom and hung me on the shower and started kicking me. I was bleeding from my back;

they poured alcohol on it to make the beating hurt more. They asked me the same questions. I stayed silent. Then they brought a syringe filled with something that looked like *mazout* and injected it under my toenails. Then they beat me some more on the soles of my feet. But I didn't tell them anything.

They kept coming to me and pointing a loaded gun at my head and pulling back the safety catch. And telling me to talk. But I didn't. Each one beat me. Once they fired a series of shots over my head. I was sleeping on the floor, without cover or mattress. My hands and legs were tied for five days. The ropes were so tight that the bones were showing. These scars are from the ropes.

After five days they said they were going to execute us. They had brought another man. We couldn't see each other because we were blindfolded. They put us both in the boot of a car and took us to Bir Hassan. There they took off the blindfolds and put me in a small cell alone.

In the end, when they got nothing out of me, after the Jebhat al-Inqadh[11] found out where I was, they let me go. I went straight to hospital and stayed there three days. For a month I couldn't walk, my feet were so swollen.

The number of people detained by Amal during the second siege is said to have been 121, of whom all but 10 had been released by 8 July. At least 60 men missing since 1985 were never found. The Movement had three main prisons: in Bir Hassan, Haret Hreik and the Murr Tower.

'My biggest problem was the children'

Bushra is a young employed woman living near her parents-in-law in Shateela. As a child, she had lived through the siege of Tell al-Za'ter. Now she was married, with two young children aged three and five years.

Right from the first day they encircled the camp. There was no way for anyone to enter or leave. Many who had just come to visit were stuck inside. My father-in-law who had gone up to Dana Mosque to pray had to stay outside the whole month. Half-way through he was able to contact us by radio and find out our news.

I had no food in the house. The next day was the end of the month and I was planning to take my salary and buy supplies at the Co-op. I had nothing in the house, no oil, no *semneh*, not even an onion. No rice. I had enough sugar to last for a few days, a bit of tomato paste and some garlic.

We stayed close to my parents-in-law. They had stocks because they are a big family. And there's my aunt who works in the kitchen of one of the Resistance groups; she brought us cooked food. My husband was here, he's with the Front, he brought me food as well. A plate from here, a plate from there . . . The Resistance kitchens made enough for everyone.

I was worried about my aunt, I wouldn't let her bring us food. Sometimes I'd go, or if it was quiet I'd send my daughter running to the kitchen. It's close. My aunt has more children than I do, and she's a widow. Her son was martyred four months before, in the 'battle of eight hours';[12] soon after that my uncle died.

When the shelling was very heavy we all sat in the corridor of the school. The school was heavily shelled and two floors fell. I was very scared because of having gone through the siege of Tell al-Za'ter. I saw whole buildings collapse there before my eyes. I thought of moving but I couldn't. Our home is near the school and near the home of my parents-in-law. All my cooking things are here.

I was especially scared for the children. They kept getting bored and wanting to go outside. We'd tell them to come in but they'd say, 'We're not afraid', and stay outside. When a family was wounded here, in front of the shelter, I stopped letting them go out.

The children were my biggest problem. They weren't frightened by the shelling. They went on playing and screaming, they talked, they quarrelled, they dared each other. My nerves were on edge but they seemed to feel nothing.

We kept the same daily routine as always. We even bathed more often, because of the dust from the shelling. Our hair became white. Also our clothes and the floor and the mats, all got covered with dust. After every bombardment I'd wash it all down and wash myself.

Water was plentiful. Mortars and shells would fall and damage the pipes, but they'd go immediately and mend them. We fixed a hosepipe to the nearest tap and brought water into my father-in-law's house, and filled from there. The hose was damaged several times but we'd go back and fix it.

This alley where we hang clothes to dry became piled with rubble. We had to keep clearing the rubble to one side to leave a path, so that we could run fast from our door to theirs.

Even though they fixed the washrooms, I couldn't stand the shelters. They were crammed with people. I would have passed out from the heat and the sweat. Even for my children's sake I couldn't go down. Once we went down when the shelling was very heavy, but we never slept there. I'd rather die here.

Once a woman who was obliged to stay in the shelter with her children came to us to wash. She had given birth in Gaza Hospital the year before, a few days before the 'Battle of the Camps' broke out. The baby was in an oxygen tent and the mother got separated from her. The baby disappeared. Six months later they found her safe and sound in the Sahel Hospital.[13] The nurses there had kept her name and the mother's name still fixed to her arm. When the father heard the news, he was mad with joy. It's a beautiful story. In the middle of so many atrocities there are still people with a heart.

If I hadn't had children I would have been more active. I did go out occasionally, to the Popular Committee and the Salvation Front. Once or twice I typed their daily news-sheet *Sumood al-Mukhayem*. It had news about the political situation as well as information about health, garbage collection and the wounded. But once when I went there the children followed me. Shelling started and my husband had to go running after them. So I thought, that's it, I won't go any more. Then they brought the typewriter here.

We didn't have electricity, but the hospital and the Popular Committee had generators. Some people even recharged their batteries from them so that they could watch the World Cup on TV. When there were no more fuel and candles in the shops, the Popular Committee distributed a bottle of petrol to each family.

I gave blood to the wounded like all the other women. It's up to us because the fighters, who weren't too well nourished, had to keep all their strength. Not being able to do much else, I spent time with the wounded. There was one who had lost an eye in the first siege and now he lost another. He is a father of three young children. He was desperate the first few days, but we did everything we could to help him accept his situation. Two others were hit in the spinal column and were paralysed.

The hardest sight, and one that I'll never forget, is what happens after the cease-fire when the families of those who fell are able to enter the camp. Maybe you saw the photo in the papers of my aunt wiping the tears of the mother of Fadia. Fadia was seventeen years old, she stayed in the camp to help, and she was killed by a bullet in the head. It's also when you leave the camp that you hear all the misfortunes of those who stayed outside: men arrested, beaten, sometimes killed; homes looted and burnt.

'We had to keep running'

With an easier military situation, the defenders were better placed than the year before to organize the infrastructure of defence including water, light and power, bread, garbage removal and burial of the dead. Abu Mujahed, Popular Committee chairman, tells how these essential kinds of work were carried out.

Electricity was cut off from the first night. They did it so that they could steal the cable and equipment from the electricity stations outside the camp. We had power for the three most important things: the hospital, the bakery and the well. We had two generators, one for the Popular Committee, the other for the Red Crescent. We used them alternately, just enough to make light for the operations room, and work the bakery, and pump water from the well. We had to keep repairing the cables – although they were underground, they kept getting cut by the shelling. We had to keep running, the Popular Committee and the volunteers, to keep the cables repaired.

The first day they destroyed six drinking-water wells outside the camp. This left us one small well on the edge of the camp. They couldn't reach it but neither could we. It was the same story with the water pipes. The hospital needs a lot of water, and we had to keep it supplied. They cut all the main pipes outside the camp but there are still a few old pipes – no one knows where the water comes from. This source they couldn't destroy, and we protected its pipes from shrapnel with sandbags. But the pipe inside the camp wasn't covered and it got broken several times. We had to mend it quickly. Sometimes we had to work all night to save water for the hospital. The bakery needs water too.

If they could have stopped the air and light from reaching us they would have done it. They blew up one of the water mains near the Sports City with the aim of flooding Shateela; but of course it didn't work.

Garbage was a problem. It began to pile up on the streets, especially near the hospital. There was dirt and blood, and flies increased. So we called for volunteers. The Popular Committee worked too, because you can't ask people to work and then just sit and watch them. We told people to bring the garbage in front of their houses to a central place. We used the fork-lift truck to push it outside, and then we burned it. We could only do this because the *shebab* had succeeded in removing Amal from certain areas around the camp. We didn't want to expand, just to defend ourselves.[14]

Burying the dead was a problem because the Mosque was already full from last year. It's very painful to dig up dead bodies, but in a war there's no *haram* and *halal*, you have to save people from sickness. We tried various things – opening the graves, bringing more earth. But it was impossible. So we closed the Mosque and began to use the Hursh.

The Hursh wasn't very safe – you can see the shell craters. But we carried out burials at night, or during lulls. The Popular Committee was responsible for burials, but we used to ask for volunteers to help. We'd ask for one and find ten. Once I saw old people standing there waiting to help. People run quickly to bury a martyr.

We had to bury without ceremony. Sometimes the *sheikh* prayed, but usually we said, 'He's a martyr, he doesn't need prayers.' So now there's one more cemetery. We are thinking of moving bodies to the Martyrs' Cemetery.[15] We don't want to live surrounded by cemeteries. It's not easy for the families to pass them every day.

The main problem now is reconstruction. The school is destroyed. We are petitioning UNRWA for a school programme next year. The Syrians have agreed to reconstruction but Amal still doesn't allow materials to enter the camp. We raise the matter at the Coordination Committee, they discuss it, we wait, and the materials don't reach the camp.

They are still kidnapping people on the street and beating them. The day before yesterday they kidnapped people in Sabra and Fakhany at night, checking ID cards and searching. We have to discuss such incidents within the alliance. We have to have patience.

We are facing another problem: emigration. It's because of insecurity and siege. There are people who haven't been outside the camp for more than a year. Maybe they think that if they go to Denmark or Germany or Sweden, things will be easier. But they're wrong. If there's unemployment in Europe, what shall we do there? Just take relief? As Palestinians we have no interests outside, we should stay here and continue our struggle for our homeland. We shouldn't expect our life to be easy.

'They forgot that there was a war outside'

Beit Atfal al-Sumood has a centre in Shateela, with thirty registered children and several young social workers. Here its local director, Jameeleh Shehadeh, a gentle, serious young woman from a pious background, tells of work with children and families.

We felt at ease in this siege, we could move and work. In the last siege there was real fear that they would enter the camp and destroy us. I felt paralysed. This time there was no real fear; I felt able to go out and work.

I think that the work of a social institution like ours is especially important during a siege. There were a number of serious social problems. Along with the sisters in other institutions like the women's union, we tried to solve them.

Take the shelters. When we visited them we found that they were very dirty. No one was taking care of them. We sat and talked with people, we tried to make them feel the importance of hygiene in the shelters, especially for small children who weren't getting any fresh air. We registered all the names and made a programme, so that each day three people would be responsible for cleaning the shelter. In each shelter we chose a committee to supervise the cleaning.

Dirty water was collected in the shelters. They didn't have a pump and neither did we, so we contacted the women's union to help us remove the water. Finally we got the Popular Committee to provide pumps for each shelter.

Because of crowding and dirt in the shelters, children began to get spots. We contacted the Red Crescent to deal with this problem. There was also diarrhoea because of the lack of clean drinking water, so they distributed pastilles for disinfecting water and told people how to look after their children, to protect them from sickness.

There are toilets and showers in the shelters. We emphasized the importance of keeping them clean, and distributed Flash, Dettol, soap and shampoo given to us by the Committee of Social Services. Every day we refilled the bottle of Dettol in each shelter. People whose homes were close could go home to wash when it was calm. But there were people from Hayy Gharbeh and the Hursh who couldn't do this.

There was one family whose children were especially dirty. Other people in the shelter were complaining about them. We found out that their mother was simple-minded. All the work fell on the oldest daughter, Huda, who was only fourteen. We explained to the mother that she must wash her children but she couldn't understand us. So we helped Huda bathe her brothers and sisters. There were four of them – six including Huda and her mother. After we had bathed the children we brought them to the Centre and gave them each a set of clean clothes.

Then we told the mother that she should also take a bath. A social worker who went to check on her found her sitting in the bathroom, doing nothing. So she stayed with her and helped her to wash herself.

While this was happening, her husband came to ask about her and found the youngest daughter, whom he loved very much, crying. This made him angry and he ran to the bathroom, wanting to open the door on his wife to beat her. I explained to him that it was we who had told her to take a bath, and he calmed down. After this, other people in the shelter accepted this family, and they – the children and the mother – felt much better psychologically because they were clean. This was the hardest case we faced. Other families looked after themselves. Sometimes there were conflicts over space, but these were easily solved.

When shelling was heavy and people couldn't get out to buy bread from the bakery, bread was distributed free. If we saw a family that couldn't afford to buy bread, we'd ask one of the committee to give it to them free. Our girls helped the Committee of Social Services distribute food supplies and made sure that the families supported by Beit Atfal, needy cases, got their rightful share. From our work in the shelters we knew which children had special need of milk, so we contacted all the bodies that had milk powder, to give them some.

We kept daily hours in the Centre, we never closed down. We said, home or Centre, it's the same. If there was heavy shelling we took shelter under the stairs; when there were lulls we went out and worked. The Centre got two direct hits. Luckily we had all just left.

This year we celebrated A'eed al-Fitr in spite of the siege. You know, it's our tradition that everyone visits the cemetery on the day of the feast. Here the cemetery is in the Mosque. It had been hit so much that it was all rubble and dust. So we met on the *woqfi*[16] and cleared the mosque of rubble, and swept it and washed it, and then we decorated it. People were very happy when they saw the Mosque clean and decorated.

Beit Atfal exists for children, so we said we must do something for them during the *a'eed*. We had some children's clothes and shoes in the Centre; we gave them out, with priority to children in the shelters. We told the mothers, 'Even though it's wartime, let your children put on these new clothes today.' We also made pretty baskets and filled them with sweets, and distributed them. The children were happy and remembered to say to each other, '*Kull 'amm wa intum bi-kheir*'.[17]

After the feast, we and the women's union dedicated two special days to the children in the shelters, with songs, and dancing to drums, and drawing with crayons. In spite of the war, most of the children's drawings were in peaceful colours, green and yellow, and about peaceful subjects such as home. While the entertainment was going on, they forgot that there was a war outside. So did we.

There was one small thing I saw that affected me a lot. A small child, a girl of about four years old, got wounded. Usually children cry when they are hurt, and this child's hand was bleeding. But she didn't cry, she kept asking for her grandmother who was wounded at the same time. 'Where is grannie?' she kept asking. She wouldn't stop until she saw her.

There was another child, a boy, one of those who was wounded outside the shelter. They took him to the hospital to treat him, and after the bleeding stopped they offered him a Bonjus.[18] He said, 'No, I'm fasting.' He was so young and yet so attached to his religion.

I feel that religion plays an important role in enabling people to stay steadfast. There were many occasions in the siege when people escaped death by a miracle. This made them say, 'God is protecting us. So what if they shell us!' This helped them to go on bearing it. The effect of the shelling on them didn't last. As soon as it calmed down a bit, they'd move, they'd bring food for their children, they'd forget fear and death. Faith helps this forgetting. People say of someone who was killed, '*Khalas*![19] His days are over. Wherever he was, he was going to die.'

'Many more leaders got killed this time'

Dr Muhammad was still trapped inside Shateela during the second siege, but with a well-staffed medical centre operating he had more time to observe people's reactions.

Young people were even more active this time than last. There were several reasons I think. One is that the siege was expected, so they were prepared. Then there's the fact that many of them had been imprisoned in the camp for a year. This made them angry. Fighting gave them a chance to get out of the prison of the camp and get rid of the frustration inside. That's why they were more active, fought harder and felt happy. Morale was very high.

The fact that there were political and military leaders in the camp this time added to the fighters' spirits. The leaders had a plan, and the fighters understood it.

But because their morale was so high, they took unnecessary risks. Many of them still don't understand that they need to be specially careful during cease-fires. They went to the edges of the camp where they were exposed to snipers. They were so sure that Amal couldn't beat them that they demonstrated their courage in foolish ways. All the most severe wounds were received during cease-fires.

Another thing: many more leaders were killed this time. Abu Adnan, Ziad Bakri – I can name you four or five leaders who were killed by sniper fire. Last year it wasn't like that. Maybe this time they wanted to demonstrate their courage to their followers. Maybe it was because they knew they hadn't been courageous the first time, and they wanted to make up for it.

In this siege I saw many people act as if there was nothing going on. You see the flowers on that roof? The man who owns the house used to water them daily, whether there was shelling or not. Once I asked him, 'Whatever are you doing up there?' He said, 'Don't worry. I have to water my flowers. They won't hit me now.'

The *shebab* felt stronger, they had weapons, they had leaders, politically we were in a strong position. They knew that if Amal tried to invade the camp there would be shelling from the mountains. Anyway, Amal wouldn't try to invade because they couldn't do it. I never saw fear on anyone's face. They said, 'If they couldn't beat us the first time when we were so weak, there's no way they can beat us now.'

This time Amal stayed shelling us from afar. This was a ruse to make us expand outside the camp so that the Syrians would hit us. Our leadership decided we would just defend our positions and let them shoot. But Amal's media announced that the Palestinians were spreading outside the camp. They did this to mobilize public opinion against us. That's why some Lebanese leaders began saying, 'No to the return of Palestinians to West Beirut!'

The *shebab* took parts of Hayy Gharbeh and the Hursh as defence positions. This is why there were fewer casualties and less destruction inside the camp than last time, because most of the shelling was on the borders. It was good tactics.

You know the Austrian Clinic on the edge of the Hursh? When the *shebab* took it they didn't attack it frontally, they got in through the roof. I don't know how they did it, but it was a neat operation, and not one of them was killed or wounded. Amal did not expect that we would try to take that building because it was strongly defended. Our people said, 'Amal think we can't take it, so we will take it.' They found this way of surprising them.

There were very few casualties during the shelling. People stayed at home, under cover. We got casualties when the shelling stopped and people came out, and then sniping or shelling started suddenly. Most of the serious wounds came in the period after the cease-fire. Most of the deaths were caused by head or chest wounds from snipers in Sabra, from those high buildings, using telescopic lens.

This time there was no lack of food or medicine or water. People were calm. Perhaps because they were less afraid, there was less closeness than the time before. Then, anyone could go into any house and eat or sleep, people were so close.

It's harder now, after the siege is over. They want to go out, to be free, but they can't. During the fighting they had this hope; now there's an anti-climax. Some react by saying, 'We were strong, we could have gone right out of the camp, but others stopped us.' You hear some of the young men cursing the leaders, or cursing the situation.

People are frustrated now; they are saying, 'Why don't they let us rebuild? Why is it taking so much time to fix water and electricity?' They are fearful about the future. When there is shelling you see the consequences immediately – a building falls, someone is killed. But this waiting and waiting is hard, especially when it's waiting for something unknown.

There have been many cases of breakdown, especially among young women who lost their husband or brother. They had to bring the wife of one of the leaders to the clinic every day for ten days for treatment.

There's a boy of twenty who had a kind of breakdown. His friend was badly wounded. He was inside the operating room and the doctors were treating him. The boy knew his friend would die and wanted to see him before he died, but the doctors wouldn't allow him in. He lost control and broke the windows of the operating room.

'The camp is our only country'

Once again there was extensive damage to housing and to public facilities. Reconstruction is the urgent concern of all. Abu Mustafa expresses both typical Palestinian optimism ('We have a project to make street lights') and a clear perception of the political obstacles to returning to normality.

We came out of this war that was imposed on us against our will with high spirits, and set about the work of reconstruction. Among the priorities is water. We managed to repair the pipes inside the camp with the help of UNICEF, but when we tried to repair the wells outside the camp we met obstacles. The brothers in Amal are setting conditions. They want to enter the camp to lay the pipes, and they want to keep the pumping station in their territory.

UNRWA couldn't agree to this because it has the responsibility of providing water to the camp. And we couldn't agree. The main well is far from the camp, near the Sports City, and has cost us a lot. Every two or three months the pump station used to be burnt out because of people interfering with it. And we used to have to pay for repairs, never less than LL8,000.

We tried to cooperate with them [Amal]. We said, 'This water will be both for you and for us. We will take two inches and give you four inches.' But no, they want to keep control of the switch. If we agree to this, they can cut off water to the camp any time they want.

A second priority is to clear the camp of rubble and garbage. The main streets are clear but there is still a lot of rubble on roofs and in the alleys that are too narrow for the bulldozer to enter. There are ten workers with a fork-lift truck and a tractor working every day; they will go on until they have cleared the smallest pebble from the camp.

Of the four electricity stations outside the camp, only the walls are standing. Everything was stolen, including the big generator which cost LL300,000. The Coordination Committee and the Syrians have helped us by putting pressure on the Electricity Company to increase the load of the only station inside the camp. But repairing the network will cost between LL30,000 and LL40,000.

We also have a project to make street lights for the main roads and inside the camp, to make life spring up again.

We have a new project, to open a shop for supplies for the people, to beat the monopoly of the little shops inside the camp that make a big profit. With the backing of the Committee of Social Services we'll set up a people's shop that will guarantee everyone's needs at a reasonable price.

We need building materials – cement, iron, pebbles, sand. Amal is still not allowing these into the camp. Not even a bag of sand. Someone whose home is destroyed can't build a roof over his children's heads. Of course we raised this matter many times at the Coordination Committee. But they [Amal] play around, they talk, they say OK, but nothing happens. It's the usual harassment. The Coordination Committee ought to stand up to them.

They search women at the entrance, they question women and children. They search bags. This isn't in accord with the agreement between us. We have to be patient because they have an aim, they want to inflame the situation. We want to make this attempt fail.

The news exaggerates the numbers of followers of Abu Ammar and makes it appear that they are the aggressors. But it isn't Arafat or the PNSF that is making attacks, it is Amal that is besieging the camp. Let them leave us in peace.

There's very little work inside or outside the camp. People are afraid to go out of the camp to look for work. Many young men and girls have been followed, and taken at checkpoints. Anyway there aren't any jobs. This is what makes many of our young men want to emigrate.

Yet the camp isn't empty. The ones who left are those whose houses were hit, or who want to put their children in schools outside because schools in the camp have been destroyed. Even if they go outside, they remain linked to the camp; they make daily visits, their wives and children often remain in the camp during the day. They try every way to get their homes repaired. Most of them are living as refugees outside, in mosques or building shelters. They have no friends there. So they are drawn to return to the camp, and to stay among familiar people and customs. The camp is our only country.

Notes

1. Serious attacks occurred on 24 August and 7 October 1985, from 28 to 30 January and from 27 March to 15 April 1986. Sticks of dynamite were often tossed into the camp at night and once a woman was killed by a night sniper. On 25 September 1985 there was a massacre of seventeen Palestinians in the nearby neighbourhood of Haret Hreik.

2. Casualty figures given for the second and third sieges are probably less accurate than for the first. They also do not include people killed between the sieges, and after the last.

3. This was Dr Chris Giannou, who lived through both the second and third sieges inside Shateela, spending an uninterrupted twenty-seven months there. He is the author of *Besieged: A Doctor's Story of Life and Death in Beirut*.

4. A medium-sized share (for families of four to six persons) contained 2 kilograms of rice, 1 kilogram of whole lentils, 1 kilogram of crushed lentils, 2

kilograms of *burghul*, 3 kilograms of sugar and ½ kilogram of crushed beans or macaroni. Food shares were distributed three times during the siege.

5. A sweet drink made from rose petals.

6. These were multi-storey buildings built by the PRM just outside Shateela, near the northwest entrance. They were later destroyed.

7. Akel Hamiyeh was military chief of Amal during the 'Battle of the Camps'. He is from the Beqa', the area from which most of the fighting elements in Amal were drawn.

8. See footnote 1 above.

9. There was a myth that all the Beirut camps were connected by underground tunnels.

10. This small camp in Wata Museitbeh remained relatively safe during the siege because it was under PSP protection.

11. Throughout the 'Battle of the Camps', contacts continued between the PNSF (Damascus-based) groups and the Amal movement.

12. On 7 October 1985.

13. A Shi'ite hospital on the road to the airport.

14. This was a sensitive issue. Anti-Palestinian groups and media accused the Palestinians of 'expansion', i.e. of trying to take over areas surrounding the camps (see pp. 102, 115 n. 11).

15. Outside the camp (see Map 3).

16. The day before the feast.

17. A ritual greeting meaning 'May you have prosperity this and every year'.

18. A locally made fruit drink.

19. *Khalas*: an expression indicating both the ending of an event or episode and the end of reflecting, worrying or suffering over it.

11. The Five-Month Siege (25 November 1986 to 6 April 1987)

The third siege again differed from the other two: it was longer, harder and complicated by severe internal tensions and splits. It was not completely unexpected, since clashes in Sidon and the South had been escalating since the summer, Rashidiyyeh had been under siege since 29 September, and Bourj Barajneh since 28 October; but Shateela's leadership had been reassuring people that their relations with Amal were good. However, when Palestinian forces captured the village of Maghdousheh (southeast of 'Ain Helweh) on 24 November, Amal riposted against Shateela.

Militarily this was the harshest siege, with new kinds of missile being used in an all-out effort at total destruction. It was also the first siege occurring in winter – a particularly wet one and a tough experience for people huddled in ruins, trenches and underground shelters. Finally, this was the first siege that brought Shateela to the brink of starvation, when family supplies of flour, food and fuel ran out completely and when, even after the entry of supplies had been negotiated, Amal militia set fire to the food lorries as they approached the camp. The underlying conflict between Fateh loyalists and the pro-Syrian groups was fanned by cease-fire proposals aimed at eliminating 'Arafatists', a manoeuvre which, although it failed during the siege, helped to produce the *harb al-dakhili* (internal war) of May/June 1988.

Casualties were high (126 killed, 200 wounded), especially in the final weeks when people seemed to lose the will to live and were easily picked off by Amal snipers as they foraged for food or wood. Casualties among children were heavier than in other sieges, with several losing limbs or eyes.

The third siege was also remarkable for the digging of a network of tunnels and trenches, some of which extended into Amal territory, and which enabled the camp's fighters and families to hold out through their longest ordeal yet.

Portrait of Emira

Emira's father was commander of a base near Jericho School. He was killed early in the siege by a *khara'a*.[1] Emire, aged six, died two months later after receiving a shrapnel wound in the head. This description was given by a young relief volunteer who was Emira's aunt.

From the beginning of the battle she felt she had to work like an adult. She put on jeans larger than her size, and espadrilles. Wherever the girls of the women's union went, Emira went with them. If they baked bread, she helped them. If they filled sandbags, she filled sandbags.

Her father loved her very much because she was so alert. He talked to her, took her with him everywhere, although there's a boy who is older. She went with him several times to his base.

The day her father was killed was an unusually bad day. Her mother said, 'Don't take Emira today.' When she heard of her father's death she behaved like an adult: she beat herself, she said, '*Ya baba*, I wish I'd died instead of you.'

During the siege she helped her mother. She fetched water, she brought firewood. Every time there was a distribution – flour, cigarettes, whatever – she claimed her mother's share. The women were amazed at the way she wriggled between their legs to get to the head of the queue. Her mother said, 'While Emira was alive, I didn't feel the siege.'

She wasn't born in Shateela. They came here after the fighting in Tripoli, in 1983. She quickly learned to find her way through all the little alleys of the camp. Adults lose their way but Emira used to go by herself to visit our relatives.

She loved to sing and dance, and she specially liked weddings. If there was going to be a wedding, she'd ask the bride, 'What are you getting for your trousseau?' and she would tell her what she ought to bring. People liked her dancing, it was like the dancing of adults, so strong! Everyone said to my brother's wife, 'Take care of that child! Be careful of people's eyes on her.'[2] She was out of the ordinary.

She was wounded when a shell landed near a group of children. All the others were lightly wounded in the legs, but Emira got a head wound. Perhaps a fragment of shrapnel entered the brain. She was unconscious for a week; the second week she seemed to improve. She began to talk and move, she recognized her sisters, she got out of bed, she asked for food. Then suddenly . . . perhaps they had run out of medicines, they couldn't treat her. There was an infection. She became unconscious again and died.

Umm Muhammad and her neighbours

This conversation was recorded in a little alley where people had not gone to the shelters. The top floors were devastated but ground floors were relatively intact.

Umm Muhammad: This building has three floors – my children built their homes above mine. But all of us were down here in the siege and the shelling. There were about fifty of us – five families in the inside room and three families in this room. We were sleeping on top of each other.

There were scabies and lice in the shelters, no water to wash, no soap. I'm afraid of the shelters – anyway, there aren't enough to take everyone. So we took the risk of being hit, we stayed in our homes, we put ourselves in God's hands. Wherever there's a house surrounded by other houses, people come and stay in it.

Neighbour: The hardest thing was not going out. We didn't even dare to go to the bathroom while the shelling was on. You see the hits on the ground here? That's where shells landed. And here is where shrapnel entered the house. Whenever the shelling calmed down a little we ran to the bathroom. If it started, we didn't wait to dress properly, we ran back inside. What can be worse than this?

Another neighbour: My home faces the Sports City, it's exposed to sniping. I'd go into the kitchen to wash before praying, and they would be sniping at me.

Umm Muhammad: We had to cook in the same room we lived in. Black [soot] on our faces, black on our clothes. There wasn't much water. My daughter used to bring it from our neighbours in a cap. There's a tap near them. I would fill a jar, my neighbour would fill a jar. It was enough for us to drink from and to wash our nightdresses every two or three weeks. We threw a little water on our heads to keep away lice.

Old woman: From fear I started to bleed – it's twelve years since I stopped menstruating. I lay in bed for twenty-five days, bleeding. Then during Ramadan, thank God, I became clean.

Neighbour: My daughter was wounded in the head at the beginning of the siege. The wound was bleeding. I brought olive oil and boiled it and wrapped it in a cloth round her head. And the wound healed.

Umm Muhammad: At the beginning I had stocks for twenty days. People like us who don't have a salaried employee in the family can only buy a little at a time. I had some *mazout*, one bottle of liquid gas and one bottle of kerosene – these were enough for a month but I made them last longer by using wood from the roof for making bread. My daughter used to go up to the roof under shelling to get it. When the wood on the roof was finished, we broke up the cupboard. All my children who had damaged cupboards brought them for firewood.

Our flour finished after two months and a bit. There was a little flour from the organizations. What did they give to a family of eight people? Two or three kilos. We adults took a mouthful of bread, less than a quarter of a *ragheef*.[3] We'd drink a drop of water with it, just so as to keep our bowels working. Our sugar gave out at the beginning of the last month. I kept a little for my grandson because he was only getting milk. I cut it from myself and the other children. I told them, 'This is your brother's son, he's only a year old, what else can he eat?' At the very end, when all food was finished, I crumbled fragments of dried bread in a little tea for him. The other children lost weight but not the baby. If I saw other people had food I'd take a little for him.

Neighbour: The last day, women organized a demonstration to open the road. One of them was in her eighth month – Hanan, the wife of Abu Faheem. He said to her, 'Go and have the baby at your mother's. It's better than staying here where there's nothing to eat.' They hit her with a sniper's bullet. And her aunt who went with her was wounded in the thigh. Four were killed in that demonstration. Not many people from this quarter went out. We heard that women who went out from Bourj Barajneh camp were shot, so we were scared. Those who were ready to take the risk went out.

Neighbour: We heard about Bourj Barajneh on the news. When the batteries finished, we took them out of the radio, put them in water on the fire, boiled them, dried them and let them cool. Then we put them back in the transistor. It worked. There were no new batteries – what else could we do? We Palestinians have big brains!

Another neighbour: Such big brains! They slaughter us, we die, and we still say what big brains we have! How many years have they been slaughtering us! And they are still doing it!

Umm Muhammad: The worst thing for me was my children being outside. I wondered, 'Will I ever see them again? And my husband?' Every week we would say, 'Next week it will finish. *Khalas*! It's going to end soon.' But *inside* we were thinking that we are going to die here and we'll never again see those who are outside.

'We still don't have a saucepan'

Like many other families in the siege, Umm Kamal and her children were from outside Shateela. They were helped by the *shebab* to escape from Hayy Gharbeh into Shateela under heavy shelling. In this conversation Umm Kamal discusses her experiences with a woman cadre, showing some differences of perspective.

Umm Kamal: Usually there's time to run away or return home – you hear a few gun shots, the beginning of a battle. But this time, they started straightaway with tanks and heavy artillery. It was impossible to leave Hayy Gharbeh. We took shelter in a room 3 x 4 metres. There were about twenty-five of us: I and my seven children; my neighbour who has six; the four daughters of another neighbour. There were babies and old people. At around 10 pm Palestinian fighters came and helped us to reach the camp.

We spent the first night in the club near the mosque. We left Hayy Gharbeh with the clothes we had on – we didn't bring a thing with us. Of course, the children were hungry. They gave us two or three loaves of bread and a tin of Picon cheese. And we found in the club 2 kilos of coarse *burghul*; we moistened it with a little water and gave it to the children. The shelling was so heavy that we couldn't reach the bakery or people we know to get food.

After five or six days they found space for us in the shelter of brother 'Ali.[4] There too we stayed without bread or food unless God sent us a woman we know who would give us a loaf. We are from Hayy Gharbeh, we don't know many people inside the camp.

Samia (a cadre): We in Jebhat al-Inqadh (the Salvation Front) began to distribute bread from the tenth day.

Umm Kamal: I'm talking about the first week, at the beginning of the battle, when the shelling was very heavy. After that, help began arriving from our brothers in Jebhat al-Inqadh and the other organizations. But there were still many difficulties, for example lack of soap.

Samia: We distributed soap three times and a cup of Tide every two or three weeks.

Umm Kamal: For seven people, I got a teacup of 'Yes'[5] every two weeks and a piece of soap the size of a shaving stick. In five months, what soap did we get? Three pieces!

Samia: No, more. But it's true that we had very little soap. Shampoo disappeared completely. I had to wash my hair with Tide.

Umm Kamal: When I wanted to wash, I hadn't got a spare dress to change into. My mother-in-law borrowed a vest and a *gallabiya*[6] for me.

Samia: The people from Hayy Gharbeh were the ones who suffered most.

Interviewer: What about things for cooking with?

Samia: Weren't there two saucepans in the shelter?

Umm Kamal: No, there weren't. There was a primus but no saucepans. If someone had a saucepan, it was just enough for her and for her children. Is she going to wash it and give it to me?

Samia: In another shelter we distributed two saucepans. Families in their homes gave them. We asked people to take turns using them.

Umm Kamal: There were 120 families in our shelter with two primuses.

Samia: The siege started and we didn't have everything we needed. Now one realizes that it's as important to have kitchen utensils as milk for babies. Clothes also. For example, I'm a 'daughter of an organization',[7] my home isn't in Shateela. I had to wash my clothes at night and wear them the next day. It was hard during the rainy months.

Umm Kamal: We left home without blankets. Abu Rashed, may God protect him, gave us a blanket. I put my children to sleep on it and covered them with a blanket that my neighbour gave me. When there was cold and wind they were shivering.

Samia: We in the Struggle Front distributed blankets to the shelter that's in front of our office. The Popular Committee didn't have blankets or mattresses. Our fighters had two blankets each. We asked them to give up one; we collected them.

Interviewer: Did rain come into the shelters?

Samia: No.

Umm Kamal: We kept on cleaning the floor; and when the shelling got less we'd go up and clean outside the shelter. For the sake of the children.

Samia: One from each family would go up to clear around the shelter and open the gutters. Each shelter had its own committee working under the supervision of the Popular Committee and the women's union. The ventilators were operated for an hour every day to take out the stale air; and there was no flooding from the toilets.

Umm Kamal: It's an experience I won't ever forget!

Samia: A marvellous one, wasn't it?

Umm Kamal: For God's sake! My heart almost failed.

How the siege started

Badr was on the periphery of the camp when the shelling began. As a member of the Coordination Committee, he was called out to negotiate the removal of fortifications, and was taken prisoner by Amal.

I went out with the representative of the Jebhat al-Inqadh to meet with the Syrian brothers and Amal near one of the entries to the camp. There we agreed to make the rounds and tell the fighters to remove the barricades they had been putting up. Amal was supposed to send a representative, but none of them came. We had with us someone from the Lebanese Army and two Syrian officers.[8]

There were *shebab* from Amal movement making piles of sand to close the road. We talked to them, suggesting that they remove these fortifications because people in the camp were taking them as a sign that Amal was planning to attack the camp. We said that we didn't want the fighting to spread.

One of them said, 'We don't want anyone from Jebhat al-Inqadh coming here.' Another jumped up: 'No, they have the right to see our fortifications, just as our leaders enter the camp to inspect theirs.' They started quarrelling. One hit the other and the one who was hit went to get his Klashin. The others tried to stop him but he managed to fire a few shots at the ground.

It was a moment of great tension. It only needed one shot to make the whole camp explode. So when this shot rang out, all the bases began to fire. Bullets rained on the camp and the camp replied. That's how it started.

We were in a place that was under Amal control. Amal people wanted to kill us, women attacked us with their shoes, a man came at me with a knife. We spread out. The other Palestinian managed to reach an Amal

office but I got blocked near the Hammadeh Villa with the Lebanese
Army man and one of the Syrians. For two hours they were quarrelling
over who would kill me. We couldn't reach the Syrian post but we finally
managed to reach an Amal office.

'I didn't worry about my children because everything is from God'

In general, mothers stay with their children while defence and social work
are carried out by *banat* (young unmarried women). But although she had a
baby less then a year old, Umm 'Issam was active.

I was here in the camp so I felt obliged to work like everyone else. I was
responsible for the Committee for the Wounded. In the morning we
brought them cigarettes and after lunch we brought them Tang. We
helped them all without discrimination. If there was a patient who
couldn't eat, I'd sit beside him and support his head with my arm, and
give him the juice drop by drop.

Some of them had no clothes, so I went and gathered all that we had,
the underclothes of my husband and son, their slippers and things, and
took them to the wounded.

I used to leave my children with a friend who was pregnant. We stayed
with her because she lives on the ground floor of a building that had five
floors. Ours had only one. I didn't worry about the children because
everything is from God. I could have been with them and something
could have hit us and they could have died.

Every night before sleeping we said the *shehadeh*,[9] so that if a shell
came, we would die in the faith. My children stayed home all the time.
Sometimes when the shelling stopped I'd take them out for a walk.
Especially the baby, I'd take him out to get some sunlight.

When there were no more glass covers for kerosene lamps we made
new ones with Tang jars. You take off the cover and insert it in the base of
the lamp. Then you take the jar and heat it on a fire; when it's hot, you dip
it in cold water so that the bottom falls out. It becomes like the cover of a
lamp. You fix it on the lamp and screw it in. Without it, the lamp would
make soot.

When kerosene gave out, we found an empty bean or tuna-fish tin,
filled it with sand mixed with *semneh*, put a wick in it and lit it. When
wicks gave out, we cut strips from jeans, soaked them in oil and made
them into wicks. Everyone did this.

Digging for survival

Speaking for the three-member Fortification Committee, Abu Samra describes the work which, as much as the fighters, saved the camp after its front-line defences were destroyed in the first week's shelling.

All the houses on the edges of the camp were destroyed in the first week. The damage was incredible; it reached 90 per cent of all houses. This created a very dangerous situation. All the camp entrances were open and not only that: the whole of the interior of the camp – its streets and offices and institutions – was exposed to sniper and artillery fire. We had to find a way to protect the inside of the camp, so as to be able to move about and carry the wounded. Our plan had two aspects: first, to raise barricades at all the main entrances to block Amal sniper and artillery fire; second, to dig trenches and tunnels to secure communication between key areas, mainly the bases and the hospital.

The first step was to form a Fortification Committee. But even with the seven comrades brought in to help from the Committee of Social Services, these were not enough to carry out the work, which called for muscular and manual effort. Such work really needed a bulldozer – all we had were spades and shovels. At the beginning it was difficult to mobilize people to help with the fortifications because of the violence of the shelling. Two or three shells were landing every minute. We built the first two barricades alone and then, as we felt that the violence of the battle would continue, we called on the organizations to send us volunteers. In addition, families in the areas where we were working spontaneously helped us.

It was the job of the Fortification Committee to look after the inside of the camp. The fighters dug the trenches, tunnels and rooms under their bases.

We worked mainly at night. We'd go out onto the streets and alleys and pile up barricades of earth, iron, rubble, sand – everything we could find. If there were burnt-out cars, we filled them with sand and stones and set them on their sides. As the barriers were raised, they shelled them. Every day there were gaps that we had to close. The work was continuous. To build one barricade would take us several nights. Often, just as we finished, tanks would destroy it and we had to start all over again.

What gave a big push to our determination was the old people who insisted on helping. These old people who had worked so hard all their lives, who had given everything, brought shovels and spades and worked side by side with the *shebab*. In addition, women worked on the fortifications as well as all the other work they did, such as making bread, nursing the wounded and distributing supplies. In fact, an all-female work group was formed which built a barricade in a very dangerous area near Hayy Farhat. While they were working, sniping began and one of the comrades was hit in the eye. The other girls took her to hospital and carried on working. We all knew that if the fortifications weren't carried out, many more people would be killed.

There was a street near the hospital directly targeted from the Sports City. The night we were digging a trench there, they started to shell that area. Several shells fell near us but we took cover in the trench and carried on digging. This trench was essential for transferring the wounded to hospital.

Another time we were helping fighters in an advanced base in the Hursh to finish their trench and underground rooms. There also we had a female comrade who was an outstanding example of work and sacrifice. She never stopped working. She was wounded there while giving first aid to a wounded comrade, and lost a leg.

The fortifications constructed in Shateela in four and a half months would have taken two years at an ordinary work pace. Everyone realized that if we didn't work quickly, we'd die quickly. But hard as we worked, we never managed to complete our plan. We finished the most basic and important part. But one barricade in a street wasn't enough, because a sniper on a fourth floor could see beyond it. We needed a series of barricades on every alley. As it was, probably more martyrs fell inside the camp from sniping than fell in the bases.

As much as we gave, our means remained limited. Everything had to be done by hand and with simple tools. On top of that, we suffered many shortages as the siege went on. At the beginning we had a fair number of spades, shovels and pick-axes because these are tools you find in every home. But each base needed its own digging equipment; and there were many other things we needed, from saws to nails. A nail in the siege was worth a kilo of gold, we used up so many. Political splits also affected us, causing some organizations to drop out of joint work.

The sandiness of the soil under Shateela was both good and bad. It made digging easy; but it meant that the trenches and tunnels were liable to cave in. This forced us to construct solid sides and ceilings to prevent collapse. We would dig a metre or two, then lay a wood scaffolding to hold up a wooden ceiling. This is why we used up all the wood that was in the camp. Luckily for us, hundreds of metres of building wood had been brought into the camp just before the siege to use in reconstruction. But we also used iron and doors to make the ceilings of the rooms and tunnels under the bases. To make them really secure we piled maybe a metre of sand and rubble on top. No shell could pierce them.

Sewage and water pipes were a problem with the advanced bases and tunnels that reached outside the camp, into Hayy Gharbeh and the Hursh. There was also the problem of electricity cables: the high-tension ones are underground and dangerous if cut. We had no way of avoiding them except to dig very deep.

The other big problem was the rain. The war was in winter and the rainfall was particularly heavy this year. All the trenches and tunnels got flooded.

I remember a time when one of the fighters was wounded in Hayy Gharbeh. The wound was a serious one, near the backbone. He had to be got back into the camp but the trench was full of water, up to the chest. There was no other way but to make him walk through the trench, with his blood flowing out.

In the Hursh all the trenches were overflowing and the room where the fighters slept was flooded. When the fighters did guard duty, they had to stand for hours in waterlogged trenches – in winter, with the cold, they had to wrap themselves in blankets – we didn't have enough winter clothes or boots for them. During all of March the trenches were flooded. The hardest time we faced was the winter season and the extreme cold. But we couldn't give up the advanced bases because Amal would have gained positions from which to shell the camp.

After the siege I was taken to see several of the underground bunkers and tunnels. The work was strong and precise, the fruit of 'Ali Abu Towq's military skill and Shateela men's years in the building trades. It was amazing to think that this work had been carried out under heavy shelling.

A front-line family

Rana is a nine-year-old girl who lost a leg in the siege, one of several child amputees. Her home is right on Abu Hassan Salameh Street, facing the Sports City. Her mother speaks.

When the fighters started, we were up on the second floor. We came down to shelter inside on the ground floor; but the shelling on this area was so heavy that we jumped from the window into the alley and ran to another house. A shell hit that house so we escaped again, from house to house, until we reached a house in the middle of the camp. After we had been there a few days, we got a direct hit. It came through the wall of the room we were sheltering in and killed my father-in-law. All of us were wounded – my mother-in-law, my husband, and the baby. Rana got that scar on her face. I got a piece of shrapnel too, only a small piece. That was in December, about fifteen days after the beginning of the battle.

After that we took refuge in the Popular Front shelter. There was hardly room to lie down. I put my little son on my lap and the other son curled up next to me. We had nothing with us. When I left home I took a few clothes for the children but everything flew when the shell came down on us. I begged for a small saucepan to boil milk for my son.

The second time Rana was hit was at the entrance of the shelter. It was at sundown. They carried her straightaway to the hospital and her leg was amputated. The operation lasted four or five hours.

When she realized that her leg was gone she cried, of course. She asked, 'Where have they put it? Will they come and fix it back on?' Then later she asked, 'Will they give me an artificial leg?' And now she cries because she wants to go to school.[10]

I put her in a private school because she's intelligent. She's our oldest child, she's nine. They say they'll take her outside to fix her an artificial leg. Think how many times she must change it before she's twenty! How can we do it? Look, these are the only clothes she has. Isn't it a shame that children should live like this?

'Amal's basic strategy was to destroy the camp'

The military account given here combines information given by leaders from both the PNSF and the DFLP. When the battle started, the organizations were divided but within days a joint military leadership was formed. Even after political splits resurfaced, the 'unity of the bases' was maintained.

From the first moment, this battle was different from past battles, in the speed with which it started, the intensity of shelling and in the rapid intervention of tanks. Another difference was that this time the bulk of the attacking forces were not Amal movement but the 6th Brigade of the Lebanese Army. It was supported by the 1st Brigade, brought from the Beqa', as well as units from two other brigades. They had T54 tanks and other vehicles equipped with artillery, from direct cannon 106mm to mortars ranging from 60mm to 160mm.

The thing that made this siege outstanding militarily was the enemy's use of *khara'at*. It was the first time they used them. They are fired from tank cannon and weigh from 18 to 20 kilos. They can pierce ten ordinary walls and take out foundation pillars of reinforced concrete. Their conventional use is against tanks or military fortifications, not breeze-block walls. Imagine their impact! They bring down houses on top of their inhabitants. In the Hursh before the digging of the trenches, our fighters were posted in a room where several *khara'at* passed through in a single day. Surely no other battle has been fought under similar conditions!

We didn't have time to prepare our defences. We expected something but not on the scale that occurred. Our situation in the first two weeks was critical. During this time, our fighters had to face tanks at the same time as digging trenches. They had to fight almost without cover, moving between walls not more than 10 centimetres thick. They surpassed all military precedents.

The trenches played a great role. Without them our fighters could not have maintained the outer defence of the camp after the destruction of the houses that were our first line of defence. The decision to dig trenches and tunnels was taken in the first two or three days. There was no other way of remaining firm in our bases.

From the time that we began digging the trenches, there was a joint military leadership in the camp. It was this that made it possible to carry out this operation successfully and fix the camp's defence lines so that they could not be breached. We made a second Shateela underground.

Amal's basic strategy was to destroy the camp, beginning with the edges, so as to squeeze the fighters back into a small area where they could easily be eliminated. They shelled the camp systematically, trying to flatten it area by area. They concentrated on every high building that blocked their aim into the heart of the camp. The Iqleem building alone received at least 1,000 shells; even after it was reduced to a pile of rubble, they went on shelling it. They wanted to destroy this building so as to have a clear view of the Red Crescent (hospital) and the Mosque.

But we used the rubble created by their shelling in our defence. We were able to make shelters for our fighters in places where no one could believe there were still people. This is what made them mad; in spite of their saturation shelling, our fighters still came out to stop every attack.

For the first fifteen days, shelling was continuous, day and night, and they made simultaneous attacks on different bases in an attempt to penetrate anywhere they could. They used to shell with greatest intensity just before launching an attack. But our fighters were hidden behind the rubble or crouching in trenches, protected from the shelling. When their fighters were confronted by our fighters, they failed and fell back. Their bodies remained lying on the ground, on the streets and the crossings. They couldn't make any advance. There was coordination between our military bases, they formed a strong and integrated chain of defence around the camp.

After the failure of all their attempts to storm the camp, the enemy adopted different tactics. They continued shelling, but from afar. They positioned their tanks so that they could shell us without our being able to see them or hit them. They fortified them with sandbags, or concealed them inside houses, or built walls of sand around them, concealing both body and mouth of the cannon. They also used heavy artillery stationed in Jnah and the southern suburbs. We couldn't see them. Not only that, we didn't have any long-range weapons. We only had B7s whose range is from 300 to 400 metres, and they were further away than that.

Once they had lost hope of defeating Shateela militarily, they turned instead to a war of attrition, using occasional shelling and sniping to cause casualties and the siege to wear down morale. The fighters continued to improve their defences – this work went on until the last month before the cease-fire. Improvement meant digging trenches in the rear and connecting the trenches to the bases. By the end, all the bases had small underground rooms for sleeping. We even made wooden bunks to protect the fighters from damp. In the first few weeks the fighters slept in the trenches.

The Army also used phosphorous shells, especially in the Hursh area. We have one badly wounded man on whom the burns are obvious. They used tear gas against the PLA building at the beginning of the battle. Amal also sprayed the camp with aeroplane petrol with the intention of setting fire to it. Another weapon employed in this siege were 'plates', French mines shaped like saucers which explode at high pressure. However, in this battle they were never able to penetrate and blow up houses at night as they did in the battle of Ramadan. They couldn't get near us, neither them nor their tanks.

In the Red Crescent hospital

In this siege as in the others, devoted medical care was as critical to *sumood* as bread lines. Regine is a French nurse who worked in the operating theatre.

This wasn't my first siege but it was certainly the hardest. The difference this time was that I felt a bit like a mother to the other nurses. It was a kind of joke – they called me 'Umm Regina'. I tried to pay attention to them, to notice when they got too tired, to send them to eat or sleep. There were two girls who were not quite as brave as the rest. I'd make them rest in a calm place when I felt they had reached the edge.

There were days without anything, there were other days when we worked twenty-four hours. We had shifts but it wasn't really possible to rest if there were many casualties, even if they told you, 'Go and sleep'. One slept if one was really tired, otherwise . . . there was always something that needed to be done – folding bandages, making compresses.

In the emergency room, there were two teams of nurses, one for night and one for day. In the operating theatre it was always the same team. There were five of us, plus two nurses for the anaesthetics. One nurse worked with the surgeons, who were always Dr Giannou and one other. Three other nurses helped with the operation, doing whatever had to be done; and one looked after the compresses, sterile clothes and instruments.

The operating theatre is underground and well protected with sandbags. On calm days it was transformed into a dormitory. The operating team slept there, although there wasn't really space.

The siege forced us to manage, to fix things up, to find new ways of doing things. Nothing was ever thrown away – they'd find a way to use it. When something was missing, we'd find a replacement. For example, when there wasn't much electricity I couldn't operate the proper sterilizing unit but used instead a small autoclave which uses very little electricity. At the end, I had to do the sterilization on a wood fire in something like a pressure cooker, but a bit larger and more complicated. There's a gauge for the temperature and pressure but basically it's the same system. You put in a little water and put it on the fire. The whole operation took three to four hours. First one had to find the wood. . . . But I managed to keep ahead by relying on the hospital laundry. The hardest part was drying things. For this I used a radio set which had a little fan. This way I always had a couple of sets of sterilized instruments in reserve. On the days when everything was really finished, I brought out these two reserve packets. Even between operations we managed to sterilize.

The winter was hard. The nights were very, very cold. And very humid. There was nothing we could do against the humidity. In the operating theatre and the main hospital it was fairly dry, the rain didn't enter. The worst place was the annexe where patients were transferred when they needed less nursing care. The cold there was terrible. The nurses working there really suffered. And the wounded! But they were really courageous. They had blankets, yes, but what could we do against the rain? Everything got wet. We put large sheets of nylon over the beds but it wasn't really waterproof; everything one touched was humid. We couldn't use electric heaters because they use too much electricity, and liquid gas was finished.

Interviewer: What was the largest number of operations you had in one day?

Regine: I don't remember. Of course, there's a limit . . . But you can't really choose. Even if you say, I can't do any more, if a casualty arrives you have to treat him. You take five or ten minutes to rest, you drink a cup of coffee, you get a grip on yourself and start again.

'. . . there were people who had nothing'

Umm Ahmad is a housewife, mother and grandmother, who lived through every siege in the camp. Her account underlines the strong code of sharing which helps Palestinians through crises.

The last siege was a game compared with this one. When the last siege ended we still had gas, flour, sugar, rice, everything. But this time it was really hard. We had stocks but there were other people who had nothing. We said it's a shame that we are eating and they aren't; so we gave a little food, here and there. We had 300 kilos of flour; we thought the siege is bound to end before we finish it; so when I baked, I gave people who had no bread two or three loaves. Every day I baked 70 to 80 loaves. There were some homes that didn't stock up with flour – they didn't have the means. But most people did. But then the flour finished and the siege went on.

I baked at home, not at the bakery. I used gas until it was almost finished, then I started baking bread in a small oven on firewood.

At first I put the oven in the courtyard. If there was shelling I'd put in a *ragheef* and stand in the doorway until it was cooked. Then I'd get it out and put in another. One day, I had just put in a *ragheef* when a shell came down in the alley next to our house. The shrapnel went up and came down like glass. After that I baked on firewood inside the house, even though it made a lot of smoke. We had to keep the door and the windows shut to keep out shrapnel. The windows have iron shutters; we tied them down with wire and left the glass open.

The drama of bread

In other sieges flour stocks had lasted. In this one, although there were large stores at the beginning, they were used wastefully. This was the direct result of the number of organizations in the camp and competition between them. But up to the fourth month, a committee continued the 'operation of the joint loaf'.

From the beginning there was a committee for directing the 'operation of the joint loaf', formed from representatives of the Jebhat al-Inqadh and from Fateh. The Popular Front contributed the bulk of the flour – most other organizations didn't have a speck – and the Popular

Committee provided the fuel oil. We distributed bread to all the fighters according to the number in each base. To families and to institutions like the Red Crescent we distributed flour and ran the bakery so that they could come and bake.

There are two bakeries in the camp. The first was shelled all the time, it was dangerous to stay there; so we carried all the equipment to the other bakery which was slightly protected by having two floors over it.

There were five or six workers allocated to the bakery. Their work was to bake the bread – no woman worker can stand in front of the furnace – and to distribute it to the organizations. The work of the women also requires expertise – they prepare the dough, divide it, roll it and cool it after it has been baked. They also sifted the flour because by the end it was full of weevils. Making the dough also meant bringing water. There were about ten women workers; each organization sent one.

The bakery baked for everyone but there were special times for different sectors. For example, the early morning was for the organizations; then came the turn of the Red Crescent; after that the civilians. The bakery was open from dawn to dusk.

There was hardly a day when shelling stopped, but women came to the bakery and faced the shelling. Amal used to see smoke coming from the bakery and hit it. As you've seen, many parts of it were damaged.

When fuel oil got scarce we began to use wood; we broke up doors and cupboards. We decided to keep the small quantity of fuel oil that was left for the hospital operations room and for pumping drinking water. Bread can be baked with many kinds of fuel but the operations room couldn't carry on without electricity. And without electricity we couldn't pump water from the wells on which we relied after all public water was cut off.

Later, when both flour and firewood began to get scarce, we decided that each organization must make its own bread using small ovens in their offices. The bakery oven needs a lot of wood to get hot whereas a small oven needs very little. It was at the beginning of the fourth month. We went on distributing enough flour to each family and organization to guarantee half a loaf a day per head but we had to stop distributing bread.

The operation of the 'joint loaf' created a feeling of unity. When it comes to bread, there's no difference between people, whatever their political belonging. Banners were raised in the camp saying that bread is united so political stands must be united.

Outside Shateela

This young woman lives in Sabra, a few hundred metres from the camp, an area controlled by Amal. Her testimony is valuable for what it tells of Shi'ite–Palestinian relations during the battles.

If they [Amal militia] know that an apartment belongs to Palestinians, they throw them out, even if they're old. This happened to eight families in our building. They turned them out and occupied their homes. And when they saw that the situation was beginning to return to normal, they took all their belongings.

Because I'm Lebanese nothing happened to me. If they had known I was married to a Palestinian they would have hassled me: 'What, you couldn't find a Lebanese good enough for you!' – that kind of thing. But because I was staying with my mother, they didn't realize. No one told them. There was just one Amal guy who knew about me but he turned out to be decent, he didn't give me away. He's our neighbour.

At night, around 7 pm, they used to bang on doors with their Klashins. If anything had happened to them, like losing a fighter, they'd vent their anger on anyone. There were many they beat and threw out. I saw them. You couldn't talk to them. If you said anything to defend Palestinian neighbours, they'd turn on you: 'Shut up, or you'll go out before them.' No, Amal were bad. But several of the Shi'ite neighbours hid Palestinian young men.

There was an old man, a Palestinian, alone. Amal went into his home, they liked it, they told him, 'Go!' One of them threw him out but he remained lying near his door. He couldn't walk much and he didn't want to leave his home. They asked me to take him away. I refused. I said, 'He's an old man. Where can he go?' He stayed sitting outside his own door – they had taken his key. Eventually an Amal leader came by and we neighbours asked him to intervene. So in the end they opened the door and let him in.

Internal politics

There were ten organizations inside Shateela. Giving each one's specific point of view is not possible and none were neutral concerning the major issues. The DFLP, though linked to Fateh, strove for national unity. Its 'responsible' speaks here of this difficult struggle and of the work of the political cadres in general.

'Responsible': We entered this battle with groups that had specific political stands and thus weren't united. The strength of the attack obliged us to unite militarily but political issues remained unsolved.

There was pressure from all sides to form joint military, political and social committees; and this was done even though some groups refused at first. But differences remained and showed up in our defence and in all our work in the camp. If we had had unity we would have been able to organize the social situation better.

The issue that caused the most serious split inside the camp was the question of Maghdousheh.[11] From the time that this became a primary issue, all the committees began to be shaken – the military committee, the social committee, even the shelters began to be affected. Everyone was arguing over this question. Some said that if we withdraw from Maghdousheh, the siege will end, the whole crisis had been created by Abu Ammar; this was the line of the PNSF. Others said, 'No, we shouldn't withdraw.'

Our first and main aim as DFLP was to stop discussion of this issue while the camp was under attack. We had to secure a minimum of political unity so that the fighters could jointly defend the camp. Many difficulties confronted us. But eventually it became clear that Maghdousheh was not a real issue but an artificial one thrown by Amal into the Palestinian arena like a football to create splits. This became obvious later, when the Resistance withdrew from Maghdousheh and they put forward new conditions. As a result of these manoeuvres, while some in Shateela were digging trenches, others were mobilizing for withdrawal from Maghdousheh. The fighter on the confrontation line was looking forward at the enemy and backwards because there were political problems.

At each stage of the siege there were different problems. After the story of Maghdousheh and the villages east of Sidon, there was the 'story of the apples', when supplies that came in for one political group were used to put political pressure on the other groups. The supplies were not distributed fairly. Some had food and cigarettes, others not. This caused quarrels between fighters and between cadres. It was a very difficult stage. We worked to stop this bad feeling from spreading and affecting the defences of the camp. We were still under siege.

Within this crisis was contained another, that of the presence of 'Arafatists' in the camp. The PNSF said that the condition for ending the siege was that Arafat's fighters should leave the camps or join other groups. We said that the real issue between us and Amal (and the groups behind Amal) was not Arafat, it was the continued presence of the Palestinian people and Resistance. Whether the Palestinian gun was in the hands of Arafat or the PNSF, it was this gun that was aimed at. This is why we opposed this proposal fiercely in public meetings. Fateh fighters were an important part of the fighting front; if they withdrew, the camp would be in danger. We said, first a cease-fire, then the withdrawal of

Amal, the entry of supplies and the evacuation of the wounded. Then we will discuss the question of Arafat. But now, under siege, to discuss this issue would be a dangerous mistake.

This campaign was very hot and all the political cadres were involved in it. In the end the people supported our point of view; we succeeded in transferring the internal struggle back against the external enemy. This was the work of the cadres, to argue and struggle around these issues and clarify them for the masses.

Interviewer: How did the splits affect people's morale?

'Responsible': They don't affect the fighters so much, but people begin to ask questions, they feel confused, they lose confidence. The fighter doesn't analyse, he thinks it's all propaganda on both sides. But people in general are very sensitive to splits. They want to know what the problem is, who is telling the truth and who is a liar. Everyone was arguing over Maghdousheh. People wanted to know who was right, but they also wanted unity. This affected their morale. Some, instead of concentrating on the battle, concentrated on political disagreements. They reached a stage where they said, 'We are ready to stay steadfast *but there must be unity.*' They lost their enthusiasm for work; their courage became less. This was why it needed a really heroic effort from the cadres to clarify the issues. It was important work. Because when Amal failed to make the camp fall through military attack, they tried to make it fall through internal splits.

Inside and outside the siege, our stand was the need to restore national unity. This is why we considered the holding of the 18th PNC[12] a major victory. Through it, Arafat returned to the national line and this ended the crisis in the camps. It took away all the pretexts from parties that claimed they were fighting deviation and corruption within the PLO. This victory was achieved while we were still under siege and we were able to publish pamphlets about it and give the good news to our people. It was a great achievement that, although closed in by the siege, we were able to stay in contact with the leaders in Algiers and hear every detail of the agreements being reached.

In the period leading up to the PNC, people used to stand outside the shelters, in this area that we call 'Red Square', waiting for news about the discussions. When there were disagreements, people got depressed. When unity was achieved, their faces showed their happiness.

As for the work of the political cadres: in the DFLP we don't have a high degree of specialization between political and military cadres. The political cadres worked at everything, the fighters also had to work at everything. Political work means politicizing the fighter as well as the masses. In the time of attacks, we had to be there in the bases. Our masses don't accept that a political cadre doesn't fight – we must be in the front line.

Communication and contacts with the leadership outside went on all the time. This was an important part of our work, enabling us to understand the political situation at every moment of the battle.

Our work was practical and varied. We didn't just sit in offices; we went round visiting the bases, looking at the trenches, working on the fortifications, supervising the kitchens and bakery and the shelters. Also in the shelters there was politicization going on; we held meetings there at every stage of the siege to explain what was going on.

Sometimes the cadres of different organizations met, but everyone spoke from a different point of view. There were nine or ten organizations grouped in three main currents.[13] Coordination in social work ended with the issue of Maghdousheh and the 'story of the apples'. Some military coordination continued because there's no way to fight separately in such a small space. More than one base was joint. Some groups were allied and trusted each other, others not at all. But political alignments changed during the siege and this crystallized more during the Algiers discussions. The PNSF lost cohesion and three groups within it got closer to our position, although they didn't leave the Front.

Interviewer: Did all the main groupings publish newspapers?

'Responsible': In fact the PNSF had two, one published by the General Command and Fateh dissidents, the other by the PFLP, PSF and PLF. Fateh brought out a paper occasionally but it was mainly concerned with military matters, such as how to dig trenches. We were in broad harmony with their position, especially in the time of 'Ali Abu Towq, so sometimes we passed them items of information and they wrote them up. Later we published information on the Tripoli Agreement and the PNC.

Information and analysis was important for us as cadres and for the masses. People were always asking us, 'Where have we reached?' We had to put them in the picture. Because if there was national unity people could stay steadfast much longer. We cadres needed to know how long the battle was likely to last, so as to specify our duties and organize our supplies. To mobilize correctly, we had to know the nature of the battle.

There were political groups but in spite of differences and even conflicts, there were many links between them. One was the need to defend the camp and to organize its social situation. At the level of the people, there were links of family and neighbourhood that crossed political lines. You find families in which one son is with Fateh, another with the Dissidents and another with the General Command. Their ties remain strong even if each one goes to a different base. They differ politically but they are all sons of the same family, all sons of the same camp.

The problem was greater at the level of the cadres. There is little kinship between them. But the shell hits everyone and the fall of the camp would harm everyone. There were warm relations between some of the cadres, though one can't say these predominated. For example, I had good relations with comrades in the PFLP, PSF and PLF. Between me and the 'responsible' of the General Command there was mutual respect. With other comrades in the PNSF there was continual argument. There was no joking but most of the time there was respect. However, there were some people with whom one couldn't talk, who were completely hostile.

During the 'stage of the apples', discord was at a maximum. We would see one another on the street – *'Marhaba'*, *'Marhaba'* – nothing more than that. One group wanted to use hunger to gain political concessions. They wanted to use apples, *halaweh* and cigarettes to draw people to their organization. I couldn't be on friendly terms with people who behaved like that.

The death of 'Ali Abu Towq

Near the *ashbal* base was a shell of a house where Umm Kamal, mother of the wounded boy, had set up a temporary home. She had seen the popular Fateh commander killed nearby, on 27 January 1987.

Umm Kamal: I worked at the bakery, making dough and rolling it. I went to all the bases, not just this one where my son was; and if the fighters needed someone to wash or cook for them, I was there. Not just me, all the women of the camp.

When they told me, 'Your son . . .' – I'd seen so many wounded, so many martyrs. And there's nothing dearer in this life than a son.

There's another Umm Kamal, she's my friend, two of her sons have been martyred. Her loss affected me a lot; I went to comfort her – I go to all women who lose their sons. My son was wounded but that was no worse than the situation everyone else was suffering.

When brother 'Ali was martyred, here in this empty area, near the tap, our nerves were broken. He worked day and night. He made rounds to all the bases and all the trenches. When Amal opened the sewers on us, he was the one who went out to secure clean water for us to drink. He loved children, whatever he had he gave them. When he was killed, everyone's morale collapsed.

Young man: Brother 'Ali was like a father to us. He didn't discriminate between people; he didn't say, this one is near to me, that one is a stranger. He used to tell people, 'If I'm killed, you must carry on as if I'm there.'

Umm Kamal: I had a house full of things. You saw it before the siege? People used to come from all over to look at my curtains. We got hit in the first siege, I repaired the damage. It got damaged again in the second siege, again I repaired it. Now it's been completely destroyed. My husband has been away in the desert thirty-seven years and now everything he worked for and I worked for has gone.

'It's true Shateela was destroyed, but we were under the rubble'

Abu Samir worked with the Fateh loyalists as administrator. On the wall of his home there was a large poster portrait of 'Ali Abu Towq, and his six-year-old son was wearing an 'Ali Abu Towq T-shirt.

Abu Samir: For a week before the battle began, Amal was stirring things up, firing at night against our bases and building fortifications. We asked our brothers in the Jebhat al-Inqadh what was going on. They said that there wouldn't be fighting in Shateela, it's a 'red line'. This reassured us and so we didn't reply to their provocations.

Then on Tuesday 25 November at 4.30 pm they began. They threw everything they had at us, like a volcano: heavy artillery, tank cannon, medium machine guns. They attacked from all sides. No one dared come out of the houses except the fighters and those who worked in first aid. They destroyed all the outer walls of the camp. They made some progress against us but the presence of our martyred brother 'Ali Abu Towq defeated them. He was the one who told us to dig the trenches and tunnels. Their gunfire was reaching into the heart of the camp and their snipers were preventing us from moving. But brother 'Ali with his military ability and enormous energy was able to unify all the military forces in the camp and set up a joint operations room. Under his leadership they succeeded in pushing the enemy back to places far behind their original positions.

It's true that Shateela was destroyed, but we were under the rubble. If we had wanted to expand outside the camp we could have done it. But for political reasons, so that there wouldn't be any talk of 'Palestinian expansion', we didn't do it. At the end, when people were starving, the leadership was thinking of making a sortie outside the camp to get food. It was possible but luckily it wasn't necessary.

Interviewer: Did 'Ali have difficulty convincing the other groups to dig trenches?

Abu Samir: No, no. Everybody worked on it, everybody agreed. Fighters and civilians dug the trenches together. All the groups took part. My wife's brother is one of the military leaders of the Jebhat al-Inqadh – ask him!

'Ali learned the system of trench-digging from the training course he took in China. That was how he escaped from Beaufort Castle when the Israelis invaded in 1978 and again in 1982. He stayed here fighting with us from after the Siege of Ramadan to his death in this siege on 27 January. He was martyred near the Political Office, he and his deputy Samir, by two French shells from outside, God knows from where.[14]

Interviewer: Is it true that he was distributing coffee to all the bases that day?

Abu Samir: No. There had been an attack on the Political Office and Amal had destroyed one of our barricades. He went to inspect the repairs and had stopped by the tap near the Political Office to drink when the shells fell.

Interviewer: What was the effect of 'Ali's death?

Abu Samir: I can't describe it. All the camp gathered near the Red Crescent – fighters, women, children, old men. They didn't notice the shelling. There was a big crowd. The doctors were telling people he was OK – they were afraid that the news of his death would affect their morale.

'Ali was part of everyone here, there wasn't a home he hadn't entered. He was an extraordinary person. He never got bored and he never got tired. He made those around him work. He supervised every detail, he cared about everyone. He had no house, no car, no possessions. He was amazing.

Interviewer: Did people despair in the last period of hunger and sniping?

Abu Samir: If we were capable of despair, Palestinians would have given up a long time ago. We instituted rationing. At the beginning our fighters were given three loaves of bread daily. Then we cut it down to two, then one. But they were never cut off completely from food. It's true that at the end there was nothing but *burghul*, lentils and Maggi soup. But I consider these good foods, better than rice.

Interviewer: People told me that some *shebab* got too weak to hold their guns.

Abu Samir: That's exaggerated. We had many shortages but we weren't completely without any kind of food. There were some weak people who predicted another Tell al-Za'ter. But we in Shateela, no. We were sure the camp wouldn't fall even if they brought the whole Lebanese Army.

Fighter in an advanced base

I visited several of the bases and was shown the underground rooms and tunnels; but I only recorded one fighter, on leave from his base which was outside Shateela, in Hayy Gharbeh.

Fighter: After the first month we began operations behind their bases. A joint force was formed which carried out an attack on the Hamdan School in Hayy Gharbeh. It was at 4 am – the Palestinian fighter always attacks at night – and we captured one of them who was telling the Syrian *mukhabarat* [intelligence agents] about the attack on a field radio. We returned with him to our bases.

During the first part of the siege they made continuous and violent attempts to penetrate the camp. These attacks were preceded by hours of heavy shelling. We stayed in our fortifications, knowing that when the shelling stopped, while dust still filled the air, they would attack. At that moment we would send out a rain of machine-gun fire and we would hear their screams rising. In general, if one of them gets hit, the rest run away, they don't try to remove him. Their bodies lay on the ground for hours; they would make a heavy artillery bombardment before taking them away.

There was a time when Amal agents in the camp put out rumours that the bases in Hayy Gharbeh and the Hursh had fallen. People were beginning to be afraid. So we formed a joint force to make a large attack to show people that not a single one of our bases had fallen. The attack was to be against an Amal base near the Sports City. After we had worked out a plan and briefed the fighters, we asked the PNSF leadership to secure us artillery cover from our brothers in the mountains. Without it our plan couldn't succeed.

We infiltrated to their nearest base and reached it at 3 am. We stayed there under their positions, waiting for the shelling from the mountains to begin, to launch our attack. But the mountain fighters didn't shell because the Syrians had confiscated their artillery.

What were we to do? We attacked; but we didn't achieve the aims we had set because of the lack of artillery cover. One of the brothers was martyred, we fell back to our bases, and they shelled our area for seven hours continuously.

The leader of our base was always thinking of operations to carry out against them. The last one we made amazed them. One of their bases was close to the Sports City. Near it was a house whose ceiling we had brought down with explosives. We crept up at night under their fortifications and their guards, towards the house with the fallen ceiling. From near the base a group of them were firing at the camp. We stayed motionless, waiting for them to stop and the guard to change. He came, still half asleep. From our hideout we wired explosives to the corners of their base, and pressed the wires. When we exploded the bomb, their shouting filled the night. We stayed without moving under the fallen ceiling. Shelling began. Every time we carried out an operation like this, they combed the area with tank and machine-gun fire. When the shelling stopped, we withdrew and went down to our base.

Interviewer: Were fighters able to leave and enter the camp in spite of the siege?

Fighter: Some went outside to look for food or medicines. Some groups managed to come in from outside bringing ammunition, blood, cigarettes. This went on all the time. At night the Palestinian fighter was completely free. Anyone who can cross the border to Occupied Palestine can cross Amal's lines. They had three lines of defence but we could penetrate all of them.

Interviewer: What was the effect on the fighters of the death of 'Ali Abu Towq?

Fighter: Of course, when there's a leader of the calibre of 'Ali Abu Towq, people are bound to be affected by his death. He was a great and heroic leader, he directed everything in the camp, he was close to people and they loved him; he dealt with them honestly and they respected him. Of course people were sad when he died but it didn't affect their will to resist. The fighters didn't leave their bases, they accepted reality.

Interviewer: Didn't the camp depend on him for military planning?

Fighter: His deputy took his place and assumed the same level of leadership. He followed the plan and the system that brother 'Ali had set up. Furthermore, brother 'Ali was with us during the hottest period of the fighting; after his death it became a defensive war on both sides, just an exchange of fire between their bases and our bases.

With us, a military leader doesn't work alone, he works with others. For example, if I'm the leader of a unit and I have a plan, I have to consult with my deputy as well as with the leader and deputy leader of the Unified Command before carrying it out. Before any military action, all the unit leaders meet with the leader of the Unified Command and his leader. They agree on a plan and it's only acted on if there's no objection or criticism.

Interviewer: There were spies in the camp?

Fighter: Yes, there were a few, about five or six, men and girls. They weren't a problem. We caught them and punished them; and after the road was opened we threw them out.

Interviewer: What did they do?

Fighter: They take a particular target, maybe a leader, they watch where he moves. They inform the enemy artillery so that they can hit the place where the leader is. Or they spread rumours to lower people's morale. Once one of them sent up flares at night from the Hursh to make people think that our bases had fallen and the Lebanese Army was there. They send messages by radio or by shooting in the air at night, according to a code. Whenever a shot went up at night we knew it was a spy; we identified the area and caught him.

Interviewer: How were spies treated?

Fighter: We treat them like Israelis, as an enemy. We interrogate them and punish them. But we don't execute them because we don't have the authority. We banish them from the camp.

Interviewer: How were the wounded moved from bases outside the camp?

Fighter: We had first-aid materials in every base. The first thing is to stop the flow of blood with gauze and cotton wool. One or two fighters in every base have first-aid training. We stop the bleeding and put the wounded on a stretcher and take him out through the tunnel. Each base has a tunnel dug under it, high and wide enough to move in. The tunnel had wooden walls and ceiling and is covered with sand so that shells can't penetrate it. There are reserves whose job is to carry the wounded. Once inside the camp, they carry the wounded to the hospital.

Interviewer: How many casualties were there in your base?

Fighter: Two martyrs and seven wounded. Sometimes fighters get fed up with staying underground, with the damp and lack of air. They come up and get hit, maybe, by a piece of shrapnel.

Interviewer: Were you affected by political conflicts?

Fighter: In the base all political conflicts are put aside. We didn't discuss politics.

Interviewer: What did you do when you weren't fighting?

Fighter: There wasn't much time for listening to the radio or even sleeping. We worked on strengthening the fortifications; if anyone had an idea about how we could strengthen them, we discussed it. At the end there was a shortage of fighters. But after the cease-fire some *shebab* were able to enter the camp without going through the Amal checkpoint, so the fighters inside could rest. We have to stay very watchful in case they launch a new attack.

Children on the street

The ages of this little group ranged from four to ten.

Child: They shelled us with B7s and mortars. A mortar fell on our house and all the windows were broken. Everybody went into the shelters because we were afraid. They shelled us because of Arafat.

Interviewer: How was it in the shelter?

Child: It was all dust, dirt and lice – disgusting! If we wanted to breathe we had to go up to the street. If we went to the bathroom there were rats and mice. Everyone who went to the bathroom had to tread on children to get there. Someone trod on the stomach of my pregnant sister and she cried from the pain.

Interviewer: Did women have babies in the shelter?

Child: No, they went to the clinic. Some of us got dizzy and vomited from the smoke. We flapped blankets to clear the air. Some people used plates or cardboard or saucepans.

Child: We made fires with wood and we went on eating *burghul*. My mother went home and she found my brother there. We ate *burghul* and *burghul* and *burghul* and *burghul* . . . We broke windows to get wood.

Child: They hit us with cannon and bullets. We ran home to get blankets and mattresses. I and my sister filled sandbags.

Child: In 'Ain Helweh the Israelis hit with airplanes and everyone was killed. Here they hit us with shells, not planes.

Child: At the end we ate *burghul* until out stomachs swelled up. Small children cried for bread. Their mothers gave them a drop of oil so their hearts wouldn't dry up. We wanted to drink but there were no cups.

Child: My little brother hid a piece of bread in his pocket. He said, 'This is my identity card.' He ate half and kept half for tomorrow.

One of the children sings a song:

> Abu Ammar, *ayooni*[15]
> Your size is like a lemon
> When you go into an office
> You are like a mother

Interviewer: How old are you?

Child: Ten. We filled sandbags in the bases and we dug trenches. Under the shelling we went to make sandbags at the Jericho base and the Austrian Clinic base.

Interviewer: Were you afraid?

Child: Not much.

Second child: I was very afraid.

'Hide us, mother!'

I could never count the number of people in this family, there seemed to be so many of them. A married daughter had given birth only a few days before the siege began. Umm Sa'eed speaks.

You feel your heart is going to fail from hunger, and your head to burst from the heaviness of the shelling. You can't breathe from the dust, you feel you are going to suffocate. And the children cry, 'Hide us, mother!' because they're frightened of the shelling. Or 'Feed us, mother!' because they're hungry.

My son Khaled stood like this, swaying. He said, 'Akh! Mother! I'm going to die from hunger.' I told him, 'Go and wash your face and drink a little water, and you'll feel better.' He'd come back and tell me, 'Mother, I feel dizzy.'

My family is big, it needs to eat. The children didn't stop crying. There was no sugar, no tea, we had nothing left. I gave them milk once a day, because they say there's something in it that prevents poisoning from phosphorus shells. But I had no sugar to put in it.

The siege isn't over. Our men are still sitting in the corners of their homes, unable to leave the camp. If they go out they face imprisonment, beating, shooting. They wait for women to go out to get them what they need.

What did we do? If you are sitting at home and they come and attack your house, aren't you going to defend yourself? If they had entered the camp they would have slaughtered us, true or not? Because this wasn't the first time. Didn't they come before and kill people sleeping in their houses? Didn't they throw their bodies on the ground like sheep?

If we had given Amal the chance they would have done the same to us. And many of us were killed. The *shebab* would go out when the shelling got heavy and come back on stretchers. Small children, three or four years old, you saw them carrying them like slaughtered birds. And what's still ahead we don't know.

A woman cadre

'Samia' is responsible for the women's bureau of one of the Resistance groups. Her description of women's many tasks in the siege points to the way that traditional work, like making bread, is mixed with radically new ones, such as digging trenches with *shebab* at night.

Everything they said about Shateela outside really happened, it wasn't exaggerated. The very first day of the battle an entire family, seven people, were killed in their home. Twenty people were killed when they blew up a building on the edge of the camp. Amal did this to break our nerves. It was terrifying to see a building of many floors crumble in front of your eyes, just like in a film. When the strongest buildings fall to the ground, there's nothing to be done except go underground. So we started digging trenches. It was mainly the job of girls because the fighters can't stay digging twenty-four hours.

Often we dug at night because the shelling then was slightly less. In the rainy season we had to repair the trenches quickly, before they caved in and endangered the base. I remember once we stayed up two nights in a row in the trenches with the comrades.

Twenty women were martyred and around twenty more were wounded. Our comrade Deeba Masriyeh lost an eye.

It was we girls who brought the flour from the Political Office to the bakery and it was our job to prepare the dough for the organizations – even though, as girls, we didn't have experience in making bread and we were spending a lot of time working on the trenches. We met many problems: crowds, people's moods, shelling . . . At the beginning making bread took three-quarters of our time. Later, when the Popular Committee got the *ajjaneh*[16] repaired, and centralized the bread-making operation, it became easier.

In addition, we shared in social work as part of the women's union. One of their jobs was to distribute milk powder to children; another was the distribution of supplies. Some of us also helped with statistics.

People don't easily accept the principle of rationing: 'What is this? One small piece of cheese! Two spoonfuls of *semneh*!' They cursed us, they accused us of keeping things for ourselves! Our people are used to eating their fill, using up everything. We could have distributed everything at one time and told them, 'Do what you want.' But they would have ended up starving. We are a vanguard, it was our job to make people understand that we were in a siege, it could drag on.

Afterwards people praised the rationing system we adopted, although at first they didn't accept it. We felt proud of such testimony. In Shateela we didn't suffer from hunger as much as they did in Bourj Barajneh.

Active girls had other roles. They sat with families in the shelters and encouraged them because, at the end, people began to despair. They felt that the battle would never end and that everyone would die. When each supply truck that entered was burned, they reached a stage of hopelessness. We had gone for twenty days without flour. People were beginning to curse the leadership. So we sat with people and told them to hang on a bit longer, help will come. It was a difficult job.

The experiences that Shateela people passed through have made their political consciousness higher than that of people outside. If you go to Mar Elias camp[17] you'll feel the difference. People here can accept a girl like me, who doesn't have a family in the camp but who was present in an office among *shebab*. As much as you give, work, produce, so much they respect you. Ordinary people here are more progressive than leaders outside.

'One would rather drink salty water than lose a child'

Children in the siege carried out domestic chores and many fell victim to snipers' bullets or shrapnel while bringing water from the tap or wood from the roof. Umm Munzher's refusal to risk her children reminds us of the many child victims. Her husband and a women's union member, Amal, join in the conversation.

Umm Munzher: Our home is in Hayy Farhat.[18] The minute the firing started we ran to the nearest shelter and we stayed there throughout.

Amal: They are refugees from before. In the first siege their house was destroyed and this time also it has been destroyed. This room was lent to them.

Umm Munzher: At the beginning we didn't have mattresses or bedding. We slept on the ground. There weren't even any mats. Later we brought bedding. We had to borrow a water container. There was a tap near the shelter, we went out and brought water from there. It's well water, salty: good drinking water was far away, near a base, we didn't dare go there. One would rather drink salty water than lose a child.

Amal: They opened the water for half an hour every day. It didn't come all the time.

Interviewer: Did you go or the children?

Umm Munzher: No, I went. I was very afraid for my children. My children sometimes went out but it was mainly I who went back and forth to the house to fetch things.

Interviewer: How did you manage about bread?

Umm Munzher: Don't ask about bread. That was a great difficulty. I baked, but not in the shelter; either in the bakery or here. My children are old enough to be sensible – the youngest is ten – I'd tell them, 'I'm going out to bring you food, or bread. You stay here.' They'd argue with me, 'No *yumma*, we'll go. We don't want you to get killed.' But they didn't roam around the way small children do. There were many tragedies. At the end we despaired, we wanted to die. People were sitting and crying, yes, crying. Because this one is killed, that one has lost his leg, this one needs blood . . . There was despair.

Amal: People were in the dark. When the fuel oil got scarce they kept it for the hospital. For a while people made their own lamps with a little *mazout*, a bottle and a wick; but by the end they were completely in the dark.

Umm Munzher: There was no bread, just *burghul* and milk. In the morning we drank milk but it doesn't fill you. We boiled *burghul* on firewood and ate it without oil or onion. Everybody had the same. People went round hunting for a piece of wood. They even went outside the camp. Nothing mattered any more, neither sniper nor shelling.

Amal: At the beginning, everything was available: flour, food supplies, fuel oil, kerosene. They lit the shelters for an hour or two every day. We brought flour and cleaning materials – soap, bags of 'Yes', Dettol for toilets. We organized the cleaning of the entrance and the stairs of the shelter; and the lavatories. Each woman kept her own area clean. Sometimes the floor was washed down with soap and all the rubbish cleared out. The old men from the shelter dug a hole and moved all the rubbish there and covered it.

Interviewer (to Amal): What did you say to people when things got bad?

Amal: What could we say? People knew the situation as well as we did. No one could say or do anything at the end.

Umm Munzher: At the end there was nothing, it was useless to ask. The children got very dirty, they got sick; there was no medicine to give them.

Interviewer: What sicknesses were there?

Umm Munzher: Coughs. Stomach colics. Skin problems. Once the doctors of the Red Crescent came down to the shelter and examined people, and gave them something for their hair and skin, against lice.

Abu Munzher: The doctors should have come to the shelter every day.

Amal: Yes, they should have done. There were many of them.

Abu Munzher: They weren't up to the mark.

Amal: If someone had typhoid, they said to bring him to the hospital. Because they couldn't come.

Abu Munzher: They couldn't come! So the mother has to carry her son under the shelling? The doctor can't come?

Amal: They came to get blood.

Abu Munzher: Why could they come to the shelter when they wanted blood but not to treat people? Why?

Amal: It was different. When the doctors came to say that so-and-so is wounded, don't you remember how everyone rushed to give blood?

Abu Munzher: Everyone gave.

Umm Munzher: Because they are our children.

Amal: There wasn't a single person in the shelter who didn't give blood, however weak they were.

Interviewer (to Umm Munzher): Did you join the women's demonstration?

Umm Munzher: Yes, I went. There was no food. Children were almost dying. Women collected near the Mosque and they said, 'Let's go out. We'll try to open the road, to bring food for our children. *Yallah*!' As soon as we got near Cinema Sharq they fired at us. Three were killed and three were wounded. We returned defeated.

The burning of a food lorry

In March, as Arab and international pressure mounted on Syria to let supplies into Shateela, Amal started a cat-and-mouse game with the beleaguered camp. They would agree to allow food supplies to enter the camp but when they arrived, they were shelled. A Popular Committee member describes one of these incidents.

By the time a second lorry with food supplies arrived, our situation in the camp was very bad. We had distributed the last consignment of flour. The Popular Committee stores were practically empty. We were waiting on Abu Hassan Salameh Street, near the shop of Abu Omar. We signalled the lorry to stop there and the driver jumped out and joined us. We had arranged to unload the supplies here first, before moving them to a safer place inside the camp. It was between midday and 1 pm.

We moved out towards the lorry to start unloading it. No sooner had we got close to it than a B7 came over our heads and exploded in a nearby building, bringing down a lot of dust and rubble. One of us, Hisham, was wounded slightly in his head and one hand.

We tried a second time and this time there was sniping. One of the *shebab* was wounded in the shoulder.

We tried a third time. The food lorry had stopped inside an angle made by a house and the burnt-out frame of a previous UNRWA supply truck. The tyres of the truck hadn't burned. Now they shot at them and they caught fire.

We contacted the camp leadership and they got in touch with the Syrians and PNSF who were standing outside. The Syrians told us, 'OK, you can go out, we are in control of the situation.' But every time the Syrians controlled one building, Amal would hit us from another one. Each building had its own leader and its own decision. However, the food lorry didn't catch fire. We planned to try to unload the supplies at night, as they had once done in Bourj Barajneh.

After a while, when Amal saw that the supplies hadn't caught fire, they shot directly at the lorry. They say it was mortar but I think it was a 107mm rocket. We saw the supplies begin to burn. It was a terrible sight. If one of us had been killed it wouldn't have mattered so much.

It must have been around 4.30 pm when the food lorry began to burn. There was nothing we could do. I was exhausted and went home to sleep for a couple of hours, until darkness.

At 7 pm I went back to see what was happening. It was like daylight. Amal was still firing at the lorry, to increase the flames. In spite of this, people had gathered near the burning lorry, mostly women and children. No woman would have gone, or sent her son, if the situation hadn't been desperate.

There's a man with eight children, Abu Riad Shehadeh. He had managed to snatch from the flames a half-burnt bag of rice and a can of *semneh* which fell from his hands, it was so hot. Then he was hit in the stomach by a sniper's bullet. He kept on crawling along the ground, clutching the supplies. When people went to help him he said, 'Don't take the rice, give it to my children.' The bag of rice was all blood when they got it to his home.

Sa'edideen Abu Shelayha, he's paralysed on one side but he went to get food for his children. Near the lorry, someone pushed him and a sniper's bullet got him in the head. He died on the spot. In that one night we lost three martyrs and had twenty-two seriously wounded.

If the sky had been spread with flares, it wouldn't have made more light than the burning food lorry.

The last days of the siege

It is appropriate to leave the last word to Abu Mujahed, Chairman of the Popular Committee:[49]

Finally there came the period when no one had any stocks left. The supplies which got in from UNRWA helped to save people from starvation. But lorries that came with food from Saudi and Kuwait never got further thy in means of resistance. I call this the stage of *sumood* and victory; it was the essence of all the preceding stages.

Negotiations were continuing all the time on conditions for ending the siege. After many public meetings and discussions, we in Shateela proposed that the question of Arafat was negotiable, but only after a complete lifting of the siege. This did not satisfy those outside. It seems there was a decision to bring the camp to its knees through hunger.

The Syrians had agreed to let supplies enter the camp and a Syrian officer with the rank of colonel accompanied the food lorries and witnessed how they were fired at. The Syrians were in control of West Beirut – no one could take a knife out of his pocket without their permission. How come the stronger power couldn't put pressure on its smaller ally? We couldn't explain it, we only knew that we were hungry. I felt that this was the final form of the plot to make the camp submit.

Surrender was not an option – that was final. Everyone was convinced that it would mean a massacre. Tell al-Za'ter was the nightmare in front of everyone in Shateela. The only choice was *sumood*. But within this choice there were two possible lines of action: a military expedition outside the camp to bring in supplies, or individual infiltration. We worked on these two alternatives. But the word coming down from the leadership outside was not to take any action that could harm political contacts. We had to be patient, to 'bite the bullet', to give the leadership outside more time for negotiation: 'Wait twenty-four hours . . . supplies are coming tomorrow . . .' Supplies did come but they didn't enter the camp; or people were killed and wounded for a handful of food.

It was at this point that women demonstrated to try to open the road. Only 100 metres away from us, in Sabra, people were living a normal life. It was like the distance between heaven and hell. The besieging force around the camp was no more than 100 metres in depth. So women got up and said, 'OK don't send us food but open the road!' They went out and Amal shot at them at a distance of 50 metres. They could see that they were women and that most of them were old. Shi'ite women in Hayy Farhat were visible to us throughout the siege, but no one thought of shooting at them.

The shooting at the women's demonstration shook us and made us realize that it was time to remind people outside of our existence. Up to then we had depended on others to deal with the media; we didn't have the time to issue statements. But now people inside Shateela felt that those outside were not reflecting our feelings. So we started to send statements to the press, giving facts.

Our media campaign was aimed at two audiences, not one. The first direction was to the Palestinian leadership and contained an implicit threat. We told them that we had enough food left for three days.[20] We had reached zero point with no choice left except a military operation. This message didn't represent any political side, neither Arafat nor PNSF, it represented Shateela.

The second audience we aimed at was the rest of the world, international, Arab and local leaderships. At that time President Asad was about to visit the USSR. We sent a telegram to Gorbachev in which we reminded him of the siege of Leningrad in World War Two. Shateela is less than one square kilometre in area but it is a thorn in the flesh of all who conspire against it.

This was an extraordinary period in the life of the camp. I remember 'the Day of the Land' 31 March. All of Shateela, all of it, came to the mosque on this occasion for a reading of the *fatiha*. I had been wounded and had only just come out of hospital but the comrades pushed me to make a speech. It was very brief. I just said that we shouldn't gnaw each other. All were tired, all were hungry. We had suffered together, we must continue together. In front of us were only two choices: *sumood* and death with honour; or surrender and death with shame.

This stage was the one in which victory came at what we can call the 'right moment'; normality returned as a reward for everything that Shateela had suffered and given. On 6 April the Coordination Committee entered the camp. The cease-fire had started the night before and supplies had successfully entered the camp. Even then we lost a martyr, our last. He was from the General Command. He was up on the lorry handing down supplies and he was hit by a sniper's bullet in the head.

The first thing that the camp did was to come to the Mosque. Everyone came spontaneously, without planning or invitation. There beside our martyrs we met. We weren't waiting for anyone from outside to come and congratulate us. People were embracing each other and weeping. Tears were falling, tears of happiness for victory, tears of sadness for the dead.

Conclusion

It is hard to establish precisely the extent of the casualties, destruction and displacement caused by the 'Battle of the Camps'. Brynen gives a total death toll of 2,500, but it is possible that the number was even higher, with Amal casualties much greater than those of the Palestinians.[21] An UNRWA source gave Palestinian deaths between 1985 and 1987 as 904, with 1,722 wounded and 207 missing. The same source said that 30,000 Palestinians had been displaced from their homes between 1982 and 1986; and that 87 per cent of housing in the camps of Central and South Lebanon had been totally destroyed. A study of displaced Palestinians carried out in 1988 found a total of 25,334 individuals (4,468 families) scattered over 87 locations.[22] There was also destruction of Shi'ite homes in the areas around the camps by Palestinian artillery in the Shouf, and displacement of Shi'ite families. Previously intermingled, the two groups now tended to separate out, with Palestinian *muhajjareen* (war-displaced) seeking areas where a Sunni majority or the PSP offered them some protection, and Shi'ites regrouping in 'their' areas.

Cease-fire arrangements after each major round of fighting reflected multiple factors: the situation 'on the ground', the interventions of regional and international bodies, and shifts within the Lebanese arena. The fact that all the negotiations for cease-fires took place in Damascus testified to the power of the Syrians to mediate and control outcomes; yet it was a power that needed increasing Syrian military involvement in West Beirut to be effective. According to the agreement worked out to end the first siege, the Damascus Accords, all except light weaponry was to be removed from the Palestinian camps, Amal was to withdraw from camp surroundings, and both sides were to release detainees. A joint Syrian/Amal/PNSF/LNRF coordination committee was set up to supervise the implementation of the Accords; the FSI (the Lebanese gendarmerie) was placed outside the camps, and the PNSF was given charge of the interior. The Damascus Accords also guaranteed the work and residence rights of Palestinians in Lebanon. After each new round of fighting the Accords were reaffirmed, with alterations notably in the nature of the force placed outside the camps, ostensibly protecting but in fact controlling them: after the second siege, this force was the Lebanese Army, reinforced by Syrian military observers; after the third siege, it was the Syrian Army and Intelligence. However, none of these bodies or resolutions protected Palestinians against Amal attacks, which continued until intra-Shi'ite fighting intensified to the point of eclipsing other conflicts.

By dragging on, Amal–Palestinian conflict attracted media attention and external interventions that were damaging for those seen to have initiated them. Throughout the whole episode, the resistance of the camps offered a focus for Arab nationalist opinion, with popular delegations visiting the camps.[23] The Iranians also took an increasingly active role, a development that could not have pleased Damascus in spite of the formal Syrian/Iranian alliance. Particularly during the first siege, press coverage was intense and extremely hostile to Amal.[24] Israeli actions such as the release of Amal/Shi'ite prisoners and air raids against Palestinian positions around Sidon underlined a tacit alliance embarrassing for Amal.

The effects on Amal of the 'Battle of the Camps' were disastrous: a great number of its members left the movement, in many cases defecting to Hizbollah. The condemnations of leading Shi'ite clerics such as Sheikh Mehdi Shamsideen and Sheikh Muhammad Hussein Fadlallah were highly discrediting; heavy losses and failure to defeat the Palestinians caused bitterness within the Shi'ite community, with many blaming Amal for acting as surrogate for the Syrians. Even though Damascus re-equipped and retrained Amal militia after each bout of fighting, relations between the two grew increasingly strained. At the same time, the 'Battle of the Camps' alerted other parties within the 'national/progressive' alliance to Amal's ambitions, provoking counter-reactions. Although groups within the alliance took different public positions, some following the Syrian line and blaming Arafat, others defending the Palestinians, the continuation of the attacks against the camps denuded Amal of its national 'cover'. Night attacks against Amal and Sixth Brigade (Lebanese Army) units in West Beirut began during the first siege and continued through later ones, a low-key form of the hostility between Amal and all the other militias that eventually erupted in February 1987, when only Syrian intervention saved the Movement from rout.

Effects for the Palestinians were more positive: the survival and autonomy of the camps was guaranteed at least for the time being. Syria's move to split the PLO was frustrated, as the PNSF broke up during the third siege, with the PFLP rejoining the PLO Executive Committee shortly before the 18th PNC. As for the pro-Syrian Resistance groups, although they had helped to defend the camps, they could not avoid being discredited by alliance with the Syrians, seen by the majority of Palestinians as the major responsible party. The fact that funds for reconstructing the camps came from Tunis and not from Damascus was another discrediting factor. Yet although the 'Battle of the Camps' served to reunify Palestinian ranks and preserved the continuing military/political role of the Resistance movement in Lebanon, its effects for the Palestinian community in Lebanon were more problematic. Palestinian–Shi'ite economic and social relations built up since 1948 through co-residence and a shared sense of deprivation were disrupted.[25] As homes were rebuilt after each siege, only to be destroyed again, many residents lost hope that there could ever be a return to 'normality'. As the majority community in Lebanon, Shi'ite hostility had disturbing long-term implications for the future, even if it was partially balanced by diminishing Maronite hostility. One Palestinian phrased the situation this way: 'Our problem in Lebanon is that the more we win, the more we lose.'

Notes

1. *Khara'a*: a type of missile that pierces through several walls, used for the first time against Shateela in this siege.

2. An allusion to the popular belief in the power of envy (or the 'evil eye') to harm children.

3. *Ragheef*: Arabic bread is made in flat rounds, about 30 centimetres in diameter, which opens like a pocket when cut. Each round is a *ragheef*.

4. 'Ali Abu Towq, commander of Fateh. The shelter near his office was named after him.

5. A cheap, local brand of soap powder.

6. *Gallabiya*: a long, loose cotton dress.

7. Young women who belong to Resistance organizations are often called this, stemming from the way they are usually identified with their families.

8. From soon after the end of the second siege, Syria sent a small military force to help supervise the cease-fire around the camps.

9. *Shehadeh*: witness; the basic avowal of the Muslim faith.

10. While I was recording with her mother, Rana hopped about cheerfully on one crutch. She kept begging her mother to send her to a newly opened kindergarten, and asked me for books.

11. The village of Maghdousheh in the hills above 'Ain Helweh was taken from Amal by a Palestinian force on 24 November, in order to put pressure on them to lift the siege of Rashidiyyeh. This sparked off the third siege of Shateela. Palestinian withdrawal from Maghdousheh became Amal's condition for ending the siege of the Beirut camps.

12. The 18th PNC was held in Algiers on 20 April 1987; an earlier preparatory meeting in Tripoli, Libya, was attended by George Habash, presaging the collapse of the PNSF and isolation of the pro-Syrian groups. The 'Battle of the Camps' directly contributed to this outcome.

13. See p. 210.

14. Later, Fateh undertook an investigation which is said to have proved that 'Ali Abu Towq was killed by an explosive placed in a trench by order of the PNSF leadership in Damascus.

15. *Ayooni*: 'my eyes', a term of endearment.

16. *Ajjaneh*: a large machine for mixing dough.

17. Mar Elias is a small camp in West Beirut in a mainly PPS/Druze area.

18. Hayy Farhat is on the eastern side of Shateela. Many Palestinians rented homes there. A mainly Shi'ite area, throughout the camp battles it was occupied by Amal.

19. See Appendix for his brief history of the siege in all its different stages.

20. Abu Mujahed specified that at this point the Popular Committee had enough stores to supply one more distribution of ½ kilogram of *burghul*, ½ kilogram of milk powder and less than this amount of flour per head.

21. R. Brynen, *Sanctuary and Survival: The PLO in Lebanon* (Boulder, CO: Westview Press, 1990), p. 190. But official casualty figures for 1985 give 4,637 killed and 6,571 wounded; for 1986, 3,985 killed, 7,004 wounded; and for 1987, 4,862 killed, 6,419 wounded (*Al-Nahar*, 5 March 1992). Although these figures are for the whole of Lebanon, these were years when the 'Battle of the Camps' formed the major source of casualties.

22. Carried out by Popular Aid for Relief and Development (PARD). Not all this displacement was caused by the 'Battle of the Camps'; much was the result of earlier fighting. The study found that 19.7 per cent had been displaced three times or more, and 75.2 per cent more than twice.

23. For example, the Egyptian opposition parties, including al-Tagammu', sent a delegation to Lebanon and Damascus in late 1986. Their detailed evaluation, highly critical of Amal movement and Syria, was published in *Al-Yawm al-Sabi'* in December (see *Journal of Palestine Studies*, no. 63, Spring 1987, p. 189).

24. International press coverage of atrocities against Palestinians outside the camps in May 1985 led to threats against journalists. On 18 June, press attention to the 'Battle of the Camps' switched to the hijacking to Beirut of a TWA aeroplane, allegedly by Hizbollah elements. Some local observers saw Amal's hand in this event.

25. This was especially clear in the South. Near Rashidiyyeh, a substantial proportion of Palestinians were employed in Shi'ite-owned plantations. In the southern suburbs, too, many kinds of economic relations were disrupted.

Epilogue

Another kind of siege

The end of the third siege on 6 April 1987 did not bring the normalization that the defenders had hoped for. Although Amal movement was broken as a political/military force, the Palestinians were prevented politically from reaping the fruits of their resistance. A Syrian force now took over Amal's positions around the Beirut camps, controlling entry and exit. Their first act was to prohibit the movement out of or into the camps of all males aged sixteen years and over. They also prohibited the entry of even the smallest quantity of building materials. These prohibitions remained in force for more than a year, turning Shateela into a prison of rubble. Yet the Syrians did not give protection: on more than one occasion Amal militia sprayed men standing near the camp's entry with bullets, killing several.

Syrian forces had been moving gradually into West Beirut since the time of the first Amal–Palestinian battle, in response to the appeals of all the 'Opposition' leaders, who were unable to find any other solution to the destruction and disorder caused by militia clashes. In July 1986, after the second round of Amal–Palestinian fighting, a small Syrian special unit was sent to Beirut to carry out a new security plan based on mixed units under Syrian/Amal supervision. In February 1987, a 4,000-strong Syrian force was despatched to Beirut as all the 'Opposition' militias rose against Amal hegemony in the fiercest street battles yet witnessed. General Ghazi Kenaan accompanied these troops as Syrian mediator.[1]

While the third siege had positive effects for the PLO, leading to the 'unification of ranks' at the 18th PNC (Algiers, 20 April), the situation of Palestinians in Lebanon remained uncertain and insecure. Amal harassment continued until the end of the year, when Berri, under pressure from Hizbollah's growing challenge, took the pretext of the Palestinian Intifada[2] to make a formal *solh* (reconciliation) with the PLO and Arafat. In the area of West Beirut, Syrian arrests of Palestinians escalated. Arrests had begun as early as June 1985, but after February 1987 they ran into hundreds.

Ostensibly aimed at 'Arafatists', they included people who were not members of any organization, forcing many to join the pro-Syrian groups as a means of protecting themselves. It was during this period that Fateh-Revolutionary Council (Abu Nidal) spread among Palestinians in Lebanon, introduced no doubt to deepen divisions and, in a period of economic hardship, attracting many 'converts' through high salaries, generous health care and help with school fees.

Women were now the only people who could move in and out of the Beirut camps relatively freely, although they were subjected to searches and interrogation. They became the communicators and suppliers, carrying in not only domestic provisions but also goods to be sold in small camp shops. They also brought in money and, in spite of the prohibitions and searches, small quantities of material for house repair. It was estimated that 80 per cent of homes had been totally destroyed and the rest severely damaged. People were living in ruins. It was months before water pipes and electricity cables were repaired.

I managed to smuggle in a tape-recorder and tapes to continue recording stories of the siege. But one day I took a photograph of the ruined main street from too near the Syrian checkpoint. I was called in, asked where I was staying and told to bring my baggage. After a search, the *mukhabarat* made me take the film out of my camera. Fearing reprisals against the people I had photographed, I succeeded in making them destroy the film.

Istanfarat (mobilizations) were another problem. Because of the tension generated by the siege, individual quarrels rapidly flared into shoot-outs and confrontations between antagonistic groups. Once, while I was visiting friends in the camp, armed men began running down the narrow alleyways outside. An 'incident' over the distribution of wood planks had degenerated into Fateh loyalists and dissidents taking up battle positions against each other. Assassinations, another symptom of external pressure, were frequent during this period. Families still living in the camp endured these dangerous conditions as best they could, waiting and hoping for a real end to the siege.

Of Shateela's three schools, Galilee and Menshiyyeh were reduced to rubble, while the third, Ariha (Jericho), did not open again until September 1988. This meant that children of families living in the camp had to go up to schools in Sabra, risking harassment by Amal militiamen on the way. Many lost three years of schooling because of the sieges. Indeed, the need for schooling was one of the major pressures on families to leave (or stay out of) the camp. Many families who had withstood all the sieges now left, living in crowded, squalid conditions in *muhajjareen* (war-displaced) centres scattered over West Beirut, just so that their children could go to school normally.

As the Syrian siege dragged on, people became very anxious about sons trapped inside the camp. Without any end in sight to the Syrian–PLO conflict, there was a growing fear that they would 'lose their future'; and linked to this fear was another, that they would be caught in the intra-Palestinian fighting that everyone predicted. It was not easy for parents to convince young men deeply imbued with the spirit of *sumood* that staying in Shateela now that the battle with Amal was over served no national purpose. Although Umm Muhammad Ahmad had been a Resistance activist since the 1960s, she decided that now the time had come to get her four adolescent sons out of Shateela – all were good students and two had university scholarships waiting for them. There were several escape routes possible – women's dress, the alleyways at night, special permission, bribes to the guards – I do not know which way she used, but eventually she got them all out, back in school and university. Those who left in this way were mainly students, young men who had taken up arms as volunteers to defend their camp; a substantial number of fighters and cadres as well as families remained inside.

Many factors now combined to increase the pressure on Palestinians to leave Lebanon. In a general sense the 'Battle of the Camps' formed one such pressure. Because of the concentration of Palestinians in Shi'ite areas, and because of the intermingling of the two populations, Shi'ite hostility had more serious long-term implications than that of the Lebanese Forces, who dominated a relatively small area from which most Palestinians had already been expelled during the Civil War of 1975/6. Shi'ite numbers would be bound to count in an eventual political restructuring of the Lebanese political system. The reconciliation between Berri and Arafat in December 1987 did not put an end to Palestinian insecurity. Indeed, when Fateh units protected Amal against Hizbollah in 1989, during their fratricidal battle in Iqleem al-Tufah, it only underlined the precariousness of the Palestinians' situation, with few choices left other than to play the role of expendable ally in intra-Lebanese battles. Unemployment and rising living costs added to insecurity in pressurizing Palestinians to leave, with or without visas. Many parents were ready to make any sacrifice to get their *shebab* out of Lebanon, even if nothing better awaited them in the country of second exile than living on government hand-outs in refugee centres. A motive for many was to obtain a foreign passport, so as to be able to move about freely, and be rid of endless hassles at frontiers. Whereas migration before 1982 had been mainly temporary, for work or study, and had involved mainly single men, since then Palestinian migration from Lebanon has included whole families, or young married couples, who hope to build better lives outside. Another difference is that post-1982 migrants have been going to Europe – Germany, Denmark, Sweden – rather than to other Arab countries. This is largely because all Arab countries except Libya are now closed to them.[3] No one knows for certain how many have left, nor how many remain; but certainly this community, once the largest in the diaspora after that of Jordan, has been considerably depleted.[4]

The Syrian siege around the Beirut camps had internal political as well as economic effects. One result was to empower the pro-Syrian Resistance groups vis-à-vis the others. Their members – or people close to them – were now the only (male) people who could freely leave or enter the camp, becoming a source of permits for other people, since they were the only ones who had *waasta* with the Syrian authorities. Located inside the camp, the pro-Syrian groups were a far more effective instrument of control than Amal had been. Fateh dissidents set up their own checkpoint next to that of the Syrian *mukhabarat*, interrogating everyone who entered even after the general ban on movement was lifted. Even family members were turned back if they were believed to be 'Arafatists' or to come from the South. Once a group of orphans was prevented from going on a summer trip abroad because it was alleged that some of their fathers had been 'Arafatists'. Bitterness between 'loyalists' and 'dissidents' was exacerbated by the fact that, although the pro-Syrian groups might control West Beirut, in the Palestinian arena as a whole they were discredited, with the Salvation Front broken up and Arafat more in control of the PLO than he had been before the PNSF campaign to arraign him as a traitor.

The intra-Fateh battle everyone had feared finally exploded in the camps at the end of April 1988, only weeks after Arafat's first meeting with President Asad since the rupture of June 1983.[5] Although all the other Resistance groups deployed intense efforts to end the fighting, and even Sa'eqa and the PFLP-GC stood aside, nonetheless the bitter fratricidal conflict continued throughout May and June. Initial 'loyalist' success in pushing the 'dissidents' to camp perimeters worked against them, since it enabled the 'dissidents' to shell the camps – Bourj Barajneh as well as Shateela – without risk of hitting their own positions. The outcome was decisively influenced by Syrian artillery and logistic support. 'Dissident' bombardment continued, shattering what was left of Shateela and causing many casualties. The 'loyalists' could not respond without hitting Lebanese residential areas.

Visiting Shateela on 23 June, just after the 48-hour pounding that brought about its final surrender, an AFP reporter found twenty-five families alongside fifteen Fateh loyalist fighters, and Women's Union leader Amneh Jibreel, who had not left the camp since May 1986. The Red Crescent hospital was shattered but still functioning. The reporter wrote: 'Shateela, symbol of resistance, is reduced to dust.'[6] At dawn on 28 June, the 'loyalists' were evacuated to Sidon under Libyan protection. A handful of residents not accused of 'Arafatism' remained. Photographs taken at the time show the camp as a mass of rubble, with not one building standing. It is hard to believe that some people continued living there through the months before water supplies were restored and rebuilding began.

The Ta'ef Accords and the Gulf War

The Lebanese situation continued to deteriorate, taking the shape of intra-sectarian conflict as rival Maronite and Shi'ite forces strove to monopolize the representation of their sect, with an eye towards an eventual restructuring of the political system. When President Amin Gemayel's mandate ended in September 1988 without the election of a new president, a period of dual government began, with an escalation in East–West artillery battles. Arab efforts to end the Lebanese crisis intensified, and during 1989 Saudi pressures succeeded in assembling Lebanese parliamentarians in Ta'ef, wringing from them a new national contract, the Ta'ef Accords (October 1989). After the assassination of newly elected President René Mo'awad in November 1989, his successor Elias Haraoui, with Omar Karameh as Prime Minister, set out early in 1991 to implement the Ta'ef Accords. The new government's first move was to disarm the unofficial militias and restore Lebanese Army control throughout the national territory.

The processes of re-stabilization set in motion by Ta'ef had several implications for the Palestinian community in Lebanon. A first step seemed promising: the renewal in April 1991 of Lebanese–PLO relations, broken in 1982.[7] The government's choice of Muhsin Ibrahim as negotiator was taken by Palestinians as a good sign.[8] However, the government's prioritization of militia disarmament meant a deaf ear to PLO arguments that the camps needed their own means of defence against continuing Israeli attack, and that Resistance fighters should be reorganized under Lebanese Army command. In July (1991), the Lebanese Army took control of areas around 'Ain Helweh after five days of fighting, leaving Resistance groups in control of the interior of the camp. This inconclusive outcome pointed, first, to a decline in Arafat's strategic interest in Lebanon, and second, to Syria's disinclination to preserve a Palestinian military potential in Lebanon. In addition it suggested that the Lebanese Army was not enthusiastic about an all-out battle against the Palestinians for the sake of a still precarious regime.[9] The essential uncertainty of this situation has been reinforced by the protracted Arab–Israeli negotiations resulting from the Gulf War.

Within the scope of negotiations over 'pacification', the Palestinian leadership in Lebanon also called for a declaration of refugee civic rights such as had been contained in the now defunct Cairo Accords.[10] In September 1991, an eleven-point memorandum was submitted to the government, calling for the reopening of the PLO's Beirut office, the right to work, autonomy for the camps, media freedom and the right to national struggle. Soon afterwards negotiations were 'frozen' by the government, pending an outcome to the Middle East settlement talks begun in Madrid in

October 1991. Efforts were exerted during 1992 to have the PLO office in West Beirut reopened, as a very minimum, but to no avail.

The regional shifts and international moves set in motion by the Gulf War of January/February 1991 have more serious implications for 'Lebanese' Palestinians than Ta'ef. Some effects were immediate: a tightening of Syrian repression, the loss of jobs in Kuwait and other Gulf countries for many, and the end of this area as a source of private and public financial support.[11] But an even more serious effect of the Gulf War was to transform the Arab environment of the Palestinian struggle, as the Arab states were polarized into those supporting and those opposing the US-directed attack against Iraq. This political polarization overlaid and partly concealed another, between the oil-rich, underpopulated states of the Gulf and the poor, overpopulated ones of the circum-Mediterranean. The wealthy Arab states, always unhappy at the threat posed by the Palestinian struggle to their relations with the West, found in the PLO's support for Iraq the pretext they needed for breaking relations with the PLO, ending financial aid, and expelling hundreds of thousands of Palestinian workers and employees. The ecoomic repercussions of this rupture have been severe not only for the PLO, but for thousands of Palestinian families in the West Bank, Jordan, Lebanon and Syria. In all these areas, almost every household had one or more members working in the Gulf.

Widespread unemployment and the cutting down of all forms of external aid, public and private, have made the economic situation of Palestinians in Lebanon increasingly harsh. The pre-Gulf War wealth of the PLO and its reputation for easy spending worked against the community now. The Lebanese call them 'the people of dollars', but since the Gulf War Palestinians are facing a situation in which all PLO sources of economic support – jobs, salaries, free medical care, educational subsidies, pensions for the families of men killed in war – have been drastically reduced. Foreign aid that flowed in after 1982 has also dwindled as the Lebanese civil war is perceived to have come to an end. UNRWA services have diminished.[12] Since the formation of the Hariri government in October 1992, regulations concerning work permits have been toughened up, with the prospect that they will be extended into the 'informal sector' where an unknown but large proportion of Palestinians eke out a living, and where in the past permits were not required.

One of the black jokes for which Palestinians are famous sums up this economic squeeze, in which all factors combine to maximize pressures towards emigration. An *ibn shaheed* (martyr's son) is talking on the telephone with his father in heaven: 'And how is your mother, my son? Does she have everything she needs? A fridge, a television, a washing machine?' The son replies: '*Yarayt! Hiyya "full automateek"*' – 'If only that were true! She's working like a washing machine.'

Difficult as their economic situation has become, Palestinians in Lebanon are even more concerned by the political consequences of the Gulf War, in the shape of the US-sponsored Arab–Israeli negotiations that began in Madrid in October 1991. Given the power disequilibrium between Israeli and Arab/Palestinian negotiators, Palestinians here are sure that if a settlement is reached, it can only be based on Palestinian concessions. Among these is expected to be the giving up of the right of return for Palestinians in exile. Whatever form of self-rule is allowed for the Occupied Territories, whether or not a settlement leaves scope for an eventual state, Israel will certainly strive to set limits on its sovereignty, and to exclude the right of 'in-gathering' of diaspora Palestinians.[13] Rejection of *towteen*, the resettlement outside Palestine of the refugees, was one of the two main starting points of the Resistance movement (the other being recovery of the land), and the centrality of this principle to its formation threatens it with a 'crisis of existence'.

To the extent that all the diaspora communities are linked by a common national cause and framework, all are equally affected by the current crisis. But each community has a specific politico-economic environment and history that affects its reactions to the possibility of *towteen*. In Lebanon, Palestinians are dangerously out of place in a readjusted sectarian political system underwritten by the post-Gulf War international/regional 'balance'. Their lack of civic rights adds to national feeling to make the prospect of no return more painful for them, perhaps, than for Palestinians in Syria, Jordan or Egypt. Given the long-term concern of the Lebanese state and much of the political leadership to reduce the size of the Palestinian community, it is logical to expect an intensification of the many measures, such as restrictions on work permits and camp sites, that have already pressured a large number into migration.

Shateela people

As for the people whose voices have been recorded in these pages, they have reacted to difficult conditions with a characteristic mix of political persistence and individual resourcefulness. A few have joined the wave of second exile out of Lebanon, but most are still here. Among those who have stayed through every battle is Abu Mustafa. The family home just outside the boundaries of the camp was completely destroyed in the first siege, and Umm Mustafa and the children were forced to spend several years in a *muhajjareen* location near Sidon. This move guaranteed the children's schooling, but for Umm Mustafa it meant weekly bus rides between Wadi Zeini and Beirut as she took on washing and cooking for two households. Reconstruction during 1991 enabled the family to return to Shateela, to a new home inside the camp. Like many other families, they have a son studying in eastern Europe. Added to the worry of how children are faring, far from home, amid political upheaval and racial violence, is the worry of whether they will find jobs when they return. But pride in a son who will one day be a doctor offsets such anxieties. One daughter is studying in the Arab University. A married daughter is back home while her husband, who lost his job in Abu Dhabi during the Gulf War, tries to establish himself in one of the Scandinavian countries. Nine children raised and educated on a cadre's meagre salary – no small achievement!

One or other member of the Haleemeh family stayed in the camp through every battle, repairing their home bit by bit, with packets of cement smuggled through in women's shopping bags. They have had more than their share of difficulties, with ten-year-old Bilal disabled by a speeding car on the motorway near the Sports City, the first time he ever left the camp alone. This accident occurred at the end of 1990. Bilal lay in a coma all through the build-up of the US-led war coalition against Iraq and the bombing that preceded the final assault. It was inspiring to watch the whole Haleemeh family – parents, grandparents, uncles, aunts, distant relatives – gathered round his bed and helping to bring him back to consciousness and mobility. Nothing could have formed a stronger contrast to the death and destruction being dealt out against the Iraqi people by Western high technology. Science teacher Ahmad still dreams of setting up a club in Shateela with a laboratory and science library, as he began to do next to Galilee School after the 1982 invasion.

Abu Mujahed has been made the chairman of all camp popular committees in Lebanon, and works from an office in Mar Elias, the small camp where many Resistance offices and social institutions are located. In this capacity he is a centre of information about conditions and developments in all the camps and settlements inhabited by Palestinians in Lebanon. A tireless organizer, he has been in the forefront of protests against the decrease in UNRWA services and the move begun in September 1992 to issue new registration cards.[14] It was from Abu Mujahed that I heard a metaphor for the Palestinian experience in Lebanon that pungently expresses its contrast between action and suppression, creativity and frustration, life and death. He said, 'Palestinians in Lebanon are like those women who have many pregnancies but never succeed in giving birth to a live child.'

Many Shateela people live outside but work inside the camp, or visit it daily. This is the case with Dr Muhammad al-Khateeb, whose account of medical care during the 'siege of Ramadan' first drew my attention to that siege's epic quality. His home in the camp has not been repaired, but he still works there as a doctor, though now with UNRWA instead of the Red Crescent, and still spends most of his off-duty time playing chess. The Red Crescent maintains its clinic in Shateela, and Umm Muhammad Farmawi is still in charge of hygiene, though living outside in a high-rise building full of *muhajjareen*. Abu and Umm Isma'een have half rebuilt their two-storey home in the camp; one or other of them visits daily to see friends and exchange news. As more of Shateela's original population returns, the camp is becoming familiar again and is losing the frightening aspect it had for so long after the 'internal war' – a mass of ruins without water or light, a 'wilderness'. In the course of 1992, two fears – fear of eviction, and fear of losing rights to space in the camp – induced many families to return. Political life is muted, and the newly plastered walls bear few posters or graffiti. But Palestinian social institutions continue to function; there is a Popular Committee and Resistance offices. Shateela still lives.

But there are others whose homes were in the neighbourhoods surrounding Shateela – Hursh, Hayy Orsan, Hayy Gharbeh, Hayy Farhat, Sabra – whose return is blocked politically as well as economically. Amal leaders have long regarded these areas as reserved for Shi'ite settlement, and would try to prevent any return of Palestinians. Homes outside camps are not eligible for UNRWA reconstruction subsidies. In addition, private rights to land in this area, in abeyance for many years, will certainly be restored as the Lebanese state reasserts its authority. Families from the outer neighbourhoods are still living in *muhajjareen* centres, under increasing threat of eviction.[15]

This is the situation of Umm 'Issam, who helped care for the wounded in the third siege. Her home used to be in the Hursh. She built it herself (as many women did) with the help of a single building worker; it was larger than homes in the camp, with a garden where she grew flowers and herbs, and where workers from the 'Austrian clinic' after the 1982 war came to drink coffee and relax. Isolated on the eighth floor of a walk-up, 'occupied' building on Rawsheh, Umm 'Issam misses Shateela badly. Her husband's salary does not allow them to rent in the camp. The void in her life is made worse by the marriage of two daughters to emigrants. Her eldest son has migrated, too. Torn between missing them and relief that they are settled outside, nostalgic for the old days of social work and visiting, Umm 'Issam epitomizes the malaise brought about by the post-siege scattering of the Shateela community. Yet, active and sociable, she has made new friends in the building, takes part in sit-ins against eviction, and last year helped in the making of a film about the famous Palestinian cartoonist, Naji al-'Ali. Most families, like hers, have sons and daughters outside, and wait for permits to enable family reunions.

Two large buildings in the heart of Sabra contain some of the most miserably lodged of the *muhajjareen*, but they do not face eviction, since these buildings belong to the Red Crescent. One of them was once Gaza Hospital; in the other the walls are not plastered nor the floors tiled, and there are no doors or windows. Families here live in single rooms, without private toilets or separate cooking space. Rabiha, the Red Crescent worker whose son disappeared in the first siege, is living in Gaza building; also Umm Kamal, who described life in the shelters in the third siege. Several families here are from Da'ouq, the little unofficial camp that was overrun by Amal during the first siege. Present hardship is made worse by uncertainty about the future: no official body – Palestinian, Lebanese or international – has come up with any plan for their eventual rehousing.

Among those who have migrated is Bushra, the young mother mentioned in the account of the second siege, who had already lived through the siege of Tell al-Za'ter in 1976, and her husband Abu Samra, who coordinated the digging of tunnels and fortifications in the third siege. Migration increasingly involves families with young children, as parents worry about the rising cost of health care and education in Lebanon. Reports that filter back from migrants are generally glowing, a fact that motivates others to follow, although no one really knows whether the migrants are telling the truth or merely, as migrants do, putting a brave face on it.

The young woman who joined a base and fought in the first siege went through a difficult time later, suffering a breakdown brought on by the disappearance of her brother. He was her widowed mother's only son, and had come home from Germany to get married just before the first 'Battle of the Camps' broke out. Amal militia took him from home and he never showed up again. But 'Samar' recovered, and was sent on a training course to Yemen. Graduated with honours, she is married now to a fellow trainee.

'Samia', the woman cadre of the dialogue with Umm Kamal, who went through the longest siege, lost the home she shared with six brothers and sisters in Sabra (both parents were killed in an Israeli air raid in 1981), but has managed to keep the 'family collective' going. Still active with the Women's Union, she is training to become a kindergarten teacher.

Umm Amal, who described an incident in a Shi'ite market after the first siege, has been to visit her village of origin in Israel. I met her with her husband at a Shateela wedding in the summer of 1992; he had just returned from twenty-five years' exile as a worker in Norway. She brought back video cassettes of weddings in her village which she will show me one day. Weddings there, she says, have brought back many traditional features dropped in Lebanon, such as painting the bridegroom's hand with henna, symbol of good luck and happiness. In her family alone, there were four weddings last summer.

Notes

1. Maronite leaders Gemayel, Chamoun and Geagea protested against the Syrian intervention of February 1987, but the United States and the Soviet

Union both welcomed the move, and none of the Arab states with the exception of Algeria criticized it. Arafat accused the Syrians of intending to support Amal's ongoing attacks against Rashidiyyeh, Bourj Barajneh and Shateela.

2. The beginning of the Intifada is generally dated from 8 December 1987, when an Israeli truck in Gaza ran into a number of cars carrying Palestinian workers, killing four.

3. It began to be difficult for 'Lebanese' Palestinians to obtain jobs in and entry permits to Gulf countries by the late 1970s, long before the Gulf War of 1990/1.

4. UNRWA statistics gave a figure of 317,376 registered refugees as of March 1992, but this figure is only approximate since a substantial number of Palestinians are not registered, nor is a record kept of migration.

5. Arafat's visit to Damascus was to attend the funeral of Abu Jihad, Fateh leader assassinated by an Israeli commando unit in Tunis on 16 April. Though not a real reconciliation, the Arafat–Asad meeting was interpreted by many as a sign of a forthcoming Syrian–PLO *rapprochement*. Some local media attributed the internal war to dissident fears that such a development would end their role. There was also speculation that Syria wanted to reinforce its control of the Beirut camps before the Lebanese presidential elections (due in September 1988), and to thwart an emerging Arafat–Hizbollah–Jumblat alliance in the South (*L'Orient/Le Jour*, 27 June 1988).

6. *L'Orient/Le Jour*, 24 June 1988.

7. For post-1982 contacts between the Lebanese government and the PLO, see R. Brynen, *Sanctuary and Survival: The PLO in Lebanon* (Boulder, CO: Westview Press, 1990), p. 228 n. 11.

8. Founder of the Organization of Communist Action, Ibrahim has always taken pro-Palestinian positions, particularly during the 'Battle of the Camps'.

9. Much of the Lebanese Army is said to have remained loyal to its commander General Aoun, who had taken over *de facto* authority from President Gemayel in 1988, tried to wage a 'war of liberation' against the Syrians during 1989, attacked the Lebanese Forces on 31 January 1990 and had finally been dislodged from Ba'bda Palace in October of the same year.

10. Unilaterally abrogated by the Lebanese government in June 1988.

11. Palestinian communities in the Gulf countries were generous funders of social projects in the camps in Lebanon.

12. See R. Sayigh, 'Palestinians in Lebanon: Uncertain future', in D. Collings (ed.), *Peace for Lebanon? From War to Reconstruction* (forthcoming, from Lynne Rienner: Boulder, CO).

13. Israeli conditions for participating in the multilateral conference on refugees in Ottawa in November 1992 required that the Palestinian delegation would not raise the issue of the return of the refugees (*L'Orient/Le Jour*, 23 October 1992).

14. UNRWA's decision in 1992 to issue new registration cards was explained as a purely administrative move. However, Palestinians saw it as a census, and as linked to settlement plans.

15. Up to February 1993 the issue of the return of the war-displaced, Lebanese or Palestinian, to their homes has not been decided, and the government has 'frozen' evictions. Nonetheless, eviction threats are being made, and are being carried out, though in piecemeal fashion.

Appendix: A Brief History of the Third Siege

An account by Abu Mujahed, Chairman of the Popular Committee

For two weeks before the battle there were daily incidents: extra checking of ID cards, searching, harassment. There were also events that showed that a battle was coming, first the siege of Rashidiyyeh, escalation in Sidon, Bourj Barajneh, then Maghdousheh. Amal began to throw up fortifications. Outside and inside the camp was like a beehive preparing for winter.

The battle didn't begin gradually like other ones. No, it began at its peak. There were thirty tanks firing 100 shells a minute at this small area, not to mention ordinary artillery and individual weapons. The scale of the attack showed the completeness of its preparation. After the siege of forty-five days we thought that, with Syrian observers around the camp, Amal would not be able to do whatever it wanted. On our side, we had no fortifications. All those from the second siege had been dismantled. Nothing could be brought into the camp without searching at the entrance. Even house repairs were forbidden without a permit from the Popular Committee; and no one was allowed to bring in more than ten bags of earth, or iron more than 6 millimetres thick.

The stage of 'living the battle'
All the camp's defence lines were destroyed, the first and second line of buildings. Where could the fighters stand? How could they fight? Of course in the first few days there was fear and confusion. The camp was defended by flesh alone.

After this the situation came under control. The first thing that had to be done was to establish a new defence system. A meeting was held on the second day. The political leadership took the decision to stay steadfast. Under the slogan 'all support to the bases', military work was given priority. But a decision was also taken to organize the social situation, and duties were allocated. We had to act fast since it was clear that Amal and the 6th Brigade were counting on knocking us out so quickly that there would be no third battle of Shateela. The fall of Shateela was supposed to be the answer to Maghdousheh and a recompense for their failure to take Bourj. They thought that they could destroy it as they had destroyed Da'ouq.

In this phase we concentrated on defence. All our resources were put to digging trenches and making fortifications. Amal destroyed the surface; our young men and women made underground roads so that our fighters could meet their attack outside the ring of destruction instead of within it. Our shooting surprised them before they even reached the destroyed positions. Their attacks failed because they didn't know where the defenders were.

There are certain parts of Shateela that were always targeted in previous battles – it's said they are marked on Lebanese Army maps. Other parts were less hit. But this time, no, the 120mm shell was used against the inner alleys, bringing down whole houses. There wasn't a single safe place in the camp. Naturally this situation created panic and fear. We had to fortify ten times more than in the past. The hospital, for example: we had to stop the *khara'a* from penetrating it. You can imagine the work that was needed, in the middle of this atmosphere of panic and the shelling that went on day and night.

There were about 3,500 people in the camp and the shelters could scarcely take 1,000. We had to dig small underground rooms – thank God that houses didn't fall on them because many families were sheltering there.

Of course people didn't expect a battle on this scale – if the leadership didn't expect it, how could ordinary people? So they needed time to get used to it. At the beginning everyone was in the shelters, everyone wanted his family to stay close to him. Parents wouldn't let their daughters go near the door of the shelter, even less outside. But this changed after about ten days. Panic ended. Ordinary people began to look for ways to help. If anyone wasn't active, others would say to him or her, 'Why are you sitting there? OK, you can't carry a gun; but you can help carry the wounded, or bury the martyrs, or carry water, or dig trenches.' This wasn't from us, it was a popular reaction.

The hospital couldn't take all the wounded. So some people took those who didn't need so much care into their homes. Everyone gave their blood. There was one girl who fainted every time she gave blood but, in spite of this, every time they needed blood she volunteered. Girls got angry if their blood wasn't taken – 'Why them, not me?' When we went to the shelters to ask for blood for a wounded fighter, no one asked, 'Who is he?' All were ready to go to the hospital under shelling to give blood to any wounded fighter.

People recovered from the shock of the first few days. It wasn't a decision from the leadership, it was the feeling of ordinary people: 'No, we will never let them enter the camp.'

Meetings began to organize the social situation. We faced many problems: the number of urgent social tasks; the exposure of all the inner part of the camp to shelling and sniping; the need to direct our human resources in a unified and systematic way.

The members of the Popular Committee were too few to do all the work, especially as some of them had other tasks. We thought that the Women's Union and other social institutions in the camp could help us. The Political Committee agreed to the unification of social work so we formed the Social Work Committee, and it had its first meeting on 5 December. Subcommittees were formed to deal with specific tasks: the Bread Committee to organize the bakery and supply bread; the Fortifications Committee to build barricades against sniping; the Committee of Wounded and Martyrs to look after everything to do with the hospital; the Shelter Committee to look after hygiene, light and supplies in the shelters; the Committee of Supplies and Distribution, which also collected statistics; and the Water Committee which mended pipes and worked the wells. All this work was supervised by the Popular Committee.

At the beginning there was also a Mobilization Committee which visited the shelters to raise people's morale. When Maghdousheh emerged as a burning issue, we had to cancel this committee; after that each organization mobilized as it wanted.

The period of military stagnation and political divisions

These six social committees worked well for a month – the period I call 'living the battle', the period of strongest attack. Then came a period of military stagnation – routine shelling, routine sniping. Daily. No news, no developments. We improved the defences and found solutions to some problems but the political conflicts that were present before the battle began to emerge again. On top of the conflict between Arafat and the PNSF came the issue of the villages east of Sidon. Initially, the Social Work Committee included all organizations, but now a process of organizational fragmentation began; some groups refused to continue working in a common front. The military leadership remained in one committee[1] but the political leadership split up and began to meet separately. The Social Work Committee remained one committee but of course its work was affected by the political atmosphere. The basic issues were outside Shateela – it wasn't a question of one group wanting to negotiate with Amal, the other not; nor that one group supported the siege, and the other opposed it. No, the issues were broader ones of national policy: how to deal with Israel and how to solve the problem of the camps in Lebanon.

Even within the PNSF there were two opinions. There were the groups whose stand was to put the defence of the camp ahead of the struggle with Arafat; and there were the other groups for whom the struggle against Arafat's deviationist line remained primary. In past sieges the PNSF had published a single news bulletin but in this one each of these two political currents put out its own publication. This didn't mean that we local cadres inside Shateela agreed with Arafat's line, but we gave priority to the fight with Amal. After all, Arafat's fighters were sharing in the defence of the camp. This position of some organizations within the PNSF prevented complete separation between the two main groups. On the Arafatist side there were people – among them 'Ali Abu Towq – who understood that the PNSF has to be the leader in the camps in Lebanon and that it has to stand alone. Even if they weren't convinced, they went along with us. There were people both in the PNSF and with Arafat – I won't call them 'moderate' because I don't like the word – who gave priority to preventing internal conflict. This meant that anyone who put forward an extreme position faced criticism from within his own organization.

The period of scarcity and suffering

On the social level we insisted on continuing unified work. But apart from political disagreements, new problems arose because the battle dragged on and the problem of scarcity began to loom. Certain kinds of cooperation continued, based on complementarity of resources. Fateh and the Popular Committee both had *mazout*, so they would distribute half of each person's share and we would distribute half: Fateh had flour and the PFLP had flour. Each had resources to offer and the work of distribution went on until these were reduced. Now a new problem emerged. Fateh people declared that they had nothing left to offer people; the little they had was hardly enough for the fighters. This was maybe three months after the beginning of the siege.

At the beginning, Fateh people said that they had sufficient stocks for six months of siege. Yet now they came along and said they had nothing left. People were saying, 'It's Arafat who rules the National Fund. Can it be true that Fateh doesn't have supplies?' I myself thought that they were saying this so as to force the Popular Committee to distribute all our supplies; then they'd have me by the neck politically, as well as making us appear impotent before the masses.

I called a meeting with some of the elders of the camp. I told them what the Fateh representative had said, and that I didn't believe him. Fateh repeated that they hardly had enough supplies for their fighters. Then I said that I was sad their supplies had finished since they were for everyone, not for Fateh alone.[2] But at the same time I was happy since this showed everyone that a small quantity of supplies well distributed is more useful than a large quantity distributed chaotically. The Popular Committee still had supplies because we had distributed systematically and fairly, on the basis of statistics. We measured by gram! Each family took according to its size. It wasn't a matter of connections or party membership. At the time people were angry at receiving such small quantities – I remember a man stepping on a piece of cheese. Later he came and apologized. People recognized that our distribution system was right.

In this stage the battle began to take a social form. In addition to political conflict, there began to be scarcity. This was the period in which sufferings exploded and, day after day, problems got worse. It was a situation of waiting, of taking blows, interrupted but continuous, with sudden bursts of shelling which caused many casualties, and threats of military escalation. As supplies dwindled, competition increased and there was fear that they would end before the siege did.

As the Popular Committee we had to make many difficult decisions. When our *mazout* began to run out we had to think what were the priorities. The hospital, the water wells and the bakery all needed *mazout*. The generator for the bakery consumed five tins a day. We said, 'Let's keep the *mazout* for the hospital and the water, and run the bakery on wood.' There was difficulty in convincing people of the necessity of this decision; there were arguments and even blows. The first day after the decision was taken, it wasn't carried out. The second day the same. The third day the decision had to be implemented by force: '*Khalas*! There's no more *mazout*. If you want bread, bring firewood!'

After we stopped giving *mazout* to the bakery, we went on giving the shelters a small amount for light. We also gave the organizations a small amount to light their underground shelters. We calculated shelters and organizations on an equal basis. But as *mazout* diminished we felt we had to keep it for the hospital and the water well and stop giving it to the shelters. Imagine how people felt when there was no more light!

The distribution of flour

But the most serious problem was that of flour. You know that bread is the basic food of the Palestinian people. If there's no bread, whatever kind of meal they have, people feel it is unsatisfying. Flour was essential for both fighters and families. When flour got scarce it made everything worse. This goes back to the failure of the organizations to institute a careful rationing system. It was clear from the beginning that this was a 'battle to break bones'; and it was the duty of the leadership to organize resistance for the longest possible time. Did this happen? To be honest, this was one of the failures.

At the beginning of the battle we were using 800 kilos of flour daily for the fighters. Later we reached a point where 200 kilos was enough. If we had used 200 from the beginning it would have lasted longer. We used to contact the political leadership daily to tell them that there's a flour crisis, we have to start rationing. They'd agree with us and do nothing about it.

The Popular Committee came out in the shadow of this situation to say, the priority is for *everybody*. The fighter and the civilian are together in this siege. The fighter can't stay steadfast in isolation from the people. It cannot be that the fighter eats two loaves and the civilian one.

Some of the organizations finished their supplies even before Fateh. We as the Popular Committee didn't want to give to them because our supplies are for ordinary people. The organizations were supposed to make their own preparations. Some of them started rationing early in the battle, eating two meals a day instead of three from the first few weeks. There were others that didn't ration themselves. So tension grew between the organizations that hadn't got supplies and the Popular Committee which wanted to give supplies only to the people.

At the same time we faced organizations that stole fuel oil. It could have been individuals rather than an organizational decision. But not a single organization punished or even questioned a member if we told them that so-and-so had stolen *mazout*. I can't over-praise the heroism of our fighters, their readiness to expose themselves over and over again to death. Nevertheless, some, if they saw some piece of private or public property, couldn't refrain from taking it. Many things that were public property, such as electric cable, were stolen during the siege.

Another problem that surfaced in this period was cigarettes – they were being sold at LL1,000 a packet, maybe more. We shouted that this was war-profiteering, they must be called to account. It was known to which organization the one who was selling the cigarettes belonged; they should have disciplined him, but they didn't. There were also a few cases of people selling rice and flour at black market prices. The political leadership did nothing about it.

I mention these negative points because they had an effect upon relations between the organizations, and upon the work of the Popular Committee. This was a period of continual tension and conflict over scarce supplies. Popular Committee members lived in a state of confrontation with their own organizations. For example, a leadership decision would be taken to distribute sugar only to children. Then a comrade comes to a Popular Committee member and asks for sugar. '*Ya 'ammi*³ your leader has just agreed in a meeting that sugar is only for children.' He says, 'Are decisions taken in meetings to be acted on outside?!' Maybe he thinks that if he takes five kilos of sugar, it won't affect supplies. But five kilos was the share of twenty-five infants for a week.

Sharing

Ordinary people, just as they had shared in defending the camp, now shared in the struggle of scarcity. When we said the bakery needed firewood, people went to search for it in fallen houses and in areas exposed to sniping. They cut up electricity poles, they broke up their own furniture.

They also shared in the matter of supplies. Whereas in the beginning they had shouted for their share, when it came to real hunger there were families who never forgot their neighbours. I remember a mother bringing a kilo of tea to the kitchen of the PFLP; and another who gave the Popular Committee two kilos of flour. These were women who had fought for their share; but when things got really tough they gave.

At first the Popular Committee didn't give supplies to the Red Crescent [hospital] because it is covered by the PLO's National Fund. But when we found that the doctors and nurses were drinking tea without sugar and going without meat and cheese so that the wounded should have these things, we were obliged to give them shares like families.

The people also played a useful role in relation to the political situation. A number of family heads went round to all the organizations to ask them about the latest developments and discuss their point of view. They tried to build bridges between these different standpoints because, as they said, the important thing is unity.

It was during this stage, the stage of scarcity and suffering, that supplies came into the camp for the PNSF. With the supplies came a delegation representing Fateh dissidents, the General Command and Sa'eqa. They brought a message. Throw out Arafat's following or the siege will continue. Instead of helping the PNSF it damaged them. All were in the same situation, yet supplies came for them and not for the other organizations. Only three of the six PNSF organizations took the supplies, the other three stood aside; and they distributed them themselves, in a chaotic way. The Popular Committee took what they didn't take and distributed to everyone. I heard women say, 'If the Popular Committee distributes it, everyone gets their share.' Even Fateh, which wasn't represented in the Popular Committee admitted this.

At this point, the three organizations of the PNSF that had not taken from the supplies set up a joint kitchen. If we had done this before, it would have prevented many problems. But each organization likes to look after itself and isn't ready to show what it has to the others.

[Abu Mujahed's account concludes on pp. 315–6.]

Notes

1. After tension increased, contact between Fateh loyalists and the PNSF was managed through a coordinator.

2. Abu Mujahed refers here to the fact that, as Chairman of the PLO, Arafat is responsible for the whole Palestinian people, not just Fateh.

3. 'O uncle!', a common form of address.

Select Bibliography

A large literature exists in Arabic of which, regrettably, only a few items are included here.

Abu-Khadra, K., *Sahafi min Filasteen yatadhakkar* (Beirut: al-Mu'assassat al'Arabiyya wa al Nashr 1985)

AbuKhalil, A., 'Druze, Sunni and Shi'ite Political Leaderships in Present-day Lebanon', *Arab Studies Quarterly*, vol. 7, no. 4, Fall 1985

AbuKhalil, A., 'Shi'ites and Palestinians: Underlying Causes of the Amal–Palestinian Conflict', in E. Hagopian (ed.), *Amal and the Palestinians: Understanding the Battle of the Camps* (Boston: AAUG, 1985)

AbuKhalil, A., 'The Palestinian–Shi'ite War in Lebanon', *Third World Affairs*, 1988

Abu-Lughod, I. and E. Ahmad (eds), 'The Invasion of Lebanon', special issue of *Race and Class*, vol. XXIV, no. 4, Spring 1983

Ajami, F., *The Vanished Imam: Musa Sadr and the Shi'a of Lebanon* (London: Tauris, 1986)

Ang, S., *From Beirut to Jerusalem: A Woman Doctor with the Palestinians* (London: Collins, 1989)

Aruri, N. and S. Farsoun, 'Palestinian Communities and the Arab Host Countries', in K. Nakhleh and E. Zureik (eds), *The Sociology of the Palestinians* (London: Croom Helm, 1980)

Aruri, N., F. Moughrabi and J. Stork, *Reagan and the Middle East* (Belmont MA: AAUG, 1983)

Aulas, M-C., 'Lebanon's Palestinians: Life at Ground Zero', *MERIP Reports*, no. 119, November–December 1983

Aulas, M-C., 'The Socio-Ideological Development of the Maronite Community: The Emergence of the Phalanges and the Lebanese Forces', *Arab Studies Quarterly*, vol. 7, no. 4, Fall 1985

Barakat, H., *Lebanon in Strife: Student Preludes to Civil War* (Austin: University of Texas Press, 1977)

Barakat, H., 'Social Factors Influencing Attitudes of University Students in

Lebanon towards the Palestinian Resistance Movement', *Journal of Palestine Studies*, vol. 1, no. 1, Autumn 1971

Barakat, H. (ed.), *Towards a Viable Lebanon* (London: Croom Helm with the Center for Contemporary Arab Studies, Georgetown, 1988)

Barrada, L., 'Sabra and Shatila: Testimonies of the Survivors', *Race and Class*, vol. XXIV, no. 4, Spring 1983

Bourgi, A. and P. Weiss, 'Israel et le Sud-Liban', *Peuples Méditerranéens* (special issue on Lebanon), no. 20, July–September 1982

Brynen, R., 'PLO Policy in Lebanon: Legacies and Lessons', *Journal of Palestine Studies*, Winter 1989

Brynen, R., *Sanctuary and Survival: The PLO in Lebanon* (Boulder: Westview Press, 1990)

Bulloch, J., *Death of a Country: The Civil War in Lebanon* (London: Weidenfeld and Nicolson, 1977)

Chomsky, N., *The Fateful Triangle: The United States, Israel and the Palestinians* (Boston: South End Press, 1983)

Cobban, H., *The Making of Modern Lebanon* (London: Hutchinson, 1985)

Cobban, H., *The Palestine Liberation Organization: Power, People and Politics* (Cambridge: CUP, 1984)

Collings, D. (ed.), *Peace for Lebanon? From War to Reconstruction* (Boulder, CO: Lynne Rienner, forthcoming)

Commission of Inquiry into the Events at the Refugee Camps in Beirut, *The Beirut Massacre: the Complete Kahan Commission Report* (New York: Karz-Cohl, 1983)

Cutting, P., *Children of the Siege*, (London: Heinemann, 1988)

Dawisha, A., *Syria and the Lebanese Crisis* (London: Macmillan, 1980)

Deeb, M., 'The External Dimensions of the Conflict in Lebanon: The Role of Syria', *Journal of South Asian and Middle Eastern Studies*, Spring 1989

Deeb, M., *The Lebanese Civil War* (New York: Praeger, 1980)

Democratic Front for the Liberation of Palestine, 'The Camps of Lebanon: Shelling, Forced Emigration, Destruction of Houses and Arrests', a report prepared by the DFLP in December 1986, in 'Documents', *Journal of Palestine Studies*, vol. xvi, no. 3, Spring 1987

Entelis, J., *Pluralism and Party Transformation: al-Kata'ib 1936–1970* (Leiden: Brill, 1974)

Faris, H., 'Lebanon and the Palestinians: Brotherhood or Fratricide?', *Arab Studies Quarterly*, vol. 3, no. 4, Fall 1981

Farsoun, S. and W. Carroll, 'The Civil War in Lebanon: Sect, Class and Imperialism', *Monthly Review*, no. 28, 1976

Farsoun, S. and R. Winegartner, 'The Palestinians in Lebanon', *SAIS Review*, Winter 1981/2

Fisk, R., *Pity the Nation: Lebanon at War* (London: Andre Deutsch, 1990)

Franjieh, S., 'How Revolutionary is the Palestinian Resistance Movement?',

Journal of Palestine Studies, vol. 1, no. 2, Autumn 1972

Gabbay, R., *A Political Study of the Arab–Jewish Conflict: The Refugee Problem* (Paris, Librairie Minard, 1959)

Genet, J., 'Four Hours in Shatila'', *Journal of Palestine Studies*, vol. XII, no. 3, Spring 1983

Giannou, C., *Besieged: A Doctor's Story of Life and Death in Beirut* (London: Bloomsbury, 1991)

Gilmour, D., *Lebanon: The Fractured Country* (London: Sphere Books, 1983)

Golan, M., *The Secret Conversations of Henry Kissinger* (New York: Quadrangle Press, 1976)

Goria, W., *Sovereignty and Leadership in Lebanon 1943–1976* (London: Ithaca Press, 1985)

Gresh, A., *The PLO: The Struggle Within* (London: Zed Books, 1985)

Hagopian, E. and S. Farsoun (eds), *South Lebanon* (Detroit: AAUG, 1978)

Hagopian, E. (ed.), *Amal and the Palestinians: Understanding the Battle of the Camps* (Belmont MA: AAUG, 1985)

Halaq, H., *Mawqif Lubnan min al-qadiyat al-Filastiniyya 1918–1952* (Beirut: PLO Research Centre, 1982)

Haley, E. and L. Snider (eds), *Lebanon in Crisis: Participants and Issues* (New York: Syracuse University Press, 1979)

Harris, W., 'Syria in Lebanon', *MERIP Reports*, no. 134, July–August 1985

Hashan, H., 'Attitudes of the Lebanese Sects towards the Palestinians', MA thesis, American University of Beirut, 1987

Hinnebusch, R., 'Syrian Policy in Lebanon and the Palestinians', *Arab Studies Quarterly*, vol. 8, no. 1, Winter 1986

Hof, F., *Galilee Divided: The Israel–Lebanese Frontier 1916–1948* (Boulder: Westview Press, 1984)

al-Hout, S., *Isharoona 'amman ti Munazzamat al-Tahrir al-Filastiniyya, 1964–1984: ahadith al-dhikrayat* (Beirut: Dar al-Istiqlal, 1986)

Hudson, M., 'The Palestinian Factor in the Lebanese Civil War', *Middle East Journal*, vol. 32, no. 3, Summer 1978

Hudson, M., *The Precarious Republic: Political Modernization in Lebanon* (Boulder: Westview Press, 1985, 2nd edn)

Jabbra, J. and N., *Elusive Peace: The Collapse of the Lebanese–Israeli Troop Withdrawal Accord of 17 May 1983* (Toronto: Canadian Institute of International Affairs, 1985)

Jaber, T., 'Le Discours shi'ite sur le pouvoir', *Peuples méditerranéens* (special issue on Lebanon), no. 20, July–September 1982

Jansen, M., *The Battle of Beirut: Why Israel Invaded Lebanon* (London: Zed Books, 1982)

Johnson, M., 'Popular Movements and Primordial Loyalties in Beirut', in T. Asad and R. Owen (eds), *Sociology of 'Developing Societies': The*

Middle East (New York: Monthly Review Press, 1983)

Joumblatt, K., *I Speak for Lebanon* (London: Zed Press, 1982)

Kamhawi, L., 'Palestinian–Arab Relations: A Study of the Political Attitudes and Activities of the Palestinians in the Arab Host-States, 1949–1967', PhD thesis, University of London

Kapeliouk, A., *Sabra and Shatila: Inquiry into a Massacre* (Belmont MA: AAUG, 1984; first published in French by Seuil, 1982)

Karam, F., 'Témoignage sur les réfugiés palestiniens', *Conférences du cénacle*, nos. 3–4, March 1949

Kassir, S., 'Au Liban, fragile domination syrienne', *Le Monde diplomatique*, March 1991

Kassir, S., 'L'affirmation des chiites libanais', *Le Monde diplomatique*, May 1985

Kassir, S., 'La Résistance nationale libanaise: quelques propositions', *Revue d'études palestiniennes*, no. 16, Summer 1985

Katz S., *Armies in Lebanon 1982–84* (London: Osprey, 1985)

Khaled, A., 'Al-fashiya al-saghira: dirasa fi suhuf wa nasharat al-qiwa al-in'aziliya', *Shu'oon Filastiniyya*, no. 56, April 1976

Khaled, L., *My People Shall Live: The Autobiography of a Revolutionary* (London: Hodder and Stoughton, 1973)

Khalidi, R., 'External Intervention and Domestic Conflict in Lebanon, 1975–1985', Wilson Centre Working Paper no. 65, June 1985

Khalidi, R., 'L'impact du mouvement national palestinien sur la politique et la societé libanaises', *Revue d'études palestiniennes*, no. 12, Summer 1984

Khalidi, R., 'The Asad Regime and the Palestinian Resistance', *Arab Studies Quarterly*, vol. 6, no. 4, Fall 1984

Khalidi, R., 'The Palestinians in Lebanon', *Middle East Journal*, Spring 1984

Khalidi, R., *Under Siege: PLO Decision-making in the 1982 War* (New York: Columbia University Press, 1986)

Khalidi, W., *Conflict and Violence in Lebanon* (Cambridge MA: Harvard Center for International Affairs, 1979)

Khater, T., 'Lebanese Politics and the Palestinian Resistance Movement', PhD thesis, State University of New York, Buffalo, 1982

Khoury, P., 'Syria and Lebanon 1943–1975', *MERIP Reports*, no. 134, July–August 1985

Kishli, M., *Al-Azma al-Lubnaniya wa al-wujood al-Filasteeni* (Beirut: Dar Ibn Khaldoon, 1980)

Kosseifi, G., 'Demographic Characteristics of the Arab Palestinian People' in K. Nakhleh and E. Zureik (eds), *The Sociology of the Palestinians*, (London: Croom Helm, 1980)

Labaki, G., *The Lebanon Crisis (1975–1985): A Bibliography* (Maryland: Center for International Development and Conflict Management, 1986)

Longrigg, S. H., *Syria and Lebanon under French Mandate* (London: OUP, 1948)

Lorch, N., *The Edge of the Sword: Israel's War of Independence 1947–1948* (Jerusalem: Massada Press, 1968)

Mandus, H., *Al-'amal wa al-'umal fi al-mukhayem al-Filasteeni: bahth maydani 'an mukhayem Tell al-Za'ter* (Beirut: PLO Research Centre, 1974)

Mansour, C., 'Au-delà des sièges des camps palestiniens de Beyrouth: la montée en puissance du mouvement Amal et ses limites', *Maghreb-Machrek*, no. 109, July–September 1985

McDermott, A. and K. Skjelsbaek, *The Multinational Force in Beirut 1982–1984* (Miami: Florida University Press, 1991)

McDowell, D., *Lebanon* (Minority Rights Group, 1984)

MERIP Reports, (originally *MERIP Reports*, this journal became *MERIP: Middle East Report* in January 1986, and *Middle East Report* in early 1988) special issues on Lebanon:

  'The War in Lebanon', no. 108/9, September–October 1982

  'Lebanon in Crisis', no. 118, October 1983

  'Lebanon's Shi'as', no. 133, June 1985

  'Lebanon's War: Any End in Sight?', no. 162, January–February 1990

Morris, B., *The Birth of the Palestinian Refugee Problem, 1947–1949*, (Cambridge: CUP, 1987)

Morris, B., 'The Initial Absorption of the Palestinian Refugees in the Arab Host Countries, 1948–49', in A. Bramwell (ed.), *Refugees in the Age of Total War* (London: Unwin Hyman, 1988)

Moughrabi, F. and N. Aruri (eds), *Lebanon: Crisis and Challenge in the Arab World* (Detroit: AAUG, 1977)

Muir, J., 'Lebanon: Arena of Conflict, Crucible of Peace', *Middle East Journal*, Spring 1984

al-Nahar, *Al-Filastiniyoon fi Lubnan: al-'Alaqat ma' al-Dowlat al-Lubnaniya, Malaff al-Nahar* (Beirut), no. 2, July 1974

Nasr, S., 'Roots of the Shi'i Movement', *MERIP Reports*, no. 133, June 1985

Nassib, S. and C. Tisdall, *Beirut: Frontline Story* (London: Pluto Press, 1983)

Natour, S., 'The Legal Situation of the Palestinians in Lebanon', n.d.

Nazzal, N., *The Palestinian Exodus from Galilee, 1948* (Beirut: Institute for Palestine Studies, 1978)

Norton, A., *Amal and the Shi'a: Struggle for the Soul of Lebanon* (Austin: University of Texas Press, 1987)

Norton, A., *External Intervention and the Politics of Lebanon* (Washington DC: Washington Institute for Values in Public Policy, 1984)

Norton, A., 'Lebanon after Ta'ef: Is the Civil War Over?', *Middle East Journal*, vol. 45, no. 3, Summer 1991

O'Brien, L., 'Campaign of Terror: Car Bombing in Lebanon', *MERIP Reports*, no. 118, October 1983

Odeh, B., *Lebanon: Dynamics of Conflict* (London, Zed Books, 1985)

Owen, R. (ed.), *Essays on the Crisis in Lebanon* (London: Ithaca Press, 1976)

Pakradouni, K., *La Paix manquée: le mandat d'Elias Sarkis (1976–1982)* (Beirut: Editions Fiches du Monde Arabe, 1984)

Pakradouni, K., *Le Piège: de la malédiction libanaise à la guerre du Golfe* (Paris: Grasset; Beirut: FMA, 1991)

Peteet, J., *Gender in Crisis: Women and the Palestinian Resistance Movement* (New York: Columbia University Press, 1991)

Peteet, J., 'Socio-Political Integration and Conflict Resolution in Palestinian Camps in Lebanon', *Journal of Palestine Studies*, vol. 16, no. 2, Winter 1987

Peteet, J., 'Women and the Palestinian Movement: No Going Back', *MERIP Reports*, no. 138, January–February 1986

Petran, T., *The Struggle over Lebanon* (New York: Monthly Review Press, 1987)

Picard, E., 'De la "communauté-classe" à la résistance nationale: pour une analyse du rôle des chi'ites dans le système politique libanais', *Revue française du science politique*, vol. 6, no. 35, December 1985

Picard, E., 'La politique de la Syrie au Liban', *Maghreb-Machrek*, no. 116, Spring 1987

Picard, E., 'Le Liban et la résistance palestinienne', *Revue française du science politique*, no. 25, February 1975

Picard, E., 'Liban: guerre civil, conflit régional', *Maghreb-Machrek*, no. 73, July–September 1976

Rabinovitch, I., *The War for Lebanon 1970–1985* (Ithaca NY: Cornell University Press, 1985)

Randal, J., *Going All the Way: Christian Warlords, Israeli Adventurers, and the War in Lebanon* (New York: Viking Press, 1983)

Revue d'études palestiniennes, 'Dossier: le siège des camps palestiniens de Beyrouth', no. 17, Autumn 1985

Rokach, L., *Israel's Sacred Terrorism* (Belmont MA: AAUG, 1980)

Rouleau, E., 'La mutinerie contre M. Yasser Arafat', *Le Monde diplomatique*, August 1983

Rubenberg, C., 'Palestinians in Lebanon: A Question of Human and Civil Rights', *Arab Studies Quarterly*, vol. VI, no. 3, Summer 1984

Rubenberg, C., *The Palestinian Liberation Organization: Its Institutional Infrastructure* (Belmont MA: Institute for Arab Studies, 1983)

Ryan, S., 'Israel's Invasion of Lebanon: Background to the Crisis', *Journal of Palestine Studies*, vol. XI, no. 4 and vol. XII, no. 1, Summer/Fall 1982

Salibi, K., *Crossroads to Civil War* (New York: Caravan Books, 1976)

Salibi, K., *The Modern History of Lebanon* (London: Weidenfeld and Nicolson, 1965)

Sayigh, R., *Palestinians: From Peasants to Revolutionaries* (London: Zed

Press, 1979)

Sayigh, R., 'Palestinians in Lebanon: Status Ambiguity, Insecurity and Flux', *Race and Class*, vol. 30, no. 1, July–September 1988

Sayigh, R., 'The Palestinian Identity among Camp Residents', *Journal of Palestine Studies*, vol. VI, no. 3, Spring 1977

Sayigh, R., 'The Struggle for Survival: Economic Conditions of Palestinian Camp Residents in Lebanon', *Journal of Palestine Studies*, vol. VII, no. 1, Winter 1977

Sayigh, Y., 'Israel's Military Performance in Lebanon, June 1982', *Journal of Palestine Studies*, vol. XIII, no. 1, Fall 1983

Sayigh, Y., 'Palestinian Military Performance in the 1982 War', *Journal of Palestine Studies*, vol. XII, no. 4, Summer 1983

Sayigh, Y., 'Struggle within, Struggle without: The Transformation of PLO Politics since 1982', *International Affairs*, vol. 65, no. 2, Spring 1989

Sayigh, Y., 'The Politics of Palestinian Exile', *Third World Quarterly*, vol. 9, no. 1, January 1987

Sayigh, Y. A., 'Implications of UNRWA Operations', MA thesis, American University of Beirut, 1952

Schechla, J., *The Iron Fist: Israel's Occupation of South Lebanon* (Washington DC: American Arab Anti-discrimination Committee, 1985)

Schiff, Z. and E. Ya'ari, *Israel's Lebanon War* (London: Allen & Unwin, 1985)

Seale, P., *Asad* (London: Tauris, 1988)

Sharif, H., 'South Lebanon: Its History and Geopolitics', in E. Hagopian and S. Farsoun (eds) (1978)

Sicking, T. and S. Khairallah, 'The Shi'a Awakening in Lebanon: A Search for Radical Change in a Traditional Way', in *Vision and Revision in Arab Society, 1974*, CEMAM Reports (Beirut: Dar el-Mashreq, 1974)

Sirhan, B., 'Palestinian Refugee Camp Life in Lebanon', *Journal of Palestine Studies*, vol. IV, no. 2, Winter 1975

Sirriyyah, H., *Lebanon: Dimensions of Conflict* (Brassey's, for the International Institute for Strategic Studies, 1989)

Snider, L., 'The Lebanese Forces: Their Origins and Role in Lebanon's Politics', *Middle East Journal*, no. 38, Winter 1984

Stoakes, F., 'The Super-Vigilantes: The Lebanese Kata'eb Party as a Builder, Surrogate and Defender of the State', *Middle Eastern Studies*, vol. II, no. 3, 1975

Stork, J., 'Israel as a Strategic Asset', in Aruri, Moughrabi and Stork, *Reagan and the Middle East*

Stork, J., 'Report from Lebanon', *MERIP Reports*, no. 118, October 1983

Stork, J., 'The War in Lebanon', *MERIP Reports*, no. 108/9, September–October 1982

Swedenburg, T., 'Problems of Oral History: The 1939 Revolt in Palestine', *Birzeit Review*, no. 2, Winter 1985/6

Swedenburg, T., 'The Palestinian Peasant as National Signifier', *Anthropological Quarterly*, vol. 63, no. 1, January 1990

Swedenburg, T., 'The Role of the Palestinian Peasantry in the Great Revolt (1936–1939)', in I. Lapidus and E. Burke (eds), *Islam, Politics and Social Movements* (Berkeley: University of California Press, 1988)

Suleiman, M., *Political Parties in Lebanon: The Challenge of a Fragmented Political Culture* (Ithaca: Cornell University Press, 1967)

TEAM International, *The Palestinian Labour Force in Lebanon* (Beirut: TEAM, 1983)

al-Turk, G., 'Mohafez of the South', in H. Abu Izzideen (ed.), *Lebanon and its Provinces* (Beirut: 1963)

Turk, M., 'Lebanese–Palestinian Relations after the Cairo Agreement', M.Litt. thesis, Oxford University, 1981

UNRWA-Lebanon, *Awda' al-Muhajareen al-Filastiniyeen fi Lubnan*, Warshat 'Amal, Sidon, 22 March 1990

Yaniv, A., *Dilemmas of Security: Politics, Strategy and the Israeli Experience in Lebanon* (New York: OUP, 1987)

Zamir, M., *The Formation of Modern Lebanon* (London: Croom Helm, 1985)

Other useful sources

Journal of Palestine Studies (has a Palestine chronology, with little on Lebanon)

Middle East International

Middle East Report

Race and Class, notes and documents

Revue d'études palestiniennes (began a chronology of South Lebanon and Golan with issue no. 26, Winter 1988)

List of Abbreviations

AHC	Arab Higher Council
ALF	Arab Liberation Front
ANM	Arab Nationalist Movement
AUB	American University of Beirut
CDC	Council for Development and Construction
DA	Democratic Alliance
DFLP	Democratic Front for the Liberation of Palestine
GUPW	General Union of Palestinian Women
IDF	Israeli Defence Forces
INM	Independent Nasserist Movement
ISA	Institute of Social Affairs
ISF	International Security Forces
LCP	Lebanese Communist Party
LF	Lebanese Forces
LNM	Lebanese National Movement
LNRF	Lebanese National Resistance Front
MNF	Multinational Forces
MOD	Movement of the Deprived
NSSP	National Syrian Socialist Party
OCA	Organization of Communist Action
PFLP	Popular Front for the Liberation of Palestine
PFLP-GC	PFLP-General Command
PLA	Palestine Liberation Army
PLF	Palestine Liberation Front
PLO	Palestine Liberation Organization
PNC	Palestine National Council
PNSF	Palestinian National Salvation Front
PPS	Parti Populaire Syrien
PRC	Palestine Research Centre
PRCS	Palestine Red Crescent Society
PRM	Palestinian Resistance movement
PSF	Palestine Struggle Front
PSP	Progressive Socialist Party
SISC	Supreme Islamic Shi'a Council
SLA	South Lebanon Army
UNRWA	United Nations Relief and Works Agency

Linguistic Glossary

abu (pl. *abawat*)	: father
a'ediyya	: money to spend at the feast
a'eed (pl. *a'yad*)	: feast (e.g. A'eed al-Fitr, which terminates Ramadan)
ahel (pl. *ahali*)	: family (*ahali al-mukhayem*: families of the camp)
ahlan!	: welcome!
a'ileh (pl. *a'ilat*)	: family
'alim (pl. *'ulema*)	: learned man, cleric
Allah yerhamu	: God have mercy on him/her (the dead)
Allahu akbar	: God is greatest
'ameel (pl. *'umala'*)	: agent, informer
aqal	: black band holding men's headscarves in place
arba'een	: the fortieth day after a death, an occasion of renewed mourning
argeeleh	: water pipe, hubble-bubble
ashbal	: see Political Glossary
'Ashoura	: Shi'ite commemoration of the death of the martyr Hussein
atfal (sing. *tifl*)	: children
awda'	: return
balanga	: a frame for hanging animal carcasses, used by butchers
bamieh	: okra
barakiyeh (pl. *barakiyat*)	: shack, hut
Basha	: Ottoman title given to an important or wealthy personage
bey/beg/bek	: a title indicating a status somewhat below a *basha*
beit (pl. *byoot*)	: house, home, household
bint (pl. *banat*)	: daughter, girl, young unmarried woman
bourj	: tower
bu(q)ra hizbiyyeh	: a focal point of political parties
burghul	: crushed wheat
dar	: part of the house where visitors are received; also used for family

darak	: police
dashsharoona	: they abandoned us
daya	: midwife
debkeh	: the dance of villagers in the Palestine–Syria–Lebanon area, originating in the collective stamping down of mud roofs; associated with weddings
diwan	: a meeting place, part of a house used for meetings; an office
effendi	: Ottoman title often given to urban notables (less than *beg*)
elbas	: baggy trousers worn by Galilean villagers, men and women
falafel	: fried bean patties
faqeer	: the poor
farah	: happiness (linked in rural culture to weddings)
fatwa	: a religious decree
fawj	: a military unit
faza'a	: rush, a movement of collective defence; related to fear; only used by villagers
feda'i (pl. *feda'yeen*)	: one who sacrifices his life for a cause, the term used for Palestinian Resistance fighters
fellah (pl. *fellaheen*, fem. *fellahat*)	: peasant
fowda	: chaos, disorder
gallabiya	: long, loose, cotton dress
hadaneh	: crèche
Hadeeth	: sayings of the Prophet Muhammad
hafleh	: party, celebration
hajj (fem. *hajji*)	: term used for someone who has made the pilgrimage to Mecca
halal	: what is permitted (opposite of *haram*)
halaqa	: circle, series
halaweh	: a sweet made of sugar, sesame paste and nuts often spread on bread (*helweh* means 'sweet')
hamal	: porter
hamuleh (pl. *hama'el*)	: clan
harakeh (pl. *harakat*)	: movement
haram	: what is forbidden, sin (opposite of *halal*)
hareeseh	: a sweet pastry; also a dish of wheat and meat; and a hot pepper sauce
harb	: war
hasab	: ties of blood
hatta	: the chequered black and white, or plain white, headscarf worn by Palestinian villagers (originally by Bedouin)
hayy (pl. *ahya'*)	: quarter, neighbourhood

hijab	:	veil or head covering; also magico–religious charm or amulet
hijra	:	migration (used for Muhammad's movement from Mecca to Medina, also for the exodus from Palestine)
hikaya (pl. *hikayat*)	:	story
hizam al-bu'us	:	poverty belt
hizb (pl. *ahzab*)	:	political party
hursh	:	forest, wood
Husseiniyyeh	:	meeting place attached to Shi'ite mosques
ibn halal	:	decent fellow (literally, a legitimate child)
iftor or *iftar*	:	breakfast; the meal that breaks the fast during Ramadan
ihtifal (pl. *ihtafalat*)	:	celebration
infiraj	:	relief, relaxation of tension
inhiraf	:	deviation
insh'allah	:	God willing
iqleem	:	region, locality
iqtisad	:	economy
istinfar	:	state of preparedness to fight, an alert
instinhad	:	state of anger, readiness to rebel
iqta	:	feudalism
istiqbal	:	reception
jabr	:	bone healing
jama'a	:	following
jaree'	:	daring
jaysh	:	army
jebha	:	front (political)
jihad	:	holy struggle
jihaz	:	trousseau
jiwaz	:	marriage
kaftan	:	robe
kahweh	:	coffee house
karameh	:	dignity, honour, generosity
keffiyyeh	:	same as *hatta*
khalas`	:	the end, often an exclamation of relief
khanq	:	strangulation
khara'a	:	a tank-fired missile
khutbeh	:	a speech, sermon; also an engagement to be married
kibbeh	:	meat pounded with burghul
kleel	:	crown (e.g. worn by a bride; colloquial for *ikleel*)
kombas	:	long robe
leban	:	clabbered milk, yoghurt (*lebneh*: strained *leban*)
mahrajanat (sing. *mahrajan*)	:	rally
mahrumeen	:	deprived, oppressed
mahwar (pl. *mahawer*)	:	base (military), also axis, theme

maktab (pl. *makateb*)	: office (*maktab siyasi*: political office)
ma'moul	: cake filled with dates or nuts, made specially for feasts
mantaqa	: area, region
maramiyyeh	: sage
marda(q)oush	: oregano
marhaba!	: hallo! (a minimum greeting)
mazout	: fuel oil
mejlis	: council (*mejlis al-shuyyukh*: council of old men)
mena(q)eesh (sing. *men(q)ousheh*)	: rounds of bread covered with oil and *za'ter*, then baked and eaten hot
mendeel	: fine headscarf worn by village women on festive occasions, usually trimmed with sequins or crochet
menfa	: exile, diaspora
men(q)al	: brazier for charcoal
merja'	: reference (used for religious leader, or centre of representation)
mihneh (pl. *mihan*)	: profession, craft
mlaya	: woman's long, black coat
mlebbes	: sugared almonds, usually offered at weddings or during the feasts
mloukhia	: Jews' mallow, a green vegetable chopped very fine and eaten in chicken stew with garlic and coriander
moda(q)adeemi	: old-fashioned style
mooni	: domestic stocks, usually food
mowlid	: birthday of the Prophet; chanting of the Quran on family occasions
mowt	: death
mu'allem	: master craftsman
mu'asker	: military camp
mudir	: director
mudun (sing. *medina*)	: cities
mu'essesseh	: institution
mu'essisseen	: founders
mughtaribeen	: returned migrants
mahajjareen	: displaced people
mujahed	: literally 'holy warrior', the term used for those who fought against the British Occupation in Palestine before 1948
mukhabarat	: intelligence agents, plain-clothes police
mukhayem	: camp
mukhtar	: village headman
muqawwimeh	: resistance
musaanid (sing. *masnad*)	: hard cushions

mustabaheen	:	animals (or people) without protection
muwashshahat	:	religious or mourning chanting (also a form of Andalusian poetry, usually sung)
nafoos	:	registration
namoora	:	a kind of cake
na'na'	:	mint
nasab	:	ties created by marriage
natour	:	guardian
nedweh (pl. *nedwaat*)	:	seminar
nekba	:	disaster
niswan	:	women
nuss	:	half
'oud	:	a stringed instrument (origin of the lute)
qa'id	:	local leader
qariya (pl. *qura*)	:	village
(q)awiyyeh (masc. *(q)awee*)	:	strong
rabb al-a'ileh	:	head of the family
ragheef	:	a flat round of Arabic bread
ra'isiyyeh	:	chief (adjective from *ra'ees*, head)
sar nasseeb	:	literally, there is good fortune, i.e. a marriage has been arranged, or has taken place
semneh	:	clarified butter used in cooking
sfoof	:	a kind of cake
shabb (pl. *shebab*)	:	young man
sha'b	:	people (adj. *sha'bi*: popular)
shaheed (pl. *shuhada'*)	:	martyr, one who falls in national struggle
sharab al-wared	:	sweet drink made from rose petals
shaweesh	:	sergeant, leader of a small military unit
sheikh (pl. *shuyyukh*)	:	old man; local leader; man known for piety
shentian	:	long trousers worn by village women under dresses
shu'oon	:	affairs, short for *shu'oon ijtima'iyya*, social affairs
suhoor	:	the last meal eaten before dawn during Ramadan
sumood	:	steadfastness, endurance, staying put
taheeneh	:	paste made from sesame seeds
tajawuzat	:	excesses
tanak	:	tin
tanzeem (pl. *tanzeemat*)	:	organization
tarha	:	train (worn by bride)
tashkees	:	creation of human likeness
tatruf	:	extremism
thawb (pl. *thawab*)	:	long shirt or tunic worn by village women, usually embroidered
thawra	:	revolution

towjihi	:	official school finishing exam in most Arab countries
towteen	:	see Political Glossary
umm (pl. *umahat*)	:	mother
'umma	:	nation; the collectivity of Muslims
ustadh	:	courtesy title given to teachers
waasta	:	connection
wadi	:	river bed
wahid	:	one
wajih (pl. *wujaha'*)	:	notable, leader of clan, village or city quarter
wallah!	:	by God!
wilayat	:	province
woqfi	:	the day before a religious feast begins
yifrah	:	to be happy (in the marriage of one's children)
yallah!	:	'let's go', or 'get out!'
za'eem (pl. *zu'ama'*)	:	leader, important politician
za'ter	:	wild thyme
zinco	:	corrugated iron (used for camp roof-tops)
zoofa	:	hyssop
zuhoorat	:	a tea or tisane made from dried herbs and flowers
zu'ran (sing. *az'ar*)	:	hooligans

Political Glossary

Amal movement (Harakat Amal): The name is an acronym, formed from Afwaj al-Muqawwimeh al-Lubnaniyyeh (Battalions of Lebanese Resistance). Founded in 1974 as the military wing of the Movement of the Deprived, Amal survived its parent movement to become a major contender for the representation of the Shi'ite community. Since 1980 Amal's leader has been Nabih Berri.

Arab Higher Council (AHC): Formed in 1936 by Hajj Amin al-Husseini to coordinate and lead the general strike, the AHC opened offices before 1948 in several Arab capitals to solicit support and buy arms. An AHC office in Beirut continued to operate until the Mufti's death in 1974.

Arab Liberation Front (ALF): A Resistance group formed of Palestinian members of the Iraqi Ba'th party.

Arab Nationalist Movement (ANM): Launched in the early 1950s from the American University of Beirut by, among others, Dr George Habash and Hani Hindi, the ANM spread rapidly to most parts of the Arab world but never took the form of a party. Associated with Nasserism, it declined after 1967 but remained an important intellectual current. It gave birth to both the PFLP and the DFLP.

Arab Socialist Action Party: A small Marxist Lebanese group formed in 1972, linked to the PFLP until 1981, based mainly in South Lebanon and the Beqa'.

Arafat, Yasser (Abu Ammar): Born in 1929 in Cairo; fought in the war of 1948; set up the Palestinian Students' Union in Gaza/Egypt before the establishment of the PLO; and was one of the core group that founded Fateh. Elected Chairman of the PLO's Executive Committee at the 5th National Assembly in 1969. With the declaration of a Palestinian state in 1988, he became its president.

al-Asad, Hafez: President of Syria since 1970, when he led a coup against the radical wing of the Ba'th party then in power. Born in 1930 near Lattaqia, he joined the Ba'th as a schoolboy. In 1951 he joined the airforce, becoming Airforce Commander in 1964, Minister of Defence in 1966.

al-As'ad, Kamel: Born in 1929, a member of the largest Shi'ite landowning family in South Lebanon. Became a deputy in 1953, and was frequently

Speaker of the National Assembly. An ally since 1975/6 of the Maronite right, he helped to get Bashir Gemayel elected president in August 1982.

Ashbal (sing. *shibl*): 'lion cubs', a physical/military/political training programme for young boys, begun by Fateh. A similar formation existed for girls, called the *zohrat* ('flowers').

Ba'th Party: Founded in 1954 in Syria by Michel Aflaq, Salah Bitar and Akram Hourani, the Ba'th party's ideology was Arab nationalist, secularist and socialist. Helped create union between Syria and Egypt in 1958 which broke up in 1961. In 1963, Ba'th party coups succeeded in Baghdad (February) and Damascus (March). Later came the split between the Arab National leadership (Aflaq) and the local Syrian leadership (Asad, 'Umran, Jedid), with the former moving to Baghdad.

Beit Atfal al-Sumood: Originally an orphanage founded by the General Union of Palestinian Women after the destruction of Tell al-Za'ter camp. After 1982, Beit Atfal became independent, changed its name and now sponsors orphans in families.

Berri, Nabih: Born in 1937 in Freetown, Sierra Leone, Berri's family was originally from Tibneen in South Lebanon. As a law student in Beirut, Berri joined the Ba'th party but later became a member of the group around Imam Sadr. Elected leader of Amal movement in 1980, Berri became a Cabinet minister in 1984, after the February uprising against the Gemayel regime.

Black September: Term used by Palestinians to refer to the confrontation between the Jordanian Army and the Resistance movement that began in Amman in September 1970 and eventually led to the expulsion of the PRM from Jordan.

Cairo Agreement: Reached in Cairo in November 1969 after the uprisings in the camps in Lebanon, the agreement was supposed to regulate Lebanese–PLO relations. It was unilaterally abrogated by the Lebanese government in June 1987.

Chamoun, Camille: Born in 1900 in Deir al-Qamar; first elected to Parliament in 1929; among the leaders of the Lebanese independence movement. Elected President in 1952; supported the pro-Western Baghdad Pact. Died in August 1987.

Chehab, Fuad: Lebanese Army commander during the civil war of 1958, Chehab kept the Army out of the fighting, was elected president after the US Marine landing in July, launching a programme of state-building and infrastructural development.

Damascus Agreement: This was the agreement that formally ended the first 'Battle of the Camps' on 17 June 1985. Its terms included a cease-fire, release of prisoners, withdrawal of Amal fighters and their replacement by the FSI (police). The agreement recognized the PNSF as the political leadership of Palestinians in Lebanon.

Da'oud, Da'oud: A Shi'ite from a border village, Da'oud was a member of Fateh in the early 1970s but turned anti-Palestinian after being punished for misconduct. He joined Amal, becoming commander of the province of Tyre.

Palestinians say that he cooperated with the Israelis before, during and after the invasion of 1982. Da'oud was assassinated in Ouzai in June 1989, during the battles between Amal and Hizbollah.

Day of the Land (Yom al-Ard): A national day, on 31 March, which commemorates the resistance by the people of Ikreet and Kfar Birim (in northern Israel) to state land confiscation, in which seven people were killed.

Democratic Front for the Liberation of Palestine (DFLP): Born from a leftist split from the PFLP led by Nayef Hawatmeh in February 1969, the DFLP initiated the 'mini-state solution' and has generally stood with Fateh against the PFLP. Recently split over the issue of peace negotiations versus armed struggle.

Deuxième Bureau (*Maktab Thani*): The Intelligence section of the army, built up by Chehab as a base of his regime, to weaken the traditional political leaders and to control the radical opposition parties.

Fadlallah, Sheikh Muhammad Hussein: Leading Shi'ite cleric and religious *merja'* (reference) in Lebanon, Sheikh Fadlallah is generally recognized as the spiritual guide of Hizbollah. Critic of the Lebanese state and the Arab regimes, he has occasionally called for an Islamic state in Lebanon.

Fateh: The name of this, the largest and one of the earliest Resistance groups, is formed by reversing the initials of Harakat at-Tahrir at-Watani al-Filastini (Palestinian National Liberation Movement). Formed in the late 1950s by Yasser Arafat, Khalil Wazir, Khaled al-Hassan and Salah Khalaf, Fateh's first announced military strike took place on 31 December 1964. It includes all ideological tendencies. Fateh-Revolutionary Council is a breakaway group headed by Abu Nidal.

Franjiyyeh, Suleiman: A leading Maronite politician from Zghorta, he took part in the 1958 uprising against Chamoun. Elected president in 1970. Formed his own militia, al-Marada, to defend his northern fiefdom against the Kata'eb and Lebanese Forces. Was Syria's candidate in the (unheld) presidential elections of 1988. Died in July 1992.

Geagea, Samir: Born in 1952, Geagea joined the Maronite rightist military forces during the 1975/6 Civil War, becoming Kata'eb and Lebanese Forces commander of North Metn. Led the LF in the Shouf battles of 1983/4. Was ousted by Hobeiqa in May 1985 but regained control in January 1986. During 1990, he survived war with General Aoun.

Gemayel, Amin: Born in 1942, older son of Pierre Gemayel, Amin was a member of the Kata'eb party, and deputy for Metn. In September 1982 he was elected president after the assassination of Bashir.

Gemayel, Bashir: Born in 1947, Bashir joined the military wing of the Kata'eb party, fighting in the 1975/6 Civil War and, at its end, fusing all the rightist militias into the Lebanese Forces. Between 1976 and 1982 he set out to control the 'Maronite enclave', eliminating his main rivals (Tony Franjiyyeh in 1978, Chamoun's 'Tigers' in 1980). Elected president in August 1982; assassinated 14 September.

Gemayel, Pierre: Born in 1905, he was one of five founders of the Kata'eb Party in 1936, and devoted himself to building it. An austere and autocratic man, he kept the Party rigidly centralized until his death in 1984. He was a pharmacist by profession.

General Union of Palestinian Women (GUPW): Formed in 1964, one of several mass unions attached to the PLO. Its Lebanon branch has always been considered one of the most active.

'Green Line': This was the line established during the Civil War of 1975/6 that cut Beirut into two sectors, one predominantly Christian, the other predominantly Muslim. Suppressed in September 1982, it reappeared after the February 1984 uprising.

Haddad, Sa'd: In October 1976 Major Haddad was set up by the Israelis in control of a border strip based on Marja'youn, and formed the South Lebanon Army. From the strip, Haddad impeded *feda'yeen* operations, shelling camps and villages throughout the South. The strip was expanded in 1978, after the Litani Operation, and again after the 1982 invasion. Haddad died in January 1984, and was succeeded by another Lebanese Army officer, Major General Antoine Lahd.

'Harb Chamoun' ('Chamoun's war'): A local expression for the 1958 uprising against Chamoun.

'Hawadis Ayar' ('events of May'): The phrase used to refer to the clashes between the Lebanese Army and the Palestinian Resistance in May 1973. Accusing the PRM of not abiding by the Cairo Agreement, the army surrounded and shelled Shateela, Bourj Barajneh and Dbeyeh camps.

Hizbollah (the party of God): Formed somewhat earlier, Hizbollah first emerged in August 1982, when it published a strong critique of Amal and Berri. Iranian backing enabled it to develop social institutions as well as a militia initially numbering 800–1,000. From 1985 the two Shi'ite formations were engaged in a bitter struggle for control of the southern suburbs and the South. After many cease-fires arranged by Iranian mediators, that of November 1990 has held.

Hobeiqa, Elie: Born in 1956 in Biskinta, he became head of LF Intelligence during the Civil War of 1975/6 where the Israelis marked him as efficient and intelligent. As well as working with Mossad, he is believed to have been Syria's man inside the LF. It was he who commanded the special unit that carried out the Sabra/Shateela massacres. Became Minister of State for Displaced Persons in the Haraoui/Karameh Cabinet of December 1990.

al-Husseini, Hajj Amin: While still a young man, Hajj Amin was elected Grand Mufti of Jerusalem with British backing, becoming head of the Supreme Muslim Council. From this basis he became the main, though not uncontested, leader of the Palestinian national movement. The Mufti escaped British arrest in 1937, spending several years in exile. After the fall of Palestine in 1948, Hajj Amin tried to set up a Palestine government in Gaza. Expelled from Egypt in 1954, he spent the rest of his life in Lebanon and died in 1974.

al-Husseini, Hussein: Born in 1937 in Ba'lbek; elected deputy for Ba'lbek–

Hermel in 1972. One of Sadr's inner circle, al-Husseini helped found the Movement of the Deprived and Amal, and headed Amal between 1978 and 1980. Speaker of Parliament from 1984 to 1992, Husseini was one of the architects of the Ta'ef Accords.

In'ash al-Mukhayem (Revival of the Camps): This is a Lebanese–Palestinian association formed soon after the 1967 war to carry out sociocultural and income-generating action in camps. In'ash started work in Shateela, establishing a teaching kindergarten, children's libraries and productive projects for women. From this grew the revival of Palestinian peasant embroidery for which In'ash is best known.

Independent Nasserist Movement (INM): The oldest and largest of several Sunni groups formed in support of Nasserist Arab nationalism, it was founded in 1958 by Ibrahim Koleilat. It had a small militia (about 600 in 1975/6), the Murabitoun. The movement was Beirut-based; other Nasserist groups existed in Beirut as well as in Sidon and Tripoli.

Intifada: The word means 'uprising'. Since December 1987, this term has been used exclusively for the Palestinian revolt in the Occupied Territories. But before this it was used for the revolt of the Fateh dissidents, and for the Amal/PSP/Murabitoun revolt against Gemayel's army in February 1984.

Islamic Amal: This small, religiously oriented group split off from Amal in 1982 under the leadership of Hussein Musawi. Based in the Beqa'.

'Al-Jaysh al-Ta'ifi' ('the Sectarian Army'): Term used of the Lebanese Army in West Beirut by 'Opposition' groups after 1982, pointing to the non-national character of its politics.

Jebhat al-Inqadh (Salvation Front): Short form of the title of the Palestine National Salvation Front formed in Damascus in March 1985 of Fateh dissidents, Sa'eqa, PFLP-GC, the PSF and PLF.

Joint Forces: A control unit formed of PLO and LNM forces.

Jumblat, Kamal: Born in 1917 of a leading Druze family; elected to Parliament in 1951, where he was the youngest deputy, he founded the Progressive Socialist Party in 1949. He took part in the revolt against Chamoun in 1958, and served in several Cabinets, often as Minister of Interior. In 1969 he launched the Lebanese National movement, a coalition of progressive nationalist groups. Assassinated in March 1977.

Jumblat, Walid: Born in 1949, son of Kamal, Walid inherited at the age of twenty-eight his father's position as leader of the PSP, LNM and the Druze community. Walid has followed a more sectarian line than his father. He dissolved the LNM during the Israeli invasion. Joined Karameh's national unity Cabinet in April 1984.

Karameh, Rashid: Member of a leading Sunni family in Tripoli, Karameh spent more time as Prime Minister than any other Sunni politician. Nicknamed 'the effendi', he was respected as honest and patriotic. Assassinated in June 1987 by a bomb in an Army helicopter.

Kata'eb Party: Also called the Phalanges, the Kata'eb was founded in 1936 by a small group of Maronites including Pierre Gemayel. Modelled on European fascist parties, the Kata'eb was paramilitary and highly disciplined, explicitly Lebanese nationalist, implicitly anti-Arab and anti-Muslim. Originally the largest of the Maronite militias, the Kata'eb armed forces broke away in 1976 under Bashir Gemayel to become the core of the Lebanese Forces.

Khalaf, Salah: One of the founding members of Fateh. Assassinated in Tunis in February 1991.

Kifah Musellah (Armed Struggle): A unit formed from the PLA to keep order in Palestinian camps after the uprisings of 1969, in accordance with the Cairo Accords.

Lebanese Communist Party (LCP): Founded in 1925, the LCP is the oldest of Lebanon's modern political formations. Its main membership has been Christian and Shi'ite. Moscow-oriented.

Lebanese Forces (LF): Formed in 1976 to coordinate the separate rightist Maronite militias, the LF were originally composed of the Kata'eb armed forces, Chamoun's 'Tigers', the Guardians of the Cedars, Franjiyyeh's Marada, the 'Organization' and other smaller groups. As LF leader, Bashir Gemayel used it to build his influence within Maronite politics.

Lebanese Front: political leadership of the Maronite right during the Civil War of 1975/6.

Lebanese National Movement (LNM): A loose coalition of progressive nationalist, Muslim and secular leftist groups formed in 1969 to oppose ultra-Maronite militarization. Its programme emphasized political reform, deconfessionalization and social justice. The LNM was dissolved by Walid Jumblat during the 1982 invasion. It was replaced by a series of pro-Syrian fronts most of which were little more than names: the National Unity Front, the Lebanese National Democratic Front, the Front of Liberation and Unity, and others.

Lebanese National Resistance Front (LNRF): Formed in September 1982 to struggle against the Israeli occupation.

Maghrib: Term for the Arab states west of Egypt (Libya, Tunisia, Algeria, Morocco, Mauritania).

Maktab Thani: Arabic for Deuxième Bureau.

Manshaqeen: Those who cause a split (used of Fateh dissidents by Fateh loyalists).

'Maronite enclave': This term was first used during the Civil War of 1975/6 by people on the national/progressive side to designate the area controlled by the rightist Maronite militias.

Mashreq: Arab states east of Egypt, including the Gulf states.

Mejlis al-Janoub (Council of the South): Body set up to compensate victims of Israeli aggression, financed by the Arab states.

Metwalis (or Matawli): A term for Shi'ites used by others in contexts of hostility or contempt.

Millet: An Ottoman administrative term used to designate minority sectarian communities.

Movement of the Deprived (Harakat al-Mahrumeen): Launched by Imam Sadr in a series of mass rallies beginning in 1973/4 as a way of pressuring the Lebanese state to redress Shi'ite grievances. The MOD was structureless and faded away after the formation of Amal, its military wing.

Mukafaha: A special unit within the Lebanese Army with 'commando' training, used against criminals, subversives, etc.

Multinational Forces: Composed of US, British, French and Italian units, the MNF was formed to supervise the evacuation of the PLO/PRM fighters from Beirut in August 1982, as part of the Habib Accords. Recalled after the Sabra/Shateela massacres to protect the civilian population, they finally withdrew after the February 1984 uprising.

Murabitoun: The largest of the Nasserist Sunni militias, the military wing of the INM. The name means 'those who are linked/committed'. The Murabitoun were closely associated with the Palestinian Resistance movement. Like other Nasserist groups they were urban-based without a national structure or leadership.

Al-Nahar: The oldest continuously published Lebanese newspaper, founded in 1933 by the father of the present owner–editor Ghassan Tueni. Pro-Western, independent and centrist in its politics, *al-Nahar*'s Arab-world circulation once rivalled that of *al-Ahram* but declined because of the war in Lebanon.

Najjadeh: Formed in 1936 by Adnan al-Hakeem, the Najjadeh was the Sunni answer to the Kata'eb, but declined in the 1950s as more vigorous Nasserist groupings emerged.

Nasserist Popular Organization: Originally the Popular Resistance, founded in 1958 by the Sidon Sunni leader Ma'rouf Sa'd as one of the forces ranged against Chamoun, renamed in 1975 by his son Mustafa. The main political and military formation in Sidon.

National Salvation Committee: Formed by President Sarkis at the beginning of the Israeli invasion of 1982, the committee included 'active forces', e.g. Bashir Gemayel, Walid Jumblat and Nabih Berri. It collapsed when Jumblat left it in August.

National Salvation Front: This short-lived front was launched in July 1983, with Syrian backing, by Franjiyyeh, Karameh and Jumblat to oppose the Lebanese–Israeli 17 May Accords.

National Syrian Socialist Party (NSSP), also known as the PPS (Parti Populaire Syrien): founded in 1932 by Antoun Sa'deh, a secular Arab national party focused on the aim of a 'Greater Syria'. Strongly disciplined and hierarchical, the PPS began by being anti-communist but gradually adopted a progressive orientation. One of the founding members of the LNM, with a substantial militia and a membership spread over most regions and communities, but split into factions.

'*nuss zayid wahid*' (half plus one): This was the formula through which Fateh dominated all PLO committees.

Organization of Communist Action (OCA): Formed in 1971, by Marxist ex-members of the Arab Nationalist movement. A founding member of the LNM; led by Muhsin Ibrahim; close to the DFLP. Supportive of the

Palestinians during the 'Battle of the Camps'.

Pakradouni, Karim: Born in 1944; leader of the Kata'eb student section; close to Bashir Geyamel; member of, and spokesman for, the Lebanese Forces Command. Pakradouni built ties for the LF with Damascus, the PLO and Baghdad. Author of two books on Lebanese politics.

Palestine Liberation Army (PLA): Established at the 1st Palestinian National Council (Jerusalem, May 1964) and recognized by the 2nd Arab Summit, September 1964. The PLA has brigades stationed in Syria, Egypt, Jordan and Iraq.

Palestine Liberation Front (PLF): One of the smaller Resistance groups.

Palestine Liberation Organization (PLO): A Palestine entity was authorized by the 1st Arab Summit (Alexandria, January 1964), and the PLO was subsequently established at the 1st Palestine National Council, called by Shuqairy in Jerusalem in May 1964. The PLO is nominally supported by all Arab League states. Its status as sole legitimate representative of the Palestinian people was recognized at the 7th Arab Summit of Rabat, October–November 1974.

Palestine National Council (PNC): The highest Palestinian body, the PNC had 388 (now 450) members representing all Palestinian communities except in Israel and the Occupied Territories. It elects the PLO Executive Committee. The PNC held its twentieth meeting in September 1991, in Algiers.

Palestine Red Crescent Society (PRCS): The first PRCS was founded during the war of 1948 but was re-created in 1968 as the medical services branch of Fateh, later achieving quasi-independent status with its own governing board. Its headquarters are now in Cairo.

Palestine Struggle Front (PSF): One of the smaller Resistance groups, the PSF had an active following in Lebanon until 1988/9 when 'frozen' by a leadership split.

Parti Populaire Syrien (PPS): See NSSP.

Popular Front for the Liberation of Palestine (PFLP): Formed out of the ANM in November 1967, under the leadership of George Habash. Fateh's main rival and critic, the PFLP has suffered from internal splits (the first giving birth to the DFLP). Its rejection of the 'mini-state solution' appealed to Lebanese Palestinians, most of whom come from areas that became part of Israel in 1948.

PFLP-General Command: A small, purely military Resistance group led by Ahmad Jibreel, a Palestinian who formerly served as a Syrian Army Intelligence officer.

Progressive Socialist Party (PSP): Founded by Kamal Jumblat in 1949, the PSP was anti-sectarian (Christians and other Muslims were among its founding members), reformist, democratic and pan-Arab. With the approach of the 1975/6 Civil War, it formed a militia wing that became the largest within the LNM. Over time the PSP has become increasingly limited to the Druze community.

Qabalan, Mufti Abdul Amir: State-appointed judge of the Ja'farai Tribunal which adjudicates in Shi'i personal status cases, hence a leading official representative of the Shi'i community. Close to Amal, his speeches often indicate the Movement's 'line'.

Quwwat al-Reda' (Arab Deterrent Forces): The ADF was set up at the Arab summit in Cairo in October 1976 which formally ended the Lebanese Civil War of 1975/6. Although several Arab countries sent contingents, the bulk of the ADF's 30,000 troops were Syrian, thus enabled legitimately to occupy most of Lebanon.

Sa'd, Mustafa: See under Nasserist Popular Organization.

Sadr, Imam Musa: Born in 1928 in Iran, Sadr accepted the post of Mufti of Tyre in 1959; became first chairman of the new Supreme Islamic Shi'a Council in 1969, launching the Movement of the Deprived (1973/4) and Amal movement (1974). Disappeared while on a visit to Libya in August 1978.

Sa'eqa (Thunderbolt): A Palestinian Resistance group formed from the Ba'th party in Syria in 1966.

Salam, Sa'eb: Leading Sunni politician based in Beirut; took a prominent part in the 1958 uprising against Chamoun. Several times Prime Minister. At first a Nasserist, Salam swung back to support of Maronite–Sunni *entente*. Supported Amin Gemayel for president in 1982, later went into self-imposed exile.

Salameh, Abu Hassan: Head of Fateh Security, Abu Hassan was entrusted with contacts with the Maronite right. Assassinated in Beirut in 1981 by Mossad agents.

SAMED: 'Workshops for the Children of Palestine Martyrs', a productive institution founded by Fateh in 1970 in Beirut to provide training and employment for the families of those killed or imprisoned during national struggle. Publishes a magazine, *SAMED al-Iqtisadi*, as well as engaging in manufacturing, farming and handicraft.

'Sawt al-Arab': An Egyptian radio programme with a strong Palestinian component, 'Sawt al-Arab' began broadcasting in the late 1950s, and was immensely popular and influential among Palestinians. Listening to it was forbidden in Palestinian camps in Lebanon. Closed down by Sadat.

'Security Zone': A narrow strip of Lebanese territory where in 1976 Israel established a surrogate Lebanese militia, the 'Security Zone' was enlarged during the 1978 invasion and again after the invasion of 1982.

Al-Shebab al-'Arabi al-Filasteeni: One of several small Palestinian nationalist groups formed in Lebanon after 1948, it merged with the Arab Nationalist movement.

Shamsideen, Sheikh Muhammad Mehdi: A Shi'ite cleric and religious authority, deputy head of the Supreme Islamic Shi'a Council.

South Lebanon Army (SLA): Paid, trained and supplied by Israel, the SLA was commanded by Major Haddad until 1984, since then by Major General Antoine Lahd.

Steadfastness Front: Formed in December 1977 by Syria in opposition to Sadat's peace overtures to Israel, the Steadfastness Front was composed of, in addition to Syria, Algeria, the PLO, the Popular Democratic Republic of Yemen, and Libya. Iraq joined briefly in 1978.

Ta'ef Accords: During 1989, after the failure to elect a president to succeed Amin Geyamel, Saudi Arabia and the Arab League exerted exceptional pressure on Lebanese parliamentarians to meet in Ta'ef (in Saudi Arabia) where, in October, they signed a pact of national reconciliation, which included mild reforms in the political system and a programme of restabilization and reconstruction of the state.

towteen (implantation): This term is always used in the context of international pressures to settle diaspora Palestinians outside Israel/ Palestine.

Tripartite Accords: A Syrian project for a settlement of the Lebanese crisis based on the three main sectarian militias (Maronite, Druze, Shi'ite). The accords were signed in Damascus in December 1985 by Hobeiqa (LF), Jumblat (PSP) and Berri (Amal), but were made obsolete within weeks by a coup organized by Geagea and President Gemayel against Hobeiqa.

United Nations Relief and Works Agency (UNRWA): Set up in 1949 to deal with the Palestinian refugee problem, UNWRA began operations in 1950 in the West Bank, Gaza, Jordan, Syria and Lebanon. UNWRA's head office was in Lebanon until 1975 when it withdrew to Amman and then to Vienna.

Wazzan, Shafeeq: Sunni politician who was briefly Prime Minister under President Sarkis and again under President Amin Gemayel.

Index

252, 259, 268, 270, 271, 274, 278, 292, 316
Mossad, 18, 132, 201
mourning, 85, 97, 146, 224, 259
Movement of the Deprived, 157, 169, 170, 177, 182, 186
Mubarak, Ignatius, 23
Mufti, 52, 72, 73, 74; influence of, 50, 59, 60
muhajjareen, 327, 329
Murabitoun, 135, 153, 182, 189, 225, 242
Muslim Brethren, 51

Najdeh, 215, 216
Nasser, Gamal Abdel, 27, 29, 51, 52, 69
Nasserism, 26, 28, 52, 73, 77, 87, 166
National Salvation Front (NSF), 3, 140, 141, 142, 186
National Syrian Socialist Party (NSSP), 140, 144
Nawal, 78, 239
Nazira, 197, 218
Nimrud, killing of, 224
nurses, 240, 293, 294, 339

oral history, Palestinian, necessity of, 4-10
Organization of Armed Struggle, 145
Organization of Communist Action, 165, 180
Ottoman period, 5, 8, 26, 158, 159, 160

Pakeezah *see* Ghazaleh, 59
Pakradouni, Karim, 141, 169, 173
Palestine Communist Party (PCP), 210
Palestine Liberation Army (PLA), 29, 91, 94, 106, 210, 211
Palestine Liberation Front (PLF), 210, 300, 301
Palestine Liberation Organization (PLO), 3, 6, 27, 28, 29, 31, 52, 60, 73, 74, 75, 95, 96, 100, 101, 105, 108, 109, 110, 111, 112, 139, 203, 207, 208-11, 213, 216, 299, 318, 321, 324, 325, 326
Palestine National Council (PNC), 29, 208, 299, 318
Palestine National Salvation Front (PNSF), 4, 6, 211, 220, 262, 278, 291, 298, 300, 301, 304, 314, 317, 318, 324, 335, 338
Palestine Red Crescent Society (PRCS), 59
Palestine Research Centre, 216
Palestine Struggle Front (PSF), 4, 209, 300, 301
Palestinian Resistance Movement (PRM), 7, 16, 19, 21, 28-31, 96, 105,

108, 109, 110, 114, 125, 144, 149, 165, 169, 174, 178, 179, 184, 190, 208, 213, 214, 218; constrained by Arab environment, 10; problem of fighters' behaviour, 179
Parti Populaire Syrien (PPS), 25, 159, 177
Popular Committees, 95, 96, 181, 197, 201, 217, 224, 236, 242, 257, 258, 262, 263, 270, 271, 273, 285, 310, 313, 335, 336, 337
popular culture, 83-6, 102-5
Popular Front for the Liberation of Palestine (PFLP), 4, 31, 93, 94, 97, 98, 201, 220, 239, 300, 301, 318, 338
post-siege trauma, 259-60
prisons, 202, 203, 268; Ansar, 131, 144, 148, 200, 204, 205, 206; Nabatiyyeh, 131
Progressive Socialist Party (PSP), 128, 130, 136, 138, 142, 145, 153, 181, 220, 233, 317

Qabalan, Mufti, 157, 190

Rabiha, 234-6
Rana, 290-1
rape, 203, 204
Reagan, Ronald, 17, 138
Red Crescent, 196, 200, 214, 215, 216, 257, 259, 262, 265, 266, 271, 273, 292, 293-5, 296, 312, 328, 329, 338
Red Cross, 232, 241
religion, 5, 51, 58, 84, 170, 183, 274
Rhodes Armistice Accords, 18

Sa'eed, Abu Ahmad, 92, 99, 102, 119
Sa'eed, Sheikha, 239
Sa'eqa, 76, 98, 180, 210, 324, 338
Sadat, Anwar, 28, 173
Sadr, Imam Musa, 31, 134, 137, 145, 146, 157, 166-70, 170-3, 182, 184
Salam, Sa'eb, 30, 53, 72, 132, 137
Salameh, Abu Hassan, 92, 99
Salvation Front, 236
SAMED, 112, 214, 215, 216
Samia, 107, 284, 309-10, 330
Sarees, Khaled, 54, 55
Saudi Arabia, 16, 27, 50, 209
sewage, 40, 70, 96, 99, 135, 197, 199, 213, 223, 289, 301
Shaheen, Rafeeq, 66, 170
Shamsideen, Sheikh Mehdi, 132, 134, 137, 146, 182, 186, 245, 318
Sharon, Ariel, 17, 19, 125, 128, 129, 207
Shateela: abandonment of, 323; as habitat, 38-41; checkpoints at, 197;